REAL ESTATE FINANCING MANUAL

A GUIDE TO MONEY-MAKING STRATEGIES

Jack Cummings

PRENTICE HALL, Englewood Cliffs, New Jersey 07632

Prentice-Hall International, Inc., *London*
Prentice-Hall of Australia, Pty. Ltd., *Sydney*
Prentice-Hall Canada, Inc., *Toronto*
Prentice-Hall of India Private Ltd., *New Delhi*
Prentice-Hall of Japan, Inc., *Tokyo*
Prentice-Hall of Southeast Asia Pte. Ltd., *Singapore*
Editora Prentice-Hall do Brasil Ltda., *Rio de Janeiro*
Prentice-Hall Hispanoamericana, S.A., *Mexico*

© 1987 by
PRENTICE-HALL, INC.
Englewood Cliffs, N.J.

10 9 8 7 6 5

10 9 8 7 6 5 4   (PBK)

Library of Congress Catalog Card Number: 87-061419

ISBN 0-13-763418-8

ISBN 0-13-762535-9 PBK

Printed in the United States of America

To my Mother, who got me started in real estate

FOREWORD

The success of any real estate venture is usually tied to the financing on that project. Quite often, a marginal real estate investment can be turned into an excellent one through the use of creative financing. Conversely, an otherwise good investment can become a financial disaster when incorrectly financed.

For several years, Jack Cummings has been considered the final answer when it comes to creative financing of real estate. I have known Jack since 1969 and have often recommended his ideas to investors. He's the one that investment experts rely on for solutions to their financing needs.

In this, his latest book, Mr. Cummings covers all of the financing bases, from using financing to solve investment problems to locating and negotiating the best possible financing for your investment, home, or development. The multitude of charts, checklists, and ideas presented here take the guesswork out of real estate financing.

If you are involved in real estate investing, buying, selling, developing, or brokering, this book needs to be on your desk.

Milt Tanzer,
author, lecturer,
realtor, investment
counseler

CONTENTS

MAXIMIZE YOUR PROFITS AND REDUCE YOUR RISK THROUGH SOLID AND CREATIVE REAL ESTATE FINANCING STRATEGIES

The objectives of this book are:

1. To provide the real estate investor, salesperson, developer, banker, seller, or would-be owner with a complete one-stop financing reference. The information is presented in easy-to-understand terms that will help you build your knowledge of powerful investing and financing strategies in a logical way. The idea is to expand your ease with deal making that only the insiders are used to.

2. To help you find highly profitable techniques that will work for you from the first day you use them. For example, in Chapter 3, "THE POWER OF NEGOTIATING," you will discover the four steps to successful negotiating that will ensure your getting started with an edge in all deals.

3. To give you both sides of the picture—in each chapter, we will take a solid look at the benefits and pitfalls of each of the dozens of methods of financing you can use to invest profitably in real estate.

4. To help you make more money in real estate as an investor, developer, banker, lender, salesperson, or seller, and become a heavyweight in real estate investing.

In writing this book, I have had the advantage of looking back over my previous real estate publications to pick and choose from the hundreds of successful ideas and techniques I have already covered in such books as *The Complete Guide to Real Estate Financing, The Complete Handbook on How to Farm Real Estate Listings and Sales, Cashless Investing in Real Estate, Successful Real Estate Investing for the Single Person,* and *$1,000 Down Can Make You Rich.* With this background, and many new and exciting examples and techniques to give you, I have provided an up-to-date book that will *help* the real estate investor *solve* the modern problems he or she faces in real estate investing. My own personal success as an investor, broker syndicator, and nationally acclaimed lecturer in the field of real estate investing.

TWENTY-THREE CHAPTERS

The twenty-three chapters in this book are devoted to making your job easier and your real estate investments more profitable. You will begin with "The Goals of Real Estate Financing," and end with "How to Deal with Foreclosure." In between, you will discover all of financing techniques you will probably ever need. You can choose the technique to fit your situation so that you stay on top of the deal and win time and time again. In Chapter 2 alone, you can find such solid ideas as setting your goals to win, developing your own comfort zone, discovering fifty-four methods of disposing of real estate. Each chapter is filled with something you can use, something that will make you more confident in your ability in real estate investing. Uncover the insider tricks to blanket mortgages in Chapter 9, and in Chapter 10 learn How to Use the Best Tool of All, *the wraparound mortgage.*

This book will aid you in every possible financing situation. If you are a builder or developer, you will find techniques that will show you how to get financing at the best terms possible and how to set up a total loan package that will serve joint ventures or syndications of any size.

Novice or first-time investors will discover that this book is *user-friendly.* No matter who you are or how much you know about real estate, you will find in the text new techniques and ideas. The novice will build a strong foundation, and the expert will add to his or her strengths.

INVESTORS WILL GAIN FLEXIBILITY

We live in a world of real estate seminars and get-rich-quick schemes that all promise wealth without effort. Some of those "build-your-fortune-seminars" present sound information, good techniques, and fundamentally good concepts, while other seminars build a program on some good concepts but fall way short of delivering on their promise.

This book presents all techniques, all potential. I review the good and the bad, and point out the advantages and the disadvantages. In Chapter 5, you will find eleven steps to help you deal with lenders. And in Chapter 6, you will discover the keys to nonconventional financing with four creative examples of matching needs, six ways to use a secondary loan and when to use secondary financing as a *last resort*.

Successfully handling a problem means finding the *right answer* to the problem. Each situation is different depending only on your goal and specific need. This book will help give you those *right answers*.

BUILDERS AND DEVELOPERS

Gone are the good old days when a builder had to fight off lenders who were trying to fill his pockets with cash so that a new project could be constructed. Financing is becoming more and more sophisticated. Builders and investors will discover this book will help them open up more doors, get more loands closed and in their pocket, and have greater success.

Chapter 8, "Land Development and Construction Loans and How to Effectively Get Them," will be more than worth the price of this book the first time it is used. It includes solid techniques such as nine steps to get top dollar and seven points for better loan negotiations.

This book will become a well-used reference book for any builder or developer who is constantly looking to expand his or her markets, get the best rate on a development loan, and to maximize overall profits.

PROFESSIONAL REAL ESTATE BROKERS AND SALESMEN

Real estate salespeople will learn how to meet the objections of the toughest seller or the tightest buyer through the expanded knowledge they will gain in this book. They will discover how the real estate broker and salesperson can use this book to make more sales and to increase commissions. No longer will the salesperson be at a loss when his or her clients demand a salesperson who is up to date and who understands creative financing techniques.

BANKERS, MORTGAGE BROKERS, AND LOAN OFFICERS

This book will help all bankers, loan officers, mortgage brokers, or lending agents better serve the real estate investor by opening more alternatives, and bringing creative financing to all investors, not just the insiders.

Making money on money is the name of the lending game, and bankers or loan officers or mortgage brokers cannot afford to overlook any technique that will work for any specific borrower. Let's face facts. Buyers want to deal with bankers and lenders who know about modern, up-to-date techniques—techniques such as the eight shown in Chapter 18 include the sliding mortgage, shared equity, double finance, and more.

STUDENTS AND FIRST-TIME INVESTORS

This book tells it as it is. There is no promise that you can make a million dollars using this or that technique. Use it incorrectly and you can go bust, yet this book will show you the right way to select the proper techniques, and how to implement them. You will build your own comfort zone following the six steps to setting up your comfort zone. You will build your confidence in yourself. You will discover the magic world of the pyramid form of investing shown in Chapter 13, and how and when to use blanket mortgages. The important element of using any tool is to know how to use it, to understand what it can do, and to realize that there are limitations to its use. The information contained in this book is detailed and comprehensive, and *is not limited to real estate financing*. This book takes a long and hard look at the factors of risk and goal setting, and the fundamental elements that enable a real estate investor to establish him- or herself, to work at building wealth in real estate by reducing risk in the market, and to maximize return by buying and selling at the best personal and market terms.

SELLERS OF REAL ESTATE

Most investors at one or more times in their life sell what they have purchased. If you have bought right and know how to sell right, your profit is at its highest level. For some sellers, the act of disposing doesn't take much talent. They set a price, someone comes along and makes an offer, and the deal is closed. But for most sellers the sale isn't that simple. *Did I get the best offer? Did I get the most money?* These are questions that keep many sellers awake at night for weeks after the contract has been signed. This book will help you get the best offer, the most money.

And what if you don't find a buyer? Many sellers are stuck in a tough market and can't sell. This book will help solve many of these sellers' problems through highly creative techniques that work. Discover in Chapter 19 the four creative techniques that put you in the driver's seat, and in Chapter 20 the creative financing techniques using benefits you didn't know you had. One of these fantastic techniques will show you how to use "sweat equity deals" as a seller. These and other strategies can help you sell the property that no one wanted to buy—even in the toughest market.

A BOOK FOR EVERYONE INVOLVED IN REAL ESTATE

Are you involved with real estate as an investor, lender, developer, salesperson, student, banker, buyer, seller, renter, landlord? Then this book will maximize your success, simplify your efforts, and increase your self-confidence through achievement of your goals and the realization of solid profits.

Chapter 1

HOW THE GOALS OF REAL ESTATE FINANCING CAN HELP YOU SOLVE SPECIFIC PROBLEMS

This chapter is designed to help you to develop a clear understanding of what financing should do, and to enable you to lay the foundation for using the tools of financing to enhance your success in real estate investing.

All success must begin somewhere, and in real estate financing it begins with the Ten Goals of Financing. You will find that you can approach any problem using these ten goals to determine whether financing can provide a solution. If, upon a review of each of the goals, you can see no benefit to be obtained, you can stop looking into financing as the source of the solution.

In this way, you will see that the solution does not depend as much on finding an immediate answer as on knowing whether financing can indeed provide an answer. You will not be able to arrive at a solution without a clear understanding of your goals.

THE TEN GOALS OF FINANCING—AND WHAT THEY WILL DO

1. Create the Highest Value. Financing should enhance the value of a property. From a buyer's standpoint, it should provide the best terms in the marketplace to give him or her the greatest value for the investment made. The seller looks at financing as a tool that provides the maximum market price.

A well-worn adage applies here: "I'll pay your price, if you'll take my terms." In other words, price often is a fluctuating factor, depending on the terms of the sale. It is clear that a property may be difficult to sell if the seller feels that he or she *must receive* all cash to effect the sale. There is, however, a balance that can exist: The lowest value for a property could well be the all-cash price, whereas the highest value could well be the price that is accompanied by the best terms—in short, the best financing.

It is important, however, that you realize that the weight of the cash available to the seller may be more critical than the highest value. Therefore, using the tools of financing to solve their problems, both parties should look at their desired goals more closely.

2. Consolidation. Financing can be used to consolidate existing financing that is overburdening the owner of a property. The goal here is to examine the owner's options using one or more financing techniques to see if consolidation can relieve the burden.

The simple refinancing of a property can work wonders in a market in which the interest rates have dropped and a high-interest loan can be replaced with a newer, more affordable loan. The increased value of a property due to years of appreciation and past cost-of-living index advances also can give the owner a substantial advantage in the total loan available on a given property. This increased loan capability can allow the owner of the property to pay off other loans on other properties, should it be desirable to do so, by consolidating a number of high-interest-rate loans into one lower-interest-rate loan.

In this age of high credit, the lowest interest rate possible on long-term investing (other than a loan against life insurance cash value) usually is a mortgage on your place of residence. If the current market was only 9.5 percent interest for that kind of loan, it would be neither prudent nor wise to have 18 percent outstanding balances in credit card payments or 20 percent interest loans for one's car if refinancing one's personal residence would produce the needed cash to retire the higher interest payments and to consolidate the other loans into more affordable circumstances.

The interest rate itself is not the only criterion to examine when you are looking into overall debt payments. You may owe on a number of different loans at various payback terms. The most specific item to note is the constant rate of payment of the loans. The term *constant rate of payment* is used within the lending industry, and you should become aware of what it is and how it is used. In Chapter 3, I provide you with details of how to use the constant rate of payment in analyzing mortgage situations.

From a consolidation point of view, you need to determine your ultimate goal and how the use of financing through consolidation can best serve you. For example, if you simply want to reduce your monthly payment to satisfy several loans (home, car, credit card company, and so on), you could consider refinancing your home to produce the added cash to retire all outstanding loans except the newly refinanced mortgage on your home. Yet, while this may seem to solve the problem, it may in fact create the additional burden of paying far more than you would have had you simply hung in there for a short period and paid off the existing loans. By removing them altogether, you can avoid committing to an additional twenty years of payments on your newly refinanced home loan.

There is no need to seek consolidation as a goal unless one or more of the following situations are present.

1. There is a need to reduce existing debt payments through the refinancing of any or all of the existing debt in such a way that the total future payments will not exceed those payments under the old finance situation.
2. There is an inability to meet current debt payments, and refinancing is the only way to meet the current payments—even though the overall payments will exceed those of the current debt structure.
3. The property is not readily marketable with the present financing structure, and a change in this situation through refinancing of this or other properties will provide a more favorable result in the marketplace.
4. A cash-out situation is needed in which the owner can mortgage above the present financing levels and put cash in his or her pocket. This must be done in such a way that by so doing the property will not become overburdened and the debt service will actually be less than the current payment structure.
5. There is the immediate need to create cash, and no other option seems to be viable at the present.

There are many ways to consolidate existing financing. Almost any form of financing will lend itself to consolidation of an existing debt. Naturally, some forms of financing will give better results than others.

3. Make Property More Salable. One of the major aspects of financing is the ability to make property more salable. This goal may seem to be the same as Goal 1, but in careful analysis you will see some very important, though subtle differences.

Creative financing may be the only way to take a property that is difficult to sell into the marketplace. The sale often is a result of more than one form of financing being put to use. A sale and lease-back, with the seller holding secondary financing (with or without cross-collateralization of the second mortgage to secure the lease), is an example of multiple techniques that can be used to facilitate the sale.

While the goal of making the property more salable generally serves the seller more than it does the buyer, there are times, such as in a strong buyer's market, when even great properties are difficult to sell because of high interest or low buyer demand, and the seller must find techniques to make his or her property stand out as a deal that can't be refused.

For example, to get the buyer in the door it is not unusual for a builder to offer mortgage financing at well below the marketplace for the first several years of the mortgage. Once attracted, buyers may discover that they can pay more cash up front and get a better price (use of the first goal) instead of the "buy-down" form of financing that the builder was offering.

The builder's buy-down mortgage offer is a technique in which the builder "pays" the lender a fee for lending money at terms that seem to be below market. In reality, buy-down loans are at market prices and are simply another form of "reducing the price" of the property. This technique is very commonly used by automotive manufacturers.

4. _Increase the Market Potential for the Property._   This is another seller-oriented financing goal. Here the goal is to expand the market potential of the property and not just make it more salable. It is possible, of course, that by doing one we will also do the other. However, one does not necessarily accomplish the other. Review the following case study.

Mr. Wallace, who wanted to sell his 25-unit apartment house, was realistic in his price and felt that at $500,000 the apartment complex represented a good buy. After all, the net operating income (NOI) on the property was $53,000, and for the current marketplace, considering the condition of the building, the area of town, and soon, this was a very good ratio of NOI to value.

However, the city was about to launch a major road and sewer project right in front of the apartment house, and there was every prospect that the complex would lose all of its tenants for at least a year. Once the work was finished, with the newly planted median and sidewalks where none had previously existed, the apartment complex would be in good shape and its value would increase.

The approach to the first goal was to make the property more salable. This was accomplished by establishing a format for a sale and lease-back for one year. By assuming the risk for the year during which the road work was to take place, the seller was in fact taking no greater risk than if he put the building up for sale and was unable to sell it during the same time period. In fact, as the specific need of the seller was to sell the building, holding onto the building was a hardship that he could not afford to take. Thus far, the goal served was to help make the property salable. Now the task was to increase the market potential for the property.

To this end, Mr. Wallace could have taken a number of directions. Keep in mind that one form of increasing the market potential of a property is to make it available to more ready, willing, and able buyers. It should be obvious that the seller of a 6,000-acre farm will have fewer buyers than if he were to offer for sale 60 acres at a time of the same farm.

As seller of the apartment building, Mr. Wallace could have turned the building into a condominium or a cooperative apartment building, seeking twenty-five different buyers at much reduced prices. In fact, it is likely that in some market areas this has been the direction that many sellers have taken, producing a greater sales price than would have been realized had the building been sold to a single investor.

Another way to increase market potential is to be more flexible in the terms one is willing to accept in the sale of the property. By the way, this flexibility is difficult for many sellers to attain because they have not properly established their own investment goals. If you have clear goals and know exactly where you want to be at any given time in the relatively near future—and you constantly review those goals—you will begin to realize that it is the attainment of the goals that is important, not the attainment of any specific terms of a sale.

Let's go back to our apartment-building seller, Mr. Wallace. If part of his long-term goal was to retire to the mountains of North Carolina with a nice cabin and 10 acres of apple trees, he would realize that if someone were to offer him an acceptable home in North Carolina or 10 acres of apple trees as partial payment on the apartment building, he would have found a buyer who may not have ever considered this apartment building. This buyer might have thought that to buy a building he was first going to have to get rid of the North Carolina property or the apple orchard.

No matter what Mr. Wallace's long-term goal is, by viewing it clearly he will begin to see that there are additional "things" to help him entice more buyers to his apartment building. At the same time, these "things" would accomplish the critical task of "getting rid of the apartment building" while moving Mr. Wallace closer to his long-term goals.

By utilizing Internal Revenue Code 1031, a buyer or seller may enter into an agreement that will have more specific benefits than a more conventional transaction because of the reduced tax liability to one or more of the parties. This option is open to you only if you know how it works and how it fits into your goals.

Mr. Wallace decided that another available option was to reduce the amount of cash needed to take control of the property. With his accountant, he worked up a rather attractive package that, when coupled with the sale lease-back technique, would allow a buyer with little cash to purchase the property. This technique enticed more buyers and produced the desired results of selling the property.

5. Increase the Cash Return from Marginal Properties.   This goal can be the most important goal for a buyer of income property. Due to its importance to buyers, it also becomes very important to sellers. While cash flow is not the only criterion for determining acceptability of one property over another, it often is highly desirable to create or to increase the spendable yield from the property. All things being equal, a buyer will pay more for a property that produces a greater cash flow. The bottom line, which is so important to most investors, can well be a function of the kind of financing that has been established on the property.

If financing is not available at the best rate or terms, the payments would take away from the potential cash flow that the investor could realize.

Most creative financing tricks learned by real estate investors are designed to soften the overall blow of the property debt. The ideal situation is one in which the investor can buy without putting up any of his or her own money so that the property is 100 percent financed—or at least 100 percent purchased—without the buyer digging around for cash. Before you jump to conclusions that can be counterproductive to your healthy attitude about buying or selling real estate this way, let me state that buying real estate without putting up any cash is not difficult to do. The primary factor is being able to make money doing it. Also the investor quite often does put some value into the transaction, but instead of money the value is some other benefit to the seller.

As this goal best serves the buyer, it is essential that you recognize that buying from a seller who is inflexible and who only wants cash over his or her existing mortgage does not give the buyer much room to be creative. In these circumstances, and assuming that the buyer wants that property and none other, one solution is to educate the seller into flexibility by examining what it is he or she wants to accomplish. By drawing out the seller's goals, it sometimes is possible to demonstrate to the seller benefits that he did not visualize earlier.

Investors will look for sellers who are flexible and with whom the investor can mix and match one or more of the techniques that will be discussed in detail within this book.

6. Generate Immediate Cash When Needed.   This goal often is overlooked. Since the principal owed in existing mortgages may decline over the years, and the value of the property may increase, it often is possible to refinance and pick up ready cash. This can be accomplished without affecting the cash flow on a property. For example: The mortgage payment for $150,000 over 15 years at 9½ percent per annum is $1,554 per month. If a new mortgage can be obtained at 10½ percent per annum but the term is 25 years, the same payment of $1,554 would allow the owner to get $179,275. This would produce $29,275 (less loan costs) in immediate cash.

While this may not appear to be dramatic, if cash is essential at that moment of need, the opportunity to get cash and use cash may be worth the increased term and interest in the debt payment. While the amount paid each month has not increased and in fact remains the same, the investor has an additional ten years to make those same payments as his or her cost to get ready cash. This would add $186,480 to the total payment (the last ten years of the 25-year term total this amount). However, this sum could be offset by the yield or need for the $29,275 gained now.

When a borrower obtains money through financing, such as getting a loan from the local savings and loan association, there may be no income tax liability on that money. In essence, as the money was not "earned" but borrowed, the borrower can in many circumstances renew his loans from time to time, increasing amounts borrowed as the values of the real estate go up, pulling out capital that is tax free, at least for the moment. When the borrower ultimately sells the property an adjustment would be made to determine what amount of loan still outstanding exceeded the basis (book value) of the property. This excess would be treated as earned income at that time and taxed accordingly. Under present IRS rules the real estate investor is able to deduct the interest paid on many real estate loans, which makes this technique a very positive aspect to real estate investing.

Your use of financing to produce cash in a transaction will depend on your ultimate goals and what it is that you are trying to accomplish at the time you desire this cash.

As you learn more of the creative techniques of financing, you will discover that getting cash in refinancing is not always the most productive or best route to take. For example, in this book you will discover a technique called *pyramiding*. With it, you will be able to take the cash needed to buy property from the first property you own by giving the seller of the second property a second mortgage on the first property. You will do this, and variations thereon, at interest rates well below those offered by the institutional lenders in your marketplace.

7. Help Solve Tax Problems.   This goal serves two masters—the buyer and the seller. When you use a form of financing to solve a tax problem, you often create a problem for the other party to the transaction. It is at this time that the most critical item that comes into play is the motivation of the parties. If the most motivated party is the seller and his or her goals are better met by selling the property, the transaction may be slanted to the buyer in tax benefits and still be able to close. On the other hand, if the most motivated party is the buyer, and his or her goals are not compromised by giving some considerations to the seller's tax problems, those needs can be incorporated into the transaction and the financing tools can be used. On some occasions, both parties can gain benefits from careful review of the transaction and the tax laws.

The items to consider vary depending on the circumstances of the parties. However, there are ten items that should be part of your checklist when either buying or selling real estate. A review of each item with careful attention to your own goals and circumstances will aid you in determining if there are any tax advantages you need to consider prior to either making the offer or at least prior to closing.

The Tax Advantages Checklist

1. What items are to be depreciated within the investment property? Buyers generally want maximum values established; sellers often want lower values set. In exchanges, both parties may want to have the depreciable items considered with different base values.
2. Should you take title to land and building and personal property equally? There are advantages to taking it differently if it fits your circumstances.
3. On what date should you close? This can have a specific advantage to one party or both if the date can be split between two tax years.
4. How should an option payment be established? This can create cash to the seller that is not taxed right away and can be highly effective in nailing down a deal.
5. Review the advantages of the wrap-around mortgage, as it might apply to the transaction contemplated.
6. In a IRC 1031 exchange, should the property be directed against the land, the building, or both?
7. What are the one-time capital gains exclusions available to you under the current tax laws?
8. If the seller is to hold financing, should part of the down payment include the maximum advance interest allowed by the IRS? (The maximum allowed as of this writing is the interest that would be earned during the balance of the year.)
9. Should the buyer buy the property or the personal interest in a corporation or trust that owns the property? This and similar questions about form of ownership can give the investor a lot to think about when he or she buys so as to establish the best form of selling interest.

8. Create Tax-Deferred Transactions.   In some instances, the only major benefit from a technique of finance might be to pass on to some future date the possible income or capital gains tax consequence. There are, of course, other nonfinance options available to the investor that may have similar results, but the idea here is to examine what benefit the investor or the seller may have and at what cost. For example, if the technique used by a buyer was to acquire a property by entering into a long-term lease with an option to buy, the seller would not have a capital gain tax to pay until the sale itself took place. If part of the rent paid was "option money" that was paid each year or month to the seller to keep alive the option to buy, and a portion of that money was to be applied toward the ultimate purchase, it is possible that the option money would not be taxed as income or as capital gain until the sale actually took place no matter how many years in the future that was.

In the IRC 1031 exchange, which is covered in detail in this book, it is possible to have a lifetime of investing and still not trigger any capital gains tax.

Many techniques have an effect on the benefits of real estate and change the long-range tax, which may be payable at some time in the future. The more you know about your own tax consequences and your future goals, the better you will be at using the laws and finance tools to your best advantage.

9. Create New Ways to Allow the Investor to Expand His or Her Portfolio. As an investor in real estate, you would learn quickly that profit in real estate is not a function of buying real estate—it is a function of use and utility of the property and the final disposition of the property.

This signifies that to be successful in real estate investing, you will benefit the most when the overall plan fits the goal. You will not succeed in investing by buying this and/or that without knowing what to do with the property after you have acquired it. There is no doubt that with sound study of the area and with the development of expertise you could recognize opportunities that other people would overlook, and be able to take advantage of those properties without having the immediate use fixed in your mind. In those cases, the use or utility of the property is simply that of a good sound investment spawn out of your unique knowledge in the area and your grasp of the opportunity.

The more you understand about the tools of financing the better equipped you will become to use them to expand your portfolio. In developing your knowledge, you are reducing your risk in the investment game.

Since some of the benefits of finance are to assist in the sale or disposition of property, your knowledge of these tools enables you to move through your portfolio to other properties and investments.

10. Provide the Finishing Touch to a Good Marketing Plan. In selling your most difficult property, the maximum appeal to the marketplace and to your own satisfaction will be in covering all details. Investors who look after details are generally the most successful investors. Your devotion to the use of the tools of finance will demand that you anticipate your ultimate marketing plan, which should include various financing approaches to suit the probable investors who will buy your property.

When the time comes for you to "need" heavy financing for a large transaction or the development of some upcoming project you have been wanting to build, success could well depend on your past history of dealing with lenders.

KNOW THE LIMITATIONS OF THE TOOLS OF FINANCING

The preceding ten goals are the keys to your use of financing as a problem solver. Yet from time to time there will be situations that you cannot solve by using any of the financing techniques. In fact, at best you will simply maintain the status quo by using these tools, and in the worst case you can ruin the property and the investment if by applying the wrong technique.

The knowledge that you develop of the financing techniques covered in this book cannot be considered absolute. There will be many tips and suggestions to help you expand your knowledge, and you should recognize that there is no single source of knowledge in any field.

In the chapters to come, I will approach many of the techniques by reviewing their advantages and their disadvantages to the buyer and seller of any property. In your review of these different points of view, you should ask yourself how you would approach a particular technique in your own circumstances. If you are reviewing this book to brush up on some of these techniques in anticipation of some specific transaction you are trying to nail down, I recommend that you also review the table of contents to spark additional recollections of other techniques as well.

It is rare for a real estate investor to use any single technique in a transaction. In most cases, combinations of techniques are offered, countered, and refined into the final document of sale. One party buys hoping to have made the best investment possible, and another sells with a similar hope in mind. Each party to the transaction may have still held onto a card that he would have thrown into the pot to sweeten the transaction were it necessary. But no more cards were required, so the deal stands as executed.

Here are some important points to remember when approaching a situation that you feel may be solved with one of the financing techniques covered in this book:

1. At least one of the ten goals described in this chapter must be met for financing to have any real benefit to the parties involved.

2. Different points of view will be held by the buyer and the seller in their interpretation of these goals. The results of the form of financing used often will affect these two parties differently.

3. Theories that work on paper are valid only if they work in real life. Remember, there often are many parties to a transaction even when only two or three are apparent. The visible ones are the buyer and seller, and often the broker. The not-so-visible ones are the lawyers, wives, girl friends, bankers, bartenders, and so on—each party having some relationship to the deal. Each party has to be dealt with when he or she impedes on the desired results of a transaction.

4. To achieve constant success in real estate investing stay as close to

your long-range goals as possible. Since so much does depend on this goal-setting ability, I have provided a detailed chapter on goal setting and development of your comfort zone. Each chapter will become a foundation to your future as a real estate investor.

5. If your role in the game of financing is that of a real estate broker, you will have the added burden of acting as fiduciary in the transaction. However, you will also have the advantage in the investment game and will find that all of the techniques covered in this book will become useful tools in helping your clients buy and sell properties.

Chapter 2

HOW TO SET GOALS FOR INVESTING IN REAL ESTATE

The importance of setting your own investment goals is so critical to getting the maximum benefit out of the financing tools that I have devoted an entire chapter to this topic.

A WORD TO THE WISE ABOUT GOAL SETTING

Proper goal setting is difficult. It should not be contemplated half-heartedly, but instead should be given thought and deliberation. Your goals should come under constant review, and you should not hesitate to alter or revise your goals once you are sure they need changing.

The fact that you may set goals does not ensure success or happiness. Many people attain wealth and happiness without having gone through any specific goal-setting process. Yet motivation within these people often is at a very high level, and while they may not have made a conscious effort to set goals, they often are driven by high ideals or are out to prove something to someone.

The kind of goal setting that I refer to relates to the prudence of setting your priorities straight. You would not get much out of training to be an Olympic swimmer by spending all your energy on the ski slopes. Time management, the act of performing the most efficient task at the time to attain the desired results, depends on knowing what the desired results should be.

So the progression of setting goals, having those goals help you in establishing your priorities, and implementating the tasks to attain those goals is not as simple as determining where you want to be five years down the road.

GETTING TO YOUR DESTINATION STARTS WITH THE DECISION OF WHERE YOU WANT TO GO

It's similar to going on vacation by car. You have to make the following determinations:

1. Do you actually want to get down the road?
2. Do you know where you want to go?
3. Do you have some mode of transportation in mind?
4. Do you know how to drive that vehicle?
5. Do you have the staying power to keep it on the road?
6. Do you have the willpower to avoid being detoured from your desired destination?
7. Will you recognize when you have arrived at your destination?
8. Will you set new destinations and start over again?

The foregoing sequence should be easy to follow. It is all a matter of goal setting and then formulating the plan to get you to your goals. It starts with the selection of the destination. Let's begin there.

DEVELOP A VISION OF THE FUTURE

In one of my all-day seminars, I go through the following session with the audience. Read over the following material and then contemplate what is going on. Better yet, have someone read this section to you and let your mind take over.

Get comfortable. Find everything about your position that is not comfortable and change it. Then, when you feel you have a comfortable position, tense every muscle in your body in any random order that works for you, then return to that comfortable position. Now close your eyes and listen to what I have to tell you.

I want you to clean the slate in your mind. I want you to think only about the things I tell you to think of, remembering things from your past only to make the scenes I describe be more vivid to you.

Now erase this mixture of colors in your mind, just as a child would wipe the black board with a dusty eraser. All you see is that misty white slate; a white mist fills your mind.

You will relax even more now. See this milky white in your mind as it changes from the white dust on the black board to a misty morning. You are somewhere where it is cool and pleasant, you are very relaxed, your mind very clear, and you now see that the mist is over a lake or pond. The water is very still, and you are very relaxed.

You are actually in a time machine, and you are passing ahead into the future. Somewhere below you as you are flying through this cool, pleasant mist you see things going on below you. It's as though you are in the clouds and cannot quite see what is going on below you.

Then it begins to clear and you realize that you are beginning to see where you are. You look around within your mind. You see yourself and you note on the wall there is a calendar. The date is nearly ten years into the future. You look around and see what is going on.

Take careful note as to what you are doing, who you are with, where you are. What kind of clothes do you have on?

When you are satisfied that you can fully describe the setting, you will return to the mist and return to present.

When I finish this, I let the audience relax for a few minutes. Then I ask several of them to describe to me, and to the audience, what it was they saw.

When you look into your future like this, you have the tendency to see your own self-image of your future. To some degree, it might be the dream of what you would want, or hopes for the future. These are the natural goals that live within you. Like computer programs that can be altered, these goals may well be the default parameters that drive you.

The critical part of these visions are that they are not accepted by you as goals but as dreams. For some people, these visions are not pleasant at all, as if some more dramatic force were taking them into the future without much hope, without much self-esteem.

VISUALIZING THE FUTURE IS ESSENTIAL TO SOUND GOALS

An athlete knows the power of visualizing winning. The runner who is able to demonstrate that she "sees" herself winning can demoralize her opponent. Likewise, the salesperson who "sees" the sale being closed and assumes that his or her efforts will be rewarded knows that his or her success in selling will be increased. So it is with goals. If you can't clearly see the end result, you may never attain the desired goals, or at best you will not attain them with the ease and satisfaction that will come through goal setting.

ARE YOUR GOALS REALISTIC?

Proper goal setting is critical because it is easy to "see" the wrong future. You must realize and accept the fact that you can change your self-image, and can set your own goals. You are not bound by the vision you first saw when you looked into the milky mist.

EXAMINE YOUR VISION CAREFULLY TO SEE WHAT IT IS YOU LIKE

In this vision, there are elements that you will want to work on. It is critical that you constantly recall this vision because you will be making changes as you get closer to it. However, the most important aspect to pay attention to is the vision, and not the specifics as to how you got to the vision.

Most people have the wrong concept about goals, and when they set them they look more to the mode of transportation rather than to the destination itself. For example, if your vision is of you and your family living on an island paradise with dozens of close friends around you at all times with nothing to do but lounge around, the first element you would establish as your goal would be *the money it will take to buy this life style*. Money is the mode of transportation, not the destination. The goal of having lots of money, "I want to be a multimillionaire," is an improper goal as it directs you to the vehicle of transport rather than to the items you think money will buy.

Mind you, money and the desire for it are very strong motivators and can drive many people so strongly that they get money but little else. It is far better for you to understand that there are people so motivated, and to use their motivation to your own benefit.

Money is relative and its worth changes. The amount of money it might take to attain your goals can be much more than your goal allows.

To understand this last statement, you need only look at what has happened to the value of money in some countries. If you were looking into your own vision twenty years ago in Argentina, your concept of the amount of money needed to become "independent" would just about buy you breakfast today. In the early 1930s in Germany, boxes of money wouldn't buy you the boxes the money was in.

The best goals then are those that follow the following guidelines:

GUIDELINES TO SETTING YOUR GOALS

1. Define your goals in terms of what you want to attain, where you want to be, what kind of life style you want to live—and not in terms of how much money you think it will take to attain your goals. The money aspect of goal setting will play its part later on.

2. Make sure that your goals fit into your abilities or the abilities you plan to attain. It should be obvious that if your vision has you doing heart transplants and you are not yet out of high school, you have a lot of work ahead of you and you must plan accordingly.

3. Goals should be set in stages. You will have to establish these visions in increments of future time zones. In other words, the greater the distance you put between now and your first vision, the tougher it will be to attain that goal. It is far better to establish deadlines that are closer together and work for those intermediate goals, attain them and move on toward the greater goal down the road. For example, for a car trip to the West Coast from New York City, you want to know exactly where you want to go (say, Beverly Hills, not just California), but equally important you want to know where you need to stop for gas alone the way.

4. Accept the fact that *failure is essential to success*. This is important because it is a realistic view of life. You have to plan for setbacks so that when they occur you will be able to move on without becoming disillusioned about your ultimate success. Learn by your failures to the extent that you review your own goals to make sure they are attainable. Remember that if your goals are too distant, it is very difficult to be able to find the opportunity to adjust in midstream.

5. Continue to "fine tune" your vision of yourself in the future. This will be a constant ongoing process. The clearer your vision, the easier it will be to attain that image. You will modify and enhance the goals as you advance toward them.

6. Be so specific that you can write down the significant elements of your goals as you visualize them. This is important because it will later give you proof that you have attained your goals. Nothing is better for your self-esteem than the personal satisfaction of attaining something you have set out to obtain. The written-down evidence is important because it is too easy to remember a goal slightly less than or greatly more than its actual realization. Some people therefore are always believing that they are right on target when they are way off base, and others continually fail because they are too harsh on themselves. Be honest with yourself and write down the goal.

7. When you have attained the goal, celebrate. You will enjoy the

success more this way and let these moments offset the moments of failure you are bound to encounter along the way.

HOW YOUR GOALS WILL HELP YOU IN REAL ESTATE AND IN THE USE OF FINANCE

Let's tie everything together and make sure we keep the continuity of goals with the concept of using the tools of real estate finance to make for better real estate financing.

As you develop goals, you will begin to visualize how the other side of the forest should look, even while you are still deep in the woods. This ability allows you to anticipate what you will need to have done, what abilities you will have to attain, and just how much money you may need to accomplish the current and upcoming tasks. You will also begin to see other ways to obtain your desired goals without using cash.

Let me give you an illustration of how this can work for you. Assume that you are a "fresh-out-of-law-school" graduate who has just started to work for some big law firm in Miami, Florida. You have worked hard to get where you are at the moment, and you want to build a future for yourself using all of your abilities. This includes taking the plunge into real estate investing.

EXAMINE ALL OF YOUR ABILITIES

One of the first stages in setting your goals is to look at exactly what you are good at and what you might want to be good at (and therefore could take a course to learn). As a budding lawyer, you might have made the following list:

Abilities

1. Good at law.
2. Can study well.
3. Know and enjoy working around the garden.
4. Have painted inside and outside houses before.
5. Can come up with $10,000 in cash to invest.
6. Can carry a moderate mortgage (rent?) payment of $1,000 per month.
7. Have a high energy level.
8. Have weekends partially free for other self-investment work.

As the list is being composed, your mind is running on the back lot side of the fence. When the abilities list is completed, you begin to look at your liabilities.

Liabilities

1. Have to be very conservative because of the new job and lack of security.
2. Can only spend a few hours per weekend on other work.
3. Have car payments.
4. Have a six-month lease I can't get out of.

Once these two elements have been taken care of, you then sit back and let yourself be immersed into that milky white substance of the clearing of the mind. You work on your vision for several weeks and decide that your destination in about ten years is to:

1. Own your own office building and law practice
2. Own your own home, somewhere in the Boca Raton area
3. Have a forty-foot (or better) sailboat
4. Be financially set for life

In a review of these four goals, you notice that you have not been specific enough concerning the levels of debt that might occur. Owning an office building, home, sailboat, and being set for life are relative to how much you want to owe and what you mean by "set for life". So you sharpen your pencil and come up with these more specific goals:

1. Owning an office building where you can have your own offices without expense, sufficient income to support any debt on the building, and a minimum of a current market rate return on your cash invested.
2. Own a home on the water in Boca Raton where you can dock your boat and own the home free of any debt.
3. Own a forty-foot sailboat free of any debt.
4. Have sufficient "outside" income to support all insurance needs, and all costs to keep and maintain a home.

ON THE WAY TO SETTING INTERMEDIATE GOALS

Once the revised goals are established, you can set your intermediate goals to guide you along the way. These intermediate goals may include a number of items that may not be necessary at first, but may at the outset go down on the list. Your preliminary list of steps to attain your goals could look like this:

1. Need to build a specialty in my law field that will support my other

goal interests. This specialty should be within the real estate field in the geographic areas in which I want to live and invest.

2. I need to develop an insight to the techniques of investing in real estate and specific contacts in the area where I want to live and invest.

3. I may want to buy some vacant land on which I can build my office building and/or home in the future.

4. I should anticipate learning how to operate a forty-foot sailboat.

5. My first step is to stop renting and start owning and building equity.

6. I shall begin Monday.

Your approach to setting your goals should follow similar stages in real life. This need not be an overnight event, and if you are married or have dependents they should be a part of this process.

WHO DO YOU LET KNOW YOUR GOALS?

Your goals have to be your own goals and not your friends' goals that have been superimposed on you. This goes for your family goals too. Yours, together—not parents' goals, not friends' goals. But what then? Whom do you entrust with this personal information? Who do you let know your secret?

The answer is: Keep your goals to yourself and only the most important members of your "advancement" team.

DEVELOP AN ADVANCEMENT TEAM

Every person who has a plan should have as part of that plan an advancement team. This team is made up of people who can advance your interests toward your goals. The available members to the team are many, and best of all their services may be totally free. Others may charge you only for their performance, while others will charge you by the hour. In any event, to attack a future without an advancement team is foolhardy.

Your advancement team consists of the following people:

General Team Members	*Specific Team Members*
Realtors	Your specific and loyal lawyer
Bankers	Your own true and true accountant
Insurance companies	Your own banker
Loan officers at savings and loans	A trusted financial advisor
A handyman you know and trust	
Local governmental officials	

Of these advancement team members, you will entrust your goals only to specific team members. The general team members should be told only what they need to know, as they need to know it. (It's like sending them behind the lines—you never know whether the enemy will get to them.)

PUT YOUR GOALS, YOUR TEAM MEMBERS, AND YOUR ABILITIES TO WORK

The total picture now comes together: You have your goals, you see your abilities and your liabilities, and you begin to develop your team members and your techniques at the same time. The only thing that is keeping you from success and attainment of your goals is fear of failure, or just fear itself. There is still one element you need to attend to. It's the development of your comfort zone. Once you have finished this last task, risk will be minimized and success is just around the corner.

PROFIT IN REAL ESTATE THROUGH YOUR COMFORT ZONE

The comfort zone is a geographic area. It is in essence the total geographic area in which you will live and invest. It is your zone of reference, your zone of total comfort and knowledge. It will be within this zone that you will reduce or eliminate all risk in activity. It will become your financial security blanket.

WHY IS A COMFORT ZONE IMPORTANT?

Every form of investing or activity has its comfort zone. If you were to make your fortune investing in stamps or coins, you would have to have an area of interest and expertise. Just as in other fields, people first become proficient and then expert in any specific talent. The singer, the dancer, the pilot—each requires something unique, something oriented to one area of risk. To intrude into another's field can be highly risky, even deadly. For the jazz singer to try to sing hard rock could be suicide, as could be true for the Sunday afternoon pilot who tries to land a 747.

All forms of investing have comfort zones in which the participants succeed once they understand the rules, the regulations, and most importantly the pitfalls of what they are doing.

Just as the windsurfer makes that sport look easy (when in reality it is almost impossible until you have spent many hours of practice), the investor with a comfort zone can create the illusion that making money is easy and simple.

What is simple is the technique. What is easy is the concept of how to make money. What is fun is the development of the comfort zone. What is difficult is making money without knowing what you are doing.

HOW THE COMFORT ZONE WORKS
FOR THE REAL ESTATE INVESTOR

Nothing lends itself to a comfort zone as much as real estate. Of course, you can develop a comfort zone in any kind of field or interest, but when it comes to making money in your backyard, real estate is it.

Basically, the reason the comfort zone works is this: Real estate is local in nature. Local real estate has very little relationship to real estate that is across the country or in another, distant town. It is specifically here and not there. It has appeal because of that fact. Its value or lack of it is due solely to where it is located. It is said that "location, location, location" are the three most important aspects of real estate.

Due to real estate's purely local nature, you cannot devise an accurate national statistic on what is going on in the market. The only important fact to keep in mind about national statistics and real estate is that while other people believe a national statistic about a decline in the value of one or more specific kinds of real estate, you can profit from knowing that they are increasing in value in your area.

The stock market expert can watch the market and become the national expert in gold, silver, or pork bellies. But someone in Chicago can never be an expert on Ashville, North Carolina, real estate unless that town is part of his or her comfort zone.

There can be a million experts in real estate, each having a different comfort zone, each knowing more about a particular area than any other person, and yet none of them ever infringe on the others. Your comfort zone then will be the totality of where you are comfortable in the opportunity to use your techniques and abilities within the real estate game. Some of you will become multinational investors who think nothing of building high-rise buildings, while others will be single-home investors who never buy any further than two miles from where you live. The whole idea is to be pleased with yourself, to have confidence in what you are doing, to achieve the goals you set for yourself, and to sleep soundly at night.

FORMING YOUR COMFORT ZONE

Prior to forming your comfort zone, you should develop the goals that I discussed earlier. Without a clear set of goals, you will not be able to formulate or benefit from your comfort zone properly.

To establish your comfort zone, begin with your goals. Remember when you role-played the lawyer whose list of four goals were the office building, the home, the sailboat, and certain economic freedom. A comfort zone would be devised to help you attain those goals. However, in getting started the comfort zone may have little relationship to the final product.

If you, as a young lawyer, began at a stage in your life where you wanted to buy office buildings and have waterfront homes in Boca Raton, Florida, you would develop as your comfort zone the specific areas that contain exactly the kind of property that you want to buy. This means that you would geographically locate a zone or territory that consists of office buildings and waterfront homes in Boca Raton.

You then would define that area in specific terms. It might be all the property along three main commercial streets in town, or all the waterfront properties along five or six canals. Whatever the area, it would begin small and work into a comprehensive area.

However, because you are just starting out, you may begin with your more immediate needs, your intermediate goals.

To this end, you still devise a geographic area, and you will follow the same techniques you will use later on as you advance to the higher, more specific areas of your dreams and goals.

HOW TO SET UP THE COMFORT ZONE AREA

You might want to establish your first ownership of real estate, or find a good investment in apartment buildings. These final types of properties that you decide you want to buy should take you closer to your final goal.

First, you have to learn how to set your priorities to the kind of property you want to own within the geographic area we now call your comfort zone. Since you cannot know everything about every area of town, you need this specific area to be well chosen and clearly defined. So decide right now that you will never stray from your comfort zone.

This "never stray out of the comfort zone" rule is not a limiting element. The concept is that you must start somewhere, and that as you develop the comfort zone you will be adding to your own confidence and therefore reducing your risk. As this process develops, the comfort zone is expanded little by little. So instead of being limiting, it is constantly allowing you to expand your opportunity awareness safely.

STEPS TO SETTING UP YOUR COMFORT ZONE

1. Review Your Goals
2. Review with Your Specific Team Members What Kind of Property Can Move You Closer to Your Goals
3. Pick a Part of Town Where You Can:
   a. Find the kind of property you want to own

     b. Feel comfortable

     c. Be able to get to easily

4. Begin to Learn All You Can about that Part of Town

     a. Start by driving around in the area. Do you like what you see?

     b. Walk and/or jog in the area during all times of day.

     c. Get your team members to help. They can provide:

       (i) Maps

       (ii) Zoning books and regulations

       (iii) Local officials names and addresses

       (iv) Local tax laws

       (v) Property ownership information

       (vi) Introductions to important people

       (vii) Invaluable contacts

     d. Go to the town hall meetings

     e. Talk with the road department

       (i) Learn what is going on, where roads are to be built

       (ii) What are the busy areas in town?

     f. Meet the planning and zoning officials in town

       (i) They know what is going on long before the newspapers

       (ii) The officials will tell you what is going on

     g. Be observant

5. Get Your Knowledge Together

     a. Get the data on the properties you want to own

     b. Contact the owner

     c. Demonstrate that you know more about that property than anyone

6. Put Your Other Talents to Play

     a. You will have more confidence in your own abilities

     b. You will reduce risk in your investment portfolio by:

       (i) Knowing what is going on in your area

       (ii) Being able to "tell" what is a good buy in your area

       (iii) Have more deals come to you because you are becoming known as the "expert" in the area

THIS CONCEPT WORKS WELL FOR INVESTORS AND REAL ESTATE SALESPEOPLE

Using the comfort zone concept, you can actually feel the power gained through knowledge. Knowledge, by the way, is the same kind of foundation that makes one real estate salesperson stand out over another. Smart real estate salespeople will learn all that they can about the area in which they want to list and sell real estate. Their demonstration of being experts in the area enables them to dazzle owners into the realization that the best person to list and sell their property is someone who knows the property like the back of his or her hand.

The investor who has established goals, has picked out a comfort zone, and is proceeding to become an expert in the area will equally demonstrate to the participants that he knows what he is doing.

The effect of all of this is multilevel. Not only will sellers be more receptive to buyers who are so knowledgeable, but lenders also will lean toward doing business with this kind of person.

Much of the art of using the tools of finance depend on your being able to convince the other side of the deal that what you propose is sound, good business for all persons involved, and should be accomplished.

The prospective investor who shows up at the local savings and loan without confidence in himself and without assurance that he can back up the property will not be well received.

A WORLD OF NAMELESS, FACELESS NEIGHBORS

The comfort zone works simply because people have a tendency to live in a world in which they keep to themselves. We don't know the names of our neighbors, we don't know values across the street, and we don't even care if the house down the block is rented, or if so, for how much. Investors buy for many reasons, often taking the word of their realtor or salesperson as to what is going on in the area. This fact may not hamper their success, since many investors obviously do succeed with this tactic of investing.

However, this involves taking more risk than is necessary for the majority of investors, and most certainly for the investor who doesn't have a lot that can be placed at risk.

The "lack of knowledge" that most people have of where they live and invest can then work for the investor who has developed his own comfort zone and works it properly.

MAKING YOUR COMFORT ZONE WORK
WITH CREATIVE TOOLS

Once your goals are firmly established in your mind and you are underway with your plan, the critical steps are just around the corner. You must implement your plan with the financing techniques, and how you use them will become an important aspect of your success in real estate investing. All of the financing techniques and tips described in this book can be utilized in combination with each other, giving you nearly endless opportunities to best solve a problem at hand or seek the best format to buy or sell your real estate to take you closer to your desired goal. The subtleties of these techniques will begin to become evident as you use them. Each will have a slightly different effect on each deal and for each user. A sale lease-back in one transaction could work wonders for you, whereas in the next deal it could be the least attractive format.

You should approach each real estate investment with the question, "Do I need to buy this?" If the answer is yes, your whole approach to the transaction may be greatly altered. In essence, you would be "forced" to find a technique that solved that basic need (to buy that property), with the secondary benefit of doing so at the best terms possible. On the other hand, if the answer was no, but that you *would buy it only if it was clearly a good deal*, you can be far more selective in the use of your financing techniques and can walk away from those deals that cannot be made on terms that enable you to "own" that property in such a way that it moves you closer to your desired goals.

Keep your goals constantly in your mind. Review them, update them, and work toward them. They are what will help keep you out of trouble. Your goals will keep you on the right track.

The following list will show you many opportunities to the end result of disposing of real estate. Review this list from time to time to remind yourself that disposition of real estate is not just selling, and in some cases not even a transfer of title. Real estate ownership can be considered the use and benefit of the real estate as much as the holding of a fee simple title.

54 METHODS OF DISPOSING OF REAL ESTATE

1. Acquisition (of additional property)
2. Adverse possession
3. Bankruptcy
4. Build to suit
5. By will
6. Charitable contribution
7. Chattel
8. Condemnation
9. Conversion
10. Demolition
11. Development
12. Discount sale with lease-back
13. Discount sale with recapture
14. Easement lease
15. Easement sale
16. Eminent domain
17. Escheat

18. Exchange all the property
19. Exchange a portion of the property
20. General corporation
21. Gift
22. Joint venture
23. Holding company
24. Insurance lease
25. Insurance mortgage
26. Improvement of building
27. Lease of air rights
28. Lease of all rights
29. Lease—Sub.
30. Limited partnership
31. Mortgage out—foreclose
32. Option-lease *uni lateral contract*
33. Option-sale
34. Partition sale
35. Prescription
36. Pyramid *acquiring additional properties through refinancing properties already owned and the reinvesting in new*
37. Reclamation
38. Refinancing
39. Rent
40. Rezoning
41. Sale—air rights
42. Sale—Improvements only
43. Sale—Land only
44. Sale—auction
45. Sale/lease riparian
46. Sale—lease-back with recapture
47. Sale or lease of leasehold
48. Sell option back
49. Subdivide
50. Subordination
51. Subordination of mortgage
52. Syndicate *two or more people investing.*
53. Tax sale
54. Trust

All of the foregoing methods to dispose of real estate can be accomplished with various tactics. The finesse that you develop as you use different methods will depend on the opportunities you have and the variety of circumstances that arise.

Once you have finished this book, plan on going over this chapter again to remind you of the importance of goals and your comfort zone.

Chapter 3

THE POWER OF NEGOTIATING

The business of real estate is negotiating. Nothing happens within the closed doors of bankers, buyers, sellers, developers, and so on that is not won or lost on the finesse of the participants to negotiate property or, for that matter, to negotiate at all.

When it comes to being a success in real estate, your total knowledge will be a waste of time if you learn nothing about negotiating or cannot have someone who does know stand in for you at this critical stage of the game.

This stage is by far the easiest of all if you know what you are doing, just as the pilot will tell you that taking off is a snap in relation to landing.

This chapter is not meant to teach you all you could learn about this fine art. Instead, it is like the first-aid course that may save your life just at that critical moment you'll need it most, as well as help keep you from needing a more specialized person to pull you out of the economic fire.

THE FOUR STEPS TO SUCCESSFUL NEGOTIATING

The following steps will guide you through the early stages of getting your act into proper gear so that you can present your case in a businesslike way, and move into the close of the transaction with clear sight of your end goal. As you move through these four steps, you will find that the most essential part of any negotiating is to have an absolutely clear vision of your goal. If you don't know what it is you are negotiating for, your end result is apt to be far different from your original desire. Also critical is your understanding that winning doesn't mean coming out ahead of the other party.

The best part of dealing with these four steps and then succeeding in the art of negotiating is that you don't require a degree or any education other than the ability to demonstrate empathy and to keep your cool. The homework that you may need to do from time to time will be easy, and there will be many people ready to help you. Sometimes the most help comes from the other side itself.

Step 1: The Foundation of the Deal

The first step in any negotiation is to make sure you have a clear understanding of the goal to be served. If the property must be purchased to allow redevelopment of an adjoining property, there will be different tactics used in the acquisition of the site than if the goal was to add a few more acres to the family farm. Write down the goal, and the way in which a successful negotiation will help attain that goal. This will help you stay on track during the negotiation process.

For example, suppose it is your desire to buy an apartment building for yourself. Within Step 1 of negotiating, you must examine the various elements involved.

1. What is the long-range goal you plan to reach through the purchase or acquisition of the apartment building? This long-term goal must be kept clearly in sight because it is too easy to overlook the original objective and to attain the desired result in such a way that you jeopardize your long-term position. Assume that your long-term goal is to establish a steady income at the end of a fifteen-year period and that the apartment complex will fill that need at that time by paying off its debt and being in a very good and very safe economic position.

Once the total goal is seen, visualized, and written down, you can move deeper into the foundation in preparation of your negotiations. One of the next stages is the review of options open to you to meet this goal. How many apartment buildings have you seen? Where do you want your apartment building? And so on. Each move toward the end result will take you deeper into more alternatives that can sway you from your intended path. It is important that you be flexible so that as you move into this jungle you won't overlook the fact that other pathways that present themselves to you might lead to improved goals. However, do not let the "greener grass syndrome" take you into an ambush by the local natives. Many a would-be investor has lost his or her head over something that looked too good, too easy, too quick.

However, look and examine the alternatives. Have you overlooked that possibility, is that a better place, is this a better kind of investment, does this take me closer to my goal? Is this in my comfort zone? Or do I need to change my goals or expand my comfort zone?

All investors who succeed ask themselves these questions over and over.

You will be set to proceed to the next step in negotiating when you are comfortable that you know just how far you are willing to go in the acquisition of the property. Even here, however, you must be flexible. The other participants may have some elements available that you don't know about, and these elements might get you where you want to go quicker than you thought. But remember this word of warning: The best negotiator is the guy who makes you believe that you have just won when in fact he has.

The foundation, therefore, is:

1. Know your goals.
2. Find properties that will take you closer to your goals.
3. Set the maximum economic cost that you feel you can afford on any specific property.
4. Keep an open mind as to how that economic cost can be handled.
5. Get ready to move to the next step.

Step 2: Doing Your Homework

There are two basic kinds of negotiation: (1) blind, and (2) open.

1. Blind. This is the most common kind of negotiation. Blind is when you have no idea who you are dealing with, and make little or no effort to find out the motivations that steer the other side of the deal. Blind negotiations occur much of the time because of blocks in the way of your finding out anything about the other side. Real estate brokers or salespeople are one such roadblock. In real estate transactions, they frequently represent the sellers and like to keep control of the situation. They want to keep the buyer and seller apart and generally feel that each party should know as little about the other party as possible. This situation is founded on the premise that many transactions are lost when the buyer and seller get together. However, it is a good idea that you know as much as possible about the other party, whether you are the buyer or the seller. This will help you put together a deal that will work. Let the broker keep you apart. That's just fine.

Blind negotiation is not a waste of time, however. The speed with which you can make an offer makes blind negotiation work when speed is the most critical element of the transaction. If you know your comfort zone well and recognize that the property offered is a bargain, you have already done your homework and that additional information on the other party may not be necessary. This points out the importance of knowing all you can about the property you want to buy or the market in which you want to sell. That homework is the most essential.

2. Open. This form of negotiation involves a lot of homework. The idea is to know as much as possible about your counterpart so that when it comes time to make the deal you won't have any surprises or anything outstanding to keep you from closing the transaction. In essence, you have made the decision that this is a deal you want and that you will do all that you can to make the deal within reason and legality. This kind of negotiation isn't as difficult as it might seem. Most of the homework you can and will do will fall into your lap, if you let it. Of course, you should rely on the help of your broker, lawyer, or accountant whenever he or she can be of assistance. Let me give you an example of one such transaction where the homework made the difference.

Charles wanted to own a home that he saw on Center Avenue. It was just a few blocks from the beach, he could walk to his office on nice days, and he liked the look of the house from the street. After only two blind offers, the seller stood firm at a price that Charles didn't think was realistic. In essence, price was standing in the way of the deal. Instead of giving up on the transaction, Charles decided to have his broker look into the motivations of the seller. Keep in mind that the broker worked for the seller, so he already knew some things about him. What Charles was interested in most was knowing what would turn the seller into a willing participant to the transaction. This was the critical stage of the transaction, because the broker didn't want to betray any secrets, but at the same time he wanted to make a deal.

This is a good time to explain the legal position of the broker in this and most deals. In the United States, the real estate broker represents the seller unless the broker represents otherwise and so notifies all parties to the transaction. If the buyer goes to a broker and hires the broker to help him buy a property, the broker must notify the seller of this situation. Ethically, if the broker was the seller's agent before the buyer asked the broker to change positions, the broker would have to refuse to represent the buyer. Loyalty would have to remain with the original client. Now, unless you were watching you might have missed the word *ethical*. Legally, the broker could change position simply by giving notice that he no longer was the agent of the seller and that he was now going to represent the buyer.

To get back to Charles' problem, he wants to buy the property, the broker wants him to buy the property, and the seller wants someone to buy his property. But so far, neither the seller nor any buyer has been able to get together to make the deal work.

Charles knows that in good negotiations there is always a way to make a deal if one side makes a greater effort than the other to put the deal to bed. Since Charles is a good businessman, he knows that there is a limit to the economic cost of the transaction for the deal to make sense to him, and he would like to get in as inexpensively as possible. Therefore, Charles wants to find out about the seller, to discover if there is some factor that will help put the deal together. If the seller must be educated, then so be it.

The homework Charles must consider may take a different tact than that which you may require to make your next deal. But all homework must follow the following outline for it to be comprehensive and to the point.

THE FOUR HOMEWORK FACTORS
THAT MAKE DEALS COME TOGETHER

1. Why Does the Other Guy Want to Buy or Sell? Simple logic will tell you that this is the toughest question to answer. If you are the buyer, you want to know the reason the seller wants to sell. The reason the broker comes up with is apt to be a figment of the broker's imagination or the seller's invention. You need to look deeper. Do some homework. Find the answers to such questions as: What are the economic factors of the property? Is there a mortgage foreclosure, are there liens filed against the property or the people? Has the owner lost his job? What is it that has occurred that causes this property to be up for sale?

The answer is not as obvious an answer as it is a review of the circumstances. The seller just bought a new home. He just divorced his wife. He lost everything he owned in the storm and wasn't insured. He drew into an inside straight. He just doesn't know what he is doing. Or whatever.

If you are the seller, knowing why the other guy wants to buy is helpful too. The answer to this question is a bit more difficult to find since the motivations of those who have money or who are in the "taker" position are more difficult to inspect.

Yet sellers can, if they play their cards right, make the buyer tell them all that they need to know through the broker.

As a seller, the important data to know is what the buyer plans to do with the property. Whether it is a home to live in, a property to build on, or just a pass through, the tenure of ownership will tell the seller something about the interest of the buyer.

Much of the homework you do is a matter of being aware of what is going on around the transaction. That information must then be tied into the form of negotiations you devise to meet any objection that stands in your way of successfully concluding the transaction.

Other parts of the homework fall into the comfort zone that we have discussed in earlier sections of this book. So far, each of these two tactics is a question of awareness and comfort. The facts are often public knowledge and easy to obtain once you know how to find them.

For example, in your community there are sources of information that can tell you a lot about the person with whom you are dealing. Some of these are:

A city cross-reference directory. This is a book much like a telephone book but it contains other data, such as place of employment, name of spouse and children. You also can check addresses to match phone numbers if you have one and not the other. Once you know where your counterpart lives and works, you can go deeper into the background of that person.

A city social directory. If you are dealing with one of the social cream, you can bet that he or she will be listed in the social directory. This book often tells you things such as the clubs the person belongs to, the name of his or her yacht, the person's summer or winter address, the names of children, where the children are going to school, and so on. A check of some of these key items can be rewarding.

County court house. Here, you can find a great deal of information about many people in your community. What real estate do they own, how much tax do they pay, what did they pay for the real estate they own? Do they have mortgages on their real estate? Is there a foreclosure in the wings? How much? Have they been sued? When and for what? Are they divorced? Married? And so on.

Credit reports. You can obtain a credit report on anyone. Look in your phonebook for companies that provide this service. If you are a member of Dun and Bradstreet, this is a good place to start. But be careful of the institutional kind of report. It often only shows up the shine, and unless the person has had a lot of bad news lately, that part may not be available for the usual D and B report.

Better Business Bureau. Give this organization a call if your counterpart in the deal is a businessperson in the community. What about his or her reputation anyway? If you find a long list of complaints, be warned that you may soon be following with one of your own.

Relying on reports such as those mentioned will give you some insight to the person and the potential problems you might have. But by themselves they will not make your deal for you. You will have to make your deal based on the final play of this game as it develops. Homework only gives you the edge; the actual play is up to you.

2. *Who Is He or She Trying to Impress?* Almost everyone has someone he or she is trying to impress. The loan officer wants to impress his boss, the guy down the street wants to impress his wife or his girlfriend, and your next-door neighbor may want to impress you. Whom do you want to impress?

While you may never discover the person the other party is trying to impress most, it should be obvious to you that knowing that information would be very important. For example, some people want to impress their parents more than anything else in the world. Other people want to impress their bosses, or employees, while others are constantly trying to impress their wives or girlfriends. Possessing this information would allow you to present an offer that would allow the person to impress that person most. If it was the mother, a casual remark made in front of the party such as, "I'll bet your mother would be proud of you at your making a deal like this" would do no harm.

Try to find out something about the other party if you can. Sometimes you can get enough insight from the real estate broker, or if the deal is big enough, and important enough, some homework in the way of research into the other party's motives or interests will help. Knowing who the other party wants to impress, and why, could be the difference between a closed deal and wasted effort.

3. Know the Timing of the Transaction Better Than the Other Party.
How much can you know about the time elements that the other person must face up to? Time often gets in the way of many deals. If it is the loan officer: When does she have to meet her quota? If it is the seller: When does he have to own up to his foreclosure? Or what about the buyer: When does she have to move out of her current home? Or office? Or when must she meet some deadline?

Find out the deadline of the other person by asking the following types of questions:

"When do you need this property?"
"Is the first of March okay?"
"Can you get an okay by June 15?"

By itself, the time element is not critical unless there is a specific urgency, such as the buyer's lease is up on the first of next month. Any time urgency works in favor of the opposing party. The party with the time urgency will make a deal that is realistic, even one that costs more than he wants to pay or gets him less than he wants to get. However, some participants will end the deal if they feel they are being delayed: "Look Charlie, I can't fool around with that guy any longer. Get me another deal . . . even if I have to pay a little more. Okay?"

If the negotiation is with a loan officer, knowing the time elements that affect the loan committee's meetings, the quota that the loan officer has to meet within a certain time period to keep from getting red marks on his chart, and other time traps can affect you in your need for money. For example, a 90-day delay while your credit is being checked when you only have 60 days to meet some contract provision to keep your deal alive can be disastrous.

4. Verify the Facts. This sounds like good, sound business practice. However, you would be surprised to learn that most deals are completed without the major factors being tested out. In many transactions, the end result is that those factors might not have mattered anyway. However, if you are trying to make the best deal you can, you owe it to yourself to make sure that the following items are verified.

As a buyer:

A. Price: Is the price quoted to you the lowest price quoted in the most recent period? Sometimes brokers get old brochures—in reality, the price may have gone down. I don't ever recall a seller telling the offering party that he had just reduced the price from $300,000 to $250,000 when the would-be buyer has just offered $275,000. Make sure your broker has double-checked the price the day you go to make the offer.

B. The Legal Description. The legal description can be, as an example "LOT 1, BLOCK 7 OF THE CUMMINGS PLAT NUMBER 1" (often followed by other information such as a tax folio number to make it easy to find the property through tax rolls). Be sure that the legal description you put in the offer is in fact the property you want to buy. This error sometimes occurs, and people have bought the wrong property. It is critical that you do this for vacant land and improved property. In addition to any legal description, I suggest that the property be described in layman's terms as well: "THAT PROPERTY LOCATED AT 2671 EAST COMMERCIAL BLVD., FORT LAUDERDALE, FLORIDA, 33308, CONSISTING OF A TWO-STORY OFFICE BUILDING CONSISTING OF 3,100 SQ. FEET ON A LOT SIZED 36' FRONTAGE ON EAST COMMERCIAL BLVD., AT A DEPTH OF 150' TO AN ALLEY TO THE NORTH, WHICH ARE THE PRESENT OFFICES OF CUMMINGS REALTY INC." It would be difficult for a problem to arise if you take this simple step. There is one additional step to add to this protection: "AS IS SHOWN ON THE ATTACHED SURVEY AND PLAT MAP."

To illustrate what can happen if you don't pay attention, let me give you an example. I purchased a vacant lot (and later built a home on it) in Fort Lauderdale. The property was the last vacant lot in an area of homes that fronted canals leading to the ocean. It was very odd to find a vacant lot in this area, and on walking the lot I realized that the reason it had remained vacant was its odd shape and the small amount of water frontage it had on the canal. The lot seemed unattractive due to vegetation on two sides of the lot (the lot itself was a corner, so it had streets on two sides, and neighbors on two sides, with a fifth side facing the canal). Along its northern boundary were a massive hedge and a tree line that ran down to the canal retaining wall to a point where there was a marker nail driven into the concrete and with a yellow circle around it. The amount of canal frontage that seemed to belong to this lot was only about 20 feet, whereas all of the neighbors had 100 feet or more of dock space. However, on reviewing the plat, it turned out that the lot actually was larger than it appeared and had about 60 feet of canal frontage with riparian rights that gave the lot an ideal dockage for boats up to 70 feet. Also, all of the hedges, trees, and barbecue, and most of the lawn sprinklers and yard of the home to the north belonged to this lot, which I bought.

I also discovered that the home to the north had gone through five owners in the past seven years. I surmised that each past owner made the discovery of just where their south lot line really was located and sold out to someone else.

The current owner of the property to the north had no idea of course. He had had the title checked, the plat checked, and a survey made, all of which were reviewed by a local attorney who had failed to do one critical thing. Neither the attorney nor the current owner had walked the property with a tape measure to locate the actual corners and side line distances. Had either of them done so, they would have known that the nail and yellow circle were the figment of an overly anxious seller.

The lesson learned here is to be sure of everything that relates to the specific property in question.

C. The Mortgages. Whether you are taking out or assuming a mortgage, be sure you understand all of its terms. The mortgage documents should be in your possession prior to your final acceptance of any offer and your lawyer should go over the mortgage with you to explain it fully. Do not let him slip by a clause by saying, "That's common." You should know what it means, and be sure you will agree to its terms.

For new mortgages, you will be able to negotiate some terms and conditions. You should question any part of a mortgage you don't like or that sounds unfair. If it doesn't sound fair, it probably isn't.

Many mortgages have clauses and conditions that can be confusing to anyone, including wise and educated lawyers and real estate brokers. These clauses include, but are by far not limited to:

1. Term of payment.
   How many payments? When can the mortgage be paid off ahead of schedule? Is it principal plus interest, or interest and principal? How is amortization calculated? Are the payments monthly, or what?
2. Balloon payments.
   One balloon or two? When? How much exactly?
3. Assumption by other parties.
4. Pay off penalty.
5. Acceleration.

6. Form of payment.
   In U.S. dollars? Monthly with principal and interest? Is the escrow included or added in a lump?

7. Escrowing.
   Why?

8. Insurance included or required.
   Can you get your own? Why is it required?

9. Title insurance.
   Can you provide your own and coinsure the lender?

D. What Is Included with the Property?   Is a comprehensive inventory attached to the contract, or do you at least have the right to make up an inventory and approve it? If you don't approve it, can you get out of the deal prior to the closing? If not, you may be making a bad deal. The only time you will get everything you think you are getting is to have it in writing. Make sure that you get an inventory that is specific: not just chairs and tables and beds, but specific chairs and tables and beds. A good idea is to go through the property with a red marker and number each item of furniture and each fixture (provided the mark does not detract from the value of the property). If you cannot mark the property itself, place a stick-on tab on the item with your initial and that of the seller. Then make a detailed list of each item. The hazard of not doing this early in the negotiation or shortly after the contract is that items will disappear and/or will be replaced with less valuable items.

The same goes for the landscaping. If there are valuable plants in the garden and you want to make sure that they remain, do an inventory of the gardens (preferably with a camera). I can give you many sad stories of sellers taking plants with them.

As the seller:

A. Exactly When Will the Closing of the Transaction Occur?   If you think that the closing date is the one that is filled into the blank following the words "The closing will occur on the ————— day of ————— in the year 19———," then you might be in for a surprise. Sharp buyers have a tendency to insert provisions in the agreement that may, at their option and often at their control, delay the closing well beyond the established date indicated on the contract. You should examine the agreement carefully to determine whether such conditions exist and what delays they may cause. One safe thing to do is to put an outside date in the agreement with wording such as: "All parties agree that under no circumstance whatsoever shall the closing occur after the following date, providing the seller is not in default in this agreement and has used due diligence to meet all obligations herein contained, and that if the buyer elects not to close on that date and the seller does not extend the closing date then this agreement will terminate and any and all deposits placed in escrow pending the closing will become liquidated, damages to the favor of the seller." Keep in mind that this is just a part of what you will need in your agreement. The wording is not as critical as the effect.

B. How Is the Price Determined, and Exactly How Much Is It? I have seen agreements that showed a price that the seller would never get due to other conditions that took away from that price. If the agreement calls for you, the seller, to pay certain costs; cover certain expenses; make repairs, additions, refurbish; give credit for changes; allow for interest to be included; have moratoriums on interest or principal or both, these are all deductions from the price.

As long as you agree with these deductions, there is no problem—but watch out if you don't. By the way, don't assume that your lawyer will tell you about these items. He is apt to look at the agreement with a legal eye instead of a business eye, thinking that whatever terms or conditions are contained in the agreement are acceptable to you.

C. What Are You Selling? For the same reason the buyer wanted to know what he was buying, you need to check very carefully what it is you are about to sell. I can tell you from first-hand experience that it is easy to slip up in this area if you own a lot of property or have complicated legal descriptions on the property being sold. The solution to this problem is exactly that as was provided for the buyer. Review that section once more.

D. How Are the Mortgages Paid? The same situation that befalls the buyer will befall you, only you as seller have other considerations to look after. If you have a large taxable income or capital gain as a result of this sale, the method of payment of the mortgage could have a major impact on your tax considerations. You may want to make some adjustments in that area prior to final agreement.

Step 3: Get Started on the Right Foot

In the art of negotiation, it is important to begin properly. You should establish, right up front, the tone of the negotiation and the pattern you wish to follow. This will be your game plan, and like all good game plans it will be flexible enough to allow you to make adjustments along the way to meet any objections.

It is my opinion that in buying real estate a direct confrontation between the buyer and the seller is not wise. Now by this I do not mean that the buyer and the seller should not know each other, nor that they should not be in communication during the negotiation process. I mean that all *confrontation* should be left to intermediaries. This works for both the buyer and the seller.

KEYS TO GETTING STARTED

1. If you already know the other party, maintain the same relationship as before if it is friendly; if it is not friendly, do nothing to aggravate the circumstances. Don't make any rash changes in the friendship. Under the circumstances, you are apt to appear to be insincere and may discredit your proposal or counterproposals.

2. As a buyer, do not criticize the property or give it praise. However, be polite in complimenting the owners on their good taste, beautiful view, and other obvious elements of the home just as you might had you been invited to tea that afternoon.

As a seller, do not knock yourself out to sell the property. You have a salesperson or broker to do that. If you are called on to give information, do so without adding post scripts: "Yes, but you know . . ."

3. Do not criticize the agents or brokers representing the deal. You never know whether the agent is the other party's brother- or sister-in-law, mother, or friend. Even if he or she is not, there is no reason to find fault with the people the other party has hired as representatives. Some buyers do this in the belief that they can divide the broker from the seller and therefore make some gain.

4. Explain your goals without expressively including the property in them. "I want to acquire a vacant tract to build an industrial park. I have had this dream for several years now and believe that now is the time for me to act on that goal. My timing is such that I wish to have a property under contract within the next 30 days so that I can lock up my financing, get my building permits, and start construction as soon as possible."

5. DO EVERYTHING YOU SAID YOU WOULD DO ON TIME, OR SOONER

If you promised the seller that you would have your lawyer call his lawyer by Friday, make sure the call takes place on Thursday. If you said you would be there at 3:00 P.M. be there by 2:55 P.M. at the latest. This sets a theme that you value your time enough to get things done and that you value other people's time so as not to waste it.

6. Critical Elements to Remember:

    a. Avoid using the other party's phone or taking calls that are about other business while in the presence of the other party. If you are at a place of business or home of the other party or his lawyer and you must use the phone for some other business, wait until you have concluded your business with that party.

    b. Do not say "We are tired of dealing with people who waste our time. I want you to know we aren't like that," or any other statement that only your actions can prove.

    c. Do not praise yourself. However, feel free to let others mention your past successes or point out your professionalism. All you have to do is be professional.

d. Do not lie. If you can't think of any good truth, say nothing. Many people lie and never get caught. However, it is the quickest way to end a negotiation or, at best, discredit everything you have said.

Step 4: Understand the Fundamentals of Negotiation

Communication becomes a step to understanding any form of negotiation. Like an argument, it is very difficult to have lasting problems if there is no communication. It is the same in negotiations. It is better to have no communication at all than to have no understanding, or bad communication.

But you must get your point across. And you do that by demonstration more than by talk. Talk is the murderer of negotiation.

How then do you negotiate? As a buyer of real estate, you do it through an offer to buy, or a letter of intent to buy. This occurs after you have concluded many elements of the transaction that less informed people want to "negotiate" their way through.

The actual negotiation should not occur until there is a confrontation. After all, if you offer $100,000 on a property that the seller has been asking $200,000 for, there is nothing to negotiate if the seller accepts. (Except you won't sleep well wondering if he would have accepted $90,000.) Only when the other party balks at what you want does negotiation begin.

Take into consideration the other form of buying and selling. In bartering, where one person asks (talks) "Would you take $100,000?", the rest of the conversation might go like this:
"Are you offering $100,000?"
"No, just wondering if I did, would you take it?"
"If I said yes, would you want to buy it?"
"If you said yes, I'd think about it."
"So why not offer the $100,000 then?"
Nothing is going on here that resembles negotiation, yet each party thinks they are negotiating pretty well.

Some years ago I was in a rug merchant shop in Tangiers, Morocco. I asked "Would you sell that for $200?"
"Would you like to own this rug?" was the reply.
"I might, if you'd sell it for $200."
"Do you want only one?"
"Yes. One is all I can afford at the moment?"
"Will you take it with you, or must I ship it to you?"
"I'll take it with me."
"You have very good taste, sir. And have made a very good buy."
How I love to meet a good salesman like that!

So don't try to negotiate anything until it is time to do so. All that you will do is make it sound as if you are trying to "feel the other guy out" and that no matter what he says, you will finally offer less.

Know who the enemy is in the game. Both the buyer and the seller are actually on the same side. They both want the same ultimate goal—the sale of the property. The enemy is that raft of truths such as:

1. Taxes
2. Death
3. Government
4. Rejection
5. Hate
6. Fear
7. Failure
8. Desire for immortality
9. Intimidation

To win any game, you must know who you are playing against, so try to let other game players help you rather than block you. It's like having your star player on the bench right when you need him in the game. The only thing you have to remember to do is not let on that you know the other guy is really on your team . . . better to let him think you are on his.

Winning in negotiation is not a matter of intimidation. Intimidation is one of the enemies. It is poise and diplomacy that win the game.

All participants in the game of negotiation want to feel that they are the winner. Good participants know just how far they can go to get the points they feel are essential and still let the other side walk away satisfied.

It is possible to nail someone's back to the wall when all their chips are down, or to play a dirty game putting them into a position where there are no other participants. I won't judge you nor will I claim there is a special morality in the matter of business or negotiation. Each player must find the kind of game they want to play. I have known very successful businesspeople who are ruthless and cunning, who had no friends, and who won their business deals by pushing their counterparts to the wall. Some of these "successful" people have hung themselves, filed bankruptcy, or fled to Rio, and they are usually sad cases. Were they successful? Only in their minds.

In the real estate field, success tends to be related to fair dealing. Much of what really goes on between the people who will help you, occurs without contract, without obligation, because all of us need people we can trust. So you will spend much of your business life finding out who you cannot trust and therefore cannot deal with.

Some of the difficult-to-negotiate-with people are just frightened or unsophisticated men and women who are in trouble and don't know who to turn to for help. These people don't want to appear to be frightened or unsophisticated, so they delay, balk, or just become uncommunicative.

You may batter down those kinds of doors, but it can be a very slow and unpredictable process.

It is a good idea to remember that the sweetner of success is failure. After all, without failure there would be no pleasure to success.

I call this to your attention because in any negotiation you will be under the pressure of "failing" at your intended task. In the case of real estate investment, the task is generally to make the best investment possible to meet or take you closer to your desired goals. To do this requires you to: (1) find properties you would want to own which serve your needs, and (2) make offers and attempt to negotiate the acquisition of those properties. All successful real estate investors fail at step 2 much of the time. Your failure in this task should not be discouraging to you, nor should you let it deter you from moving along to another property.

You should fail from time to time in step 2 because, if you don't, you are doing one of two things.

1. You are buying property on terms that are not favorable to your goals. This could be because of your inexperience, or lack of clear understanding of your goals.
2. You aren't making enough offers to buy property. If you pick the property, and stick to terms that you know will help you reach your goal, you will not be able to buy every property you find. Not all sellers will be that cooperative.

Whatever the case, your failures will be positive and allow you to learn more about the use of the tools of the negotiation process. Never avoid a conflict because you fear you can not succeed. But never let a failure go buy without being a learning process.

Chapter 4

HOW TO MAXIMIZE LEVERAGE IN REAL ESTATE FINANCING

Leverage is one of the most misunderstood factors of real estate financing, and its understanding is a prerequisite to the application of the tools of financing. While it often is thought that leverage and risk go hand in hand, and that the greater you have of one the greater you have of the other, this is not always the case. In fact, once you realize just how leverage works, you will see that if this financing tool has been used to its maximum benefit, the greater the leverage the lower the risk.

Nonetheless, the concept of highly leveraged properties as being risky will continue to be deemed as investments to avoid. When you run into this kind of viewpoint, you will have the leisure of knowing that you are dealing with someone who operates under the myth rather than the reality of this factor of financing.

WHAT IS LEVERAGE?

Leverage is the result of borrowing money at a constant rate lower than the Net Operating Income Rate generated by the property. With this in

mind, you should note that the concept of leverage appears only in property that has or is capable of producing income.

For example, suppose you buy a strip store (a common term for a
small shopping center or commercial building that is generally one-level
high and constructed so that all the businesses face the street, and open
out to a walkway in front of the store or office). The store is selling for
$200,000 cash and there is no mortgage. The price you paid then was 100
percent cash. If the Net Operating Income (which is the Total Collected
Rents less the Total Operating Expenses) on this free and clear property
was $22,000 each year, you would have a return on your investment prior
to income tax computations of 11 percent of your cash invested. In this
situation, there is no leverage to calculate because there is no financing.
Without financing, therefore, nothing is leveraged. Leverage only occurs
when there is borrowed money.

On the other hand, if you had purchased this same property and had
used one or more of the financing tools available to you, there would have
been one of three results as to leverage: positive leverage, negative leverage, or no leverage at all. Of these three elements, it is very rare to have
no leverage effect one way or the other because of other factors that can
come to play in the calculations. Thus, this chapter only will discuss
positive and negative leverage.

Assume for this case study that you had put $25,000 down on this
strip store, and had obtained a total of $175,000 in financing. This fi-
nancing might be in one new mortgage obtained from the First Forever
Savings and Loan Association, or a combination of mortgages you finesse
out of the transaction. Assume for a moment that the transaction only has
one mortgage that is held by the seller in the amount of $175,000. The
terms of this mortgage are one annual payment per year of $18,000 until
the mortgage is paid off. This payment of $18,000 per year now represents
a constant annual payment of 10.28 percent per annum. (The constant
payment takes into consideration both principal and interest, and the rate
is an initial percentage which reflects the payment in relation to the *original
amount* of the principal owed.)

Since the total purchase price was $200,000 and the net operating
income was $22,000, if we now have a mortgage payment of $18,000 there
will be a sum of $4,000 left over after all expenses and debt payment.

The leverage factor is viewed as follows: In this case, we have a debt
of $175,000 that has a constant payment of 10.28 percent, or $18,000 per
year. The net operating income is $22,000 when based on the "free and
clear" investment of 11 percent of an all-cash investment. As financing
is introduced into the investment, you will notice that there is to be a
change in the interest yield of the cash invested.

If you only invested $25,000 and had a cash flow (gross income less
all expenses and all debt service payments) of $4,000, you have a cash
yield of 16 percent (16% of $25,000 = $4,000). This means that in this

transaction you have created a positive leverage by increasing the yield on the invested capital from 11 to 16 percent. This increase has come solely from the effect of the financing applied. It is possible that you may have created even greater increase in yield through the use of other financing techniques.

There are many different kinds of financing that you could apply in a situation such as this previous one. The idea of effective use of financing isn't to create the highest positive leverage, as you will soon see can have some disadvantages. The concept of effective use in your application of financing is to utilize the best format to do the most to get you closer to your goals.

In the balance of this chapter, we will delve into leverage and try to show you how to put it to work for you. I will also cover the elements of overleverage and leverage that should be kept at a minimum or a maximum. As in all aspects of anything good, there are pitfalls that must be discussed, and they come in the term *overextension*.

WATCH THE COMBINED EFFECT OF THE CONSTANT RATE ON THE MORTGAGE TO CASH FLOW

The effect of leverage is always examined with its relationship to the constant rate of the mortgages and the constant cash flow rate of the net operating income. As has been mentioned, the combined principal and interest payments of the total mortgages make up the constant rate. This constant rate is fixed at the time of the mortgage for that investor. For example, if you bought the strip store and had one loan for 30 years, with an interest rate of 8.47 percent per annum and the principal balance of the mortgage at the closing of the purchase was $175,000, your annual payment would be $16,000, with a monthly payment each month for 30 years of $1,333.33. The constant rate would be found by dividing the total annual payment by the amount of principal owned ($16,000 divided by $175,000 = 0.0914). To show this as an interest rate, move the decimal two places to the right—9.14 percent.

The constant rate is important as a way to gage the overall effect of financing. Since interest rates only tell you the economic cost of the money you have borrowed, they cannot be the final criteria in the overall cost of the financing. Because the constant rate contains both interest and principal payback, its rate is more of a guide in helping you determine your final cash-flow circumstances.

The constant rate is a function of time and interest, however, and the two elements that will change the constant rate must be examined. As shown in the following table, a $100,000 loan has a combination of constant rates, depending on the functions of time and interest.

A VIEW OF CONSTANT RATES FOR A $100,000 LOAN

Interest	Years	Monthly payment	Annual constant rate
10	25	$ 901.13	10.814 PERCENT
11	30	943.65	11.324
9	10	1,256.93	15.083
8	4	2,423.76	29.086

In this table, you quickly notice that while the lowest interest rate is 8 percent, due to the short payout of four years it has the highest constant payment and therefore the highest constant payment rate.

In the potential refinancing of older properties, it is not uncommon to discover mortgages that can be assumed at rates well below the current market conditions. These mortgages may be attractive to assume on first glance at their interest rate. Yet when you discover the actual cost, the sacrifice to get the attractive interest rate may not be worth the loss of cash flow due to the excessive constant rate.

Your review of the options available to you, and the creative way in which you reduce the overall constant rate, can mean additional cash flow to you and increased value in the property. Each of these two elements satisfy financing goals covered in the first chapter of this book.

VALUE TO LEVERAGE: THE BOTTOM LINE CAN BE
THE MOST IMPORTANT

Investment properties are valued to a great extent by the cash flow they produce. A buyer will pay a price for a return based on the yield he gets from the cash invested. If the risk demand for the investment for this investor is 10 percent, the maximum amount of money the investor may be willing to spend would be the amount that would then earn that desired rate.

Nonetheless, bottom line is not always the most important element when there are specific benefits that can be seen to the investor as a tradeoff for reduced cash flow and yield. This should be obvious with the investment into vacant nonincome-producing property. As there is no income to be leveraged into a higher yield, the sole criteria may become the actual cost to carry the specific property. If the property were to be developed within a year or so, short-term financing may be absorbed into the transaction even though it might have an excessive constant rate in comparison to the actual market conditions of financing.

SIX KEY FACTORS IN REAL ESTATE LEVERAGE

1. The structure of financing will affect the amount of leverage you receive. A short payout of a mortgage may have a very high constant and may eliminate the cash flow entirely. On the other hand, an interest-only mortgage will reduce the constant rate to a lower level for the early term of the loan, even though it may create havoc in the cash flow of later years. The goals of the investor form the basis of the way to establish the leverage best suited for the transaction if the investor has the option available to alter the financing at all.

In many transactions, the investor is limited to the creativity of the circumstances of the deal. Existing mortgages have to be assumed or paid off, rental incomes cannot be immediately increased, and the like. The other side of the investment present roadblocks to everything creative, and yet, the emotion to *own* this property cause the investor to do the best he or she can and to make the best investment he or she is capable of. The techniques within this book are designed to help you accomplish exactly the best you can under the circumstances possible.

2. Leverage calculations themselves are merely a comparison of the yield changes, and should be used only to show the differences between the financing methods that could be used. The actual amount of yield that is increased or decreased is not the specific criteria for the use of the financing tool. However, it is helpful to see how the leverages can be increased or decreased, and know what element is affecting the outcome.

Some of the discount transactions you will have available to you will enable you to increase the amount of loan at zero or very low constant rate. This kind of financing can enable you to average out very low rates.

3. Maximum leverage may not be possible under the circumstances, nor may it be the most advisable. The options available to the buyer or to the seller usually are limited by the circumstances and the goals of both parties. In the give and take of the negotiations, each party may give in to some demand of the other party. In addition to these demands, the factors of finance dictate that some weight must be given to the tradeoff elements of finance by one or more of the parties. It is generally the buyer who has maximum flexibility in this area, and his or her attention to goals and the specifics of the financing tool being used will allow for the buyer to get the maximum out of the financing, even if it is not maximum leverage.

In the tradeoff between elements of financing, these are the items to be balanced toward your desired goal.

Appreciation: Appreciation is the increase in the value of a property over a period of time. While financing has only a passive effect on appreciation, it is nonetheless very real. As income properties are valued as per their income based on the desired yield, a mortgage or set of financing tools that reduce or eliminate the increase of income and set for a long term the yield an investor could earn, the appreciation of this property would be slowed or eliminated. Some financing tools can maximize the immediate cash flow and hold back future increases of value. If the immediate cash flow were the most important aspect of the purchase, that loss would not be a sacrifice at all.

On the other hand, for some investors appreciation is the most important aspect and whole estates are planned on the ultimate growth of a portfolio.

Equity Buildup. This is the slow-and-steady payoff of the principal owed on the debt against the property. An interest-only mortgage would have no principal payback and would therefore have no equity buildup at all. Other mortgages that have a negative payment, which is one where the monthly payment is not sufficient to pay the interest due so unpaid interest is added to the principal owed, actually reduce equity by building onto the amount owed. This kind of financing is good only where the need for cash and the assumed appreciation of the property support taking out the future equity now through greater cash flow.

Cash Flow. This usually is the desired goal for many investors. However, when the existing financing is at a low interest rate, despite the high constant rate of a short-term payback, the sacrifice might well be the cash flow to obtain greater yields later on by increasing the equity buildup for the early years.

Tax Credits. Some investors want greater tax credits and lower immediate cash flow. These investors would want to see financing tools that would provide for maximum tax credits at a sacrifice of cash flow. Some of the tools that increase cash flow have the effect of reducing tax credits. This is all a part of the balance between these four elements.

Use of Funds Available. The maximum use of your investment funds may demand that you get the highest mortgage you can and invest the least cash possible. This frequently is done with the idea that eventual income levels can be increased. This causes investors to go in on a shoe string. Great fortunes can be made this way . . . and lost.

Nonetheless, if you know your comfort zone and have strong and visible goals, you will find that the risk you would have on such an investment may be well below that of the typical investor in the marketplace.

4. The amount of leverage you generate in the use of financing is not the final criteria. Remember, while you can make a marginal deal acceptable, you cannot turn a bad deal into a good deal. Overworking a transaction generally means you are looking for some rationalization to enable you to make the investment. While it may be okay for you to make the investment, do not kid yourself that something that looks good on paper (using figures you have forced) is, in reality, good.

5. Remember that the leverage available to you as a real estate investor is the maximum form of leverage offered to any investor in any field. This is due to the ease and acceptability of real estate as a collateral for mortgage financing. However, we often take this for granted without re-

alizing that in many cultures loans on real estate are unheard of. In some countries, the land and real estate is state owned. In other countries, much of the land is "leasehold" and all of the users are only tenants on land owned by the crown, or state, or old families who have handed down townships over generations. In other parts of the world, the land may be private ownership but have no value as a security on a mortgage due to the lack of confidence the banks would have in "taking that land" as a security.

Real estate has proven itself in most areas of the world as the single most secure form of investment. For this and other reasons, the institutional lender has no hesitation of making a loan based on some reliable estimate of value. This fact has given rise to a strong secondary market for real estate loans. The creative power available to investors comes through this secondary loan source. The most acceptable and best source of all mortgage loans for the investor is the seller.

6. Leverage is just a function of financing, but it is the temperature gage of what you are doing. Understanding financing well means understanding the overall picture of what happens when mortgages are paid down and equity is built up.

THE PITFALL OF LEVERAGE: OVEREXTENSION

Overextension occurs when the cost of the debt exceeds the abilities of the borrower. This event can occur with the most conservative approach to a mortgage on one property when the borrower has gotten in over his or her head on another property. In fact, this seems to be true for many foreclosures.

In the case of income properties, the proper approach to financing is to try not to overexpose the ability of that property. Naturally, there are times when you are looking for increases in rents to support the added debt to the property, and sometimes those increased rents just don't occur.

While there is no single test for you to use to keep from going in deeper than you can swim, there are some guidelines you can follow that would help you stay out of overextension.

SEVEN GUIDES OF HOW TO AVOID OVEREXTENSION

1. Make sure you are investing within your comfort zone. This means a comfort zone you have been working and know like the back of your hand. The fastest way to become overextended is to buy something out of your comfort zone area.
2. Be very sure the investment will move you closer to your goals. That means do not fool yourself. Does the purchase of that property bring you closer to your goals? Can you write down why?

3. Is it within your physical abilities? Don't take on anything that you cannot handle just because it looks good.

4. Have you "worked" the purchase negotiations? This means: Have you been a part of the transaction, or was it brought to you? If you have worked it or have been involved with the transaction for a while, it is likely you will have a better understanding for items 1, 2, and 3 above.

5. Can you carry the property for the estimated time plus an additional 50% of the estimated time needed to generate the income it would take to support the property 100 percent? In short, a low down payment and tons of leverage won't help if you promptly go bankrupt because it took nine months to get the tenants you anticipated you would have in six months.

6. Are you jeopardizing everything for this one deal? If so, you had better make sure you are all set on items 1, 2, 3, 4, and 5.

7. If things go astray, be sure you don't hold onto the sinking ship for too long. Too many investors fail because they tried to save something they were incapable of saving. If they had simply stepped out of the deal at the time they knew the ship was actually going to sink, they would have been a lot wiser.

Chapter 5

CONVENTIONAL FINANCING: THE FIRST MORTGAGE AND WHERE TO FIND IT AND HOW TO GET ONE AT THE BEST TERMS

This chapter will delve into the complex world of institutional mortgages and other financing generally referred to as "conventional financing." The goal of this chapter is to give you the edge on getting a mortgage for the best terms available in the market at the time you need the loan.

Conventional financing of any sort is generally understood as to be loans obtained from sources such as savings and loan associations, commercial banks, pension funds, insurance companies, and any other source that will lend on the same terms and standards as these institutions.

The term *conventional financing* often is misleading because the loan that is "conventional" need not be "institutional," but merely be a loan along the same general terms and conditions as a loan that might be provided by one of the institutional sources. This factor in itself is not that significant, but on occasion you may find that a purchase agreement provides for you to obtain financing from an "institutional lender," and in that context that would exclude you from finding the funds from a private source on institutional terms. Nonetheless, as the structure of the loan is important, you should be aware of the difference between institutional and conventional.

This chapter will cover the different types of first mortgages offered by the institutional lenders and will examine some of the advantages of dealing with private "conventional" sources over lending institutions. In all instances, however, there are different techniques of dealing with the different kinds of lenders and I will attempt to provide you with a full and comprehensive outline to aid you in obtaining any kind of a first mortgage.

WHEN IS A FIRST MORTGAGE A FIRST MORTGAGE, AND WHAT IS IT?

A first mortgage, or first deed of trust as it is called in some states, is a document that gives the lender a right, or lien, to the title of the property that is pledged as security to the loan. The mortgage document itself is not evidence of the amount of money owed, as it is only the evidence of the security of the mortgage. The document that describes the amount of money owed, the method of payments, and the like is called the *note* and is sometimes attached to the mortgage document.

When a borrower obtains a mortgage, the lender arranges to provide the needed funds. On the execution of the final papers, the borrower gives the lender the mortgage and note and the lender advances the money. The lender in this transaction will generally always require that the title of the property that is to become the security to the loan be checked by a title company and/or lawyers working for the lender. This title is frequently checked prior to the loan, and then once again after the mortgage document and note have been executed. This final check is to ensure that the borrower has not managed to "hit" several lenders in a short timespan using the same property as security on several loans. Until the lender is secure that was not the case, it will generally hold up on giving the borrower the proceeds of the loan.

As title has not passed to the lender, the borrower still owns the property and has full use of it. The lender however has obtained the right or lien against the property and should the borrower default on the note the lender can exercise its rights as would be provided for in the mortgage and by state and federal law. The rights to foreclose or to accelerate the demand of repayment are two of the rights the lender has to govern the force it can exert on the borrower to "get" its money back.

There is one form of mortgage in which title is retained by the lender. This is generally a seller-held mortgage, although sellers sometimes sell these mortgages to third parties. This is the contract for deed, or land contract. There could be other terms used by sellers or realtors in your area that would be in fact the same kind of mortgage. No matter what it is called, if it fits the example I will give in the next paragraph, be aware of its conditions.

The contract for deed is a situation in which a purchase of a property has been made. At this time, the seller and the buyer enter into an agreement where the buyer puts a down payment in the hands of the seller, and then makes a series of monthly payments over a period of time. At the end of this payment period, the amount owed on the purchase price would then be retired and the property title would be delivered to the buyer. Now this looks a bit like the usual mortgage you might get if you bought a home and owed the seller for the balance of the purchase price after making a down payment. The difference is who holds the title of the property. In the contract for deed, the seller holds the title. In a mortgage situation, the borrower holds the title and pledges that title as security.

Of these two kinds of transactions, most investors would avoid the contract for deed as it has a number of problems that become more evident the longer the term of payment. Sellers often "sell" their bulk packages of collections or sometimes go out of business and if the payment period was fifteen to twenty years it is possible that when it is all paid off there is no one to get the title from. Private deals using the contract for deed are okay as long as you follow the advice of your lawyer, and you don't let the term of payback be more than a few years. Even in those instances, keep the use of the technique to land sales only.

A first mortgage of the usual kind can be satisfied simply by paying off the amount owed, plus any interest or other assessments that are due. When the mortgage is paid off, the lender will give the borrower (or who ever holds title to the property at that time) a document titled *mortgage satisfaction*. It is up to the borrower to be sure that he gets this document and that it is properly executed by the lender, and that this document is then recorded in the county where the property is located. Unless this satisfaction of mortgage is recorded, there could be a cloud on the title at a later date as to the status of this mortgage. If it were many years later, it could be costly and timely to find such a document, or to obtain a new one.

If the borrower fails to make the payments on time, nothing happens until the grace period has expired. This grace period can be any time period that the parties establish, but in general use it is 15 to 30 days.

If the payments due are not made by the last day of the grace period, the mortgage is in default and subject to the wrath or pleasure of the lender. In the chapter, called "How to Deal with Foreclosure," I look into the horrors of this event. I suggest it as required reading and will only comment briefly on foreclosure in this chapter.

Foreclosure often is very cumbersome and expensive for lenders, and they will avoid taking a property owner into foreclosure if at all possible. It is not uncommon for savings and loan associations to let their borrowers get well behind in their payments prior to actually filing foreclosure documents. Nonetheless, as the final step they will do all they can to collect the amounts owed. No lender likes foreclosure, but they all have gotten so they can do it with the least possible inconvenience. Yet, almost all of them will work with the borrower who is in trouble and who comes to them and presents his or her case (see "How To Deal with Foreclosure," Chapter 00).

The position the lender has in a first mortgage exceeds any right any other lender would have. Secondary loans that are made behind (later on) the first mortgage or that were actually made prior to the first mortgage but subordinated (allowed the rights of another to exceed their rights) to the first mortgage are junior to the first mortgage. Any junior mortgage right will not collect in the event of a foreclosure until the superior mortgage has been paid out in full. This assumes that the borrower has not filed bankruptcy, which would upset this sequence and in those events the end result may be that a court decides who gets what.

The position of the mortgage with respect to this junior or superior rank is not always what appears and should be examined carefully. For example, the document that says "This is a first mortgage" is not always a first mortgage. The rank of a mortgage with respect of the position of rights of the lender has to do with the *time of recording*. When a mortgage is executed, the lender will take that document, along with the note, and make sure that it is recorded within the county or township of the state where the property is located. The intention of the lender may be to have a first mortgage; however, if the borrower has given another mortgage to another party (thinking it was a second mortgage) and the mortgage that was to be the second mortgage was recorded ahead of the mortgage that was to be the first mortgage, the *time of recording* becomes the critical element and not the intention or the title of the document.

In taking back a mortgage as a lender (if you were to sell your own property or to make a loan to another party), you would want to be absolutely sure that the mortgage is indeed what it has been reported to be. In short, no matter how much you trust the people, make sure that the actual recording dates are verified. Errors by lawyers, title companies, or county recording offices could have positioned another mortgage ahead of that "first mortgage" you thought you were holding.

This situation explains the requirements of most lenders to check the title of a property after they have actually made the loan, but prior to funding the money.

WHO IS THE MORTGAGOR AND WHO IS THE MORTGAGEE?

In the jargon of mortgages, you will frequently hear the terms *mortgagee* and *mortgagor*. The mortgagor is the person who gives the mortgage document to the lender (the mortgagee). The mixup in these words comes from this last sentence. The common practice is to say "I will go to the bank and get a mortgage." In actual fact, you go to the bank to "get money" and by doing so to "give a mortgage." Any words that end in "-er" or "-or" generally denote the "giver of the item." For example, the mortgagor, lender, grantor, leasor, and so on are all people who have given something to someone else. That someone else is the "ee" of the same term: mortgagee, lendee, grantee, leasee, and so on. So the mortgagee is the person who gets the document called a mortgage . . . and gives the money.

Still not clear? Okay, think of it this way. When you borrow money from a lender who demands security in the form of a mortgage, you give that lender a right to your property by giving it a mortgage document. That document says that if you don't make your payments on time or in any other way default, you risk actions by the lender that are not pleasant and where the end result is that you can lose your property. In essence, you pay up on time "or else". You give others rights to your property and you have to make good or else. Remember that you are the mortgagor when you get money, and all else will fall into place.

STANDARDS THAT MAKE A LOAN "CONVENTIONAL"

When you are dealing with the conventional loan market, you will find a standard that tends to prevail throughout the country. There will be little variance in the basic format of the loan once you are within the same category; however, many aspects of the loan can differ between states and even within the same city. Lending is a business, and a very big business at that. The people who make loans, the organizations who provide the money, and the policy behind it all is open to negotiation. If you know what you want and what the competition is offering, you usually can improve your position.

Understanding the difference between government restriction and lender policy is critical in order to know just how far you can go in hammering out good terms. The policy is the flexible part. The government restriction is the inflexible portion of the deal. Savings and loan associations are governed by either state or federal regulations and these regulations often restrict the percentage the lender can lend in two areas. The first is the overall loan portfolio of the institution. How much money can be lent in commercial areas, in investor-held residential property, and in owner-held residential property. This restriction will not hamper your ability to negotiate with the lender as long as it still has room to make the loan within its portfolio requirements. However, when the lender is nearly out of its allocation for commercial loans, things begin to get tough and lenders get very picky. Make sure the lender has money to lend prior to knocking yourself out to win one or two points in your favor when there is nothing to win in the long run. "Sure," the loan officer tells you, "we'll make the loan at 8¾ percent per annum, only we don't have any money to lend."

Other restrictions that affect you as a borrower are the percentage of loan-to-value ratio that the lender is allowed to lend. This percentage depends on the kind or category of loan and may vary between lenders. For example, most savings and loans (both state and federal) are allowed to lend up to 95 percent of the value of the property if the property is to be owner-occupied, and the amount of the loan does not exceed $150,000. Yet many of these same institutions will have an internal policy that will restrict this amount to a lower figure. To some degree, this depends on the market for the area. Beverly Hills, California, is apt to have loans in the upper percentage while Camden, South Carolina, will have loans in the middle range of what is allowed.

MAKE CONTACTS WITH LOAN OFFICERS

One of the best ways to obtain information about the policy of a lending institution is to sit down with one or more loan officers within that institution and have the rules, regulations, and policy explained to you. You may discover that the loan officers are discovering which is which at about the same time you are, because policy *is* regulation to the employees and they often don't attempt to distinguish between the two until someone else forces the issue.

Using the opportunity to make contact at a learning session, you will get updated data on these regulations and policy. Remember, the key to this exercise is to discover the policy; it is here that you will be able to win points and obtain better loan conditions and terms from one lender over the other. But you *must* know policy. For example, the regulation may limit the maximum investor-nonresident owner loan on a single-family home to 80 percent of the value of the property, yet the loan officer may tell you that the maximum the bank will loan is 75 percent of the loan value. In this case, the policy is 75 percent, not the regulation. Policy can be negotiated, whereas regulation is fixed. Another element of this example is the loan value percentage. The regulation generally states that the percentage of the loan is based on the value of the property. Value is somewhat of an opinion, and to help smooth out this potential problem, many lenders temper this regulation and add policy that should be something like this following: " . . . and value will be determined as the lower of the contract price or the appraisal." The wording can be rephrased a thousand different ways, but the idea should be clear to you. The lender wants to see your contract of purchase and will reserve the right to use that as the value.

Knowing then that loan percentages are dependent on *value*, you should recognize that the lender can make the loan based on value and not contract price. If you bought the property for a song, you should be able to utilize the real value for the basis of the loan and not the "contract value" as the limitation to the deal. After all, if you already owned the property (say you bought it ten years ago), the actual price you paid would have no bearing, would it?

OVER 100 PERCENT FINANCING USING REGULATIONS AGAINST POLICY

I was reviewing the needs of a friend and client one day when he told me that he wanted to buy a 10,000-square-foot industrial building in Fort Lauderdale, Florida. He was very familiar with the building since he had worked as manager of an industrial parts distribution business that had occupied the structure for nearly seven years. The owner of the distribution business (who was at that time the owner of the building) acquired another company in Miami and moved the distribution business to that city. In the meantime, he leased out the Fort Lauderdale building to another firm, which was about to move out, leaving the building vacant. The owner had no real interest in owning the Fort Lauderdale building, and he did not want to get into the problems of management at a distance.

My friend suggested to the owner that he buy the building. He would then relocate the business that had moved to Miami back into the building and operate as the firm's representative rather than as a company-owned outlet. The concept made economic sense to the owner. He could rid himself of a real estate problem and at the same time remove the management headaches of the company store in Miami.

With my help, my friend worked out a contract to buy the building for what was a very good price of $105,000.

In a review of the capital needs of my friend, we determined that he would need all of his capital to get the business going and would not have sufficient funds to pay the $105,000 price unless that sum could be financed. From the way the numbers looked, I didn't think there would be any problem financing not only the purchase price, but the loan costs and some improvement money as well.

To accomplish this, my friend and I developed a pro forma and an evaluation of the building as it would be as of the time of sale. We were not interested in the actual current value of the building, only what the value would be under the upcoming circumstances and use.

In doing this study and obtaining the backup material, I showed that the value of this building after the sale and with the fixup intended and the new use of the facility, the actual value would be $175,000. I had followed the Mortgage Request Outline, which is shown on p. *89.* I was satisfied that I had sufficient material to support the following request:

Value of the Structure

Loan Requested: $122,500

Use of the funds:

To Seller	$105,000
Remodel	10,000
Loan Costs	3,850
To Borrower	3,650
Total of Loan	$122,500

$$\frac{\$175,000 \times \text{Loan-to Value Percent} = 70\%}{\$122,500.00}$$

What I had not anticipated was being thrown out of the first two savings and loan associations because the loan officer could not understand how he could request a loan based on value and not just the contract price.

The end result: My friend got his building without having to spend any of his own money, and the lender got a good deal. The value of the building was as it had been represented, so the parties made a very good loan-to-value ratio.

Once the contact had been made with the loan officer at the lending institution, it was a matter of "educating the lender" as to policy versus regulation.

No matter what your current needs in real estate financing, if you plan to become an investor you will need to shop for a loan. Since lending is a very big business, you will want to have friends in as many places as you can find to ease your way into the loan committee's good graces. Visit several potential lenders now and make the proper contact well before you need it.

LOAN CONDITIONS COMMON TO SAVINGS AND LOAN ASSOCIATIONS

Maximum Loan (%)	Term (yrs.)	Type of property	Conditions
90	30	Single family and condos	Percent of loan is based on the contract price or an appraisal, whichever is the lower amount. The total loan is usually under $45,000.

Maximum Loan (%)	Term (yrs.)	Type of property	Conditions
95	30	Single family and condos	Same as above, except private mortgage insurance is required. These loans usually are below $40,000.
80	30	One to four multifamily dwelling units	Appraisal value will take market conditions of rental area and vacancies into account.
75	25	Five or more units Commercial real estate	Greater emphasis on the person behind the loan. Appraisals will also be more detailed and the term of years reduced.
75	3 5	Developed lots Developed lots	Terms for builders more than two lots. Terms for individuals are longer. Usual provisions on which the lots are built within the term of loan.
100	12	New mobile homes	Based on invoice price.
100	8	Used mobile homes	Wholesale value.

It is interesting to note that almost all loans over 80 percent of loan to value follow these limitations:

1. Monthly payments must include principal, interest, and a pro rata buildup for an escrow of taxes and hazard insurance.
2. If the property is a residence of the borrower (and therefore qualifying for a better term mortgage), there must be a certification that the property will indeed be the borrower's home.
3. At the time of the loan, no secondary or junior loans can be made or placed on the property.

Of course, each lender may implement any term or condition it considers reasonable or obtainable in the market. Banks, savings and loan associations, and other lenders are in the business of providing loans to borrowers for a specific business reason: profit. If the lending institution cannot make a profit, it is apt to slip slowly but surely into the oblivion of bankruptcy. As any business can go out of business, it should not be a surprise that in the economic world competition can have the same affect as in any other business.

The affect of competition on the borrower's ability to obtain loan terms that are better from one lender to another is something that has been around for a long time. One of the goals of this book is to assist any lender to recognize what the options are in seeking these better terms, and how to distinguish what is better instead of just different.

INTEREST, POINTS, AND COST

Interest rates are not regulated except by state law, which sets usury, which then establishes the maximum rate that can be charged. Interest charged is generally somewhat competitive, and on the surface it may not seem to vary much between lenders. However, as the jargon of finance is somewhat concealing, the total outcome of one loan that looks to be close to another can be most costly in the end.

The actual cost per $1,000 loaned is the best way to determine the overall cost of the total term of the loan. By comparing overall cost to actual cost, you gain a composite view of the potential economic picture. I say potential picture as some loan terms are not possible to forecast accurately. For example, if you take out a loan that is adjustable in the future, the lender has a formula that allows it to adjust the interest charged against the outstanding balance owed. This adjustment is frequently tied to the interest charged on an average of the U.S. Treasury Bills. If this is the case, the interest can go up or down (but generally up) from the original loan rate. Some lenders attract borrowers to their institutions by offering interest rates below the market for the first year or so and then "bank" on the adjustment being sufficiently beneficial to the lender to make up for the "come on" rate. In this ploy to lend money, different lenders will offer different packages in their adjustment loan package. Maximum adjustments each year, or over the life of the loan, as well as different terms for adjustments do more to confuse the borrower (and make it far more difficult to calculate the actual cost in comparison to another lender) than to serve the public. One way to combat this is to take a "best" and a "worst" appraisal of specific loans. In essence, look at the actual cost to you if the loan rates are adjusted at both the maximum and the minimum rates. This will then give you the parameters for any specific loan, and in the end the absolute comparison between different loans.

Fixed-rate loans were once the only kind of loan available. However, even then the kinds of fixed interest rates were varied. For example, automobile loans often are quoted at an "add on" interest rate and the final cost of an add-on rate is nearly double that of the same rate on a common interest loan. The reason for this is the way interest is calculated. In a typical real estate mortgage or loan, interest is quoted as an annual percent charged against the amount of the loan (the principal) outstanding for the term that the interest is paid. For example: If the principal of a mortgage was $100,000 at the start of the year, and no payments were made to reduce the principal during the year, and there was an annual interest payment due at 12 percent per annum, at the end of the year the interest due would be $12,000. If the interest payments were due each month, the borrower would owe $\frac{1}{12}$ the interest rate monthly, which in this case would result in 1 percent per month being due. In a mathematical sense, the monthly $1,000 appears equal to the annual $12,000, but economically it is not.

As a borrower, you would find it to your benefit to pay annually at $12,000 rather than monthly at $1,000. The situation should be obvious as you could take the $1,000 each month and put it in a savings account (at 12 percent over the year you would have accumulated $682.25 of interest based on your making the payment to the savings account at the end of the month for the entire year). If you then made your mortgage payment, you would pay a net of $11,317.75 as the interest in your account goes to you and not the lender. The actual cost of the annual payment (if you can earn 12 percent) of this mortgage is not 12 percent but only 11.3175 percent. While this may not sound like a lot of difference, it can add up.

On the other hand, the way the game is played by lenders is reversed. Lenders want interest as often as once a month. As you saw in this example, your bank account earned an interest of $682.25 by paying the interest monthly; therefore the lender will be able to earn that rate instead of you. So the lender gets your 12 percent in this example, plus a bonus of $682.25. As the amount of the principal has not changed due to the lack of principal payments, the bonus is 0.68225 percent for the year. In real terms, the lender makes 12.68225 percent on the loan in comparison to your paying 11.31775 percent on an annual payout.

Let's review the mathematics involved in the previous paragraph: $682.25 interest divided by the principal of $100,000 equals 0.0068225, which is the mathematical decimal for 0.68225 percent. Remember that whenever you divide dollars you will get the mathematical percent and not the actual rate, which first must be multiplied by 100. Equally, when you want to multiply a number, say $50,000 by 12 percent, you must first translate that percent to the mathematical decimal by dividing by 100 to make it 0.12.

The relation to the interest you pay and the method of payment should be clearly understood so that you can make maximum use of the loans offered, and obtain the best terms to suit your goals.

Interest then becomes another of the elements of the mortgage that can be negotiated between the borrower and the lender. Not just the rate of interest is involved, but how it is paid. As we have just seen, the frequency of payment during the year has a relationship to the total cost of the mortgage. This cost should be considered in the complete relationship of the circumstance. For example, if the interest is a deductible expense and will reduce another out-of-pocket cost, such as income tax, then the increase of the interest cost, if offset by some other element, may cause the borrower to give in on the higher interest (thereby increasing the yield to the lender at no net cost to the borrower). An example of this would be in a tradeoff to a lender who might be holding out for some other factor besides the interest. One such factor is participation in the transaction. This hidden interest is commonplace in large commercial transactions where the lender not only gets paid an interest, but also takes a percentage of ownership of the property or a percentage of gross income from the venture.

If this were the case, the wise borrower takes a hard, cold look at the potential cost of that participation and calculates the overall cost of a higher interest rate, which will have a definite termination point—that being when the mortgage is finally paid off, whereas the participation may be for the duration of ownership of the property.

Another example of a tradeoff in which the tax advantages of higher interest may be desirable is in situations where the amount of the loan is higher than that loan possible at a lower interest rate. The borrower again has to weigh the cost of the money, and in this case the use of the funds, or in many events, the need for the funds to complete the transaction at hand.

INTEREST AND PRINCIPAL PAYMENTS COMBINED

As interest rates increase, the combined effect of interest and principal make for high monthly payments. To counterbalance this, lenders have come up with a form of mortgage that has negative amortization. Amortization is that element of a mortgage that is the reduction of the principal owed. In most mortgages, the monthly payment does not change during the base term of the mortgage. If the mortgage had a 25-year term with no balloon, over the period of 25 years, which may be seen as 300 months, the monthly payment would contain two amounts of money that would total one steady monthly payment. For example, if the amount of the loan was $100,000 and the rate of interest was 12 percent per annum, over a 300-month mortgage with regular amortization the payment would be $1,042.79 per month (a total of $312,837 over 300 months.)

If the lender was unable to lend sufficient money to meet its lending requirements with these terms, it could reduce the payback sum by either reducing the interest or increasing the term of the loan to cut the payments and therefore attract more borrowers. However, by increasing the term from 25 to 35 years, the payment only drops to $1,005.49.

This would mean that the borrower would pay back a total of $422,307.82 if he or she lived those 35 years and still owned the property. As you can see, spreading out the total term doesn't help, and the lender will not want to reduce the interest if there is another alternative.

Thus, negative amortization mortgage is born. In this kind of mortgage, the payment is set at an attractive amount. How about $600 per month for the first two years, $700 per month for another two years, and so on, increasing the monthly payment every few years until the mortgage reaches the end of the tenth year, at which time the whole thing balloons.

NEGATIVE AMORTIZATION MORTGAGE TABLE
Principal at the start of the term: $100,000
A Ten-Year Mortgage with 12% interest and monthly payments shown.

Year	Monthly payments	Amount of unpaid interest added to the principal	Principal at the end of the year
1	$ 600 per month	$4,996.91	$104,996.91
2	600 per month	5,630.64	110,627.55
3	700 per month	5,063.81	115,691.36
4	700 per month	5,706.03	121,397.39
5	800 per month	5,148.77	126,546.16
6	800 per month	5,801.76	132,347.92
7	900 per month	5,256.63	137,604.55
8	900 per month	5,923.37	143,527.86
9	1,000 per month	5,393.60	148,921.46
10	1,000 per month	6,077.64	154,999.10

Total payments made over 120 months: $96,000 on the $100,000 loan and the borrower still owes $154,999.10.

Most lenders have discovered that with this kind of lending two catastrophic things often occurred. The first was that many borrowers found that they were into a debt they shouldn't have had in the first place. The second event was that the property often didn't keep pace with the increased principal owed on the mortgage. If the original loan had been at a 90 percent loan-to-value ratio, the original value would have been $111,111 (90% of $111,111. is $100,000). At the end of the third year, if the actual value of the property had not increased, the borrower would have no "profit" in the property and foreclosure by the lender would soon follow.

In looking at negative interest mortgages, you must be critically aware of the overall effect. If you take all of these elements into consideration, you will then be able to proceed to make value judgments that will direct you closer to your goals.

When we get to secondary financing, I will show you how many of these aspects thus far discussed will be put to play to give you the advantage as either buyer or seller. When you are dealing with the institutional market, and therefore the conventional form of financing, you have less creativity available to you in private dealings.

DEALING WITH THE POINTS AND CLOSING COSTS
OF CONVENTIONAL FINANCING

All lenders seek to cover their expenses in any transaction. The first line of defense of such costs and expenses comes in the way of "points." The origin of the "points" that lenders charge was to discount the amount lent so that when you paid back the total amount the lender would get an additional yield. For example: If I borrow $10,000 and the lender charges $500 in points (5 percent of the amount borrowed), I only get $9,500 but have to pay back the $10,000. All interest is calculated on the $10,000, so you can see the lender's advantage.

When we get to FHA loans, you will see that the "points" charges have this effect. The lender gets a higher yield because it takes back from the seller of a property some up front money to make the loan so the seller can sell his property with a lower interest rate than available from the general market.

However, points have become so commonplace in the conventional market that it has become a situation of the lender getting back from the borrower as much as it can to increase its yield and to make the interest rate appear lower. Points are an up front deduction or expense from the borrower. If the lender wants 5 points and the loan is $1 million, we are talking about a lot of money.

However, most lenders will talk about reducing their points just as they will talk about other factors of their loans with which they have some leeway.

Another cost for conventional lenders and secondary lenders are "out-of-pocket expenses." In essence, lenders make a list of expenses they have incurred over the last year and charge it to you as out-of-pocket expenses. So far, competition in the industry has kept this list down to a minimum, but you should question every item that is going to be charged to you prior to signing the mortgage and note.

The list is apt to include items such as:

1. Legal expenses
2. Title review
3. Abstract review
4. Document preparation
5. Post-recording title check
6. Mortgage insurance
8. Title insurance
9. Recording of title and other documents
10. Staff review of documentation
11. Credit report
12. Review of credit report

13. Field investigation
14. Survey check
15. Property inspection
16. Miscellaneous expenses

Many of these items are duplications and your lenders may think of more creative titles for some of their expenses. You will end up paying for most of the expenses the lender wants to charge. However, there are apt to be some expenses that will save you money if you know about them in advance, and others that may be eliminated.

For example, lenders often charge you for a title insurance policy to cover the amount of the loan. If you are not careful and observant you could end up with paying for two policies: one for the lender which would be insufficient to cover the total value of the property, and a separate one in a greater amount to cover the amount of your investment. The proper and least expensive way is to make sure you get one policy to cover the value of your investment, and provide (at a small expense) for a coinsured provision in the policy to cover the lender.

Find out all of the items the lender wants to charge you for. Ask if you can have them done elsewhere, and then get a price quote from several other sources. You might find that the lender is the best price around, or the worst.

Some lenders try to sell you all sorts of other insurance. Extra insurance comes in two forms: Hazard insurance covers the property against storms, fire, and other disasters, and mortgage insurance pays back the lender should you die before the mortgage has been paid in full. Mortgage insurance is usually very expensive for what you get, and you may already have life insurance that can be partially assigned to the lender in the unlikely event of your death. Even if you don't have any other insurance, make sure to ask an independent insurance agency for the price of life insurance that will pay off your mortgage, if necessary.

Another factor that comes to play in these costs is the loan-to-value ratio. This is one of the strongest factors in lending. Is the loan 50 percent of the value, or 95 percent, or somewhere in between? The lender likes a large spread in the loan-to-value ratio, so if you have done your homework well and utilized all of the steps provided in this book, you can maximize your loan and at the same time minimize the payback cost of the loan. One step in that direction will be to do all you can to show the maximum value of the property you are buying. Remember the industrial building that was discussed. Your contract doesn't establish the value of the property, and you must provide backup data to support the real value, which you believe to be higher than your contract price (if it is a new property), or provide as much detail to support the appreciated value if you have held the property for some time.

Later in this chapter you will find an outline for a loan request.

Follow its guides for all loans except for development loans, which are discussed in a later chapter.

WHERE DO CONVENTIONAL LOANS COME FROM?

You will find conventional loans from these following sources:

Savings and Loan Associations   Thrift Savings Associations
Credit Unions   Commercial Banks
Mortgage Bankers   Mortgage Brokers

HOW TO DETERMINE WHICH SOURCE TO APPROACH

Which lender in your area will be the best for you? That is a difficult question to answer. The economic market in lending fluctuates greatly from time to time, and the lender with the best secondary market going for it will be apt to be the most liberal lender. The majority of the money that you borrow comes from the secondary marketplace. This is the market to which the lenders sell their loan packages. Savings and loans, credit unions, and commercial banks maintain the added advantage of having their depositors' money as well, but the secondary market rules as king. Unfortunately this secondary market is not available to you unless you need to borrow large sums of money for development, and even then the possibility of your entry into the secondary market is slight. What this secondary market is and how it effects your determination of who to go to for your loan is simply this: insurance companies, the Federal National Mortgage Corporation, and the Government Insured Mortgage Corporation buy mortgages in large packages. Mutual funds are being formed also to buy mortgages.

THE BEST SOURCE WILL BE THE ONE
THAT LIKES YOU MOST

In all business dealings, the element of like and trust mean a lot. Naturally, there must be good, sound business principals at work, and in the moment of compromise between you and someone else the soundness of the loan might weigh more than friendship. However, never underestimate the power of your contacts. What this means, of course, is if you don't have any contacts you had better start establishing them. Your contacts should not be only in the banking field, but in all areas where one person could mean the difference between your success and your failure. In this book, you will find that lesson brought out constantly, as I feel very strongly about the power of personal attraction. There will be more on this aspect in Chapter "The Power and Glory of Negotiation."

THE PERSON YOU TALK TO IS NOT LOANING YOU HIS OR HER MONEY

You will rarely, if ever, sit down with someone who will give you money out of his own pocket in the conventional mortgage market. You will be dealing at a distance through the institution's agents, employees, or whatever. You will be dealing with people, and no matter what the institution is or how small or large it is, the person you meet face to face is an obstacle on your way to a loan.

It is rare for any mortgage or loan board in any institution to grant a loan that the loan officer has a "funny feeling" about. Somewhere along the way between your first encounter with the institution and that person, you will be judged in a variety of ways. Many of these judgments will have nothing to do with your ability to pay back the loan. Some simply are personal, others are purely business or even based on envy, jealousy, or hate.

It's people business: the attitude one person gets of another, or how well a prospective borrower is prepared to meet any objection the loan officer can throw his or her way.

Power players in any game or business abound. These people will cause or invent problems to test and pressure you. For example, your loan officer might try to improve the loan-to-value ratio, thereby increasing the security to the lending institution, and to test your vulnerability he might spring something like this on you: "You know, Mr. Cummings, in the preliminary review of your loan request several questions came up that centered around the magnitude of your request. Do you suppose you could reduce your request by $1 million?"

There are several reasons for this kind of approach—one is as I suggested and another is to set me up for some other term consideration that I would not want to give in on unless absolutely necessary, such as "Of course, Mr. Cummings, I realize how important it is for you to keep the loan at the requested amount. I offered one suggestion as a compromise in the committee. What do you think, Mr. Cummings, of a $300,000 reduction instead of $1 million, and you accept a small increase in the interest rate to 11 percent?"

You'll be better equipped to handle this type of approach.

You must understand that all of these people that you deal with need to have some personal satisfaction from their job, just as you must from yours. It isn't critical that you understand what position the other person has taken in his or her own mental game, but only that you do not infringe on that position.

We all play some kind of mental game in our business dealings, and while some of us are quarterbacks in that game, others are owners of the team.

In the lending business, loan officers get lots of red marks when loans they have recommended go sour. It was not their direct and personal mistake, but they got the red marks just the same. They will avoid red marks whenever possible.

However, loan officers must make loans. They also get red marks when they aren't doing the business for which they are hired. When the institution has money and word has come down to lend out the money, the loan officer is anxiously looking for you to help him avoid red marks. You will do that by knowing how to deal with different institutions, and what it is that they need.

Part of your success then will be in making sure that you have developed some kind of relationship that is on the professional and business level. You can socialize with the loan officer, but if you had to socialize with anyone at the bank try the president first, vice presidents second, and so on. Remember that the higher your contacts, the easier it is in dealing with the lower echelons.

DEALING WITH THE SAVINGS AND LOAN ASSOCIATIONS

When you are in the market for a first mortgage, the first source you should turn to is the savings and loan association closest to that property. We have already seen some of the basic restrictions of the savings and loan associations, but it is not the restrictions that will affect you the most, it is the policy that institution has that will determine just how far you might get with the loan you want or need.

If the savings and loan closest is not one with which you are familiar, go in and establish your position as an investor of real estate. I don't care what your job is, you can and most likely will become an investor of real estate. For your original and first encounter, you should dress in neat business apparel. There is an old axiom in lending, "If you need it, you don't get it; if you don't need it, you'll get it."

Walk right up to some employee other than the person seated behind the desk that says "Information" and ask where to find the president's office. On the way to the president's office, ask someone else the name of the president's secretary. Armed with this information, you are on your way to making your first and most effective contact: the secretary of the president of the institution.

SIX ADVANTAGES IN DEALING WITH A SAVINGS
AND LOAN

1. Local in Nature. Unlike some sources, the savings and loan is local in nature. The loan officers are on the spot, and you will find them easy to get to and for the most part highly helpful. You usually have direct contact with the savings and loan official and are not dealing through some other party, such as a real estate broker or mortgage broker. If you develop a success pattern, this local aspect of the savings and loan will be far more visible than at a more distant lender. It is critical, however, to make sure that the decisions for the loan are as local as possible. With the branch banking that is found in most states, the savings and loan two blocks away from the home you want to buy *could* be in direct control of an institution 3,000 miles away. This may not work against you, but your approach and the details you provide would be different if you knew that. As you shop for a loan, make sure that all of the savings and loans you visit are not controlled at a great distance. Find out by asking the direct and obvious question: "Where is the loan committee, who sits on it, and are they all from this area?"

Like most local businesses, the savings and loans and commercial bank like to pride themselves on community spirit. You can and should take advantage of that whenever possible and whenever there is something unique about the loan request that has some specific benefit to the community.

In rough times, savings and loans don't like to spoil their community spirit and friendly neighbor image. If you keep your rapport with the institution, they can be most understanding. This is one of their most rewarding advantages and one of the reasons for their success.

But this is not the way it is with all savings and loans. Some are cold and distant in more ways than one. You will find great differences in personnel, attitude, and service. However, if they are truly local in thought, policy, service, and attitude, find a loan officer in that institution with whom you can work.

2. Inexpensive Appraisals. This is a side benefit of the local nature of savings and loan. Since they are in the community, they usually have their own appraisal division or department. This department keeps up-to-date records on what is going on in the community and on the evaluations of property in that area. But more than that, they are aware of what is happening with future growth, new developments that you may not be aware of that can have some positive effect on your loan. You will note this difference far more positively when you deal with a distant lender who knows nothing about your area (or assumes they don't) and needs to be taught everything that is going on. Appraisals to satisfy these lenders can be expensive and long in coming. Naturally, the accuracy of the appraisal made by the savings and loan can work against you if it low balls it. Give them all necessary data. This will only lend credence to the fact that you are on top of the game.

3. Confidence in Area.   Lenders must have confidence in the growth potential of an area. In essence, they are forced into this confidence. Remember, the savings and loan exists because of the need to loan money. Naturally, areas can change, and more than one savings and loan was closed due to bad loans and a declining number of depositors. Like all businesses, savings and loans are not immune to failure and they can and do go out of business. Nonetheless, their desire to be in business works for you.

4. Attractive Terms.   For all lending institutions, the amount of competition for borrowers will vary with the circumstances of the market. In the middle 1980s, for example, the lending business grew with a multitude of companies vying for borrowers. For the first time in a long while, there seemed to be competition for the lenders. Along with competition usually come benefits for the consumer in the form of lower prices or, in the case of lending, better borrowing terms. When it comes to this kind of competition, the savings and loans are well equipped to match any of the other lenders, or better them—and quite often they do. However, you still must shop around not only between the savings and loans, but with other lenders as well.

5. Better Loan-to-Value Ratios in the Favor of the Borrower.   With the exception of government loan programs such as VA and FHA loans, the 90 to 95 percent of the value that can be borrowed on many types of property and circumstances is most attractive to some borrowers. Keep in mind that the maximum loan from any institution or any lender will generally carry with it a penalty of higher interest than a lower loan-to-value ratio. This is because of the added risk to the lender, or to cover the insurance the lender puts into the transaction to cover the upper limits of the loan in the event of a default. This added risk or cost gets passed on to the borrower, who may, as many do, still find that loan to be the one that enables him to reach his goal.

6. Lower Qualification Standards.   Among local S&Ls, there seems to be a drive to provide loans wherever possible, often making the local savings and loan the most lenient of all sources. However, I do expect this to change and for the savings and loans to pay much more attention to the credit of their borrowers and to the appraisals and evaluations of the properties they take as security on their loans in the future. From the middle 1970s to early 1980s, savings and loans lost money with some of the creative lending techniques they devised that did little more than encourage borrowers to maximize their loans. The lending institutions took the blunt of a decline in growth in many areas and a real decline in property values in some parts of the country.

Let's face it, as branch banking takes hold of an area, the local nature of the S&L is going to slip to some degree. Different areas of the country within the same savings and loan association will vie to be the top lender, with the lowest foreclosure rate of all other branches. As that kind of competition takes hold, the qualifications for a loan will go up, and savings and loans will be as tough as other lenders.

Another factor to consider is the growing demands of the secondary market. For example, insurance companies buy portfolios of loans totaling millions of dollars on a regular basis from savings and loans and other lenders. As these companies increase their standards or impose restrictions on the kind of loan they will buy or the area in which they will buy, lenders who must rely on these secondary markets to bank their loans will quickly comply with that secondary market demand.

ELEVEN STEPS IN APPROACHING AND DEALING WITH LENDERS

1. Get to know the savings and loans and other kinds of lenders within your comfort zone. This should include commercial banks and mortgage brokers. Begin by looking in the Yellow Pages to get the names of the institutions and their branch offices. Make note of those that are closest to your area, keeping in mind that any of the institutions in your county and most in the state may actually be able to serve your needs. However, you will begin with three different institutions and follow each of the next ten steps with them until you have a working relationship with a minimum of three such savings and loan offices.

2. Make your first contact the most important one. This means you should call on the president or manager of that association. Find out the person's title by calling the savings and loan and asking the receptionist to connect you with the secretary for the president of that facility. Be sure to ascertain first that you have reached the facility you want, and not a central phone number that was answered five hundred miles away. This can happen, and it is very frustrating when it does. It only demonstrates a slipping away from the local, friendly neighbor policy savings and loans have prided themnselves on over the years.

The receptionist will give you the proper title to use, and it will frequently be "president."

The ultimate contact is, of course, the president. However, from a practical point of view, it is the secretary of the president that you want to win over to your side. We shall assume that by going to the top of the line with bosses, we have also gotten to the best secretary available for the position. Once you take that position and treat her accordingly, you will find that no matter how slight your relationship with the president, you will have access to him or her through the secretary.

Your quest to know the president shouldn't be more than a professional visit. Call, make the appointment (through the secretary), and introduce yourself as a real estate investor who plans to buy property in the area. State that you have been told (by me) that meeting the president would be productive for you both. Oh . . . no. You don't have an account at that savings and loan just yet. Perhaps that can come later, if there is to be a mutual understanding. (If you have a small savings account somewhere and don't have much action in the deposit side, why have that prejudice the loan officer when he wants to know about your account history.)

Begin at the top, but move quickly into the ranks because it is here that you will find the loan officer who will help you get the money you need. To keep you from wasting time, ask your friend, the president's secretary, if she could recommend one of the loan officers that she feels would be good for you to meet.

Word from the secretary—no matter if it is to the President of the United States or the manager of the branch office—has a sting that is not unlike that of the top guy himself. After all, who passes on the president's words if not his secretary.

A call from you to "Fran," with a simple request that sounds like this, is very effective: "Oh, Fran, seems like I remember you liked concerts. Well, could you do me a favor? My wife and I can't make the Pavarroti concert next week and I'm going to drop in the mail two tickets to the concert. Please see they get good use, would you? Oh yes, Charles (the president) said I should call if you could help with any introductions. Anyway, I would like to meet with one of the loan officers. You know, Fran, I like dealing with an officer who isn't one of the old-timers or the new guy in the department. Who would you recommend I meet with?"

When Fran comes up with a name or two, follow up with: "Fran, look, I don't want to bother Charlie about this, would you please call this fellow you just recommended and ask him when it would be convenient to meet with him. I've got next Tuesday at 10 or Wednesday at 2 open. Can I call you back on this tomorrow?"

What happens now is Fran will call the loan officer she recommended, and her request to meet with you will sound like an absolute order directly from the president of the association himself.

The next part of this step is to make the meeting, find out for yourself if this is indeed someone with whom you can work. If for any reason you feel uncomfortable with the loan officer, give your friend, the secretary, a call: "How was the concert . . . ?" Thank her for setting up the meeting and let her know that you would now like to meet another loan officer so that you can meet as many officers in the association as possible to better determine which would work well with you.

Finally, make sure you have at least two meetings with the loan officer of your choice.

It will be in these meetings that you set the foundation for the loan requests you may submit in the future.

3. *Learn the procedures of the institution.* The procedures of each

savings and loan will vary slightly. Some require very detailed forms to be filled out for any loan request; others are less complicated. Collect all of the forms you must ultimately fill out and go over them so you understand exactly what the institution wants, *and why.*

You will want to know these things:

(a) How often does the loan committee meet?

(b) What day do they meet?

(c) What is the deadline to get a request in any meeting?

(d) Does the association do its own appraisals?

(e) If not, who does?

(f) What are the current loan rates, terms, and policy?

(g) What kind of property does the aslsociation *not like* to lend on?

(h) What kind of property does the association *like* to lend on?

You will be collecting a lot of data by visiting the institution, and as you make calls on several savings and loans and other kinds of lenders you will find you are receiving quite an education. In fact, it is a good idea to make two practice calls on savings and loans that are on the other side of town to get the feel for things. Play as dumb as you want on those calls. Ask the loan officer to explain anything and everything until you are absolutely sure you understand the terms he or she is using and the reasons behind everything.

4. *When you get ready to ask for a loan, plan your submission well.* Later in this chapter, you will find an outline for a loan request. It contains all of the information the lender would need to know about you and the property except some very minor details it may want to know just because of some local quirk. You should have already discovered through your contacts with the loan officers what data that association will look at most. If one institution looks very hard at the loan-to-value ratio, it is critical that you pay more attention to that aspect of the request. Another loan officer may have told you that the economics of the transaction and pro formas are the key factor for the kind of property you know you want to buy. It is important, however, that you pay some attention to all of the items in the loan request. In the lending business, it is impossible to provide too many answers. Remember, the more detailed your request and backup data, the heavier your report, the more time you have spent on specifics and background, the better your loan officer will feel about backing you in the loan committee. Don't forget that that loan officer doesn't want to get red marks against him, and the best way to avoid this is to give the impression that he did his job—so do yours.

5. *Make your loan requirements known.* You should be able to support that request fully, of course, but be as specific as possible, and have a margin for negotiations in the request—small, but some margin.

What I mean here is you have to ask for an amount of money and show the terms you expect to be able to pay based on the project or property. For example, you might ask for $125,000 with a payback over 18 years, with a monthly payment not to exceed $1,319.22. In this way, you have established what would be an 11 percent mortgage for eighteen years with a normal payback to amortize the mortgage for that term. The lender has room to match many of the criteria of the mortgage and still better its position if it can and if you will let them. For example, if they said okay to the monthly payment and total amount of the loan, but that at the end of the eighteen years you will have a balloon of $6,000, they will have increased their yield to 11.12 percent. This balloon may not mean anything to you since you don't plan to keep the property for the full eighteen years anyway, and by keeping the constant payment rate the same for the term you may agree to that slight increase in interest.

As you go through this book and as you find the opportunity to use it as a reference tool in later years, it will become more and more obvious that the more you know about the functions of finance and where the tradeoffs lay, the better you will be at developing more attractive loan portfolios for yourself and your property.

6. *Don't rush the loan committee.* You will know their schedule and the general policy with which they function from earlier contacts. Plan your submission well and submit it on time so you don't have to use up any of your "credits" by asking the loan officer to "please get this processed for me." The presentation is important also. If your package is complete and up to date, and you have anticipated all of the loose ends that might occur, the approval will be sped up anyway. Loan requests often are held up due to many items that the applicant could have taken care of in the beginning. The savings and loan association will have to go back and ask an applicant again and again for this or that document that is lacking in the files. Don't let that happen to you. If you do leave out something, make sure that you take care of it the moment it comes to your attention.

7. *Don't take no for an answer.* Not everything you do is going to succeed. The same is true with loan requests. If the loan committee comes back with a direct turndown on a request, which is unusual, go back to the loan officer and ask if the head of the department could sit in on the meeting to explain what happened and why the loan was turned down.

As I said, a direct turndown is unusual. Generally, the loan officer will come back to you with some change in the terms you requested. It might be a decrease in loan amount, an increase in interest rate, a shorter term, a balloon payment, or all of these changes. Some loan officers will give you an idea about what went on in the committee. Just before leaving his office, you might turn to him and say:

"Oh, I have a lot of confidence in you, Frank. Let me give this some thought for a couple of days. I know you have spent a lot of time and effort on this, and if there is any way we can work something out we will." As you start to leave, turn to him and say, "Only it's hard to understand how your institution could be so much below the others," and slowly let the door close.

Some lenders just won't make the loan no matter what. It might be that they don't have the funds or that they have filled that kind of loan in their portfolio for the month. Most likely, it is that they must change to meet the needs of their secondary market.

If the lender won't give you the loan, don't beat a dead horse. It is far better just to shop around for another lending institution.

8. *Use your influence.* You either already have some, or you can develop some quickly. If you don't now belong to some success-oriented kind of organization, take a look at the partial list below and select one that sounds good and is located in your area. Pay them a visit. You will find that within these organizations are the leaders of the community or the future leaders of the community.

Toastmasters International   SME International
DECA   Junior Achievement
Junior Chamber of Commerce   United Way

Of course, there are other such organizations but they are social fraternal organizations. I have nothing against the Lions, the Elks, or the Italian-American Clubs and the like—they are important too. But, if you want to develop influence and do it in a hurry, pick one or several of the organizations listed to get moving.

If more than one such club exists in your area, pick the one that meets for breakfast. Remember the adage: The early bird gets the worm.

As you develop your comfort zone, you will be following a pattern also designed to expand on your potential influence. One of the steps in comfort zone development is attending city and county counsel meetings, going to the city hall, court house, and building departments to meet key people. As you are doing this, you should also be making sure that the people you meet are also meeting you. Through proper follow up, you will find that they will remember you—so if you have left a good impression you're on your way.

Be careful not to abuse your hospitality or influence. If you work for a company that has an account with a potential lender, don't threaten to remove your company's account unless (1) it is absolutely the final straw and you are so burned up you don't care about burning your bridges behind you, or (2) you are so secure in your position that you don't care what your boss thinks about that threat.

9. *Remain calm.* It is not the end of the world, and there will be another opportunity along in a few minutes. There are times when you have to step back and take a hard, cold look at what it is you are trying to do. One turndown doesn't mean you need to make any changes, but if you are consistently being turned down then something you are doing isn't winning people over to your cause. So back off. Don't push the cause

until you have the opportunity to sift out the bugs. Your friendly loan officer should help here if he can and will. Ask him anyway. If he turns you down too, he should be replaced.

However, never fade into the background. Send a thank you note to the loan officer and anyone else who worked on your project. Tell them you appreciated their sincere help and that you are sorry things didn't work out with that lending institution on that project (never admit that you were wrong or that you failed in getting the loan somewhere else). Tell them you will keep in touch and that because of their efforts you will contact them on your next transaction.

10. *Keep up your rapport with the institution between loan requests and projects.* Maintain some kind of contact from time to time—a lunch, a note in the mail, a copy of a book you have read about the decline of the savings and loans, whatever might give you the opportunity to keep your name in front of the people who may help you out when you need it.

11. *Avoid direct confrontation and comparison of one lender to the other.* There is a temptation to invent offers that you have had from other lenders, such as, "Yeah! Well, you know that American National Federal has offered me $125,000 at 7 percent."

However, as long as you have made it clear in a sound business way that you are talking to at least one other lender, you will keep them on their toes. If you are talking with twenty lenders, don't let that get around. In fact, talk about your loan with no fewer than four lenders, but do not let them know you are dealing with more than two. You don't want to give the impression that you fear the failure of one lender, but simply that you want to get the best terms from the best lenders around.

These eleven steps are not easy to follow, and apply to other kinds of lenders as well as the savings and loans. As you follow the eleven steps, you will learn more about the lending business than you could in any book. Best of all, you will be giving yourself a better foundation to deal with other aspects of the real estate finance and investment arena.

As you progress in this book and in your own experiences in real estate investing and financing, you will discover that the creativity of bankers and lenders is often quite shallow. Perhaps that was not a fair statement because you will find several bankers or lenders who are progressive and most astute at what they do. However, they must limit that progressive and astute behavior to their own industry. As an independent investor, you have far more tools at your disposal to attack the problem of financing or investing. Your creative power and finesse then will exceed the ability of many lenders to provide compatible responses to your circumstance. This is not to be viewed as a detriment to you, but as a challenge to expand on your own opportunities because of the institutional lenders' limitations.

To best take advantage of those opportunities, you must be open to all of your options and attempt to utilize a particular tool or option that is best suited to take you closer to your goals. By becoming proficient with the eleven steps in approaching lenders, you will quickly see that there are ways to use the institutional lender to the maximum benefit.

For example, one financing tool we have not yet covered, but will in great detail, is open to you through the very best lender of all—the seller. As we get into seller-held financing, you will see that there are times when you can utilize the institutional lender with a conventional loan and the seller to provide you with more money than you need to acquire the property.

Several years ago, I helped a client of mine do exactly that when he was buying an expensive single-family property. The property consisted of two ocean-front lots in Fort Lauderdale, Florida. On the two lots, there was one single-family home. The home was livable, but was 35 years old and in great need of remodeling. The most conservative cost estimate to put the home into livable shape was $150,000.

The buyer was very well-qualified financially and had a good personal statement; however, he wanted to keep his cash in reserve for his business and for any unforeseen event.

His intention was to build a modern home on the same location as the existing one, either through extensive remodeling or new construction. He had correctly concluded that the price he paid for the property was just for the lots, and it was a good buy at that.

Like a lot of home buyers, my client owned another home that he was living in at the moment. His existing home was to go on the market for $150,000. As that home had a first mortgage of $30,000, he had $120,000 of equity in his present home. After the sale and deduction of all expenses, he could count on a profit of about $105,000.

His need at the moment was to buy the ocean-front property without putting any cash into that deal, sell his existing home, and prior to moving rebuild the ocean-front property for his own use. Since he didn't know at this time how extensive the remodeling or construction would be, he could not apply for a development loan.

The savings and loan association that he had a good relationship with had indicated that they would lend 75 percent of the contract price now, and when he knew what his plans would be they would renew the loan to include the new construction.

This 75 percent loan would account for $150,000 of the purchase of the ocean-front land, but my client still would have to come up with $50,000 out of his own pocket, and he didn't want to part with that cash.

So in the negotiations with the seller of the ocean-front property, the following deal was worked out.

The seller agreed to sell the ocean-front property for $200,000, taking a $100,000 cash down payment at the closing. The balance of $100,000 was to be held by the seller in a mortgage secured by my client's existing home. There was a stipulation that on the sale of the existing home the $100,000 would be paid off.

Now we went back to the savings and loan and borrowed the $150,000 that they said they would lend in the first place. They had the first mortgage on the ocean-front lots, and out of the proceeds of the mortgage my client gave the seller of the lots $100,000, paid the lender for the costs involved in the mortgage, and put about $46,000 cash in his pocket.

Everything about this transaction was legal and ethical. However, the savings and loan that made the loan first objected to the concept. When I pointed out that they did have the first mortgage on the ocean-front property and that there was no secondary financing on that property, they realized that they had made a good loan.

In a follow up some eight years later, my client is now looking to sell the home and move elsewhere. He has invested over $300,000 in the new home on top of his lot purchase and will make a nice profit when his home sells in the $1,250,000 range.

DEALING WITH COMMERCIAL BANKS

While savings and loans are the major source of first mortgage funds, there are times when the commercial banks, both state and federal chartered banks, will be the most interested in your submissions. Commercial banks and savings and loans often look alike and offer many of the same services; however, commercial banks differ in many ways and are one of the sources for conventional real estate loans. FHA and VA loans are generally arranged through commercial banks and mortgage bankers. No matter who else you contact, you will want to know what is available from the commercial bank you deal with.

Unlike the savings and loans, commercial banks are very protective of their clientele. This means that unless you are looking for a major development loan or plan to shift your commercial account to another bank, you will stick to the commercial bank you deal with. This is, by the way, an important lesson in why it is good to have accounts in more than one commercial bank.

THE PLUS FACTORS OF THE COMMERCIAL BANK

Many of the same features found in savings and loans are also found in the commercial bank. Nonetheless, take a look at the four big reasons that commercial banks can be a good choice for real estate loans.

1. *They are local in nature.* To some degree, the commercial bank is actually more local in nature than the savings and loan. At least they

used to be until the savings and loans around the country began to offer checking accounts.

However, commercial banks are still the heaviest suppliers for checking accounts, so the average person will visit or in some way use the services of their commercial bank several times a week.

The commercial bank is in the primary business of loaning money to many commercial ventures of which real estate is just one factor. Because of this, the bank gets involved with many of the community's basic foundations: Car loans, inventory financing, home improvement loans, boat loans, business lines of credit, letters of credit, and so on. The more access you have had to any of these kinds of services, the greater your awareness of how commercial banks operate.

2. *They have good insight into the real estate market in the community.* Perhaps they do not have as broad an approach as the savings and loan when it comes to total business in that sector of their operation, but they do keep on top of things that are important to them. The closer the property is to their front door, the better they like it. Mind you, some commercial banks will lend on projects around the world and can do so without any security other than a line of credit or personal signature.

3. *They offer lower loan fees than found in many savings and loans.* Now be careful about this one: The banker can find some way to offset this lower cost by finding a higher cost somewhere else. However, commercial banks can be most competitive in any of their usual services.

4. *They offer a wider range of projects they will loan on.* In real estate, this becomes critical as the savings and loan associations will rarely lend on vacant land unless it is tied into a development program. The commercial bank, however, can be a big source of funds for developers as well as investors who want to tie up a lot or two for the future.

DISADVANTAGES OF DEALING WITH COMMERCIAL BANKS FOR CONVENTIONAL LOANS

1. Commercial banks are older than savings and loans and often have a more conservative approach to lending. This conservatism can present some distinct disadvantages to the borrower. Some of the more pronounced are:

   (a) A low loan-to-value ratio. The bank will look hard at the loan and examine the value of the property very carefully. They would rather be conservative and lose the loan than produce a high loan-to-value ratio and risk taking back a property. Commercial banks do not like to lend their own funds above the 75 percent loan-to-value ratio. Of course, when it comes to FHA- or VA-insured loans, that is another matter and the bank will go all the way on those.

   (b) They generally require that the borrower be a client of the bank. This sometimes means that the borrower also has to keep a substantial deposit in the bank during the term of the loan. This goes back to the concept that if you have it you don't need it so that's when we'll give it to you.

(c) Interest rates can be higher than current rates from other sources. However, as the commercial bank is usually the fastest lender on any kinds of properties, the extra interest paid can be worth the cost later on down the line.

2. Prepayment of mortgage loans will generally carry a penalty or some other stipulation that limits the amount of principal that can be paid off at any given time or during any year. This may not seem to be a problem, but if you want to sell the property in a few years and the new buyer must refinance to make the transaction work for him or her, a penalty to get the old loan off the books can get in the way of a successful closing or can come out of your pocket.

3. The term of years a mortgage is amortized is generally shorter with commercial banks than with savings and loans. However, this aspect is changing as many savings and loans are using loan instruments that have a seven-year call term on a longer amortization basis. For example, this means that even though the loan looks as though it is good for twenty-five years, the lender or the company that the lender has sold the mortgage to can call the loan at the end of seven years. If that is the comparison loan at the local savings and loan, the seven- to ten-year term at the commercial bank will look attractive.

HOW TO DEAL WITH THE MORTGAGE BROKER

Mortgage brokers and mortgage bankers can be worth their weight in gold. It is a very good idea to have at least one or two contacts with a mortgage brokerage firm in your area. These companies either act as a "finder" for money for you or actually bank the loan with their own sources. They deal with many of the prime money sources around which you would have no direct contact were it not for these brokers or bankers. These sources are the pension funds, insurance companies, large out-of-the-area commercial banks and savings and loan associations, offshore money, real estate investment trusts, and so on.

When you deal with a mortgage broker, it is similar to going to a real estate broker who'll find you a house—only the mortgage broker finds a lender who will make your loan for you.

Since the mortgage broker shops around for you, you sometimes can save time and effort by using his or her services. However, any benefit can come at a high penalty because you may be lax in seeking other sources for the funds. You may find in the end that the mortgage broker was unable to make your loan or does in fact place it with the savings and loan around the corner from where you work.

However, there are many loans that cannot be made without the help of a good mortgage broker. So make a contact with a mortgage broker in the same way you would with a loan officer of a savings and loan. Do it well before you need to borrow the money.

PRIME SOURCES FOR CONVENTIONAL LOANS

The following sources for conventional money may or may not be available to you on a direct basis. Most often, the following lenders are buyers of mortgage packages from savings and loans, commercial banks, or mortgage bankers. However, sometimes you do have access to them, and if that is the case these lenders can offer the very best terms for your borrowing needs.

INSURANCE COMPANIES

Insurance companies are a good source for funds and supply a major amount of cash outside the governmental reserves into the conventional lending systems. Unless you are a major borrower (in need of $1 million or more), it is unlikely that you will have a loan directly placed with an insurance company. However, some insurance companies will look at smaller loan requests through their representative mortgage brokers and mortgage bankers.

Insurance companies have very strong motives to lend out money if they have it. Unlike savings and loans who may be packing loans to sell to secondary buyers, insurance companies have their own cash and they must put it somewhere. The investments the insurance companies make include a wide range of items, of which mortgages are just a part. However, if you need a lot of money, this is usually where you will get it.

Dealing through a representative, such as the mortgage broker, is different than dealing with the loan officer at the local commercial or savings and loan association. As the lender is usually distant from you and your property, loan committees generally require far more details and information than the local lender.

There are several drawbacks in dealing with insurance companies other than their distance. These drawbacks may not be a problem for you, and if not you should make sure that your mortgage broker has included one or more insurance companies in his or her search for a lender to take you loan. Naturally, this assumes that your loan request meets the minimum loan requirements by the specific insurance company.

The most notable drawback is the problem of good news–bad news. Since insurance companies are a good source for major loans, they frequently have a lot of requests for the funds available. This enables the institution to be selective and that makes their money difficult to get at times. This also leads to a time element that can be the killer for most borrowers who have a need to get the funds relatively quickly. Of all lenders, insurance companies can be the slowest to approve a loan. Of course, this time factor varies between different lenders and projects, but when you couple the extra data needed, frequently the requirement of having an M.A.I. appraisal in addition to all the other back-up material, plus a thirty- to sixty-day shuffle through loan committee, you can see that the commercial bank or savings and loan can be a good alternative.

REAL ESTATE INVESTMENT TRUSTS (REITS)

There are three basic types of REITS:

1. *The Equity REIT.* This is similar to a mutual fund except the investors own an interest in whatever real estate the organization acquires. The form of ownership is like a corporation, only the income and losses are treated, for the investor, as though this were individual ownership of that percentage of the transaction. The equity REIT is a major buyer of office buildings, shopping centers, and the like. They take part in joint ventures, develop, build, and otherwise are involved in many forms of real estate investing.

2. *The Mortgage REIT.* This form of real estate trust is designed for lending. They vary in size but are very potential in the lending game. They got into trouble in the early 1970s by being overly zealous with their lending practices. Many of their loans went bad and they ended up owning property through foreclosures. Some of the mortgage REITS found themselves in irreversible trouble as they made construction loans on projects that failed prior to the permanent loan paying off the REIT. As the earlier mortgage REIT based its success on a shorter duration loan—i.e., the development loan—it was not a surprise that these REITs have undergone the greatest change over the years. Where they still exist, they are more often found as a part of the third form of REIT.

3. *The Hybrid REIT.* This is a mixture of the two earlier forms of REITs. Some of these REITs were formed by accident, others by design. They have found the best and worst of both worlds, but in a counterbalance they seem to now make up the majority of REITs. Hybrids generally participate in the project, lending money and taking a percentage of ownership or override on income.

REITS fall into the same category as insurance companies in that they are prime sources for funds, but their access is generally remote and distant unless you are a major borrower or developer. Nonetheless, keep them in mind. When they have money to lend, they can be very aggressive to lend it. As a joint venture partner, the REITS can be one of the first lenders to call.

PENSION FUNDS AND CREDIT UNIONS

These organizations collect massive amounts of funds and then make investments to suit their charters and goals. They act much like insurance companies but are often more accessible to fund or union members than other larger lenders. For example, if you are a member of a credit union there are many services that that organization can provide to you besides lending money. Pension funds vary in the services they offer their members—find out what services they offer, if any.

GENERAL COMMENTS ABOUT INSTITUTIONAL LENDERS

The whole finance game seems to revolve around major lenders. The secondary market that buys packages from savings and loans, commercial banks, and the United States government plays a big roll through the Federal Reserve Monetary Policy.

The economics of government intervention in the free enterprise system is subject to argument by just about any economist you will find. The problem seems to be that no two economists seem to agree as to the exact definition of the problem or its potential solution. The theory of control by the government to provide checks and pushes to the nation's economy are based on the principal that if nothing is done things will work out.

The United States is both a lender and a borrower. It is a lender in that its insurance to banks, savings and loans, and for FHA and VA loans makes a marketplace for borrowers that may not exist otherwise. The money borrowed through the sale of bonds and the like is a real debt that is repaid through new loans made (more bonds sold).

The government is such an enormous borrower that it affects the market by taking out of it money that might go into other resources.

IF YOU ARE A BIG BORROWER, THE PENSION FUND CAN BE THE ONLY WAY TO GO

No one will disagree with this statement, except the other lenders hoping to make the same loan. The only answer, of course, is to shop around and find out for yourself just who is the best source for you at the time you need the money.

A SUMMARY OF ADVANTAGES AND DISADVANTAGES

	Advantages	Disadvantages
Savings and Loans	Local and on the spot Know property and area Have confidence in area Long pay out High percent of loan to value More lenient in qualifying both the property and the borrower	High points Personal liability Nonassumable at times Prepayment penalty
Commercial Banks	Local and on the spot Know property and area Have confidence in area Lower points Construction and land loans	Low percent of loan to value Want other business Higher interest rate Sometimes prepayment penalty Shorter term of years
Insurance Companies	Have ample money Like big borrowers Lower interest rate (often) Low points Permanent loan usually not personally guaranteed	Not local Can be impersonal Highly selective Demand greatest qualification on property and borrower Long processing time
REITS	Same as insurance companies Less conservative Loan terms more flexible	Not local Can be impersonal Generally short-term lender Long processing time
Pension Funds	Same as insurance companies	Same as REITS
The Seller	Depends on the situation and the seller No points at all Usually best rate No processing time to worry about	Seller may be limited in the amount he can hold Term usually shorter

AN OVERLOOKED SOURCE FOR FIRST MORTGAGES

One of the best sources for first mortgages is the seller. There are many advantages to this source, and oddly enough it is the seller that is often the first source that is overlooked. The biggest advantage to you is that there is no middleman. You are the middleman, and the saving of loan points and time are valuable to all parties of the transaction. This chapter will not deal with the methods of approaching the seller. Other chapters will cover this aspect in greater detail. Yet, you should never overlook this as perhaps the best source of all.

MORTGAGE SOURCE CHECKLIST

What kind of loan needed	Where to go to get the money	When to use this source to its best advantage	How to get the most from this source
	Start with the local savings and loan association and make at least two or three applications.	When you need between an 80 to 90% loan and total loan is under $50,000.	Follow the procedure given in this chapter.
Single family residence (first mortgage under $80,000 in value)	Your commercial banks. Pick one you deal with.	For loans over $50,000. Or when you are well respected by his commercial bank or you struck out at the savings and loan.	Follow the procedure given in this chapter. Remind them how much they respect you.
	Insurance companies: Deal with your mortgage broker. Often, they will be in the market for single family loans.	When you cannot get anywhere with the other sources. Or, if you know the mortgage broker is hot to make a deal.	Deal only with a reputable mortgage broker. Do not try to deal directly with an insurance company.

What kind of loan needed	Where to go to get the money	When to use this source to its best advantage	How to get the most from this source
Single family residence (first mortgage over $80,000 in value)	Start with the local savings and loan and make at least three applications.	When you need no more than 80% loan to value ratio and total loan is under $100,000.	Give more of your financial details, as well as comprehensive sales data.
Residential lots for ready development —single buyer	Commercial banks. Same as previous mortgage.	For loans over $100,000 you may find the commercial bank the best bet.	Negotiate for good terms and use your financial statement.
Multifamily (up to 5 units)	Start with the local savings and loan. Make as many applications as possible.	Maximum loan possible is 80%, but your chance is improved if you ask for only 75%.	Have detailed loan request ready for each savings and loan.
Residential lots for builder-developer use	Commercial banks—talk to them first. If they have money available, make several applications.	When you need only 70% loan to value ratio or less.	Have detailed loan request and stress the buyer as much as the property.
Multifamily (6 to 20 units)	Start with the local savings and loan. Make at least three applications.	When the loan to value ratio does not exceed 75%.	Have detailed loan request with past years' statements available.

What kind of loan needed	Where to go to get the money	When to use this source to its best advantage	How to get the most from this source
Commercial properties up to $500,000 in value	Commercial banks may be good market here; but this will depend on the bank, the property, and the person. Check around.	If you can get the seller to hold some paper and only need a 50% loan.	Show strong management capability of buyer and good past history.
	Insurance companies: REITS and funds.	When the value is over $300,000 these sources may be interested.	Use good mortgage broker and detailed loan request.
Multifamily (20 to 100 units)	Savings and loans. Make at least three applications.	Will find 70% of economic value with conservative approach the best loan ratio.	Do your homework and have detailed loan request.
Commercial properties ($500,000 to $2,000,000 in value)	Insurance companies, REITS and pension funds.	If the value is over $1,000,000 these may be the only source.	Mortgage broker and loan requests are necessities.
Multifamily (over 100 units) and Commercial properties (over $2,000,000 in value)	Insurance companies, REITS, pension funds, and trust funds.	You have little choice: these are about the only sources you have.	Mortgage broker and very detailed loan request.

What kind of loan needed	Where to go to get the money	When to use this source to its best advantage	How to get the most from this source
Shopping center development with major tenants (over $1,000,000 in value)	Commercial banks	Very rare; but if you are close to one you might have luck.	Pray.
Restaurants and special single-use properties	Insurance companies	Loan to value ratio 50%.	Detailed loan request, and heavy input on ability of buyer and past records.

PRIVATE MONEY: WHERE IT IS AND HOW TO FIND IT

Because private money is not institutional, it is often not classified along with conventional financing. But as conventional financing is a type of loan, and not limited by the source, I have chosen to include a brief section on private money. Because the use of private money varies greatly in its advantages and disadvantages, it is safe to say that it can have both the advantages and the disadvantages of all other sources.

Each private lender is an independent lender, and reacts to a loan request by seeking the most profitable deal based on what the market and his requirements dictate. In general, rates will be the highest and the amounts limited. Some private sources seem to be well financed, but these are few.

However, finding the private money is easier than getting it. A look in the Yellow Pages or newspaper classifieds will be a good start. Many mortgage brokers and stock brokers know of private money.

Deal with private money very carefully. It is best to have any and all mortgage documents examined by an attorney.

HOW TO PUT TOGETHER A LOAN INFORMATION PACKAGE WHICH WILL GET THE BEST TERMS AND THE MOST MONEY

Whenever you have a loan request in excess of $100,000, and always when you are putting a commercial venture together, you will need to have a loan request package. This folio of information will be used by the lending institution to help justify the loan, and to give you the best advantage at improving the amount of money you get and the terms offered.

The information used in the package should already be known to you. If the property is your listing, then you most certainly will have the data. If, on the other hand, the property is the listing of another office, you may have to do some digging to get all the information needed. All the data pertaining to the property and the improvements can be, and should be, part of your selling tools. The only additional data you will need to add to the package will be the portions that refer to the loan request amount and terms and personal data on the buyer. Naturally, other supporting documents, such as copy of the contract, bank forms, and so on will be added as well.

I have included in this chapter an outline which you can follow in the preparation of a Mortgage Loan Request (Figure 4-1). The request you formulate should be as complete as possible. Because the outline can become the index to all your loan applications and requests, you should have several of them run off in your office. A quick review of this chapter prior to making up a request will aid in preparing a more complete and professional presentation.

OUTLINE FOR MORTGAGE LOAN REQUEST

I. THE PROPERTY
   A. General Description
   B. Legal Description
   C. Location
   D. Location Sketch
   E. Aerial Photo
   F. Location Benefits
   G. Location Drawbacks
   H. General Statistics
      (1) Demographics
      (2) Average Rent
      (3) Traffic Count
   I. General Site Data
      (1) Legal
      (2) Size and Square Feet of Land and Site Coverage
      (3) Use of Site
      (4) Zoning
      (5) Utilities
      (6) Access
      (7) Sketch of Lots Sharing Building Location
      (8) Survey

J. Land Value
    (1) Estimated Value of Site
    (2) Comparable Land Sales and Values
II. THE IMPROVEMENTS
    A. Description
    B. General Statistics
        (1) Date Built
        (2) Year Remodeled
        (3) Type of Construction
        (4) Other Structural and Mechanical Data
        (5) Floor Area
        (6) Parking
        (7) Other Data
    C. Sketch—Ground Floor
        (1) Show Tenants
        (2) Show Square Feet
        (3) Show Approximate Sizes
        (4) Building Plans (if new building, or if lender is not in area,
            or if requested)
    D. Sketch—Second Floor
        (1) Show Tenants
        (2) Show Square Feet
        (3) Show Approximate Sizes
        (4) Building Plans (if new building, or if lender is not in area,
            or if requested)
    E. Sketch—Third Floor
        (1) Show Tenants
        (2) Show Square Feet
        (3) Show Approximate Sizes
        (4) Building Plans (if new building, or if lender is not in area,
            or if requested)
    F. Personal Property
        (1) Inventory
        (2) Value
    G. Statement of Condition of Property
    H. Replacement Cost of Structure
        (1) Original Cost
        (2) Replacement Cost
    I. Comparable Sales of Improved Property of Similar Nature in
        the Area
    J. The Economics (Actual)
        (1) Income
        (2) Expense
        (3) Net Operating Income
        (4) Economic Value
        (5) Rent Roll

(6) Sample Lease

(7) Past Records of Income and Expense

K. Opinion of Economics

(1) Relationship to Average Square Foot Rent for Area

(2) Average of Square Foot for this Building

(3) General Opinion

(4) Estimated Future Income

L. General Summary of Value

(1) Land Values

(2) Replacement Value

(3) Personal Property Value

(4) Estimated Present Value

(5) Economic Value at Present Income

(6) Comparable Value

(7) Contract Price

(8) Copy of Contract

(9) Value Justified

III. THE PERSON

A. Name

B. Address

C. Occupation

D. General Data

E. Net Worth

F. Supporting Documents

(1) Net Worth Statement

(2) Schedule of Assets

(3) Schedule of Liabilities

(4) References

(5) Position of Employment

(6) Verification of Salary

(7) Estimated Annual Earnings

(8) Credit Report of Applicant

(9) Other Forms Supplied for Application

IV. THE LOAN REQUEST

A. Amount

B. Terms and Conditions

Four Key Steps in Formulating the Loan Package

1. Keep your sales material up-to-date and accurate. This will mean knowing all there is to know about the property you are to sell.

2. Accumulate the various sketches, photographs, past records, and other supporting documents you will use. These are shown in the Presentation Index as you go from listing to marketing.

3. Develop an understanding with the lenders you will approach to make sure what parts of the presentation they want emphasized. Remem-

ber, some lenders pay more attention to the person, others the property. You will want to know just how far you should go with the economics on the property. I prefer to limit the economic data to a minimum. Past records going back two or three years are helpful, and of course current data is a must. Expenses are almost more important than income and should be realistic. In most cases, you will have to increase the expenses the seller gives you. Avoid *pro formas* showing the next five years or more. Some of the new computer printouts enable you to run a ten year, or longer, projection of income and expenses. This is a waste of time on two counts. First, no one will read them with any real belief that they are correct. Second, they will not be correct. You cannot effectively project into the future, so don't go beyond one or two years at most.

    4. Get into the habit of using the package on all your loan applications.

Chapter 6

HOW TO USE NONCONVENTIONAL FINANCING TO BE A DEAL MAKER

The creative aspect of financing rarely occurs on the conventional side of financing. Indeed, your success in dealing with conventional financing will often occur using it in conjunction with one or more of the nonconventional techniques we will discuss in this chapter.

Nonconventional real estate financing is made up of elements that on the surface will at times not appear to be financing at all. For example, land leases are not usually thought of as a financing technique nor would a banker call a time-share hotel a financing tool. Nonetheless, these two methods of shifting equities are exactly that—financing tools that are available to you.

Once you understand the concept of shifting equities you will have a much easier time using some of the more complex techniques to be developed for you later on in this book. Best of all, you will find that you will begin to combine different techniques to fit your specific situation and transaction.

FINANCING IS A SHIFT OF EQUITY

If you owned a home that had no mortgage and was worth $100,000, your total equity would be the $100,000 within the value of the home. Now if you go to a local savings and loan and give them a mortgage, and they lend you $60,000 against your home, your equity is still $100,000, only you have *shifted* part of it ($60,000, in fact) into your pocket in the form of the cash (which the savings and loan gave you when you borrowed from them). The remaining equity of $40,000 is still in the house. Assume also that you want to acquire another property. You find that the seller of the other property will take your house as partial payment. Assume that it is a farm and the price is $70,000. You have $40,000 equity in your home, so to match the price you would owe $30,000 on the farm.

For the sake of this example, assume that the owner of the farm is holding the balance you would owe on a mortgage. You still have the $60,000 you borrowed, you have another $40,000 in the farm that is worth $70,000. What happened to your original $100,000 equity? Nothing, except a shift of equity has occurred.

The critical part of this example is that you must keep open all of your options in using financing to your best benefit. You will find that you can shift equity and ownership at the same time to get closer to your goals. Or you could have taken another tact, such as might occur in a land lease with option to recapture where you give up ownership, but keep the use of the property until you decide if you want ownership back again. All a shift.

One of the reasons this concept is important is that many people look at real estate as a two-sided affair. You buy it, and you sell it. Many people think that the immediate step to buying one property is to sell the property they currently own. For many people, this is the exact pattern they should follow; but there are other ways to attain your goals than just selling one property to be able to buy another. In fact, I will show you techniques that will help you buy two properties easier than you could buy one, and other techniques that help you get the maximum value out of the property you should dispose of so you can buy the property that will take you closer to your goal.

Conventional financing is by far the majority of financing done within the single-home market and can be one of the ways you will go in your quest for the ideal conclusion to your real estate need.

RANKING OF MORTGAGES

As we get into the nonconventional financing arena, we will find that we for the most part are now dealing with a mixture of first and second mortgages. There will be times when the mortgage looks like a conventional mortgage and appears to be a first mortgage just as its savings and loan counterpart would be. But if you go by the label and you are the seller in the situation, you might find yourself on the losing end of that rope pull.

So as we develop the basics of secondary and other creative financing, take a look at how mortgages are ranked and the significance of those rankings.

A FIRST MORTGAGE COMES FIRST—BUT IT ISN'T ALWAYS

The rank of a mortgage is its position to the other mortgage liens recorded against the property. The important word here is *position*. When a mortgage is given to a lender, it is taken down to the courthouse and the document is recorded as a lien against the property.

Assume for a moment that you have just sold your home for $100,000, and after getting $30,000 cash at the closing you took back a mortgage for the balance of $70,000. The buyer had the standard forms, and the document said *first mortgage* right on the top line. In fact, the buyer was so nice that he said he would drop the papers off at the courthouse for you. He did so the day after he recorded his title, and he took out from another lender another first mortgage in the amount of $80,000. If the second lender was able to get the buyer's mortgage document recorded prior to yours, it would have the first mortgage and you would have a second position.

WATCH OUT FOR SUBORDINATION TO A LATTER RECORDED MORTGAGE

Assume that there are mortgages on a property. This is the order in which they were recorded: (1) a $30,000 mortgage; (2) a $25,000 mortgage; and (3) a $50,000 mortgage. Since the recording was in the order indicated, the first mortgage is the $30,000 mortgage, unless something else had also happened—that something is subordination.

Subordination is a term that relates to holding rank in order or recordation, but allowing that rank to be taken by another mortgage or mortgages. For example, at one time there was only one mortgage on the above property. When the property was sold to Mr. Smyth, it was done so on the specific terms that he could get a total of $25,000 in additional financing, which would be ranked ahead of the existing mortgage. (Naturally, this provision would have to be either already in the existing mortgage terms or the mortgagee would have to agree to its conditions for the agreement with Smyth to have any substance.) The $50,000 mortgage may have been put on the property at a later date when Smyth sold it to a third party.

The significance of this subordination is the position of the mortgages and to illustrate that in some circumstances the position and rank can change. The $30,000 mortgage was a first mortgage at one time, and it was ranked ahead of any other mortgage until the subordination provision was inserted. When the second mortgage was recorded in the amount of $25,000, it actually became the first mortgage. The last mortgage remained the third mortgage. However, the wording of the subordination provision could have been something like the following: "and the mortgagee does herein agree that during the life of this mortgage and until such date that all principal and unpaid interest shall be satisfied to the benefit of the mortgagee, this mortgage will be, at the option of the mortgagor or his successors in title, subordinated to a debt of up to but not to exceed $25,000, provided that the payment of that debt shall not be an interest rate to exceed ___ percent per annum, with total payments of interest and principal per year not to exceed $ ___ in any given year.

It isn't the form of the statement that is important. What you want to look for is an open-ended form of subordination. What would happen here is that if the second recorded mortgage of $25,000 was to be paid off, an amount of $25,000 of what was the third-ranked mortgage could then become the first mortgage. The point is that rank can change because of the terms and conditions in other mortgages no matter what is said within a specific mortgage.

Knowing the whole story when you buy or sell property or deal in discounting of mortgages, which will be a separate chapter in this book, it becomes critical for you to see and read and then understand the terms of all the underlying mortgages.

Please make careful note: Never rely on the mortgagor to give you the whole story or even the truth when it comes to the terms and conditions of a mortgage that person, company, bank, or savings and loan may be holding. It has been my sad experience that lending institutions give out information about mortgages they hold that is wrong, misleading, incorrect, and, in general terms, a lie.

That is a strong statement, but it has been true in the majority of situations and circumstances involving my clients. There are reasons for this that do not include intent to commit fraud, such as inexperienced staff, change in loan policy and loan forms, deneighborhoodization of the institute or bank so it is possible that the forms are a thousand miles away, and so on. But if you have not read the terms, get them and don't even bother to ask the lender.

Make sure your lawyer has read them too. And be sure he has understood what they said. There are many ways to write mortgage terms, and those terms can sound so similar to methods used by lawyers that they too could slip up.

SECONDARY FINANCING IS A DEAL MAKER

In the sale of real estate it is not unusual for a seller to be asked to take back a second mortgage. This second mortgage in its usual form is nothing more than an additional mortgage that runs concurrent to the existing financing.

It will be the terms of the secondary mortgage that give you the flexibility to use financing to adjust the benefits of the real estate investments so that it fits your needs. The secondary financing that you develop will follow the same techniques that will work for first mortgages or in conjunction with several techniques. It could well be that you establish both conventional and secondary financing at the same time.

I WILL PAY YOUR PRICE—IF YOU ACCEPT MY TERMS

By adjusting the form of financing you use in your offers to acquire real estate or in the methods used to negotiate to sell your own real estate, you will find that price can be the least important aspect of a transaction.

Many transactions have failed to be put together when both the buyer and the seller had already had a meeting of the minds—only they didn't know it. For example: A seller has made up his mind that he will never take less than $50,000 for a vacant lot he owns. Along comes a buyer who has made up his mind that he will not pay more than $47,000 for the property. However, out of this seemingly impossible transaction the seller has indicated that one or more of the following factors apply to the deal:

1. He wants to take $25,000 of the sale and travel around the world on a cruise ship with his wife.
2. Since he paid only $5,000 for the lot five years earlier, he will have a heavy gains tax to pay.
3. He plans to buy a yacht with the cash.
4. He will take as little as $10,000 down and get the balance over a period of up to 15 years (putting that in the bank for his grandson's future college education).

Working with any of the above factors would have made this transaction work. Let's look at each one in more detail:

1. The buyer gets additional information from the broker about the desired cruise. The buyer then goes to a travel agency and talks to the owner: "I plan to buy real estate by giving away cruises that you sell. I want you to pay me a commission on these cruises. Give me a list of cruises that pay top commissions." The travel agent will produce some cruises that have 25 percent and more commission. The buyer will select one of these as his "offering proposal" and will book space in the names

of the sellers in question. Assume that the specific cruise costs $25,000 (for the type of accommodation the buyer books) and that the commission the buyer gets back from the travel agency is exactly $3,000. This means that the transaction will now close with the buyer buying no more than the $47,000 while the seller gets his $50,000 of real value.

	Buyer pays	Seller Gets
Cruise tickets	$22,000	$25,000
Balance of Property	25,000	25,000
Total	$47,000	$50,000

2. Realizing that the seller has a capital gains problem, the buyer approaches the situation with an installment sale. This is a provision where the seller takes the purchase price spread over more than one year. He saves on tax as he does so since the total gain does not increase his income to the point that his overall tax rate is increased excessively.

This technique can be coupled with the "split payment" method. Where the actual price is shown as $50,000 but the payments are divided into several years. If the buyer's cash can earn him extra dividends elsewhere, the ability to spread the total payment of the purchase over one or two additional years may make up part or all of the $3,000 over the desired payment of $47,000.

3. The desire to buy a yacht is even easier to handle than the cruise around the world. The buyer pays a visit to one or more yacht brokers or companies and makes a deal to "sell" one or more of their yachts. As the term *yacht* indicates the likelihood that the purchase price of the boat is apt to be greater than the property, the actual offer to the property owner can be: "$50,000 to be applied against the purchase of any yacht costing that much or more acquired through the following yacht brokers within 24 months following the close of this transaction." The buyer puts $50,000 in the bank, and whenever the deal goes through he can collect back the $3,000 or more that would be his commission from the yacht deal. Other benefits might include interest on the $50,000, which was in the bank during the decision process.

4. Anytime a seller indicates that he will hold secondary financing and spread the payments on the balance over time, he is telling the buyer that the most critical aspect of the deal is the price, but that the terms are somewhat flexible.

As financing is simply adjustment of values to interest rates over time, the buyer can make up his needed $3,000 over a ten- to fifteen-year term. In fact, this could be done in a much shorter time period. For example, a $40,000 mortgage at 10 percent interest per annum over 7 years (84 months) will have a monthly payment of $658.55, while a $37,000 mortgage for 7 years with a monthly payment of $658.55 has an interest rate of 12.63 percent per annum. By getting the seller to agree to accept a payment of $658.55 over the term, it becomes a matter of point of view as to the actual amount. Is it $40,000 at 10 percent, or $37,000 at 12.63 percent? Keep in mind that from the seller's point of view he's apt to want to look at it as $40,000 at 10 percent since his overall tax bite will be slightly less. The buyer can rationalize that he got his deal the way he wanted it—and why not? A deal was made when it might not have been made otherwise.

The basic structure of the financing technique used should then be devised to meet your goal and close the transaction.

All transactions must have a proper and satisfactory close or there is no transaction. Real estate investors who make a living and build substantial wealth through their investments know that there is a time and place for talk, and that a deal that drags along for a long time is most likely a deal that will never be made. Reluctant sellers, difficult situations that cannot be resolved simply or quickly, or buyers that cannot make up their minds kill more deals than anything.

Real estate salespeople know the power of "now" and act to nail down deals while the decision process is working. In any secondary financing, a good real estate salesperson will help you take advantage of this power, whether you are the buyer or the seller.

ADVANTAGES AND DISADVANTAGES OF SECOND MORTGAGES

This is how the second mortgages look to lenders and borrowers.

The institutional or private lender:

1. More risky the higher the position (seconds more than firsts, thirds more than seconds, etc.).
2. The more the risk, the higher the rate.
3. Borrower should be strictly qualified.
4. Keep the term short.

5. Obtain other security.

6. Be quick to foreclose.

The borrower:

1. Can reduce equity in the property and leverage up the return.

2. Can mean a high rate on the money borrowed.

3. May be hard to get.

4. Term too short to make a reasonable payment schedule.

5. Other security can tie up other property.

6. Even slight default can bring pressure.

A lender will examine all superior financing when considering making a loan on a property. The value of the property and the percentage of existing financing will dictate the amount of risk he is taking. Obviously, the lower the percentage of existing financing to total value, the lower the risk to the lender. If the property is valued at $50,000 and the first mortgage is $20,000, a second mortgage of $10,000 is a fairly safe gamble for the lender. The rate and term of years can be adjusted to account for the level of risk.

Lower-ranking mortgages, such as third or fourth mortgages, will command even higher rates as the risk increases and as the position or rank decreases. From a practical point of view, there are few institutional or private money sources that will lend on third or fourth mortgages.

WHEN SECONDARY LOANS ARE NEEDED

Because not all real estage transactions involve the use of secondary financing, it will be helpful for you to know when you should look to this form of financing as a deal maker. The first step in ascertaining when the secondary form of financing is needed is to fully understand what the second loan can do.

Six Things a Secondary Loan Can Do

1. It can enable the buyer to structure the total financing so that he can afford the required equity down payment. Because the terms of the secondary financing may vary, the overall debt service may require lower monthly payments due to the combined financing, when compared to other alternatives. Of course, there are times when the new first mortgage money market will not permit the loan to value ratio needed, and the secondary financing may be the only way to achieve that ratio.

2. It can increase the cash flow yield on the cash invested in an income property transaction by reducing the amount of cash to be invested; and by establishing a constant rate of payment on the secondary financing which is lower than the prior cash flow yield, then the new cash flow yield will be increased.

3. It can leverage a seller's return on the paper. If the seller were to receive $50,000 in cash, where could (or would) he invest the sum or money and at what interest rate? On the other hand, if the seller were able to obtain a 15 percent return or better from a secure second mortgage on his previously owned property, he might be interested. The wrap-around may do this, and is one of the better forms of secondary financing.

4. It can spread risk and separate values. Because secondary financing covers such a broad spectrum, it includes such creative forms of financing as: land leases, wrap-around mortgages, blanket mortgages, cross-collateralized purchase money financing, subordinated interest, interest-only payments, moratorium on all payments, percentage override sale of divided interest, and on and on. These various techniques, that are covered in this book, are used in secondary financing.

You will be able to sell a building, for example, but keep the land, which is then leased to the purchaser (this is a form of secondary financing).

5. There may be a limit to other choices. If the new money market is tight, seller-held secondary money may be the only possibility for structuring a high loan-to-value ratio.

6. The secondary loan can substantiate value. If the seller will hold a substantial second or third mortgage, at good terms, a sale at a higher price may be attained. There is normally a trade-off in this situation. The seller accepts lower than current interest over the term of the mortgage and the buyer pays more for the property than he might have if he had more cash invested. The judgment of which is better for the buyer or the seller depends on the alternatives that are actually present. It will do no good to assume it would be better to take cash instead of a mortgage, unless someone actually is offering cash and someone else is offering a mortgage.

Of the six things that secondary financing can do, not all may be present in every situation. In fact, to have two or three would be exceptional. Now that you have seen what secondary financing can do, look at the circumstances that will cause you to look to it as the most effective method of financing a transaction.

When to Use Different Types of Secondary Mortgages

THE TYPE OF SECONDARY FINANCING TO USE—1.

*   *   *

Start with seller-held secondary financing. If the seller won't hold a normal secondary loan, then approach him with a wrap-around structure.

*   *   *

THE CIRCUMSTANCES—1.

New money is tight and expensive. Closing costs and points are high, and loan to value ratios are 80% or less. The property has an existing financing that totals 50% or more of value and has a reasonable constant rate of payment. The buyer has a limited amount of cash to invest and must raise the loan to value ratio.

A land lease subordinated to existing financing will separate values and reduce the cash needed for the down payment.

*   *   *

If the seller will not take the paper, look to other markets for the secondary loan.

*   *   *

Possible cross-collateralization of other property may provide sufficient equity to support the loan for the seller or other lenders.

THE TYPE OF SECONDARY FINANCING TO USE—2.
*   *   *

Use other property the buyer has for the security of the secondary financing, and go into the new money market for a first mortgage.
*   *   *

In some situations the lender will not look at a land lease that is subordinated to the first mortgage as secondary financing, and this alternative can be used.
*   *   *

Leaving the seller in the deal, with a right to buy him out in the future, is a form of secondary financing.
*   *   *

Establishing a royalty fee on overages of income can provide income to a seller, and will not affect the lender's restrictions on new money.

THE CIRCUMSTANCES—2.

New money is tight and expensive as in the previous situation. Loan to value ratios are not sufficient to give the amount of financing needed, and the lender will not permit secondary financing on the property. The existing mortgage is very low (below 30% of value) or the property is free and clear.

THE TYPE OF SECONDARY FINANCING TO USE—3.

Look to the seller as the prime secondary lender.
*   *   *

If the amount of the secondary financing needed is small, and the commission substantial, the broker will often hold the paper.
*   *   *

The land lease and other provisions mentioned earlier may be useful in this type of situation.

THE CIRCUMSTANCES—3.

New money is available at reasonable rates. Loan to value ratios are high, and the property is free and clear or has a low percentage of existing financing. However, the buyer still needs extra financing.

The above three situations are most frequently encountered. There are many variations, of course, and secondary financing can be used in any deal. However, there are times when secondary financing is not effective and you should be aware of these.

When Secondary Financing Should Be Used Only as a Last Resort

1. Avoid using secondary financing when the buyer is financially weak and the transaction must be forced to meet his economic ability. If a buyer is putting down his last dime on an income property, he may be destined for trouble. Overextension of loan to value ratios will create debt service that may be more than the property or the buyer can handle.

2. Avoid seconds if the new money market is good, the existing financing on the property is low, and the equity needed with this type of financing is available from the buyer. Do not use secondary financing simply to increase this extension at the sacrifice of leverage. You should, however, first analyze the leverage and extension of a property to be sure you are arriving at a proper level. Use the Leverage Calculation Chart discussed earlier.

3. If a property has a number of secondary loans, you may still use secondary financing, but see if it is possible to eliminate some of the current loans with the cash down or from a new first mortgage.

4. Avoid a package of combined financing that has a constant rate which is more than 3 points above the possible existing financing, unless there is a good reason (such as an existing mortgage that is to retire in a few years, and the cash flow can be sacrificed for the period of time for future gains).

Remember that the greater the percentage of loan to value ratio, the more risky the secondary loans become. There are exceptions to every rule mentioned about secondary financing. The needs of the parties involved, their capabilities, and their willingness to risk capital need to be considered.

WHERE TO GO TO FIND SECONDARY FINANCING

The few sources of secondary financing are listed below:

1. *The Seller.* He is the best. (See sections of this chapter which follow for more detailed information.)

2. *Commercial Banks and Savings and Loans.* These sources are available for secondary financing in the form of home improvement loans. These loans should not be overlooked, because the buyer often anticipates additions to a property and plans on using cash after the sale for these improvements. Transfer cash to the down payment and finance the improvements with a home improvement loan. Some commercial banks are good sources for personal loans secured by

real estate. This is a changing market, however, and will depend on the bank and the person.

3. *Mortgage Companies.* Most communities have several mortgage companies that deal in the secondary loan market. They are effective, although often expensive. Check your area to locate them. Then use the same methods of establishing rapport with them as you would for a lender (discussed in the previous chapter).

4. *Private Investors.* This source is hard to find, and often there are investors that deal with the mortgage companies. Sometimes, however, you will find them advertising in the classified section of the local newspaper. They should be found before you need them. Your commercial bank may know of some.

5. *The Broker.* In the large commercial transactions, brokers are often asked to hold a part of the risk in the transaction by holding some of the paper. Some brokers will, and others will not.

HOW TO DEAL WITH SECONDARY LOAN MAKERS

Each of the preceding five sources will require a slightly different approach. Not all five will be available for all transactions. The banks, for example, will not be very useful in secondary financing over a first mortgage that represents at least 75 percent of the value. The effectiveness of mortgage companies diminishes when there is existing financing of at least 80 percent of the value.

Therefore, in the order of their acceptability to the transaction, look at the major sources of secondary loans and learn how to deal with them.

Dealing with the Seller on Secondary Financing

The seller is the most motivated of all possible lenders. When you deal with the seller, you don't have to justify the value or pay points. But sellers require special handling.

Third-party loans, made by outside lenders, banks, or private parties, are not highly negotiable. The end result will be a loan in the amount and at the terms the lender feels he can live with. The seller, on the other hand, is not bound by the same restrictions and can be more flexible. Some brokers mistakenly feel that the sellers who don't need the money (wealthy sellers) are the best candidates for purchase money secondary financing. Naturally, these sellers are good sources and are often receptive to this form of financing. However, they can sometimes be very independent. They may take the attitude that they will hold out until a cash buyer comes along. Wealthy sellers sometimes expect all buyers to have money.

The seller who doesn't have money and needs some money is generally the one who will take the secondary financing. Why? Look back on the motivation. If he needs money, the sale of the property becomes the important aspect. It could be that he is being transferred, or just cannot afford to keep the home or property being sold. In this situation, the need to make the sale will motivate the seller to hold some reasonable paper. Many sales are lost because the realtor assumes the seller will not hold secondary paper. The fact may be that the seller cannot afford *not* to be flexible.

How to Lay the Groundwork for Secondary Financing to Be Held by the Seller: Four Key Steps

1. *First make sure you know the goals and needs of the seller.* If he needs a quick sale or money in a hurry, then your entire marketing program may take on a different approach than if he were not pressed. You may find secondary financing becomes more important and crucial as the motivation of the seller increases.

2. *Examine the property carefully.* If you believe the first or existing financing is good and adds to the saleability of the property, start talking about the possibility of the seller holding paper or other forms of secondary financing rather then new financing. When the money market does not provide suitable or reasonable terms for new financing, then seek a form of secondary financing as a solution to the marketing problems. Remember, the seller is the best such source.

3. *Know the options you have in providing secondary financing.* Do not forget that it is not a first mortgage, it is a secondary or junior loan, and secondary financing is not just mortgages. It can be a land lease or building lease. The combinations are many, and you can utilize this book as a reference source for reviewing those options.

How to Deal with Commercial Banks and Savings and Loan Associations for Secondary Financing

There are usually two forms of commercial banks in any area—state and federal. There are slightly different regulations that govern each of them, and the individual bank policy on secondary financing may very widely. It is necessary, therefore, that you follow the guide below in order to obtain good secondary financing from these institutions.

The savings and loans also follow similar guidelines, so you may consider this section as a combined guide for both these institutions. Keep in mind, however, that each loan situation is different and, as with all loans, one bank or association will look for different criteria in their analysis of the risk. Here are five important guidelines:

- Know the policy of the institution before you go in to talk about a loan.
- When you make a loan presentation, have all the necessary back-up material you know the institution will require in order to reach a decision.
- Precondition your buyer to the possibility that he may need a co-signer for the note. Sometimes a relative will be glad to do this.
- Do not approach this form of secondary financing unless you could not arrange satisfactory financing with the seller or get new money.
- Find out, ahead of time, what additional collateral your buyer has that can be used as security on the loan needed. Often, stocks can be pledged, eliminating the need for a second mortgage on the property, or at least assuring the availability of a second mortgage.

How to Deal with Mortgage Companies

Mortgage companies are also regulated, but not to the same degree as normal banks or savings and loan institutions. These companies are either private firms or credit institutions. They may be a branch of union dealing primarily with its own members, or backed by insurance companies or trust funds. Their interest rates vary—from higher than any other source to lower.

The first step is to locate them and the best place to start is the yellow pages of your phone book. They will be listed under "Mortgages," "Loans," and sometimes "Trust Funds-Credit Unions." If you fail to locate any in this way, contact your commercial bank and ask if they have a list of the public as well as private mortgage companies that are in the area.

Once you have found them, learn what their lending policy will be in various types of deals. Some of these lenders will not touch anything but single family, while others will go into hotels and other commercial transactions.

This source is large and seems to have a lot of money most of the time. However, before you deal with any such lender do the following:

- Sit down with one of their representatives and find out how their operation works.
- Ask if they will give you information on their company.
- Get a list of references.
- Check out the references they give, but also ask others about them.
- A check with the Better Business Bureau may disclose some interesting facts about the firm.

- Get a clear understanding of their charges and interest rates.
- Be sure that the mortgage company is indeed reputable.

Finding Private Lenders and Dealing with Them

This is the most difficult source of all to find, but can be one of the best. These investors are usually wealthy persons who have substantial cash and/or the ability to borrow cash at better rates than you can. They will then lend the cash out at a higher rate, picking up the leverage. Secondary loans that are secure are a good form of investment for many people and those who are in that field seem to do well. It is not, however, a market for the occasional investor, and you should avoid the casual investor who says he will take a second mortgage on a property if it is exceptional. Look for the full-time investor.

These investors are found in the most unlikely places. They will normally deal with mortgage brokers or mortgage lenders to some degree, but the mortgage broker or lender will guard the identity of this investor and you will not find out who he is. Sometimes they work from leads they cultivate with commercial banks, and this contact is more accessible to you.

Some advertise in the newspaper, usually in the classified section under "Venture Capital" or "Capital Available." Various newspapers have different headings for this type of ad so look around. You can, of course, advertise for this source yourself, but this is rarely very productive. About the only way is to keep your eyes and ears open and to ask your commercial bank president and other lenders.

Because the private lender uses a lawyer in closing his transactions, you may find that if you send a letter to attorneys in your area, asking them if they know of private investors dealing in first and second mortgages, you may locate this elusive investor.

The private lender has an advantage over you and your buyer. He knows it and takes advantage of that situation. He is, after all, usually the last person you and other borrowers will turn to. Because of this fact, the private lender will either take the loan or not.

The harshness of the terms will depend mostly on the general market for other investments. If the investor is able to obtain nonrisk investments elsewhere at a good rate, then the rate he will demand on a second loan will be considerably higher, depending on the risk involved. You can do very little to change the outcome of a loan from such a lender. Nonetheless, you may find that the need for the money will be great enough to warrant the cost.

There are times when the private lender will lend at comparative terms when all things are considered. Usually, the closing costs are a fraction of those available from commercial banks and mortgage companies.

When dealing with private lenders, keep the following two cautions in mind:

1. Be sure the lender's attorney does not represent your buyer in closing the real estate transaction.
2. Have an attorney go over the loan document before you sign it.

WHEN AND HOW THE BROKER CAN HOLD SOME OF THE PAPER

If the transaction has a substantial commission, and the buyer is just a little short of cash to close the deal, the broker may be asked to take some of the paper as a deferred commission. Of course, this situation, can come up in almost any transaction, and this becomes an individual matter that some brokers will agree to do while others will not. It is important, however, that certain factors be understood about deferred commissions.

- If the broker takes a note, or other form of loan equivalent to a deferred commission, it is likely the IRS will tax the full amount of the commission the year the note was taken, rather than in subsequent years when payment is received.
- A fee conditioned on the future collection of a debt held by the seller may avoid the tax situation shown above, as the future payments are in a sense based on continued performance.

Chapter 7

HOW TO USE GOVERNMENT-INSURED LOANS TO FINANCE YOUR REAL ESTATE PURCHASES AND SALES

When it comes to providing options to finance your investments and to aid in the sale of your properties, you will want to learn as much as you can about government-insured loans and programs. The most notable of these loan programs are the VA and FHA loan programs for single-family home buyers. However, government loan programs are wide reaching and take into account a substantial amount of loans for many different kinds of residential and commercial ventures.

When it comes to government programs, you will want to deal with a good mortgage broker who is up to date in this kind of market and who deals with the specific type of loan you may want or that will best suit your needs. The information provided in this chapter is as up to date as possible, and while there may be no changes by the time you read it, government loan programs are constantly reviewed for alterations. Generally, the changes that may be enacted will improve the programs since the loan amounts are revised upward on a frequent basis.

The first step, however, is to have a general understanding of what the government programs do and how you can benefit from them.

Keep in mind that you should think of two factors of each loan program: (1) how it will help you to buy a given property, and (2) how you can use that technique to sell a property you own. Since not all loan programs apply to everyone, it is possible that you cannot use some of the loan programs offered. However, as a seller, many of your properties will find an increased market through the VA or FHA programs to be discussed.

Once you have reviewed this chapter, go out and find a good mortgage broker who is familiar with these types of programs. You will find mortgage brokers listed in the Yellow Pages under that title, and the answers to a few simple questions will tell you if you are talking with someone who may be worth meeting.

QUESTIONS AND ANSWERS TO FIND A QUALIFIED MORTGAGE BROKER

Q. 1. Does your company have a loan officer who specializes in FHA loans, VA loans?

A. 1. Yes. (If any other answer is given, you need to call another broker.)

Q. 2. (To that specialist) Do you specialize in single-family loans and investment loan programs within the VA and FHA programs?

A. 2. Yes. (Or better: No, I specialize only in the single-family loans. Mr. Jones of our office is the government loan specialist for investments.)

Q. 3. I would like to sit down and discuss my investment needs. Would there be any charge for the opportunity to discover if you can help me?

A. 3. No. When would you like to get together? If you want to include investments as well as single-family homes, I'll ask Mr. Jones to join us.

You will find that while there may be programs on the books that look as if they are exactly what you need, the actual availability of that program will depend on the determination of the area's needs and the amount of money that has been allocated to that specific area of loan assistance. For example, there are loan programs that are designed to assist in the construction of low-cost housing for the poor or the elderly. These programs open and close for specific areas of the country on the needs for housing in those areas. Some builders and investors follow these programs around the country, looking for opportunities when they open up.

PROVIDES INSURANCE, NOT LOANS

The first thing you should know about government loans is that in most instances the government does not make the loan. Instead it merely insures a portion of the loan, thereby reducing the risk to the lender who actually provides the funds. This insurance then makes more money available from conventional lenders for these programs since the loans are more secure than noninsured loans in the same category.

In addition, since such loans are less risky, the lender is willing to increase the amount of the loan. Some government loans provide 100 percent of the funds needed for the buyer to acquire the property. In turn, this increases the number of ready and willing buyers, which enables many real estate developers to find an easy market for their properties. As a buyer, this is good news if you can qualify for the program; as a seller, this is great news if your property meets the requirements for the program.

The insurance premium is paid by the buyer. The mortgage insurance premium (MIP) was implemented as a lump sum in 1983 and two methods of payment are allowed. One hundred percent of the payment can be financed, or the borrower can pay the premium in cash at the closing.

The following example is based on the One-Time MIP Factor Table.

LOAN REPAYMENT TERM IN YEARS

Portion of MIP financed by the buyer (%)	18 years or less	18–22 years	23–25 years	Over 25 years
100	0.02400	0.03000	0.03600	0.03800
0	0.02344	0.02913	0.03475	0.03661

Suppose that Abercoumbe took out a loan through one of the government programs in the amount of $80,000. The term was 25 years. At the closing of the loan, he could either pay cash or have the loan financed. If he had decided to finance the amount of the loan, it would be added to the total loan, and he would then pay back the loan based on the larger amount. First, he calculated the two different amounts:

100 Percent Finance Amount

Amount of the loan	$80,000	
Multiplied by	× .03600	(found in the 100% finance line under the 23–25 year term)
Insurance due	$ 2,880	(if financed).
Add loan amount	80,000	
Actual loan	$82,880	

Paid at Closing Amount

Amount of the loan	$80,000
Multiplied by	× .03475 (found in the 0% line under 23–25 year term)
Insurance due in cash at closing	$ 2,780

WHO MAKES THE GOVERNMENT LOANS?

Loans that are insured by the government are obtained from most institutional lenders. Local savings and loans, commercial banks, and other forms of mortgage bankers make these loans. These loans are then frequently sold to major investors such as insurance companies, pension funds, mutual funds, as well as back through government securities funds, which hold large blocks of these mortgages and sell shares to investors.

HOW DO THE INVESTORS MAKE OUT?

The lender or investor who buys the loan portfolio finds that usually it is going to benefit from ownership of the loan in two areas. First, a contract rate is paid by the borrower to the lender. This rate usually is slightly lower than the same conventional rate that would have been offered for the similar loan. However, as the risk is less, some investors feel this rate, and the next item to come, makes these loans very attractive investments. When the loan is made, a discount is paid by the seller. This discount is a cost that is required to be paid by the seller and adjusts the yield to the lender to increase the actual percentage earned by the lender above the contract rate. For example, if the contract rate were 10 percent on a loan of $80,000, the interest paid by the buyer the first year would be approximately $8,000. On this same loan, the seller may have paid a discount (points) of 4 percent, or $3,200, which would have reduced the actual amount of the funds provided by the lender by the same amount. The lender then actually paid out only $76,800. However, the loan is set at a contract rate of 10 percent on $80,000. In this case, the actual interest yield to the lender is about 10.54 percent if the loan was a 25-year loan and was not prepaid. Since the lender gets an additional bonus if the loan is prepaid, and as most loans are prepaid within seven to twelve years, the lender could earn an average yield of 11 percent or more on this example.

When you review the chapters on mortgage discounts and wraparound mortgages, you will find other examples of how this discount can be put to use.

THE VETERANS ADMINISTRATION AND THE GI LOAN

Veterans of the United States Armed Forces number well over 30 million. This is a sizable number of prospective applicants for loans, and many have not taken advantage of the opportunities available to them through the VA loan programs offered. THe veteran loan is often referred to as the GI loan, and it will be discussed here in detail. As in all aspects of government loan programs, the requirements and loan amounts and costs are subject to change.

WHO IS ELIGIBLE FOR A GI LOAN?

According to the most recent guidelines available from the VA, the following people are eligible for guaranteed or insured GI loans:

1. A veteran who has served a minimum of at least 90 days active service between *September 16, 1940 and July 25, 1947* (WW II vets); *June 27, 1950 to January 31, 1955* (Korean Vets); and *August 5, 1964 to May 7, 1975* (Vietnam vets); provided that the veteran was not discharged dishonorably. If the veteran within the above dates was discharged due to a service-incurred disability, the active service could be less than 90 days.

2. A veteran who served active duty for a period of 181 days or more and any part of which occurred after January 31, 1955, who does not meet the exact dates shown above for the 90 days active duty, and who was discharged or released under conditions other than dishonorable or who was discharged or released after such date for a service-connected disability.

3. Widows of men who served during the stated periods and who died as a result of the service.

4. Any member of the Women's Army Auxiliary Corps who served for at least 90 days and who was honorably discharged for a disability incurred in the conduct of service causing her to be unable to physically perform service in the Corps or in the Women's Army Corps. (*Note:* This provision is applicable only to discharges prior to the integration of that Corps into the Women's Army Corps, pursuant to Public Law 110, 78th Congress.)

5. Certain United States citizens who served in the Armed Forces of a government allied with the United States in World War II.

6. A serviceman or -woman who served on active duty for 181 days or more not already covered, provided that the enlistment into active service occurred prior to September 7, 1980, and that any discharge or release was other than dishonorable.

7. An enlistment after September 7, 1980, would require the serviceman or -woman to have served two years of active duty except if discharged for a disability whether or not service-connected; discharged for a hardship; or any case in which it is established that the person is suffering from a service-connected disability not the result of willful misconduct and not incurred during a period of unauthorized absence.

8. Unremarried widows of veterans of service personnel described in items (2) (6) and (7) above, who died as a result of service.

9. The wife of any member of the Armed Forces serving on active duty who is listed as missing in action or is a prisoner of war and has been so listed for a total of more than 90 days.

10. A serviceman who is on active duty at present and has served at least 181 days but not the full two years of duty will be granted an eligibility certificate conditioned on the veteran remaining on continuous active duty.

These ten categories indicate those persons who may be entitled to obtain a GI loan. This ability depends on the criteria mentioned and the prior use of this opportunity. Once a veteran has met the aforementioned rules or requirements, he or she automatically obtains an *entitlement*. This means that he or she can "draw" on his or her right for a GI loan. The entitlement is a term that relates to the amount of a loan the government will insure. At the moment, this amount is $27,500. Keep in mind that the entitlement is not the loan amount, but the insured amount. Lenders look at the entitlement as the top portion of the loan and will issue loans in multiples of this amount. In general, the lender will advance a loan equal to four times the entitlement. That means that at present the maximum loan on the GI program that *would not require the buyer to put any money down* would be $110,000 (4 × $27,500).

The veteran can increase the loan amount by "self-insuring" an additional amount by putting a cash down payment of 25 percent above the $110,000. This would increase the total loan to $135,000. If the veteran wanted to buy a house worth $143,333, he or she could get a loan for $135,000 if the down payment equalled $8,333.

REINSTATEMENT OR RESTORATION
OF THE VA ENTITLEMENT

A veteran who has previously purchased a property with a GI loan may be eligible for a second loan if he or she meets the following specific conditions:

1. The previous property must have been sold and the original loan paid off.

2. Another veteran assumed the GI loan and substituted his or her entitlement, thereby freeing the first veteran's eligibility for another loan.

In addition to these two circumstances, it is possible that the veteran didn't use all of the entitlement that he has obtained. One reason for this possibility is that the amount of the entitlement has continually increased over the years. You can see from the following chart the dates and amounts that established these increases. If you used the total entitlement available to you during an early year and then the entitlement was increased, you now have new entitlement coming to you.

ENTITLEMENTS AND DATES THEY WERE ESTABLISHED

Date	Amount
Prior to September 1, 1951	$ 4,000.00
Changed September 1, 1951	7,500.00
Changed May 7, 1951	12,500.00
Changed December 31, 1974	17,500.00
Changed October 1, 1978	25,000.00
Changed October 1, 1980	27,500.00

By following the chart, it would be obvious that a veteran who obtained a mortgage on July 1, 1951, has only used $4,000 of his or her entitlement. The veteran would now have a new entitlement of $23,500 available, and if he or she met the requirements of the reinstatement, the full $27,500 would be available to him or her at this time.

In addition to the automatic restoration or reinstatement of the entitlement to the veteran, there are three other ways in which the entitlement can be renewed. These occur when the security for the loan has been:

1. Taken by the United States or any state, or local government agency for public use (through condemnation or otherwise).
2. Destroyed or damaged by fire or other natural hazard to the extent that occupancy, use or restoration is impractical, which destruction or damage is not a result from an act or omission willfully designed by the veteran to bring about such destruction or damage.
3. Disposed of because of other compelling reasons devoid of fault on the part of the veteran. These reasons may include health, employment, voluntary conveyance in lieu of condemnation, or other reasons felt to be compelling.

The VA loan can be used for a variety of real estate ventures and is not limited just to single-family homes. The following is a list of the different kinds of properties the veteran can purchase using the GI loan program:

1. A single-family home
2. A residential unit in an approved condominium project
3. New construction of a single family home
4. Repair, alter, or improve a home
5. Refinance an existing home loan
6. A mobile home
7. Farm land, buildings, livestock, equipment, machinery, etc.
8. Business land, buildings, supplies, equipment, etc.
9. Apartment buildings up to four units (plus one additional unit for each additional veteran living on the property who cosigns on the mortgage)
10. Refinance property so it may be sold with improved financing

INCOME REQUIREMENTS TO OBTAIN A LOAN

The VA has set a basic qualification formula that must be met by every applicant for a GI loan. This formula sets the maximum loan available in most cases. The essence of this formula is to assure the lender that the borrower has reasonable income and credit to repay the loan. Therefore, in addition to being declared eligible for a GI loan based on his or her period of service, the veteran must meet the requirements of the governing law in respect to income and credit. This income credit takes into consideration more than the property and the respective mortgage payments that will become due as a result of the financing. It also takes into account other obligations confronting the veteran, which include dependents and other expenses that he or she may have. At the time an applicant is filing for a loan, the pertinent data will be used in the final calculations as to the credit of the borrower. The wife's or spouse's income will also be included in the total family income. Prior to going for an interview for an application, there is some specific information that you should have available.

DATA NEEDED FOR ANY MORTGAGE APPLICATION

1. The veteran and spouse's name and current address.
2. Entitlement amount. (Obtain through the VA office.)
3. Entitlement certificate. (Obtain through the VA office.)
4. Place of employment for veteran and spouse, with name for verification.

5. Last four years IRS 1040 or other form.
6. All sources of income, with documentation.
7. Three personal references, names, phone, addresses.
8. Bank, savings and loan, investment brokerage account, thrift institution address, and account number, and exact name on the account.
9. Loan information, lender's address, amount owned, and loan number.
10. Credit card numbers.
11. List with values of all major assets, and amounts owed against each.
12. Total (with breakdown) of all loan payments.
13. Details on any unusual expenses, which may be temporary or permanent.

THE PROCEDURE WITH A VA OR GI LOAN

Under the current law, there are several elements about the GI loan that both the buyer and the seller need to be aware of. The VA is very specific about what costs the veteran can pay and which costs he is not allowed to pay. The importance is that the seller is required to pay certain costs with respect to a sale to a veteran through the GI loan. Of course, there is no limit to what the seller may be required to pay under the contract, but it is critical that the seller understand that if the contract calls for the veteran to pay for cost the VA will not allow him or her to pay, the contract will not close in accordance with its provisions. At or prior to the closing, the parties will have to have an understanding based on the following items:

Items the veteran can pay if he or she is the buyer	Items the veteran cannot pay if he or she is the buyer
1. The veteran's lawyer	1. Discount (points)
2. Title insurance (if no charges for abstract)	2. Photographs
3. Survey	3. Preparation of deed
4. Credit report	4. Surtax on deed
5. Appraisal (if obtained in his or her name)	5. Assignment of mortgage
6. Intangible tax on mortgage	6. Mortgage satisfaction
7. State stamps on note, if any	7. Recording of item 6
8. Repairs	8. Documentary stamps on deed
9. Funding fee of 1 percent	9. Inspections
	10. Appraisal in another's name

All properties on which a GI loan application is to be made must be properly appraised by the VA office or an appointed and approved appraiser. The VA will only appraise property for veterans. The appraisal fees are apt to vary but will be approximately $110.00 for single-family homes; $120 for duplexes; $135 for triplexes; and $145 for four-unit apartments.

FHA appraisals cost a little more, but they can be used in the VA loan process. This is important for sellers who are not veterans and who wish to get the appraisal to facilitate a sale through the GI loan program, or one of the FHA loan programs.

There are a variety of types of loans the veteran can obtain with this program. Most follow conventional patterns similar to those loans offered by savings and loan associations to the general public. GI loans are limited in amount and have restrictions that make them available only to qualified veterans. Lenders benefit because of the reduced risk, sellers are able to sell property they might not have been able to without the GI loan (even though it cost them more to do this), and veterans get the opportunity to purchase a property they may not have been able to buy otherwise.

All veterans need to understand that when they take out a GI loan, they are on that loan until either it is paid off or they are replaced by another veteran. The significance of this is that loan remains as an outstanding liability to the original veteran no matter how many sales take place on the specific property. If the buyers are not veterans, or if a buying veteran has no entitlement to use to replace the original, then the vet is there for the duration. This may not present any economic hardship for anyone, but when the veteran sells the property he or she would be best advised to sell to another veteran who will remove him or her entirely, and thereby restore and reinstate the entitlement back to the original veteran.

FHA LOAN PROGRAMS

The Federal Housing Administration provides loans that are similar to GI loans, except there is a required down payment by the borrower. The most used FHA program is the Section 203 (b) loan, which is open to anyone, including a non-United States citizen. The property being purchased can be owner-occupied or investment property. The basic terms would be 30-year payback on the mortgage, with loan amounts as follows:

FHA 203 (B) LOAN PROGRAM

Loan maximums	
Single-family homes	$ 87,500
Duplexes	97,500
Three-family buildings	116,500
Four-unit apartments	133,100

Down payment required	
Minimums	
3% of the first $25,000 purchase price	
3% of everything over the first $25,000	
Appraisal fees	
Single-family homes	$125
Duplexes	140
Three-family buildings	160
Four-unit apartments	180

In keeping with the institutional lenders' creative form of financing, the FHA has developed the Section 245 (a) program, which is a graduated payment mortgage. As in all graduated payment mortgages (GPM), the initial monthly payment is less than would cover the interest and insurance costs of the loan. The unpaid interest and insurance is added to the principal owed, making the total amount owed on the mortgage increase in the early years of the GPM. As the amount of payment is increased, this trend reverses and the payment begins to cover all costs on the mortgage and amortization of principal owned.

The 245(a) offers the borrower three different loan programs depending on the initial term and the increases in payment. All three programs have a total 30-year payout term, and are as follows:

Plan 1 Five years of monthly payments that increase 2.5% annually, then remain constant for the remainder.

Plan 2 Five years of monthly payments that increase 5% annually, then remain constant for the remainder.

Plan 3 Five years of monthly payments that increase 7.5% annually, then remain constant for the remainder.

SPECIFIC ELEMENTS OF THE 245(a)

1. Cannot be used to refinance a present-level mortgage.
2. Maximum amounts set for specific areas of the country by HUD.
3. Can be assumed as with other FHA programs.
4. Down payment is greater than with the 203 (b) program and is reviewed on a case-by-case basis.
5. Maximum mortgage amount is $87,500 but some areas may be limited to less.

FHA 245(B)

This program is similar to the 245(a), but is available to first-time home buyers, and buyers who have not held title within three years of a home.

Buyers cannot qualify under any other FHA program. If qualified for the 245 (B), the buyer is required to have only 5 percent down payment, and the payments are similar to those of the 245(a).

How to Get Information

The following list includes all the regional offices of the Veterans Administration. Any correspondence should be directed to the *Director* of the corresponding office in your area. You may request additional data from the office to assist you in your use of the VA loan program. One caution, however. Much of the material they will send you is out-of-date, and you should not rely on this information if it applies to interest rates, dollar amounts, and current programs. Local lenders dealing with loans can provide this up-to-date information. The VA sends notices on minor changes on a very frequent basis, and there is no way you can keep abreast of these changes unless you have the time to sift through all the notices which the VA sends out.

VA Regional Office
Aronov Building
474 South Court Street
Montgomery, AL 36104

VA Regional Office
Federal Building
230 North First Avenue
Phoenix, AZ 85025

VA Regional Office
Federal Office Building
700 West Capitol Avenue
Little Rock, AK 72201

VA Regional Office
Federal Building
11000 Wilshire Boulevard
Los Angeles, CA 90024

VA Regional Office
211 Main Street
San Francisco, CA 94105

VA Regional Office
Denver Federal Center
Denver, CO 80225

VA Regional Office
450 Main Street
Hartford, CN 06103
Note: Loan guaranty consoli-
    dated with Philadelphia.

VA Center
1601 Kirkwood Highway
Wilmington, DE 19805

Veterans Benefits Office
Veterans Administration
2033 M. Street, NW
Washington, DC 20421

VA Regional Office
P.O. Box 1437
144 First Avenue, South
St. Petersburg, FL 33731

VA Regional Office
730 Peachtree Street, NE
Atlanta, GA 30308

VA Regional Office
P.O. Box 3198
680 Ala Moana Boulevard
Honolulu, HI 96801

VA Regional Office
Federal Building & U.S. Court-
  house
550 West Fort Street
Box 044
Boise, ID 83724

VA Regional Office
2030 West Taylor Street
Chicago, IL 60680

VA Regional Office
36 South Pennsylvania Street
Indianapolis, IN 46204

VA Regional Office
210 Walnut Street
Des Moines, IA 50309

VA Center
5500 East Kellogg
Wichita, KS 67218

VA Regional Office
600 Federal Place
Louisville, KY 40202

VA Regional Office
701 Loyola Avenue
New Orleans, LA 70113

VA Center
Togus, ME 04330

VA Regional Office
Federal Building
31 Hopkins Plaza
Baltimore, MD 21201

VA Regional Office
J.F.K. Federal Building
Government Center
Boston, MA 02203

VA Regional Office
801 West Baltimore at Third
P.O. Box 1117-A
Detroit, MI 48232

VA Regional Office
252 Seventh Avenue (at 24th St.)
New York, NY 10001

VA Center
Federal Building
Fort Snelling
St. Paul, MN 55111

VA Center
1500 East Woodrow Wilson Ave.
Jackson, MS 39216

VA Regional Office
Room 4705, Federal Building
1520 Market Street
St. Louis, MO 63103

VA Center
Fort Harrison, MT 59636

VA Regional Office
220 South 17th Street
Lincoln, NB 68508

VA Regional Office
1201 Terminal Way
Reno, NV 89502

Note: Loan Guaranty consoli-
  dated with San Francisco.
  Loan Guaranty activities for
  Clark and Lincoln Counties,
  Nevada consolidated with Los
  Angeles.

VA Regional Office
497 Silver Street
Manchester, NH 03103

VA Regional Office
20 Washington Place
Newark, NJ 07102

VA Regional Office
500 Gold Avenue, SW
Albuquerque, NM 87101

VA Regional Office
Federal Office Building
111 West Huron Street
Buffalo, NY 14202

VA Regional Office
1801 Assembly Street
Columbia, SC 29201

VA Regional Office
Wachovia Building
301 North Main Street
Winston-Salem, NC 27102

VA Center
Fargo, ND 58102
Note: Loan Guaranty consoli-
   dated with St. Paul.

VA Regional Office
Federal Office Building
1240 East Ninth Street
Cleveland, OH 44199

VA Regional Office
Second and Court Streets
Muskogee, OK 74401

VA Regional Office
426 Southwest Stark Street
Portland, OR 97204

VA Center
P.O. Box 8079
5000 Wissahickon Avenue
Philadelphia, PA 19101

VA Regional Office
1000 Liberty Avenue
Pittsburgh, PA 15222

VA Center
Barrio Monacillos
GPO Box 4867
Rio Piedras, PR 00936

VA Regional Center
Federal Building, Kennedy Plaza
Providence, RI 02903
Note: Loan Guaranty consoli-
   dated with Boston

VA Center
Sioux Falls, SD 57101

Note: Loan Guaranty consolidated with St. Paul.

VA Regional Office
U.S. Courthouse
801 Broadway
Nashville, TN 37203

VA Regional Office
515 Rusk Avenue
Houston, TX 77061

VA Regional Office
1400 North Valley Mills Dr.
Waco, TX 76710

VA Regional Office
125 South State Street
Salt Lake City, UT 84138

VA Center
White River Junction, VT 05001

VA Regional Office
211 West Campbell Avenue
Roanoke, VA 24011

VA Regional Office
Sixth and Lenora Building
Seattle, WA 98121

VA Regional Office
502 Eighth Street
Huntington, WV 25701

VA Regional Office
342 North Water Street
Milwaukee, WI 53202

Note: Wyoming consolidated
   with Denver

Mortgage and Rent Assistance Programs for Multifamily Structures

Section 207 .... Rental project housing and mobile home
                          parks
Section 213 .... Cooperative housing

Section 220 .... Urban renewal housing
Section 220 (h) .... Rental project housing improvement loans
                                in urban renewal areas
Section 221 (d) (3)–(4) ... Low- or moderate-income family housing
                                below market rate—income not limited
Section 221 (h) .... Low-income rehabilitation housing
Section 231 .... Housing for elderly
Section 233 .... Experimental housing
Section 234 (d) (f) .... Condominium housing
Section 236 .... Rental housing for lower-income families
Section 241 .... Supplemental loans

Land Development

TITLE X .... Purchase and development of land; "New
                                Towns" development

Medical

TITLE XI .... Medical group practice facilities
Section 232 .... Nursing homes and hospitals

You should become familiar with the titles of the various FHA programs by their section numbers. In conservation, FHA programs are simply referred to as "a 236," "a 203," and so on.

Because these programs may vary slightly from year to year as new programs are added or old ones are changed, it is necessary that you continuously update the information contained in this chapter. This can be done simply by keeping in touch with the mortgage broker you plan to deal with in all FHA or VA matters.

Naturally, it is not necessary for you to deal with a mortgage broker. You can handle the applications yourself. However, unless you plan to devote a major part of your time to keeping up-to-date with FHA and VA regulations, do not attempt to handle your own applications or the applications of your clients.

HOW TO USE THE FHA PROGRAMS
TO CLOSE MORE DEALS

The FHA covers far more ground than the VA. Therefore, it will offer more opportunities for selling real estate.

The Federal Housing Administration was created by the National Housing Act, which was approved on June 27, 1934. The purpose of the FHA was to encourage improvement in housing standards and to offer lenders incentives to have a broader lending policy, thereby stabilizing the mortgage market. All these things were needed in 1934; and in retrospect, the FHA programs first offered to the public had considerable impact on lending policies.

In 1965, the office of the Federal Housing Administration was transferred to the Department of Housing and Urban Development. As a result, the FHA is now an organizational unit within the Department of Housing and Urban Development (HUD). Like the VA loan program, the FHA does not give loans, but insurance on loans. The FHA provides insurance for private lenders against loss on mortgages that they give to finance homes, multifamily projects, land development projects, and other programs that will be discussed in this chapter.

Here is a list of some of the current, existing programs that indicate the involvement of the FHA in mortgage assistance.

Homes and Units Up to 4-Plex

TITLE II

Section 203 (b)	1- to 4-family housing units
Section 203 (h)	Disaster housing
Section 203 (i)	Low-cost homes in outlying areas
Section 203 (k)	Home improvement loans
Section 203 (m)	Seasonal, leisure, or vacation homes
Section 213	Sales of individual housing cooperative units
Section 220	Urban renewal housing
Section 220 (h)	Home improvement loans in urban renewal areas
Section 221 (d) (2)	Low-cost homes for families displaced by urban renewal, etc.
Section 221 (h)	Low income rehabilitation housing
Section 222	Servicemen's homes
Section 233	Experimental homes
Section 234 (c)	Sales of individual condominium housing units
Section 235	Home ownership for lower-income families
Section 237	Marginal credit risk
Section 245 (a) (b)	Graduated payment mortgages

FHA Program Chart

Figure 6-1 illustrates the more useful FHA programs, showing the VA or GI loan as a comparison. You will find this chart helpful as a quick reference to the program number and the general aspects of that program.

Keep in mind that this chapter is not designed to make you an expert in FHA or VA financing. Books containing far more pages than this one could not accomplish that. The more you work with the VA and the FHA, the greater your understanding will be of the workings of these government programs. There can be no doubt that both VA and FHA are more complex than conventional financing. And generally, the time periods required to obtain the commitments and funding can be greater than those required in obtaining conventional financing.

In viewing the chart, take the minimums and maximums shown as the amounts or periods that can be obtained under ideal conditions. In some cases, those maximum amounts can be altered upward, but such circumstances would be highly unusual and cannot be counted on. A lot of the actual funding has to do with the favor in which the particular program finds itself at any given point of time. For example, if the FHA has decided to cut back on the Title XI program for medical facilities, you can have the finest presentation and the worthiest cause and not get anywhere. On the other hand, if Section 207 is pushing mobile home parks and money is flowing into this area, it might be to your advantage to know this and to look for clients who may want to build mobile home parks.

The Advantages and Disadvantages of Dealing with VA and FHA Financing

In the first place, it is necessary to find out the advantages and disadvantages of the three parties involved—the buyer, the seller, and the broker.

The pros and cons of VA-FHA for the buyer. Since financing has a long-range effect on the property, the buyer will generally see the majority of the advantages and disadvantages. Nonetheless, it is necessary to compare the VA or the FHA loan with alternatives. In many cases, there are no alternatives, and hence no real comparisons to make. The VA, for example, is the only way to buy with no down payment, since no conventional financing is available to match that capability. On the other hand, if you have a buyer who has between 5 and 10 percent that he can put down, and he insists on going ahead with a VA loan, then you should show him the effect of going with a conventional loan, having coinsurance which will allow 10 percent down. Since the seller is to pay the discount under VA and FHA, the savings that can accrue to the buyer may make it feasible and desirable to buy conventionally, even though he must put cash down.

The long-term pay-out provided for in most VA and FHA loans can be most advantageous. Once the loan is placed with an interest rate (due to the discount policy) below the market rate, the loan becomes valuable in its own right.

The value of low interest and long terms is seen when the property is placed back on the market in a few years. If you buy a property worth $50,000 and have a $50,000 mortgage, and in three years hope to get

USEFUL FHA & VA PROGRAMS

FHA programs	Loans on	Maximum loan amount	Down payment required	Section 203 (v) Maximum term	General information
Section 203 (b)	1 to 4 family homes; existing, under construction, or proposed	1-family: $87,500 2-family: $97,500 3-family: $116,500 4-family: $133,100	Construction approved by FHA for house over 1 yr. old: 3% of 1st $25,000 5% above $25,000 Existing construction, less than 1 yr. old and not approved by FHA before construction: 10% of the total cost to buy.	30 years	+ Single people are eligible. + In property not owner occupied, mtg. amount is 85% of mtg. amount for owner occupied (if over 1 yr. old & built to FHA requirements 85% or max. mtg. allowable if home not built under FHA requirements.
Section 203 (h)	Disaster housing	100% estimated value	No down payment as property is generally owned	30 years or ¾ remaining life	Mtgs. given to finance the replacement of homes destroyed or damaged by major disasters.

Program	Property	Max loan	Down payment	Term	Remarks
			25% maximum	30 yrs.	As these homes are not required to be lived in year-round, they need not meet full FHA restrictions. S&Ls can loan $5,000 without secured high 1st mtg.
Section 203 (v)— with veteran buyer	One-family homes; existing, under construction, or proposed	1-family: $87,500	No down payment on 1st $25,000 5% above $25,000	30 yrs.	+Veteran must have had 90 days of continuous service on active duty in any branch at any time. Eligibility never expires. There is a minimum investment of $200 on the 1st $25,000 of value. This $200 can be applied toward costs. +National Guard and Reserves are eligible.
	with a 3 percent down payment				

USEFUL FHA & VA PROGRAMS (CONT.)

FHA programs	Loans on	Maximum loan amount	Not owner occupied Down payment required	Section 221(d) Maximum term	General information
Section 207	Mobile homes and mobile parks	Mobile homes—up to 100% Parks: $2,500 per space; $1,000,000 per park	No down payment required by FHA. Some lenders may however, require small equity.	145 mo.	While FHA will insure for over 12 yrs., such term is not generally available in the market.
			Development provision will vary depending on size of park.	40 yrs.	In high cost areas, max. loan amounts can be increased up to 45%.
Section 207	Rental housing—8 or more family units (new or rehabilitated)	90 percent of face value, max. established per project	10% minimum	40 yrs.	No discrimination permitted against families with children.
Section 213	Coops of 5 or more units	Varies—follows completed formula	Varies as to maximum loan requirements	40 yrs.	Mortgagor must be nonprofit organization. Individual units to be owned by a

					closely defined group usually a part of the non-profit organization.
Section 220	Improvement loans (1 to 4 units)	Usually follows 203(b) maximums	Usually follows 203(b)	40 yrs.	Mortgagor can seek funds through FNMA under this program when local lenders are not available.
Section 221 (d) (2)	1- to 4-family; existing, proposed or rehabilitated; for low- and moderate-income families	1-family: $42,000 2-family: $45,000 3-family: $57,600 4-family: $68,400	If mortgagor is non-profit organization there is a down payment required. Minimum of 3% of total acquisition cost, which may include FHA estimate of value plus closing costs and prepayables. (221 Certificate holders— minimum investment $200).	40 yrs.	+ There must be family relationship by blood or marriage, except if mortgagor is 62 or older. + Single people not eligible unless mortgagor is 62 or older. + Some FHA offices have income limits, others don't.

USEFUL FHA & VA PROGRAMS (CONT.)

FHA programs	Loans on	Maximum loan amount Not owner occupied	Down payment required	VA Program Maximum term	General information
Section 222	1-family; existing or proposed; home or condo, provided condo is insured under FHA Section 234 (c). For members of armed forces on active duty.	1-family: $87,500	Construction approved by FHA: 3% of 1st $25,000 5% over $25,000. / Construction not approved by FHA: 10% of total cost to buy.	30 years	
Title X	Land development	$25 million each project. Based on: (1) 79% finished value, or (2) 50% of raw land value + 90% improvements; whichever is lowest.	Balance of equity required to acquire land and meet development formula.	10 years (but can be extended in many cases)	Under this program, land can be brought to development to ready to build stage. Loan covers all aspects. Releases are made available at 10% *pro rata* lot to mtg. value.

	Type of housing	Maximum loan amount	Down payment required	Maximum term	General information
Title XI	Medical group practice facilities, medicine, optometry, dentistry	Up to $5 million per facility; 90% of costs	10%	25 years	Mortgagor must be nonprofit. However the facility can be leased to a profit-making group. This program can be used by practitioners who form a nonprofit organization then lease the facility as a profit-making group. Equipment can be included in cost.

VA program	Type of housing	Maximum loan amount	Down payment required	Maximum term	General information
	1- to 4-family homes; existing, under construction, or proposed; owner occupied	VA does not set a maximum mortgage amount. However, many mortgagees limit amount to $135,000	No down payment is required by VA. However, a down payment may sometimes help chances for approval.	30 years	See list of nine categories in this chapter. Must live in home.

$60,000, you can offer the property for sale with excellent financing already on it. Your VA-FHA loan will still have nearly $48,500 in principal, and will have up to twenty-seven years to go at an interest rate which should be well below the market rate. In essence, you have over 80 percent financing available which can be *assumed* at no cost to close the loan. This type of financing on a home may well mean a better opportunity to sell at a higher price.

The ups and downs for the seller. The seller takes the big bite when he pays the discount on the VA-FHA loan. A minor disadvantage comes in taking the property off the market while the appraisal is made and the buyer is undergoing the qualification process. Time thus becomes the major nonmonetary stumbling block for the seller.

Nonetheless, the sale via VA or FHA may still be the best way to go, or the only way to go. The arguments made by the seller over discount are usually unwarranted, since he would have dropped his price anyway. But this usually means that sellers increase the price to cover the cost. Of course, the appraisal should include this price, and history has indicated that it generally does.

The biggest problem for the seller in this whole transaction is the waiting period—or worse, having taken the property off the market while the buyer is going through the approval period. In addition, the seller will not know the exact amount of the discount at the times he places the property on the market, nor will he know the totality of repairs that the VA or FHA appraisal will indicate must be made.

The advantage to the seller is the obvious expansion of the market place for this property. There are many buyers who would not qualify for any other form of loan except the VA or FHA loan, and if that is the only way to sell that property then there are no drawbacks, only benefits.

The broker's problems come in two packages. First, the problem for both the buyer and seller in that unless they are dealing with a broker who is qualified and knowledgeable with the ins and outs of the government insurance programs then a lot of time can be lost. Second, as this kind of loan program is complicated, many brokers shy away from getting involved. Rather than bring in someone who does know, brokers often will try to divert the clients to a more conventional program or will give bad advice.

WHERE TO OBTAIN FHA INFORMATION

Figure 7-2 lists the addresses for the regional offices of the Department of Housing and Urban Development (HUD). Drop one of their offices a card and ask for their current literature and to be put on their mailing list.

Region I
26 Federal Plaza
New York, NY 10007

Connecticut, Maine, Massachusetts, New Hampshire, New York, Rhode Island, Vermont

Region II
Curtis Building
Sixth & Walnut Streets
Philadelphia, PA 19106

Delaware, District of Columbia, Maryland, New Jersey, Pennsylvania, Virginia, West Virginia

Region III
645 Peachtree—7th Building
Atlanta, GA 30323

Alabama, Florida, Georgia, Kentucky, Mississippi, North Carolina, South Carolina, Tennessee

Region IV
Room 1500
360 North Michigan Ave.
Chicago, IL 60601

Illinois, Indiana, Iowa, Michigan, Minnesota, Nebraska, North Dakota, Ohio, South Dakota, Wisconsin

Region V
Federal Office Building
Room 13A01
819 Taylor St.
Fort Worth, TX 76102

Arkansas, Colorado, Kansas, Louisiana, Missouri, New Mexico, Oklahoma, Texas

Region VI
450 Golden Gate Ave.
P.O. Box 36003
San Francisco, CA 94102

Northern California, Guam, Hawaii, northern Nevada, southern Idaho, Utah, Wyoming

226 Arcade Plaza Building
1321 Second Avenue
Seattle, WA 98101

Alaska, Montana, northern Idaho, Oregon, Washington

Room 1015
312 North Spring Street
Los Angeles, CA 90012

Arizona, southern California, southern Nevada

Region VII
Ponce De Leon Avenue &
  Bolivia Street
P.O. Box 3869, GPO
San Juan, PR 00936

Virgin Islands, Puerto Rico

Chapter 8

HOW TO SECURE LAND DEVELOPMENT AND CONSTRUCTION LOANS

Two loans are used as a foundation to the real estate market: the land development loan and the construction loan. Each of these loan forms is very similar to the other in many respects, yet in some critical aspects each differs greatly.

The purpose of this chapter is to examine each loan format and look at how they are obtained and what you can do to maximize your ultimate end result to best fit your needs and goals.

THE LAND DEVELOPMENT LOAN

The land development loan is given to a property owner for the specific purpose of development of that property. This kind of loan might be used later for construction of buildings and can be tied into a construction loan as well, or simply land development.

Oscar owned 125 acres of prime timber land about forty-five miles west of Boston, Maine. The timber had not been fully cut in over thirty years, and except for one time about ten years ago when Oscar had all the soft wood culled out for pulp, no trees had been taken.

Due to the property's proximity to Boston and the nature of the surrounding area, Oscar decided he would develop the land into five-acre homesteads. He would then sell the homesteads to Bostonians who would like to have a retreat a short drive from the city.

To help finance the cost of development, Oscar planned to sell off a lot of the hard wood on the land. By being selective with the cutting, he would however maintain a heavy growth on the property.

He contacted several buyers of hardwood in the furniture industry. They were all interested until they found out that Oscar wanted to be as selective as he planned in the tree cutting. This would increase the cost to remove the trees, and would require a longer cutting period for the amount of board feet that would be removed.

In the end, Oscar got a good price, but it was far less than he had hoped. He realized he would have to get additional funds to put in the types of improvements needed to sell the sites.

Oscar discovered that the cost of development of land was going to be far greater than he ever anticipated, and because of that, the cost of the ultimate product was going to be greater than he had planned. This series of events "forced" Oscar to plan a few more improvements than he originally thought would be needed to upgrade the product.

Oscar found that the days of running in a dirt road and selling off lots were gone.

PUTTING TOGETHER A PRESENTATION TO THE LENDER

Oscar reviewed what he needed in the way of funds.

Road way costs	$ 75,000
Power line costs	28,000
Sales brochures	2,500
Interest on loan needed during selling time	12,000
Miscellaneous costs	5,000
Total development cost not including the land	$122,500
Less the net from the timber sales	45,000
Cash Needed	$ 77,500

At this point, the cost of the land has not been calculated into this transaction. Oscar has owned the land for over seventeen years, and his actual cost was only $50 per acre. A more realistic value of the land today would be $1,500 per acre. This matches the current sales of similar raw land in the area that does not have valuable timber on the land. To provide values in the project that relate to the profit from the development, and not profit from appreciation of the land, Oscar has set up a development corporation that will handle all development, sales, and the like. In essence, he has "sold" his land to that new company at $1,500 per acre. In addition, the sale of the timber will not be calculated into the sale of the sites. Oscar can anticipate his cash needs as indicated above, but in the sales calculations the timber proceeds will not be shown.

A good lawyer and CPA are suggested in setting up this kind of situation to get the most out of the federal and state tax laws. In Oscar's case, he didn't want to lose the potential capital gain treatment from the sale of the land at its current value, because the profit from the development will be taxed at earned income rates.

There are ways to protect your capital gain rights, but they vary between states and from year to year with the federal government.

Oscar then reviewed his potential sales. From the 125 acres he owned he expected to obtain 22 tracts that would average about 5 acres in size including the roadway access, which would be kept private and not become a public dedicated way. Oscar had decided to keep the roadways private for two reasons. First, he didn't want the public having access to the area; second, by keeping the roadways private, he didn't have to build a roadway to the local road department's specifications, which would have more than doubled the cost of the road.

Oscar looked at the market to determine what other similar product was available to investors in an attempt to price his tracts. He discovered that there was nothing around that would compare with his end product, especially when he took into account the beauty of the hardwood trees, which was very unique to his site. Nonetheless, there was other property available that people from Boston and surrounding towns could buy, so Oscar determined that the maximum price he could ask would be $30,000 per tract.

FINDING THE NET SALES VALUE

Gross Sales: $30,000 per tract × 22 tracts:		$660,000
Less Direct Cost of Sales		
Commissions to sales staff	$66,000	
Legal costs to close	11,000	
Miscellaneous costs	4,400	
		81,400
	Net Sales	$579,600

Now Oscar had to determine his proposed profit, so from the net sales amount he had to deduct:

Net cost of development	−122,500
Cost of land to development	−187,500
Profit on the Project	$269,600

Armed with this information, Oscar was ready to have the loan processed.

THE LAND DEVELOPMENT LOAN PRESENTATION

In Oscar's case, the land development loan would follow this example:

Current Value of the Property:		$187,500
Cost of Improvements:		122,500
	Base Cost of Site	$310,000
Amount of Net Sales:	$579,600	
Less Base Cost	310,000	
Profit	$269,600	
Loan Request:	$184,800	
Loan-to-profit ratio	50%	
Term of Loan Requested:	Draws against development costs as presented, with $62,300. in advance for land acquisition cost. Three year pay back, interest only at 11 percent.	
	USE OF FUNDS	
Advanced funds:		$ 62,300
To be paid to seller (Oscar) of land. The balance owed to the seller is subordinated to the development loan and will be paid out of final proceeds plus interest.		
Development costs:		
Roadway		75,000
Powerline		28,000
Miscellaneous		5,000
Sales Cost:		
Brochures		2,500
Other Costs:		
Interest and other legal costs		12,000
TOTAL		$184,800

The advanced funds of $63,800 were part of the deal Oscar made in setting up the development company. Through his lawyer's help, he "sold" the land to a general contractor, who was going to do the actual work. In doing this, Oscar took this advance payment as the down payment, and held the mortgage on the property that provided for subordination to the development loan, with releases as the sites were sold. Properly done, this allowed Oscar to participate in profits in the development that would be taxed at earned income, but the initial profit in the land that came through the seventeen years of appreciation was retained on a capital gain basis.

This would be critical to any project where the land had been owned for a long time and had a substantial profit built in.

The lenders that would look at this kind of loan would vary depending on your local situation. Some lenders don't like development loans, while others thrive on this kind of project.

You would be best advised to look to your local savings and loan as a start, following up with a good mortgage broker to examine the best sources for these kinds of funds.

ULTIMATE SALES FIGURES

Each lender will look at the ultimate sales figures and make its assessment of a prudent loan-to-value ratio. In this illustration, the loan request was based on a 50 percent LOAN-TO-PROFIT RATIO, which is conservative. In reality, a much higher loan would have been available in most market areas.

A review of Oscar's situation and how it was handled may give you some ideas of how you might have handled it differently. There is no doubt that the pattern could have been different, and the end results better suited to your own specific needs and goals. The lessons to be learned from Oscar's example is the need to examine all potential problems, and to look beyond the basic idea to find methods that get you to your desired location quicker, and with fewer problems.

A CONSTRUCTION LOAN

Along comes Bill, who is a general contractor of large office buildings in the Boston area. He wants to buy one of Oscar's lots so he can build a small cabin away from the big city. He makes his deal with Oscar and puts down $5,000 on the tract he is buying. He gets Oscar to subordinate his remaining interest to a construction loan to finance the cabin. Bill plans to replace the construction loan with a permanent loan from one of the savings and loans in the area as soon as he is finished building the cabin. That, at least, is his plan.

So far so good, however, as there is no problem with Oscar. He gets sufficient money out of the down payment to release the development loan he has to pay off, and doesn't mind holding the balance owned on the land since Bill is paying good interest.

Bill discovers that he can't get a regular construction loan as he is accustomed. In large construction, you frequently have two lenders, the short-term lender who takes care of the construction loan and the long-term lender who takes care of paying off the construction loan and then makes the long-term payout available to the investor.

The lenders, however, seeing the smallness of the loan, are reluctant to get involved.

THE COMBINED LOAN

The majority of all construction loans are combined loans. The combination of a construction and a development loan is in reality a circumstance where the lender advances the funds for the construction. When the property has been completed, the loan automatically converts to a long-term loan. The ideal source for this kind of loan is the local savings and loan and other savings or thrift organizations, but as lending habits are quickly changing, these loans can be found from almost any lender.

The straight construction loan and the combined loan differ only in the effort it takes to nail them down. Combined loans are generally smaller than divided loans, where the construction loan is obtained from one source and the permanent loan is obtained from another source. For that reason, combined loans are often much easier to get than if you had to deal with double paperwork for the smaller amounts. Nonetheless, there are lenders for both, and often the same foundation source of money will fund both. For example, many insurance companies buy commerical paper from banks that support construction loans and at the same time buy long-term paper from savings and loan associations.

In this chapter, you will want to keep these factors in mind as we look at the ways in which you will deal with lenders to maximize your loan proceeds while minimizing your costs and interest.

WHY DEVELOPMENT AND CONSTRUCTION LOANS ARE IMPORTANT

These forms of financing are important because they form the basis for all new development. Very few projects will get off the ground unless the cost of development can be financed. It is necessary, therefore, for you to understand the workings of these types of financing and how to find lenders willing to look at your presentation.

The ability to provide for development loans is also important. Many brokers are able to sell properties solely because they know what funds are available for specific projects. If you know in advance of the general market what can be financed, you will have a jump that may be sufficient to put you ahead of your competition. Naturally, this advantage will come as good news to your clients—both buyers and sellers.

Before we get to the fine points for developing this advance knowledge, let's examine these two forms of financing.

The Development or Construction Loan Usually Depends on the Permanent End Loan

The permanent end loan is the final mortgage that will be placed on the property. This loan may have a term of twenty years or as long as forty years on pay-back. These permanent loans are made by commercial banks, savings and loan associations, credit unions, insurance companies, REITS, pension funds, and other sources. These loans are the pay-off for the earlier development and construction loan.

The permanent loan is not placed on the property until construction is completed. Construction cannot start until the construction loan is made and advances issued. The construction loan cannot be made until the land is ready for building, which means the development loan began the sequence. It is very difficult, if not economically dangerous, to begin this sequence in the first place without having a commitment for the end, or permanent, financing.

Development and construction loans are predicated on the amount of the final permanent commitment. If you are going to build 100 apartment units and you obtain a commitment from one or more lenders to lend $1,500,000, provided the final product meets the specifications of your submission, you will find the maximum development or construction loan available will not exceed the $1,500,000. In fact, it will generally be considerably below that amount, depending on the size of the project and cost overrun averages for the area.

Because the permanent financing has such a profound effect on the nature and amount of development and construction funding you may obtain, we will look at the proper way to examine new developments.

Nine Steps for Achieving Top Dollar in Development and Construction Funding

1. Feel out the market to see what the permanent lenders favor. Once some specifics are known in this area, the builder or developer can move to the other stages. For this example, assume the developer finds that the major permanent lenders are looking favorably at projects of single-family homes in the $40,000 range; shopping centers located in new growing suburban areas; and mobile home parks that have a density no greater than six sites per acre.

2. The smart developer will follow the money. In the above case it appears that the favorites are single-family projects, shopping centers, and

mobile home parks. There may be many other areas that will be open to funding, and it is natural for lenders to disagree on their favorite type of project. What is hot in one area of the country may be cool to cold in others. If the developer has the flexibility to move from one endeavor which is out of favor to another in vogue, he will do better in the long run than the builder who will only build warehouses—whether they can be financed or not. Our hypothetical builder has this flexibility, and wants to look at either mobile home parks or single family projects. This will offer him some choice as he looks for the site and in making the final project selection.

3. Armed with advance knowledge of the type of project, the builder now attempts to find sites that the lenders may prefer. Remember, the builder is still concerned with the permanent lender. He will either use a mortgage broker or his own contacts with the permanent lenders to find out whether they have any areas in the community which they prefer. You will be surprised to find that many lenders maintain comprehensive statistics on the growth of areas in which they invest their funds.

4. The builder may still not know which of the two types of projects he will consider, or he may have narrowed it down to single-family homes. If this were the situation, he would begin to price out the competition in the areas in which he is looking. Brokers and salesmen reading this chapter will hope that by now he has aligned himself with a broker to help him in the final selection. But the fact of the matter is that he may not have, and it is not uncommon for the developer to work with a mortgage broker at this stage of the game or to be on his own. Nevertheless, he is out looking for the right site.

5. A site is selected and negotiations begin. The developer may attempt to get an option on the raw land so he can take his package to some lenders to feel out the market for this site. The option may be for 90 to 180 days so he has time to obtain a response from the permanent lender. During the first week or so of the option, the builder, the mortgage broker, and usually a land planner or two enter the picture to lay out a master plan for the development. If the plan is to go from raw land to finished product, including homes, the option will be longer than 90 days. On the other hand, if the site is ready to go now, 90 days may be enough.

6. With a commitment in hand from the permanent lender, the builder is now ready to talk to a development or construction lender. At times, the permanent lender will also make the interim loans leading up to the permanent loan. In this case, a combined package of construction and permanent loan can be arranged. But more often than not, there will be two different lenders on the large projects. *Keep in mind, however, that on small projects requiring less than $1 million, the local savings and loan associations can compete favorably with other lenders by making a package development and permanent loan.*

7. In commercial projects such as strip stores, this stage would begin with negotiations on the terms of the construction loan. If the builder had

a commitment for an end loan of $2,000,000, he would take this commitment to several commercial banks in the area and shop for the best terms on the construction loan. Because the terms of the end loan may call for placement not earlier than 24 months from the present date to no later than 36 months, the builder will look to the longest take-out construction loan possible, or 36 months.

Many permanent end loans have a floor loan amount and a maximum amount. The spread between the two sums is generally based on the break-even rent roll as projected. The lender will calculate the projected break-even rent schedule, then deduct a percentage he feels is reasonable for the market conditions. Based on the resulting net operating income, he will establish a floor or lowest amount which will be extended on the end loan. The maximum amount of the loan will be paid if a percentage of net operating income, as determined by the lender and agreed to by the builder in advance, is met. There is generally a time period in which the builder has to meet that rent roll, and if he fails to meet it he will never get a shot at the maximum loan again.

This spread in the two sums often leaves the builder short of loan funds to finish the job.

8. This is where "gap financing" comes in. This is another part of the development and construction loan process. The gap loan is a secondary form of financing that is used to literally fill the gap between the floor amount of the loan and the maximum, or the construction loan amount and the permanent loan. The source of these loans is often a mortgage banker or private party. At times commercial banks will take up the call here but these loans are often very expensive for builders and should be used only when absolutely necessary. The only redeeming factor on a gap loan is that it is usually for a short term. This means that even though the interest rate is high, it will not last for long.

9. With the end loan commitment obtained, the construction loan set, and the development loan tied down, the builder can now proceed with the expectation that he will not need any other financing. The project gets started, and as one loan is paid off by another, the progression of financing from development loan to end loan takes place.

There can be no denying the fact that the foregoing nine steps cover an ideal situation. All aspects of this development seemed to go smoothly. They often do, and when you are dealing with professional mortgage men all the way down the line you will usually have a smooth transition.

However, one clog in a long progression and a mess can occur. These clogs can appear with amazing speed and never seem to disappear. They take the form of title problems, legal hassles, attorney's errors, and nit-picking; fights over wording in legals, contracts, mortgage documents, or releases; delays caused by documents lost in the mail, pages missing from commitment letters, or documents not properly signed or witnessed. There is no doubt that if things don't go right, it can be a mess.

Of course, the fact that all goes smoothly at first doesn't mean it will stay that way from the day construction starts until the day the end loan is placed. In the first place, the terms of the commitment must be met. That means that the building to be constructed must be exactly as the plans and specifications indicated when the commitment was issued. Any changes must be approved by the lender. This is where many loans have gone astray. A lender who wants to withdraw from a loan he committed himself to two years earlier when interest rates were 2 points lower than the current rate, will look very hard to see if there is a way to get out of it.

The construction lender gets very anxious about this type of talk from permanent lenders. The construction lender is in the project for a short time, he hopes, and enjoys the high interest rate he gets on the construction loan. But he is not ready to take over a project that fails to close on the end loan. If the end loan does not close because you did something wrong, you will have made an enemy.

GETTING A DEVELOPMENT OR CONSTRUCTION LOAN WITHOUT AN END LOAN

This was very popular at one time, and as you might suspect, due to its dangers, has lost the favor it once had. This type of financing gained support when the permanent market all but dried up. Builders, sensing that the money market was very tight on a long-term loan but still relatively soft in the construction money market, went out on a limb and started projects without effective end loans.

Not many lenders would make development loans without the end loan commitment first. Then, some of the big builders persuaded their banks to go with them on the idea that by the time construction of a big project was finished one, two, or three years later, the permanent market would be back in the swing of things and that type of money would be available again.

Other builders took advantage of commitment letters from mortgage brokers, bankers, and other sources, who in effect sold these letters to the builders. In essence, the commitment letter would state that an end loan was available. This would satisfy the construction lender and the loan would be made. However, these commitment letters were for throwaway loans. The terms of the end loan under many of these letters were so onerous that to take the loan would have been a financial disaster.

The idea was this: Pay for the letter to satisfy the construction lender that an end loan was available, then wait for better years ahead in the long-term end loan market. As the best plans of mice and men don't always work out, the commitment letter format was not very effective. The permanent money market remained firm and the commitment letters were called to take out the construction loans. In some cases, the commitment letters were found to be worthless and projects got into trouble one after the other.

The lesson to be learned is simple and sweet. There are few reasons to obtain a construction loan without having an end loan. It is much better to have the end loan before you start.

WHY THE SIZE OF THE PROJECT DOESN'T MATTER

The size of the development or construction project is not the main criterion for understanding and using this form of financing. It is natural, of course, that in projects under $100,000 the local savings and loan association may compete favorably with a two-part loan—the construction loan that is replaced by the permanent loan. The combined package loan that most savings and loan associations and other lenders offer puts both aspects of the two separate loans into one document. Still, builders of single-family homes will operate with separate construction loans rather than have this combination package of end loan and construction loan as an automatic event.

USING THE DEVELOPMENT OR CONSTRUCTION LOAN TO MAKE MORE SALES

Putting the whole ball of wax together may be your role. If you are dealing in developable types of land, the redevelopment of urban areas, or in any type of real estate that calls for some form of development or construction, then you must have a working knowledge of this tool.

To be specific, the ability to package a deal will require a considerable amount of expertise in many areas. In some of these areas you need only have the sense to get someone else on your team. Planning and engineering, for example, will no doubt be beyond the scope of most salesmen. To be sure, moving from a listing to a sale can be an immense task for some salesmen on some properties.

How One Broker Made a $4 Million Deal

Jackson had just listed a very interesting property in Fort Lauderdale. The site was about 15 acres of prime, business-zoned land located on a major highway. Its uniqueness was that it was the largest vacant property in the city that had deep water access to the Atlantic Ocean. The site was located in a high-income area of town and adjoined a major shopping center.

The drawbacks in marketing the property were the general economy and the price. The economy was still struggling to make a comeback and the price quoted by the sellers was eight dollars per square foot. The price was not high when compared to other smaller sites in comparable locations. In fact, smaller lots similarly zoned had sold for over $15 per square foot. However, the size of this tract and the fact that it could not be subdivided made prospective buyers scarce.

It was clear to Jackson that what was needed to entice an investor was an economic use. A use that could not be financed was not going to be productive, so Jackson had to find a use that *could* be financed. Therefore, Jackson tried to determine all the possible uses the site could be put to. He and others made a list of all the possibilities no matter how silly they sounded at the time.

Armed with this list, Jackson approached several lenders and mortgage brokers that he had dealt with in the past and presented the problem to them. He was not asking for money, only assistance in solving a problem. What were the possible uses for the tract which could be financed? Several new possible uses were added to the list by the lenders.

Then Jackson put this question to each of them: "Of all the possible uses on this list, which is most financeable assuming that the economics work out?" Many of the suggested uses were eliminated. Some sound ideas were cast off as being overbuilt for the area or impractical for other reasons. The list was narrowed down to five possible uses that could be financed if the economics did work out.

Jackson knew that for the economics to work out, a conservative approach to development, income, and expenses would have to show the project to be profitable. Once he had some possible lendable projects, he went to work to see if the numbers would work.

One by one the projects failed to work out on paper. Then two concepts began to make economic sense. Jackson took his numbers to a mortgage broker. The mortgage broker went over the numbers and made some changes and suggestions, then sat back and agreed. It did look as though there were two types of projects that might work economically.

Jackson didn't stop there. He went to his builder and management friends and smoothed out the figures even further. With the refined projections, he returned to the mortgage brokers. Several brokers got excited about the two concepts. They could see the possibility of making a nice loan fee, so they in turn talked to several of their lenders. Before Jackson knew it lenders were hot to go. He knew that his job was now almost completed.

The result of Jackson's efforts was that the property was sold. He had developed two concepts that in turn attracted lenders and buyers' interest in the property. Interest that was prequalified, and able to recognize that the proposals were sound and feasible. What Jackson sold was not the land but the *concept*.

HOW TO INCREASE THE AMOUNT OF MONEY YOU CAN BORROW ON A DEVELOPMENT LOAN

It is possible to obtain 100 percent of the funds needed for the development and construction of many projects. In many cases, you can even include the land in this mortgage amount and enter into a development with little or no cash.

Your ability to do this will depend on several simple factors. Experience by the way, is not necessariuly one of these factors. The following list will outline the factors which must be developed in order to obtain the highest possible loan.

Eight Factors in Getting the Maximum Loan

1. *Seek the lender's favorite type of project.* Follow Jackson's example of finding out what the lenders like and then go for that type of loan.

2. *Don't jump in too soon in asking for the funds.* Plan out your project. Some lenders will ask for a feasibility study if you move too quickly. Wait until you have done your own study. If you have done it well enough you may not need a feasibility study.

3. *Have the right numbers.* Don't take one person's advice on what rent you should be able to collect on a proposed office building until you have checked out the actual market as it now stands.

4. *Have the property tied up.* If you don't own it already, be sure you have some tie on it. You have a lot of work ahead of you, and unless you can hold onto the land you may end up with a commitment and then be unable to buy the property or have to pay more than you expected.

5. *When ready, act forcibly.* Bravado is important in asking for money, so have plenty of it (bravado is a nice word for guts). Don't, however, try to cover up lack of knowledge with smugness. Point out good features instead.

6. *Leave inexperience at home—yours or your client's as the case may be.* What is important is the project, the numbers, and ability. Note the word *ability* and not *experience*. The fact that it may be your first shopping center or strip store, or ten times larger than anything you have ever built is not important.

7. *Negotiate for more.* Your lender will usually offer less than you ask for. Hold firm if you can try to get what you feel you need. Remember, if you say you must have $500,000 you may then have to explain why you are willing to take $425,000.

8. *Offer incentives to the lender.* When the need for venture capital is overwhelming, you may have to resort to tradeouts with the lender. In order to increase the loan amount closer to 100 percent, you may often have to give the lender a percentage of the action. This can

occur in many ways, which will be covered later in this chapter. Be careful, however, since the lender knows all the tricks and controls the purse strings.

HOW TO PUT TOGETHER A PRESENTATION
FOR A DEVELOPMENT LOAN

In Chapter 4, the basic loan presentation was outlined. This format should be used in all loan presentations that cover existing properties. Its adaptation so it can also be used for presentations on proposed projects will be covered in this chapter. In essence, greater detail must be included to cover the potential of the project. You cannot rely on past performance, which in the case of a new development does not exist.

The presentation itself will take on the aspects of a feasibility study. It is often thought that all feasibility studies ascertain the best use of a given site. However, this is only one type of feasibility study. More commonly, a lender may request that a study be made to indicate the potential for success a given project may have. The lender's reason for requesting this study is to use the data obtained to help the money managers come to a decision as to whether or not the money requested should be lent.

Unfortunately, the whole system of feasibility studies has gone somewhat astray. There is the classic story of a major lender from the northeast. This lender was presented with a well-planned hotel project that looked fantastic on paper. The developers were experienced, the designers were well qualified, and all the right things had seemingly been done. But the lender needed a third-party reference, so the loan was not going to be granted unless a feasibility study was made. At considerable cost, therefore, such a study was hastily ordered and sent to the lender as soon as it came off the press.

The loan was made. But after several years of development, and one failure after another, the project developers went into bankruptcy. The lender had to take the project into his portfolio and finish the construction. Some time later, a bright young lawyer in the lender's office read the feasibility study. The study had predicted that the project had merit and, based on the then present statistics of competition, would be successful. However, the study continued, there were over forty-seven similar ventures currently on the drawing boards, which would no doubt enter competition around the time of the proposed hotel development. The study went on to disclose the statistics, the number of projects and their locations.

The mistake in this situation is obvious. The venture under consideration was a hotel, and the existing hotels in the area would not be able to handle the demand for rooms that the future Disney World complex would provide. So, what else but a hotel would be a good idea? Unfortunately, what's good for the goose is not always good for the geese.

The lender was anxious to make the loan, and once the study came in it was most likely glanced over and then filed. In reality, he had paid for a study that recommended that the project not be started in the first place.

HOW TO APPROACH A FEASIBILITY STUDY

In many respects, the feasibility study is similar to the loan request shown in Chapter 4. However, the differences are sufficient for you to follow a new outline. In Figure 8–1, I have provided an outline for you to use when compiling feasibility studies.

OUTLINE FOR A FEASIBILITY STUDY

I. THE PROJECT
  A. General Description
  B. Site Plan
    (1) Breakdown of project to square footage of improvements
    (2) Use of project
    (3) Stages to be built or developed
  C. Economics of Project
    (1) Cost estimates
      a. builders' bid on other supporting data
    (2) Operating expenses
      a. during development
      b. marketing expenses
      c. preleased agreements (if applicable)
    (3) Cash flow—expense vs. income chart
  D. Feasibility of Project
    (1) Economy of area
      a. aerial photo showing location of similar projects in competing area
      b. description of competing projects
      c. economics of competing projects
      d. future growth proposed and documented
      e. future demand on type of project (including supporting documents)
      f. summary of economics of competing projects
    (2) Opinion of use based on area economics
  E. Value of Completed Project
    (1) Estimated potential cash flow on finished project (if income

property shows Operational statement, 12 month estimate after project completed)

   (2) Market value based on cash flow (capitalized at current investor demand rate)

   (3) Value of existing projects of similar nature (refer to same projects covered in earlier description of competing projects)

II. THE PROPERTY
- A. General Description
- B. Legal Description
- C. Locations
- D. Location Sketch
- E. Aerial Photo
- F. Location Benefits
- G. Location Drawbacks
- H. General Statistics
  - (1) Demographics
  - (2) Average rent
  - (3) Traffic count
- I. General Site Data
  - (1) Legal
  - (2) Size and square feet of land and site coverage
  - (3) Use of site
  - (4) Zoning
  - (5) Utilities
  - (6) Access
  - (7) Sketch of lots sharing building location
  - (8) Survey
- J. Land Value
  - (1) Estimated value of site
  - (2) Comparable land sales and values

III. THE DEVELOPER
- A. Name
- B. Address
- C. Occupation
- D. General Data
- E. Net Worth
- F. Supporting Documents (not included, but will be on forms institution supplies)
  - (1) Net worth statement
  - (2) Schedule of assets
  - (3) Schedule of liabilities
  - (4) References
  - (5) Position of employment
  - (6) Verification of salary

(7) Estimated annual earnings
(8) Credit report if applicable
(9) Other forms supplied for application

IV. THE LOAN REQUEST (for End Loans)
   A. Recap Value of Finished Product
   B. Recap Development Cost
   C. Add Land Cost to Development Cost
   D. Show Relation to Total Estimated Value and Total Cost to Develop
   E. Amount of Loan Requested
   F. Terms and Conditions Requested (for Construction or Development Loan)
   A. Recap Value of Finished Product
   B. Recap Development Cost
   C. Add Land Cost to Development Cost
   D. Show Relation to Total Estimated Value and Total Cost to Develop
   E. Copy of End Loan Commitment
   F. Amount of Construction or Development Loan Requested
   G. Terms and Conditions Requested

V. SUPPORTING DOCUMENTS
   A. Full Set of Working Plans (if available)
   B. Topography (if needed)
   C. Preleased Documents (if applicable)

WHERE TO GO TO OBTAIN A DEVELOPMENT OR CONSTRUCTION LOAN

Many lenders will provide such funds, and for the most part all normal institutional leaders have involved themselves from time to time in this type of financing. However, some sources are better than others, depending on the size of the loan and the nature of the project.

I have provided a chart that illustrates the best lenders for the various situations which may appear. Keep in mind that much of this will have to do with the lending experiences of the lender. If the commercial bank has been burned with construction loans, they may not be ready to jump back into that market. Nonetheless, commercial banks tend to be the better source for short-term construction funds.

Never forget the private money sources. These funds can be available when all other sources dry up. In essence, they are costly monies to borrow, but can compete favorably in a very tight money market. When you have to borrow, the cost may be immaterial.

Examine the chart and use it only as a reference as to where to start first. The fact that savings and loans are not generally in the construction loan market will not mean that you should not ask them if all other avenues fail.

Seven Points to Remember in Negotiations
with the Lender or the Lender's Agent

1. Distance Requires More Support.   The farther you get from the lender in the chain of command, the more the decision to lend is based on the opinions of other people. This is human nature. The loan officer at a local savings and loan will act without having to check with as many people as the mortgage representative at a major insurance company a thousand miles away. Because of this, try to obtain as many outside opinions yourself. Then document them in your presentation. These outside statements of market conditions, rental *pro formas*, expenses, and operating costs can be found without much effort. Fellow brokers, banks, property managers, owners of similar properties, and so on will often be glad to help. When you do get information from them, don't just refer to the facts—put a copy of the memo they sent you or the letter from the property manager in your report. This padding will become third-party support material that people who make the final decision can hang their hats on.

2. You Can't Really Lose.   Do as much of the initial work as you can yourself. The first time you make one of these studies you will be amazed at how little you knew about the area, the project, and your perseverance. By the time you have finished the study, you will know more than much of your competition about this type of property and development. That is not a bad side-benefit, no matter what happens to the development. After you have gone through several such studies you will have the formula down pat.

3. Continue to Expand Your Abilities.   At first, there will be some aspects that you may need assistance with. If you are dealing with a mortgage broker, he can usually provide help. Brokers are often able to go over the numbers with you, and once they see a feasible project they will get excited as hell. If they can make the loan, then everyone will benefit.

4. Be Ready to Negotiate for the Money.   When money is tight, lenders will take advantage of the scarcity of funds to make as favorable a deal as they can. This may mean they will demand a percentage of the action, which can take many forms. The most usual are shown here:

a. *An override*—This form of percentage-of-the-operation is based on the lender receiving a preset percentage of all income that exceeds certain amounts. For example: A $10,000 loan on a shopping center has a provision that the lender will receive 10 percent of gross income in excess of $2,000,000. Once the loan is satisfied, this provision does not continue.

LOAN SOURCES

Lender	Land development loan	Construction loan	Package: Development and construction	Package: Development, construction, and permanent
Commercial Banks	Bank policy varies as to local situation. Development loans must generally be backed by high credit or take out from end loan. Rare to find loans which exceed one million dollars except from majors.	The ideal place to look when an end loan is already committed. Loan will be set at a rate depending on the project. Often very competitive.	Are available from some commercial banks. The end loan commitment will be a major factor here.	Long-term lending will vary from bank to bank. Rates and years to pay back may not be as good as other lenders.
Savings and Loans			Some possibility here. Depends on bank policy, situation, and type of project—but very rare.	Ideal for single family or condo-type development. S&Ls may bring in other S&Ls to combine funds to make big deals.

Insurance Companies	Some companies have been very active in this area in the past, primarily when the project is land sales rather than continued development. Good source. Funds are not limited, but prefer over $500,000.	Rare, but some companies have made such loans in the past. Better to look elsewhere.	Rare	For big projects this may be a good source. The lender often gets a piece of the action on this type of loan. Rates and closing costs may be lowest from this source.
REITS	When REITS have money they will look at almost anything. Some look only to the short-term loan (the development or construction loan). Others like the long-term loan. As of this writing, however, REITS have lost the potency they had in the early 1970s. But that is likely to change and they should make a comeback. Make friends now as they may well become the best source again—for all forms. They prefer the larger loan, and have made some of the biggest.			
Pension Funds	Don't like high-risk deals, so won't be in this field except for closely connected loans.	Same as Development Loan	Same as Development Loan	Are becoming effective lenders in this area. Try them for deals over $500,000. Like proven track record.

153

LOAN SOURCES (CONT.)

Lender	Land development loan	Construction loan	Package: Development and construction	Package: Development, construction, and permanent
Mortgage Bankers	Yes. Depending on the banker, funds are often available for good, sound developments that have end loan take out already committed.	Same as Development Loan	Same as Development Loan	Can fund many moderate size deals. Beyond that they will seek coventure funds. Can be expensive money, but often available when others are dry.
Credit Unions	Credit unions, like the REITS, vary greatly. They have growing masses of funds like the pension funds, but like to lend first within their own circle. Yet, their managers will often allocate percentages to long- and short-term lending. They can be good for developments within their own area: teachers credit unions lending to a textbook publisher and the like.			

b. *Land ownership*—The lender takes title to the land and leases it to the developer. The lease may be reasonable, and in essence the lender becomes a partner in the venture. The loan covers the development of the land. Once the loan is paid off, the land lease still goes on. This way the lender continues to benefit even though the loan has been satisfied.

c. *Coventure*—This can take many forms. The percentage of coventure will depend on the lender and the deal. It is not uncommon that a lender will put up all the money and then take 50 percent of the venture. Usually, only builders of outstanding reputation can get these deals. However, when money is flowing, these builders can make deals without having to give up an percentage to a lender, or at most very little.

5. Don't Take "No" for an Answer.　For the most part, you are dealing with very conservative people. They take lending the money of their employers very seriously. Therefore, you may get a "no," especially if you approach the lender prematurely. So, if you think you have a hot item, hang it on the possibility of getting the money. However, do not be overly pushy.

6. Bounce Right Back from a Defeat.　Nothing should keep a good guy down for long. When you have made your most fantastic presentation for the greatest project you have ever thought of and on the hottest site in town, and can't get a lender to sound interested, try to find out why. One mortgage broker I have dealt with in the past may smile if he is very excited. The rest of the time he speaks of doom as though it came two hours ago. He tells me this is his way of maintaining his sanity in the business he is in. From your point of view, his negativism can sound like lack of interest. If one mortgage broker or lender gets to you in this way, go on to another. Always be ready to accept the fact that your idea is not sound—and if it's not, find one that is.

7. Watch Out for Too Much Praise.　This is the one thing that concerns me. If all I hear is good news about a project I am working on, I start to worry. (I call my mortgage broker friend from item 6 and know he will have something bad to say.) You need to find someone you can count on to cut the project you are working on to ribbons. You won't get ahead riding the crest of disinterested praise.

FINE-TUNE YOUR FINESSE IN THE USE OF CONSTRUCTION AND DEVELOPMENT LOANS

There are many techniques that you can apply to development and construction loans to make them easier to obtain and to keep down their overall costs. The goal of most of these techniques is: Buy the property right. Thus far in this book, I have emphasized the need for proper attention to your own goals and abilities. When you are able to approach the "buying" moment with the end result in mind, you will be far more successful at attaining your desired goal.

However, from a practical viewpoint, things don't always work out that way. Keep your long-range goal in sight, of course, but if you are watching your comfort zone correctly, you will find it too difficult to pass up "bargain" property—even though you may see no benefit from the property that would blend with your goals.

Later, as you are proven right about the "bargain," you may want to develop the property. At this time, the need for development of construction money may arise. If you try to take this potential need into account, no matter how remote it maybe, you can be successful at obtaining your needed financing without excess cost.

You need to look at many factors in any transaction where there will be a future need for development or construction loans. Begin with the following eleven factors.

ELEVEN KEY FACTORS TO WATCH FOR IN EXISTING FINANCING

Make a chart of all of the existing financing on the property and make sure you have all the answers to these questions.

1. *What is the term of the loan?*

This is important simply because it is the most basic of all elements of the mortgage. Some mortgages seem to have a term of one set of years due to a statement in the mortgage document that looks like this: "And the mortgage will be paid out over a 25-year amortization schedule." At this point, you might think you have a 25-year term . . . but three pages later there is a paragraph that has this phrase or something like it imbedded in the fine print: " . . .and at the call of the lender, to be given at any time at the option of the lender following the seventh year with a ninety-day notice, the loan is to be due and payable in full." This loan could be good for only seven years.

2. *What is the exact date of the last scheduled payment?*

This can be a minor issue. However, sometimes mortgages are so devised that this date is never specifically shown. When a property is closed, the people taking care of these details often don't have the necessary equipment on hand (a math table and calculator) to show the amortization properly. Therefore, there can be a difference between a stated amount that should retire a loan within the desired and thought-to-be term between the parties at hand. When a third party enters the picture, there is a sudden rememberance of the incorrect math that set up a mortgage that will take another five years to pay out. This can be absolute death to any refinancing ideas since the amount to pay off the mortgage at any given moment will also be incorrect.

3. *Is there a balloon anywhere in the payment, and how much it is?*

Much the same is true with balloon payments as with other terms in the mortgage. The words used might not be the words you are accustomed to. For example, "ending the 50th quarter of the formation of the lien, its full and complete satisfaction to the mortgagee is herein demanded." Interpretation: A balloon payment is due at the end of 150 months. This might make what would look like a subordinate mortgage useless.

4. *What is the interest charged?*

There are many ways to increase interest without the mortgagee realizing what is happening. Penalties, increases due to "adjustments to the All Items Index as published by the United States Government," would be just one way. If any such provisions exist, make sure you know what they are and how they can affect you.

5. *Does the interest change at any time? If so how and when?*

Most modern mortgages have provisions that will limit the long-term obligation of the lender if you sell to someone else. In the mid-1970s and early 1980s, lenders began to enforce provisions that gave the lender the right to change the interest rate charged when a property was sold or leased on a long-term lease. Many property owners tried to get around these provisions, but most failed in the attempt.

6. *Can you prepay principal without penalty? If not, what is the penalty?*

This single element has ruined many potential new loans, which can of course include construction and development loans. One very good rule to follow is: Don't accept a loan that has a penalty for any prepayment, and if you are buying a property that has a mortgage with that kind of provision either get it removed (you don't care if the seller has to "pay" to have it removed) or build the penalty into your offer.

7. *Is there any subordination available in any of the financing? If so, what, where, when, how much, for what?*

Subordination is that event where the mortgagee has agreed to a provision that would permit some lien not yet in existence to be place above the position of the mortgage—or, if there were existing liens that were behind the rank of the mortgage, to move ahead. This increases the risk in all loans, and while warranted some of the time and essential for many investors, the provision itself may not provide what you think. When buying a property with the idea of future development and the seller is holding paper, try to get the seller to agree to allow new financing above that mortgage. For example, you could state that new financing and the remaining balance owed to the seller would not exceed a specific percent of loan to appraised value of the property.

8. *Will the mortgage permit the security to be changed?*

This is a sliding mortgage technique that would allow you to move the security for the note to another property. In Oscar's sale to Bill, had Bill made this kind of provision with Oscar he would have been able to shift the mortgage to another property. The advantage to this is it will "free and clear" the specific property on which you plan to place a construction or development loan. This makes the task of getting good terms that much easier.

9. *Can you sell or replace any of the assets of the property freely?*

Sometimes an existing loan will have a chattel as additional security. This has the effect of locking in different assets such as furniture, fixtures, equipment, and so on. Sometimes the chattel is so poorly drafted that it will not allow for replacement of the item. This requires careful attention if you plan to remodel a property completely and throw out all the old equipment and furniture.

10. *Is there a release of property from the mortgage? If so, what, how, what pattern, what conditions, what payment?*

In the development of a property or construction on part of a property you have just bought or currently own, you must have the right to separate that property from any other mortgage prior to placing a new first mortgage on the property. If the underlying mortgage does not have provisions that allow releases, you must attempt to have the mortgage modified. Otherwise, you will be faced with having to pay off a mortgage at the very moment you might need available every penny from the construction loan—or worse, because of the added economic drain you may not be able to get the financing at all.

11. *Is the lender local, a person, or an institution?*

Where the lender is based has become critical. The more remote the home office is from the branch office, the more difficult it will be to get facts straight. It is unfortunate that in an age of computer data it has become impossible to communicate from Florida to California to get the current pay off or terms to a specific mortgage and feel you have the right data. When it comes time to ask for any modification of any mortgage, you will find that the private party will be the best to deal with. He may extract some penalty or ask for some benefit given in exchange for what you ask, but that is far better than going to Federated Federal Savings and Loan only to find out that they have sold your mortgage along with several thousand others to an insurance company located in Mexico City.

Buying any real estate that you plan to develop or on which you are going to build requires your attention to these eleven factors whenever there is existing financing or the seller will be holding the financing. Remember the following phrase: "Assume that your future goals are unknown—plan for everything." By this, I mean that you should anticipate the need for as much flexibility as possible. It will not do you any good later on if you have overlooked one of these eleven factors.

Another element to the development and/or construction loan is your *credit*. This is something about which you can plan and improve. All lenders want you to have good credit and to provide them with good business references. The lender must be able to "check" on your credit and your references and credit checks cannot be performed unless you leave some history of credit. And the idea is to leave *good history*. References should be cultivated, and they should know that they are your references. To build good credit and excellent references, follow these steps:

TEN STEPS TO IMPROVED CREDIT AND EXCELLENT CREDIT REFERENCES

1. *Obtain several credit cards and use them.* Credit cards are not as difficult to obtain as some people think. Start with local shops, oil companies, bank cards, and so on. Work up to one or two cards that you use most of the time, taking advantage of the "credit payment plan" offered for a month or two. Then pay off the balance. Once you have done that with your bank card (or American Express or another similar card), write and ask for an increased line of credit. Find out the maximum credit offered and work up to that. Always pay early, since you want to build a history of responsibility.

2. *Meet your commercial bank president.* Make sure that he or she knows you. Keep in touch with this person and inquire about what loans are available. Start with a small loan, *even if you don't need the money.* You can pay it back early, and the small cost will be worth the effort since it will build more good history into your credit check.

3. *Do business with people on a regular basis, and make sure you know the owner or manager of the business and that he or she knows you are a regular client.* If the business has "charge accounts," get one, ask for the maximum line of credit, and always charge—then pay early.

4. *Tell everyone you deal with from item 3 above that you are going to be taking out a loan soon and that you would like to use them as a credit reference.* Ask them to respond to any inquiry as promptly as possible since it may mean the difference between your getting the loan and not getting it.

5. *Write a short personal reference letter.* It should touch on those aspects that are critical to the potential loan, as well as give your personal background: where you live, who your wife and kids are, what school you went to, and so on. Everything in this personal reference letter should be positive.

6. Give this letter to those people who may be called on to be your credit references. This letter will also improve your relationship with these people as they will find out things about you they didn't know.

7. *Build a list of credit references.* This list should include all your

business contacts indicated in item 3 above as well as your CPA, banker president friends, professional associates, and so on. It should not be a Christmas card list, but a solid and impressive list of known business people in your community. If you do not know any such people, go to the library and get a copy of the local social register book. Make a list of people you recognize, and make a point of meeting them. References must be cultivated, for if you neglect them, they will be worthless.

8. Add the list of credit references to your reference letter, updating each from time to time. Each new person sees that he or she is in good company on your list.

9. *Get a letter of recommendation.*

This is a letter from your selected reference that tells whom it may concern that you are a highly trustworthy and honest person who is respected in your community. Get this letter by sending your "public relations package" to this person and asking for a letter of introduction or recommendation because of an upcoming business deal with important people out of town (the big lender in far-off lands). Your P.R. package is made up of your personal reference letter, your list of references, and a sample letter of introduction. In your letter, mention that you know their time is valuable, so you have enclosed a short sample letter indicating what you need. It is important here that each sample letter you send is different and as personally oriented as possible. The sample letter should give the impression that it has been written specifically by that person. For example. "As State Representative from Florida, I can introduce and recommend Mr. Cummings with the clear conviction that he is one of the leaders of the South Florida community. Having served with him on a number of local committees . . ." It is important to be specific and that each letter be different because it is likely that the letter will be returned to you exactly as you wrote it.

10. Get a new letter from the same person every couple of years. If there has been a change in your biography or reference list, send it along, and attach to your new sample letter a copy of the last letter. Make the new letter a little more favorable than the last.

Obtaining the maximum loan at the most favorable terms is now a matter of good planning and sound business practice. If you are to succeed at both, you should start to fill in any of the missing blanks in your plan. Learn the things you don't know, improve on those you do. And remember, when it comes to loans, a full, complete package wins out in the long run.

Chapter 9

BLANKET MORTGAGES AID IN FINANCING

The blanket mortgage often is mistaken or confused with the wraparound mortgage. Blanket mortgages are mortgages that cover more than one parcel of property. Wraparound mortgages are mortgages that encompass other mortgages. The purpose of this chapter is to take a hard look at the blanket mortgage and see how it can be used to assist in other forms of financing. Later on in this book, the wraparound mortgage will be discussed in detail.

Any basic form of mortgage, including a wraparound, can be used to encompass more than one property. The moment more than one property is security for the mortgage, you have a blanket mortgage. For example, an investor I knew owned three duplexes that were side by side. He wanted to refinance the mortgages on two of them, but found it was to his advantage to refinance all three under one mortgage. The resulting mortgage was a blanket mortgage.

As you read through this chapter, you will see the many advantages of the blanket mortgage. There are drawbacks as well, and these will also be examined.

WHO CAN UTILIZE THE BLANKET MORTGAGE?

The criterion for using a blanket mortgage is easy enough. You must have at least two parcels of property. It helps if they are adjoining, but this is not necessary. It is not unusual to have a blanket mortgage on two or more properties that are neither adjoining nor in the same area. A home and a lot, an apartment building and a warehouse, or vacant land and a duplex are some of the many combinations of dissimilar properties which can be combined in a blanket mortgage. Some mortgages of a blanket nature can include dozens of properties.

Most investors seeking to obtain maximum leverage will find the blanket mortgage helpful in obtaining the highest yield on their invested capital. Since maximum financing is one of the benefits that is attained from its use, let's look at this as well as the other benefits that can be derived from the blanket mortgage.

WHAT CAN BLANKET MORTGAGES DO?

1. *Provide maximum financing.* Generally, if you can include more than one property as security for a loan, it is possible to borrow in excess of the value of a part of the total security. With this in mind, blanket mortgages can provide 100 percent financing for new ventures and throw off cash to boot. In the refinancing of several properties, the combined effect of the security can make the package presented to the lender more secure and thereby increase the amount to be lent.

2. *Allow the mortgagor to obtain better terms and conditions on the loan.* It follows that if the loan is more secure, then you have room to bargain for better terms. Of the terms to be considered, the interest rate and annual payment will be most important. If you can decrease the percentage of loan to value ratio, thereby decreasing the lender's risk, you will find the terms should ease considerably. For example, Simon, a local investor, wanted to purchase a ten-unit apartment house fairly priced at $145,000. The property had a low first mortgage of $30,000. The seller indicated he would hold up to $20,000 in a second mortgage, and wanted cash above that. Simon discovered that within the new money market, the best he could come up with, after mortgage cost, was $102,000. This left him short the difference needed to buy the property, even if the seller held the $20,000 paper. The best terms available from a local savings and loan association were 24 years at 9¾ percent with 4 points closing.

However, he did own a small lot that was across the street from the apartment house. It was free and clear and he hoped to build on it one day. Its value was $35,000.

He went to the bank again and offered to put the lot up as additional security on the loan. The lot was appraised at the $35,000 value, thus a total value of $180,000 was created. The bank was told a 72 percent loan to value ratio, or a $129,600 mortgage, was all that was needed. This ratio was lower than that which the bank was willing to lend, so they gave in on the terms. A 27-year mortgage at 9½ percent was obtained. Points came to only 3 percent instead of 4 percent. Simon was able to have provisions put into the mortgage that would enable him to release the lot once the principal was reduced by $26,000. This would enable him to build at a future date without having to pay off the entire amount of the first loan.

Simon ended up with the ten units with no cash down, since the seller held the balance of the paper against the property.

3. *Consolidate properties for refinancing.* Some investors have put together a considerable array of properties over the years. Mortgages have different payment schedules and termination dates. Sometimes it is feasible to add several properties to a refinancing package of another property to provide a larger base and reduce the overall loan-to-value ratio. In this type of blanket mortgage, the properties should be similar types of realty when dealing with institutional lenders. However, private lenders may not care.

Another local investor, Aston, had nearly a dozen small warehouses across town. Each of them was fully rented and none had a mortgage greater than 50 percent of its value. Two of the larger warehouses had mortgages that were at very high interest rates as compared to the present market. Aston decided to refinance them all under one blanket mortgage. He obtained an excellent commitment from one of the local savings and loan associations in the area, and another almost equally good from a local commercial bank.

I had the opportunity to see Aston just before he made his deal with the savings and loan. In looking over the package, I discovered he had two warehouses that had 5½ percent loans. While these loans were low in ratio of loan-to-value, their term was still 14 years to go. (They must have been FHA or VA in origin.) I suggested he keep these loans and let the lender hold second position on those two warehouses. This would lower the overall payment and probably not affect the amount of money lent.

The savings and loan did not go along with that idea, but the commercial bank did. The total loan was far in excess of the pay-off of the existing financing, and Aston withdrew from the property nearly $175,000—which was not taxable.* His annual payment increased only $5,000 over his previous debt service on the earlier financing.

4. *Lock in the property.* This can be an advantage as well as a disadvantage. If you were Aston and had ideas of selling some of the warehouses in a few years, you would have to have release provisions as a part of the mortgage terms. Some lenders will go along with this, but others won't. However, if you are selling property, the features of the

---

*Funds obtained in a mortgage loan that do not exceed the basis (book value) of the property are not considered to be income therefore are not taxable as such.

blanket mortgage can be made to work for you if you are asked to hold paper. You can have the buyer include other properties which will become security to the transaction. This becomes both a buyer and a seller provision, depending on the circumstances and point of view.

5. *Lock in other assets.* There is no reason why the blanket mortgage should be limited to real estate. As in the above situation, the buyer or seller can offer or require other assets to be pledged as security. A liquor license, for example, may be tied to a bar in this way. Stocks or other collateral can be given as additional security via the blanket aspects of the mortgage.

In both of these examples, the assets can be pledged by the mortgagor or a cosigner. For example: Walters wanted to buy a home that had existing financing of $50,000 and $40,000 in equity. He had no cash to put down, but did have a father-in-law anxious to see his daughter move out of the guest house and into her own home. The father-in-law offered a second mortgage on his own home as additional security to the seller. In the end, the seller took a blanket second on the home being sold, with a second position on the father-in-law's home. The total equity was more than enough and this saved the deal.

WHERE TO GET BLANKET MORTGAGES

Not all lenders will consider a situation that calls for a blanket provision in the mortgage. However, the big lenders, such as insurance companies and REITS, have made such loans. Also, many of the more local lenders, such as commercial banks and mortgage bankers, will frequently lend with blanket provisions. The whole idea of blanket provisions is to make the loan more secure, and virtually all lenders will make blanket loans given the right circumstances.

The best place to look for money when you are willing to offer additional property as supplemental security is to the seller. The increased equity gained by virtue of this form of financing often can sway the seller into holding large amounts of paper. Other private sources, such as investors, private lenders, and mortgage brokers, also like the blanket mortgage and should not be overlooked.

WHEN TO USE A BLANKET MORTGAGE

When you are considering the use of a blanket mortgage, reexamine the 5 things it can do:

1. Provide maximum financing

2. Provide a stronger position for negotiating the terms and conditions of the loan

3. Consolidate properties for refinancing

4. Lock in the property

5. Lock in other assets

Situations that call for blanket financing require the satisfaction of one or more of the above five items. Since items (1) and (2) are rather general, it is important to remember that there are many different forms of financing that can accomplish these two desired goals. But when the best form for the borrower is unacceptable to the lender, then a blanket mortgage may be the answer.

Providing maximum financing may not be worth the cost or the disadvantages that result from both excessive leverage and overextension. Because of this, the use of blanket mortgages must be compared to the other alternatives. Once you have a basis for determining which form is the most advantageous to you, then you can proceed to see if you can work out the transaction on those more favorable terms.

HOW TO DETERMINE THE ACCEPTABILITY
OF A BLANKET MORTGAGE

The acceptability of a blanket mortgage can be seen from both sides of the transaction. As in all forms of mortgages the effect may differ from transaction to transaction and from buyer to seller. Unless you can pinpoint what makes the blanket mortgage acceptable, you may not know when to use it.

Blanket Mortgages as Seen from the Buyer's Point of View

The buyer must understand that in order to use this form of financing, it is necessary to encumber more than one piece of property. If the transaction itself contains these separate properties, there may be no reason to hesitate—providing the buyer can obtain releases that may be necessary (such as purchasing four lots from one seller). It is not unusual for the buyer to add security to the blanket mortgage from property already owned.

The majority of blanket mortgages do occur with this extra outside security as a part of the transaction. The buyer uses equity in other property to assist in new financing. To some degree it is seen in pyramiding and other forms of high leverage and extension buying. Nonetheless, the buyer must understand the disadvantages, as well as the advantages, of this format, and must weigh these in determining whether it is wise to use a blanket mortgage.

Disadvantages of blanket mortgages for buyers

1. They place a burden on other properties. Whenever a second property is pledged as additional security on a blanket mortgage, that property is in jeopardy if the mortgage falters.
2. They can make a separation difficult or impossible. Of course, this will depend on the terms of the blanket mortgage. But to some degree, the mortgagor is hampered in his ability to sell the other properties. A buyer can, however, buy subject to the blanket mortgage, and if the principal of the mortgage is less than the amount of financing held there is no disadvantage.
3. Assets can be locked in. This works as both an advantage and a disadvantage. In this instance, the combined effect of tying two or more assets together can cause unforeseen hardships in the future if the mortgagor needs to separate those assets.

You can see that the main disadvantage is the combining of other properties with the inability to separate them when or if the need arises. With this in mind, you can then look to the blanket mortgage as a useful tool when the criteria which follow can be met.

Buyers' criteria for blanket mortgages

1. Other conventional forms of financing do not generate the viable financing required to meet the cash requirements of the buyer.
2. Other properties exist which have sufficient equity that will be accepted by the seller or mortgagee as additional security to arrange the financing required.
3. Total income generated from all properties covered with the blanket mortgage is sufficient to meet the pay-out requirements of the debt service to be created. A reasonable leeway should provide for a drop of income before the break-even is reached. This will depend on the situation of course. Some transactions may be approached with a deficit—the mortgagor coming out-of-pocket for a time until new income from the property can be generated (as in the case of a new development, construction, or other income increasing methods).
4. The mortgagor can project that he will not need to separate the properties from the mortgage in the relatively near future. Even if he has release provisions, they will no doubt be costly, so it may be dangerous to enter into a blanket mortgage if he anticipates that early separation will be necessary. This will not be the case if the mortgagor is anticipating a complete refinancing and has confidence he can recast the mortgage and obtain separation in that way. Nonetheless, the risk remains that it may be costly to obtain separation.

In summarizing the blanket mortgage from the buyer's point of view, if the buyer can meet the four criteria and he understands the disadvantages of this form, he can use the mortgage.

Blanket Mortgages as Seen from the Seller's Point of View

Like the buyer, the seller and other mortgagees should know all the ins and outs of the blanket mortgage. Yet, because this format is designed to increase the security, the advantages are more often weighted in the seller's and the mortgagee's favor. However, disadvantages do exist.

Disadvantages of blanket mortgages for sellers and other mortgagees

1. The blanket mortgage may cause overextension of the property. This in turn could lead to the mortgagor failing to make his payments. The seller can always look to the properties held as security, but to move into a foreclosure can be most unpleasant, costly, and to no one's ultimate benefit—if there is a choice. The mortgagee can take all precautions to see that this does not occur, but when the buyer is into the property with no cash, or at best very little, then the security may be dependent on what occurs with the other property.

   For example: Curtis bought a 15-unit apartment house that had a fair market value of $200,000 and a good first mortgage of $140,000. He gave the seller a blanket second in the amount of $60,000 on the 15-units that also covered (by first mortgage) a lot he owned across town. The value of the lot was estimated to be $30,000. The seller felt secure that he had $90,000 of equity covering his $60,000 second mortgage.

   As it turned out, the lot was worth only about $10,000. Curtis milked the apartments for a few years, got behind on his mortgage payments, and then walked away from a foreclosure. The seller had to step in and rescue the 15 units from the first mortgage, and spend several thousand dollars as well to repair them.

2. Blanket mortgages generally reduce the cash at closing. This happens because the blanket aspect is used to supply additional security to a mortgage greater than the seller is willing to hold otherwise. The effect is to reduce the amount of cash he will receive. All things being equal, this in itself is not a disadvantage, but merely a characteristic of this form of financing. However, all things are rarely equal, and equity rarely equals cash.

   The other advantages in blanket mortgages are of a more technical nature, and have to do with the possible legal terminology used in the document itself. I have found that most lawyers are able to draft a blanket mortgage which will adequately protect their clients.

I suggest, however, that you never have the lawyer for the seller draw up the mortgage for both parties (or the other way around for that matter). Most lawyers will not do this, but I have seen some who will do exactly that. Each party should have separate legal representation for this and all mortgages.

Criteria for mortgagees holding blanket mortgages

SELLERS HOLD	THIRD-PARTY LOANS
1. Must have strong motivation to sell or hold the blanket mortgage. It is possible that the blanket is sold, and more than provides the security. Usually, the overwhelming motive is the need to be relieved of superior debt, or is sick to death of the property.	1. Is the security good, sound, and acceptable?
2. The security checks out. The combined equity which secures the blanket mortgage should be well over the principal amount of the mortgage itself. This will vary, depending on the type of property and the existence of superior mortgages. Do not rely on the value as stated by the buyer or his agent. Seek an independent appraisal, or at least ask the advice of other Realtors in the area.	2. Are the terms of the loan good, sound, and acceptable?
3. Some cash can be a part of the deal. All buyers should put some cash into a transaction. Of course, the amount will depend on many factors. But it does have a solidifying effect.	3. Is the return on the mortgage good enough, nonusurious, and acceptable?
	4. Is the mortgagor good, sound, and acceptable?

HOW TO INCREASE SALES BY USING THE BLANKET MORTGAGE AS A TOOL

Blanket mortgages have a function as a sales tool in some types of transactions. If you are selling property from a large inventory within the same owner's portfolio, such as tract lots or other subdivided property, the seller can offer packages of lots or parcels to investors with the blanket mortgage. In this way, the buyers would have two or more pieces of land covered by one mortgage. The seller would agree to release some of the lots as the mortgage is paid down. The release would be the same kind that could be used in any form of financing that may provide for the division of a property. The actual wording of the release could be predetermined by the seller to afford him the maximum protection in this type of transaction.

The advantage to the seller in this type of mortgage is mainly the increased sales potential. The risk to the seller over other forms of financing is negligible, if the land in question is substantially worth the price. The buyer can compare the blanket mortgage to other forms of financing to see how it will affect him. In the following example, you will find one such comparison.

McMoore was a land developer and had over 50 lots remaining in his most recent subdivision. He was not a builder, so he preferred to sell the lots rather than get into the housing business. While homes were moving at a fair pace, he could not attract private buyers and home builders were not interested in his normal sales terms. McMoore had been selling his finished lots at about one a week and was asking $12,000 for each one. In the past, McMoore wanted and had gotten $3,480 down and was holding the balance for one year. Some buyers had paid cash, financing the paper with their own sources.

McMoore's broker, who had sold him the raw land nearly three years previously, suggested that he make a quick deal for a sellout and move on to the next land development program they had been working on. The broker reasoned that if the proper terms were given, they would be able to get some home builders to buy the remaining lots. They came up with this plan: The lots would be put into groups of five. This meant they had 10 packages to offer to the local builders or investors. The average price per package was $60,000. The down payment, however, was $6,000, instead of the $17,500 which was based on the normal down payment McMoore had gotten on the other lots. The mortgage terms offered were interest only for three years at 8 percent per annum on the balance. This marketing of the package at 10 percent down was bound to produce the desired results. McMoore knew this and wanted to make sure he was secure in the transaction.

What he did was to require that $12,000 be paid against the purchase price for a lot to be released from the mortgage. The releases were for the purpose of building homes for later resale. So McMoore took a second mortgage position on the home back into the blanket as additional security. That second would be removed when the next lot was released—and a new second would be placed on the second home. This would continue until the first four lots were released. On the last lot, only the remaining $12,000 plus interest had to be paid. Each builder had three years to build before the balloon came due on the unpaid balance.

HOW THIS TRANSACTION LOOKED TO THE BUILDERS
THAT BOUGHT THE PACKAGES

It was a good deal. McMoore had priced the lots fairly and the housing market was strong enough to warrant tying up the initial cash. McMoore had also made the down payment reasonable, so once the builders had invested the $6,000 they could go ahead with preparations to build. They would arrange construction financing through local lenders to cover the cost of the home (plus a little overage). The excess of the loan, if any, would help pay off the lot. When they were ready to go, the mortgage to McMoore was reduced by $6,000 and the first lot was released.

The giving up of a second position to McMoore was no hardship to the builders. They knew that as soon as they sold the home they would merely move on to another one anyway. If they sold a new home from the model, they only had to pay down $12,000 cash and build on another lot. There was to be only one second lien at a time. In the meanwhile, the cost to carry the remaining lots was not overburdening them and they liked the idea.

The real key to this formula was simply the security for the seller. The blanket formula of holding all the unreleased lots into the mortgage was part of the security. The idea of adding the second mortgage on each new home as it was built, releasing the previous one, put the icing on the cake for the seller and didn't affect the buyer.

SUMMARY OF BLANKET MORTGAGES

The concepts inherent in blanket mortgages are also found in other forms of equity liens. If you remember that the ability to add other assets in order to bind the mortgage is the concept behind the blanket mortgage, then you can apply this idea to leases as well.

In the lease, the term used to cover this concept is *cross-collateralization*. The main use of the blanket lease is in sale lease-backs. In this situation the seller of a property becomes the lessee to the buyer. If the seller holds a mortgage as a part of the sale (e.g., sale price: $150,000— seller holds $50,000 in paper and takes $1000,000 down), the mortgage may be given as additional security on the lease. This has a very strong affect in securing the lease.

Blanket mortgages can be in any position on the scale of superior or junior liens. The mortgage can actually take different positions on the various properties it covers. Usually, however, the same position on all the properties is attained, but the fact that this is not necessary is most important.

It is always possible to hold individual mortgages instead of a blanket. From the seller's point of view, if the two mortgages are offered at the same term, interest rate, and principal, then the only advantage in the blanket would be the lock-in provision. This would, of course, depend on the situation and what assets or property the seller wanted to lock into the transaction.

Buyers will use this form of financing to cover a down payment. However, even the buyer can take the alternative route and offer secondary paper on the existing property. Usually, the blanket mortgage is used in circumstances when the buyer is looking for the combined effect of one seller-held mortgage that is supported by his equity in other property, rather than an exchange of equity by virtue of paper offered on something else. It is a matter of negotiation. And, it often sounds better to offer a blanket mortgage secured by the purchased property and the buyer's equity in his vacant lot, instead of a mortgage to the seller and a mortgage on the lot. Of course, if several additional properties are used to add security, the blanket mortgage is easier to work with.

Chapter 10

HOW TO USE THE WRAPAROUND MORTGAGE EFFECTIVELY

When it comes to single tools that have a wide and flexible beneficial use to both the buyer and the seller, the wraparound mortgage fills the job with ease.

Yet wraparounds are also one of the most misunderstood of all mortgage formats, and are frequently used incorrectly because of their complexity, the different ways in which they are mistaken for other forms of mortgage such as blanket mortgages, or the incorrect ways in which yields are calculated.

Nonetheless, if you are to become successful in financing you should plan on spending some time with this chapter to get familiar with the wraparound mortgage. It has its easy and its tough elements, but once you understand how and why it works, you will find that it will facilitate transactions in which you as an investor need something to make the deal work.

In this chapter, you will find several examples of wraparound mortgages that demonstrate the major elements of the technique. As with all tools in this book, I frequently will use a technique in conjunction with other forms of finance without reexplaining elements of a transaction contained in other chapters. For this reason, you will find examples of other wraparound deals in other chapters as part of a total package of financing tools that get the job done.

In this chapter, however, I will stick close to the wrap. There is no simple way to explain some of its workings other than by example, and there is no simple way to calculate the yield except by following the method contained herein at least once to see if the program you are calculating is correct.

As you will discover, there are several different kinds of yields available in wraparound mortgages. The average yield is the usual one that computers give, but that is not the most effective yield. When you get the average yield, you have found nothing useful.

WHAT IS THE WRAPAROUND MORTGAGE?

A simple example of a wraparound mortgage is: Bobby wants to buy to Jeff's house for $120,000. There is an existing first mortgage on the house of $50,000, which is payable over 20 years at a fixed interest rate of 8.5 percent per annum, with monthly payments of $433.92.

Bobby offers Jeff a down payment of $25,000 and a second mortgage of $45,000 at an interest-only payment of 10 percent for 10 years with a balloon payment at that time, with assumption of the existing mortgage. Under these terms, Bobby would have a combined monthly payment between the two mortgages of $808.92.

Jeff counters by offering to take the $25,000 down payment and hold a $95,000 wraparound mortgage with a 10 percent interest-only payment for 10 years with a balloon payment at that time. In these terms, the payment Bobby must make is only $791.66. As this amount is less than the payment in his own offer, Bobby accepts Jeff's deal. Both sides have won.

As far as Bobby is concerned, the wraparound that Jeff is holding is really one mortgage in the amount of $95,000. However, from Jeff's point of view, there are three mortgages: mortgage A is the existing first mortgage of $50,000 that has a mortgage payment of $433.92 per month for 20 years; mortgage B is the wraparound mortgage in the amount of $95,000, which Bobby pays to Jeff ($791.66); and mortgage C is the difference between the existing and the wraparound mortgages. The wraparound mortgage of $95,000 less $50,000 gives Jeff a difference of $45,000.

In reality, Bobby is paying as if he held the single $95,000 mortgage that was interest-only for 10 years. Jeff continues to make payments on the existing financing, and puts the left over money in his pocket. Since he collects $791.66 and pays out $433.92, he has $357.75 left over each month for himself. That amounts to $4,293 per year, which appears to be only 8.59 percent per annum on the $45,000 difference.

However, since the wraparound mortgage paid by Bobby is interest-only while the existing mortgage is being paid off by Jeff, at the end of each year Bobby still owes Jeff $95,000, while Jeff owes less on the first mortgage. As an example, at the end of the first 12 months the original $50,000 mortgage is now paid down to $49,007.00, which would put another $993 in Jeff's pocket if the mortgage were paid off at that time. This would increase Jeff's cash in pocket to a total of $5,286 and his yield to 11.75 percent per annum.

Bobby won because he decreased his debt service, and Jeff won because he increased his overall effective yield on the wrap.

Other things occur too, but there will be time to discuss those factors later in this chapter.

THE PURPOSE OF THIS CHAPTER

The primary purpose of this chapter is to open the door to wraparound mortgages to you and your future transactions. To get the most out of this chapter, read it carefully without trying to get into the math calculations. Then go back and pay more attention to some of the problems and their solutions.

THE MOST IMPORTANT FACTOR ABOUT WRAPAROUNDS

If there is a single, most important factor about wraparounds, it would be that a wraparound mortgage is just a tool. Depending on your knowledge of the tool and your goals, it has a lot of uses, it can be the best thing for your situation, or it can do nothing at all to take you closer to your goals.

WHAT THE WRAPAROUND IS NOT

To get a good grasp on what the wraparound is, it might be helpful to see what it is not.

Wraparound Mortgages
1. Are not a cure-all form of financing. This can be said of any technique in this book. Nothing will do everything, and nothing is so inflexible that some other technique may not work just as well depending on the people, the property, and your needs and goals.

2. Are *never in first position*. The very nature of a wraparound mortgage causes the situation to contain existing financing on the property. It could be possible for a mortgage to be called "The First Wraparound Mortgage." Even though this term might be used wrongly, it could refer to a transaction that had more than one wraparound mortgage in existence

on the same property. An example of that is a property Al wants to buy. The current financing consists of a wraparound in the amount of $100,000 that consists of the wrap of $100,000, a first mortgage of $60,000, and a difference of $40,000. In addition to the wraparound mortgage, the seller placed another mortgage on the property several years ago in the amount of $25,000. This would be a "third" mortgage as the rank of mortgages at this point would be: (1) the existing first mortgage; (2) the wraparound; (3) the $25,000 mortgage. In this transaction, Al wants the seller to hold a fourth mortgage for $35,000. The seller could do exactly that, or he would have the following options that would involve new forms of wraparounds.

The seller could:

1. Hold a second wraparound, which covers all the existing financing, including the new fourth mortgage in a gross amount show below:

1st Wrap:	$100,000	($60,000 first plus 40,000 difference)
3rd Management	25,000	
New		
Difference	35,000	
2nd Wrap	$160,000	

If the seller did this, Al would make one payment on the second wrap of $160,000 as would be indicated by the terms of that mortgage. In turn, the seller would make payments on the first wrap (which would include the first mortgage payment and the difference to the holder of that wrap), and make the payment on the third mortgage, keeping the balance left over as the payment on the new difference.

Or the seller could:

2. Create a wraparound mortgage solely around the third mortgage. In this case, Al would make two monthly payments: one on the first wraparound, and a second to the seller on a wraparound at a face amount of $60,000 ($25,000 + $35,000). Out of that payment by Al, the seller would have to meet the obligations of the third mortgage.

Or the seller could:

3. Take a fourth mortgage, which Al would pay along with the wrap and the third mortgage.

3. Wraparounds Are Not Required to Enclose All Existing Mortgages. The foregoing example was a good illustration of that. This is important to remember because if you buy a property with a wraparound do not assume that there are not other mortgages you need to pay.

4. Wraparound Mortgages Are Not All the Same. Since this is a technique and not a specific form that can be bought at a stationery store, you must recognize that this tool is very flexible, and apt to be different each time you see it. No matter how similar one form looks, you have to be very careful with the exact terms contained within the document. Later, there will be more on this aspect of wraparounds.

ANOTHER EXAMPLE OF A WRAPAROUND MORTGAGE

Pallsen wanted to sell his large home and put a price of $155,000 on it. He had an old low interest existing first mortgage in the amount of $75,000 that had twenty years remaining in its payout at an interest of only 8 percent per annum.

Along comes Beck, the investor, who offers to pay $35,000 down, assume the first mortgage, and let Pallsen hold the balance of $40,000 in secondary financing. Like many sellers, Pallsen balked at that, saying the risk was too high and the yield was too low. Beck reconsidered and countered with the following terms:

Price	$150,000	
Cash down	$ 35,000	
Wraparound	$115,000	(20-year payout at 10 percent)

Beck's broker presented the new offer. He explained to Pallsen what a wraparound was and went over the advantages to Pallsen in this offer.

The broker showed Pallsen how this wraparound would return a yield of over 13 percent over the term of the mortgage. Take a look at the illustrations the broker used.

PALLSEN'S WRAPAROUND MORTGAGE

In the transaction, Beck will make payments on one mortgage: the $115,000 wraparound. It will be set up with a 20-year amortization at 10 percent per annum. The total annual payment will be $13,317.55.

Pallsen will be required to set up a method of collection of that mortgage from Beck so that from Beck's monthly check the payment required on the existing first mortgage can be made. That payment is $7,527.75, which comes out of the $13,317.55, leaving $5,789.25 for Pallsen each year for 20 years. This means that Pallsen will be getting a monthly payment of $482.44 for the 20 years (unless he sells the mortgage or uses it to exchange into another property in the mean time). This payment, on a difference of $40,000, would correspond to a monthly payment based on a 20-year payout at 13.5 percent.

HOW WAS THE YIELD ON PALLSEN'S MORTGAGE CALCULATED?

This was a simple calculation on a wraparound mortgage. There was only one existing mortgage, and the wraparound was for the same term as the existing mortgage. In essence, by the end of the term (20 years) each mortgage would be retired. Beck would make one payment each month that would total $13,317.55 per year for 20 years. During this same time, Pallsen or any successor holder of that mortgage would pay the existing payments of $7,527.75 per year and would collect on the difference of $40,000 an annual total of $5,789.25. To find the actual effective yield on this wrap for the total term of the mortgage (20 years), you simply need to find the *constant rate* on the payment toward the difference. As long as the terms of the existing mortgage and the wrap are identical and no interim balloon occurs, the following is a quick math solution to the problem.

FIND THE CONSTANT RATE OF PAYMENT ON THE DIFFERENCE

Step One.   Once you have the annual payment of $5,789.25, which you obtained by taking the total payment on the wrap and by deducting the payment to the existing mortgage, you then divide that amount by the total amount owed on the difference. The difference in this example is $40,000 and is found by subtracting the existing mortgage from the gross amount of the wraparound mortgage.

Step Two.   The sum of $5,789.25 divided by $40,000 equals 0.1447312.

Step Three.   Convert the answer, 0.1447312, into a percentage amount by moving the decimal two places to the right. The percentage is now 14.47312.

Step Four.   Look at Table A in the appendix under the 20-year column until you find a constant percent that comes closest to the 14.47312.

Step Five.   Discover these two percentages, 14.273 followed by 14.488. These correspond to the different interest rates for that term of years.

% Interest	20 Years
13.25	14.273
13.5	14.488

As the desired percent is more than that shown for 13.25 percent interest but slightly less than that for 13.5 percent interest, the actual effective interest yield on the difference for the full term of the wraparound would be about 13.45 percent per year.

WHAT ALL THIS MEANS THUS FAR

If Pallsen were to hold onto this mortgage for the full 20 years, his effective yield would be 13.45 percent per year.

WHAT HAPPENS IF THE MORTGAGE IS PAID OFF EARLY?

A strange thing happens in wraparounds that gives the holder a bonus when the mortgage gets paid off early. Assume for a moment that Beck sells the property at the end of the first year and the new owner refinances the wrap, paying off the amount *then owed*. To see what happens, let's first get the facts.

WHAT THE MORTGAGES LOOK LIKE AT THE END
OF THE FIRST YEAR

	The wraparound mortgage	The existing mortgage
Original amount	$115,000.00	$75,000.00
Annual payment	$ 13,317.55	$ 7,527.75
Term of years	20	20
Interest rate	10%	8%
End of which year	1	1
Remaining term	19 years	19 years
Amount still owed	$113,100.21	$73,412.81

This last amount is found by finding the *constant rate* for the remaining term, at the interest rate for the mortgage, and then dividing that rate into the annual payment.

If Beck paid off the wrap it would cost him $113,100.21 out of which Pallsen would have to pay $73,412.81 leaving him a balance of $39,687.39 from the original $40,000 difference. At the end of the first year then, Pallsen would have gotten:

In monthly payments	$ 5,789.25
Payoff at the end of the year	39,687.39
Total Paid to Pallsen	$45,476.64
Subtract Original Principal Amount	40,000.00
Net Interest for That First Year	$ 5,476.64

Actual effective yield based on an annual return for the first year based on a payoff of the existing mortgage and the wrap at that time would be found by dividing the original principal amount of $40,000 into the net interest for the year. The sum of $5,476.64 divided by $40,000 equals 13.692 percent per annum.

The point to this illustration is that in a wraparound mortgage the general rule is that the actual effective yield will be higher if the mortgage is paid off early than if held to maturity. This mortgage yield went from 13.45 percent to 13.692 percent on the prepayment of the first year. The yield earned at the end of a first-year payoff in a mortgage such as described will be its maximum annual yield. Each year thereafter, the mortgage yield will move closer to the 13.45 percent per annum.

Later on in the Hodges Shopping Center example, you will see how existing mortgages are affecting the total wrap balance and the relationship to the difference.

Keep in mind that in the Pallsen example everything was at its simplest. In the real life use of the wraparound, it is usual to have more than one mortgage and more than one term of years within the existing financing. These factors make the wraparound a rather complicated mortgage to calculate, so don't be surprised if you have to apply some extra thought to this chapter. It will be worth it in the long and profitable run.

THE 12 MOST COMMON USES OF A WRAPAROUND MORTGAGE

1. Use this tool as a method of leveraging a seller's position upward with the idea of increasing the effective yield earned on the mortgage. The ability to increase the return on funds mortgaged is the primary benefit of the wraparound.

2. To induce the seller to hold secondary paper. The benefits of the increased return may help a broker convince a reluctant seller to take treater paper, or any paper at all for that matter. Many transactions are saved simply because the sellers were made aware of the benefits of this tool.

3. When the existing financing is at a relatively low rate and the constant payment percentage is relatively low, the green flag is out that a

wraparound is potentially viable. The key factor here is the constant rate. More about that later.

4. If the existing financing has any provisions that make prepayment difficult or costly, then the wraparound mortgage may provide an effective solution to the inability to economically obtain new primary financing. When there are several mortgages encumbering a property, there may be one or more with provisions that will create such problems. It is best to consider the wraparound when such conditions are present. Sellers unwilling to approach the wraparound should be made aware of the full impact of their present financing.

5. A nonassumption clause in the existing financing may be an indication that the wraparound mortgage can be used. Institutional lenders almost always use these provisions in their loans. When a property is sold, the buyer must make application to the lender to be permitted to assume the obligation. Some lending institutions have taken a harder stand than others, but most will allow the wrap if the first is assumed. The lenders, however, generally reserve the right to adjust the interest rate when such a new assumption takes place.

Nonetheless, a wraparound mortgage does not require the buyer to assume the existing financing. This is a key factor in the whole structure of the wraparound mortgage, and indirectly has created the difficulty for third parties to lend on the wrap. When a buyer purchases a property and gives the seller a wraparound mortgage, the existing financing remains the obligation of the seller. The seller makes the payments directly or causes them to be made on the existing mortgages. Some secondary financing which may be encompassed within the wrap may have absolute provisions which would make the wraparound difficult.

6. The increase of cash flow is a definite benefit which can be accomplished by using the wrap. Therefore, when the sale of a property is hampered by a low cash flow, look to the wraparound. In essence, there are only a few ways to increase cash flow. Assuming a status quo in all other factors, the increase of income will accomplish this. If this fails, a reduction of expenses will also increase the cash flow. A combined effect of increased income (via more rents, etc.) and lowered expenses often will solve the problem and make the wrap unnecessary. Normally, however, the seller is already maximizing income and minimizing expenses. The resulting Net Operating Income (NOI) can only show an increased cash flow based on lowered debt service. The yield resulting from the cash flow, based on the invested capital, must meet the demand rate. In the general marketing of an income property, the cash down is often based on the seller holding some paper, or with new financing necessary. The cash flow yield may be too low with this form of financing to warrant the investment. The wraparound can, and often does, solve this problem nicely.

7. Tight mortgage markets bring out the best in the wraparound. When you find yourself marketing a property which cannot be readily financed due to the current market conditions, you must look to all the

possible alternatives. The toughness of the market need only be relative to the overall rate on the existing financing. This means that if you have a property that has very low rates, and the current market is a point or two above those rates, then you should examine the possibility of the wrap. Of course, the complete inability to refinance for any reason within the economics of the deal will bring the wrap into play more quickly and with more dramatic results.

8. Refinancing costs can sometimes be a major problem, and this factor can be a good reason to look to the wrap. The overall effect of placing a wraparound mortgage is less costly to administer than new financing. The seller need only charge whatever legal cost is involved in the preparation of the loan document, and this should not be much more than the cost of preparing a standard form for a secondary loan.

9. Multimortgaged properties can often be very difficult to sell or market simply because of the number of mortgages present. If you have a property that has three or more existing mortgages, the wrap can convert these into one. The buyer, after all, makes only one payment on the wrap, even though the seller must direct payments out to the encompassed mortgages.

10. A short balloon in existing financing can create many difficulties in selling property. If the property is an income producer and the possibilities of refinancing it to cover the balloon payment are slim, then the wraparound can provide a solution. Naturally, the amount of the balloon must be considered. But if it is due to close and is not excessive, then the wrap may work out.

11. Marketing a property with sound financing can bring about a quicker sale and less negotiating of the price. When a property has only a moderate extension of financing, that is to say a low ratio of the loan to value, the seller's equity will come under attack by buyers anxious to buy at a lower price. It is obvious that a home offered at $100,000 with an $85,000 mortgage leaves only $15,000 to negotiate with. Buyers expect some equity, and will haggle on only the upper limits of such a transaction. The broker utilizes this technique and obtains a committment from the seller (or a third party lender for that matter), and quotes the wraparound mortgage in his presentations. This extending of the loan to value ratio will benefit the negotiations. As the buyer approaches the close of the sale, full ramifications of the underlying mortgages encompassed by the wrap will, of course, be disclosed. The first examination, however, need only show the higher wrap.

12. Buyers will look to the wrap as a tool to be used for their benefit as often as a seller. The buyers' benefits are in the overall comparison with the existing mortgage market, rather than in seller-held, conventional secondary financing. There are a few examples where the buyer will benefit from a wrap, such as when the seller will hold a usual second mortgage for the same terms and rates. The seller will, however, hold a wrap for longer, and often at lower rates than a usual second. Therefore, the buyer

can benefit by approaching any situation that may call for refinancing and offer the seller terms only slightly less costly to the buyer in the general lending market. In this way he obtains better terms from the seller than he could at an institutional lender, saves the points, and at the same time passes on to the seller the full benefits of the wrap.

If the primary reason for using the wraparound is to increase the cash flow on the income property for sale, there may be a sacrifice in some other area. The nature of the wraparound and its effect on the dollar amounts paid and received by the seller or lender should be clearly understood. In the first place, it is normal for the balance of the "difference" owed to increase for a period of time. Remember, the word "difference" in wraparound terms refers to the amount of the total wraparound mortgage that is left whenever you deduct the then present amount owed to the existing financing. A wraparound in the amount of $100,000 that encompasses a first and a second totaling $80,000 will have an original "difference" of $20,000. This term is not universal, and in some areas this amount the ($20,000) is called the "wrap difference," the "lender's position," or "new money." I shall continue to refer to it as the "difference." This difference will not remain constant throughout the mortgage and normally grows in the early years. To best illustrate what happens to this difference, examine the following case history.

THE FUNCTION OF THE AMORTIZATION AND ITS EFFECT ON THE DIFFERENCE IN WRAPAROUND MORTGAGES

Hodges sold a shopping center for $2,500,000. He received $350,000 down and held a wraparound for the balance. The wraparound was for a face amount of $2,150,000, and was payable over a period of 20 years at 9% per annum in equal monthly installments which totaled $235,532.50. The existing financing was a first mortgage ($1,200,000) at 7½% with 19 years remaining. Annual payment was $120,492. There was a second mortgage in the amount of $700,000 payable over 15 years at 8%. The annual payment was $81,781.

	Mortgages	Face amount	Annual payments
	Wraparound	$2,150,000	$235,532.50
Less:	1st Mortgage	$1,200,000	$120,492.00
Less:	2nd Mortgage	$ 700,000	$ 81,781.00
	Original Difference	$ 250,000	$ 33,259.50

The foregoing calculation is correct only for the moment the wraparound is made. Each year the balances due on the mortgage will alter.

The payment allocation to the difference will also change when the existing mortgages retire.

Here's what occurs at the end of the first year:

Mtg. balance at start of 1st year		Total payment Principal	Interest	Balance owed at end of 1st year
Wraparound	$2,150,000	$42,032	$193,500	$2,107,967
Less: 1st Mortgage	$1,200,000	$30,492	$ 90,000	$1,169,508
Less: 2nd Mortgage	$ 700,000	$25,781	$ 56,000	$ 674,219
Difference	$ 250,000	($14,241)	$ 47,500	$ 264,240

What has happened is this: The balance owed on the wraparound has declined by the principal paid of $42,032. However, the existing mortgages have declined $56,273. The total owed or remaining as a principal balance on the wrap is $2,107,967. If the mortgage were paid off by the buyer at that time and the existing mortgages satisfied, then $264,240 would remain to apply to the mortgagee or the seller. The original amount at the beginning of the year was only $250,000. The $264,240 is the difference at the end of the first year. This is ($14,241) greater than the original difference of $250,000. What happened shows up in the interest column. The interest on the wraparound mortgage is $47,500 greater than the combined interest on the first and second mortgages. This $47,500 is net interest earned by the holder of the mortgage, but since he received only $33,259.50 (see previous chart) the total principal amortized on the existing financing exceeded that amortized on the wraparound. The deficit ($14,241) had to be deducted from the total interest, then added to the balance owed. This constant adding of the deficit interest to the balance applicable to the difference will continue as the mortgage progresses. This is what happens in the second year.

Mtg. balance at start of 2nd year		Total payment Principal	Interest	Balance owed at end of 2nd year
Wraparound	$2,107,967	$45,815	$189,717	$2,062,152
Less: 1st Mortgage	$1,169,508	$32,779	$ 87,713	$1,136,729
Less: 2nd Mortgage	$ 674,219	$27,843	$ 53,937	$ 646,375
Difference	$ 264,240	($14,807)	$ 48,067	$ 279,048

The holder of the wrap still only gets the $33,259.50 cash left after the total payment is received less the existing payments on the first and second mortgages (see first chart). In this year, however, the balance applicable to the difference has grown to $279,048.

The reason for this build-up is not simply explained. It is a function of several factors that combine to create the major leverage to the difference. In the first place, leverage is present in the spread of mortgage rates. The interest charged on the wraparound is greater than the combined effect of interest charges against the total existing financing. You should be cautioned at this point not to jump to conclusions that all the underlying mortgages must have interest rates below that of the wrap. It is the combined effect you must look at. In a multimortgaged property you may have one or more mortgages with greater interest rates than the wraparound and still have a build-up of difference owed.

Therefore, the function of the amortization on the balance applicable to the difference will generally be that the amount owed will grow each year until there is a satisfaction of at least one existing mortgage. Keep in mind, however, that this is not always the case, and the actual calculation to determine this factor must be done. To recap the amortization of the wraparound in this case study, I have provided a breakdown of the mortgages and the difference throughout the full term of the loan. This breakdown is necessary in the understanding of the effective yield gained on the wraparound and will be used in the larger analysis of this yield later on. The amortization of the mortgages shown in Figure 13-1 gives the amounts owed at the end of the periods shown. Generally, you are dealing with amortizing loans which will have one constant monthly or annual payment that includes interest and principal. Because of this, neither the interest or the principal payments in each period are equal to other previous payments. Therefore, the corresponding balances of each mortgage and the difference must be calculated for each period. In analyzing a mortgage, you can be fairly accurate with year-end totals. Only in this way will you know what the pay-off amount applicable to the difference is at any given point of time.

In Figure 13-1, each mortgage is shown with the principal balance outstanding at the end of each period. For example, at the end of 8 years the balance outstanding on the wraparound mortgage is $1,686,446 (A), the 1st $881,469 (B) the 2nd $452,777 (C), and the difference has grown to $379,200 (E).

THE EFFECTIVE RATE EARNED ON THE WRAPAROUND

This is the most difficult part of the wraparound to fully comprehend. The big question is simply this: What is the real (or effective) return to the holder of the wrap?

In looking at the Hodges Shopping Center Analysis Sheet (Figure 10-1), we can see numerous yields. At first glance we see that the seller will receive, after all payments on the existing financing, a balance of $33,259.50 for the time that the existing mortgage debt service remains unchanged. This amount of return, in cash, represents 13.30% of the original balance of the difference ($33,259.50 ÷ $250,000 = 13.30%). However, the balance of the difference does not diminish during the period of full existing debt service. And should the mortgagor pay off the wrap before any of the existing debt is satisfied, the holder will obtain the full $250,000 plus a bonus of built-up interest which was earned but not received. This bonus is in addition to the interest of $33,259.50 received or retained. With this in mind then, until the outstanding difference drops below its original sum, we can treat the wrap as an interest-only return to the mortgagee with the effective yield being this original 13.30% plus the bonus rate.

Therefore, when analyzing the wraparound there will be more than one rate which you must recognize. First, there is the rate on the retained cash. This represents that sum of money that is actually received net of payments on the existing financing less amortization of the difference. In Figure 10-1, the total cash received on the difference (Column F) is $33,259.50 for the term of the existing financing and will increase when the second is retired. As there is no amortization of the difference during this period, the Retained Total (H) equals Column F. Since the original investment by the mortgagee is $250,000, and that balance owed remains at or above that sum during the term of the existing financing, then the retained cash is 13.30% for that period of time only. This rate becomes the CAP rate of the difference.

In reference to Figure 10-1, you will notice that this annual payment of retained cash changes when the second mortgage is satisfied. All calculations on wraparound effective rates must be broken down to the periods of the existing financing. When there is no amortization of the difference, which generally will occur only in the first period, the cash received will equal the retained cash. In addition to the effective rate of 13.30% for the retained cash, a bonus also occurs. This bonus is earned but not retained. It cannot be accurately computed until the mortgagee benefits from that sum at some time in the future.

FINDING THE OVERALL EFFECTIVE YIELD OF A WRAPAROUND MORTGAGE

The first step in finding the effective yield of the bonus is to fill out the wraparound analysis chart (Figure 10-1). In looking at the amortization chart for the wraparound mortgage and the existing financing, you will be able to note the year in which the build-up of difference stops and amortization of that balance begins. This is significant since it establishes the year the bonus is benefiting the mortgagee. In the Hodges Shopping Center Case Study (Figure 10-1), this occurs on the 15th year. When there is a build-up or accrual of bonus, the change generally occurs when all or part of the existing financing retires. In some mortgages, the retirement of one mortgage is not sufficient to increase the payment to the difference.

Because the bonus amount is important, and because the data necessary to obtain an accurate effective rate of return is dependent on the Analysis Sheet (Figure 10-1), a brief discussion of how to fill out this sheet is in order. Examine the chart. Notice that there are columns A through J. These ten columns will accommodate a wraparound and three existing mortgages. If you have a situation where you have more than three existing mortgages, you need to add D1, D2, etc., for each additional mortgage.

HOW TO USE THE WRAPAROUND MORTGAGE ANALYSIS SHEET

Column (A): The basic information needed which pertains to the wrap should be filled in at the top. The term of years, annual interest rate charged, and annual payment of P & I are important for reference. At the *End of Period O*, you should place the face amount or original balance owed on the wraparound. In the following years, as the column extends down the page, you can put the principal balances owed at the end of each successive year. This is a purely mathematical calculation which can be done easily with a two-memory calculator or can be obtained from an amortization schedule. It should be noted that the years shown are the *end of that period*, and in order to find the balance owed at the *beginning of a year* you need to look to the balance owed at the end of the previous year.

Columns (B), (C), and (D): These columns contain the same type of information as Column A, except that they are for the currently existing mortgages. Most sellers will have amortization schedules for this information.

Column (E): This is the balance owed on the *difference* and the most important part of this computation. If there is no amortization of the difference, as will usually be the case in early years, this amount will grow. The total in this column represents the net payoff to the mortgagee at the end of any given year. This column will indicate when the difference peaks out and begins to amortize. Subtracting the original balance of the *difference* from the amount in this column at the end of any year will give you the amount of the *bonus* thus far accrued (to be shown on Column J).

Column (F): The *total cash received* on the difference is the amount of net cash left over after the existing mortgage payments are deducted from the payments received on the wraparound. These payments will remain constant for the separate periods of the existing financing. If you have only one existing mortgage that is satisfied before the end of the wrap, you will have only two periods. This column is very easy to calculate and should present no difficulty.

HODGES SHOPPING CENTER—CASE STUDY ANALYSIS

The wraparound principal balance @	Existing financing principal balance at end of period		
$2,150,000 Wraparound mtg. Yrs. __20__ Rate __9%__ Payment $235,532.50	$1,200,000 1st Mtg. Yrs. __19__ Rate 7½% Payment $120,492	$700,000 2nd Mtg. Yrs. __15__ Rate __8%__ Payment $ 81,781	3rd Mtg. Yrs. _____ Rate _____ Payment _____
End of period (A)	(B)	(C)	(D)
0 $2,150,000	$1,200,200	$700,000	
1 2,107,967	1,169,508	674,219	
2 2,062,152	1,136,792	646,375	
3 2,012,213	1,101,492	616,035	
4 1,957,780	1,063,612	583,828	
5 1,898,448	1,022,891	548,753	
6 1,833,775	979,115	510,872	
7 1,763,283	932,057	469,961	
8 1,686,446	881,469	452,777	
9 1,602,693	827,087	378,058	
10 1,511,403	768,627	326,522	
11 1,411,897	705,781	270,863	
12 1,303,435	638,223	210,750	
13 1,185,212	565,598	145,830	
14 1,056,348	487,525	75,715	
15 915,887	403,598	0	
16 762,785	313,376	0	
17 595,903	216,387	0	
18 414,002	112,124	0	
19 215,729	0	0	
20 0	0	0	
21			
22			
23			
24			
25			

Column (G): *Difference Amortized.* This column will contain amounts only for the years when the difference is declining. These amounts are found by looking at Column E. In Column E you have the amount of the difference as it increases and then declines. You need not be concerned with the increase in the Column G calculation, only the decline. The

	Difference $250,000 20 yrs. varies (E)	Difference Total cash received on difference $33,259.50 (F)	Difference amortized (G)	Retained interest (H)	Annual interest rate (I)	Earned but not retained bonus (J)
0	$250,000					
1	264,240	$ 33,259.50	0	$33,259.50	13.30%	$ 14,240
2	279,048	33,259.50	0	33,259.50	13.30%	29,048
3	294,416	33,259.50	0	33,259.50	13.30%	44,416
4	310,340	33,259.50	0	33,259.50	13.30%	60,340
5	326,804	33,259.50	0	33,259.50	13.30%	76,804
6	343,788	33,259.50	0	33,259.50	13.30%	93,788
7	361,265	33,259.50	0	33,259.50	13.30%	111,265
8	379,200	33,259.50	0	33,259.50	13.30%	129,200
9	397,548	33,259.50	0	33,259.50	13.30%	147,548
10	416,254	33,259.50	0	33,259.50	13.30%	166,254
11	435,253	33,259.50	0	33,259.50	13.30%	185,253
12	454,462	33,259.50	0	33,259.50	13.30%	204,462
13	473,784	33,259.50	0	33,259.50	13.30%	223,784
14	493,108	33,259.50	0	33,259.50	13.30%	243,108
15	512,289	33,259.50	0	33,259.50	13.30%	262,289
16	449,409	115,040.50	62,880	52,160.50	10.18%	199,409
17	379,516	115,040.50	69,893	45,147.50	10.05%	129,516
18	301,878	115,040.50	77,638	37,402.50	9.86%	51,878
19	215,729	115,040.50	86,149	28,891.50	9.57%	34,271
20	0	235,532.50	215,729	19,803.50	9.18%	
21						
22						
23						
24						
25						

amount amortized is the amount of decline each year as seen in the reduction of Column E. When the total in Column E does begin to drop, deduct the end of the year amount from the previous year.

Columns (H) & (I): It is generally best to do these two columns as one calculation. The Retained Interest and Annual Interest Rate are found as follows: The Retained Interest—Column F total cash received on difference) less Column G (difference amortized). The result will be the interest portion of the total cash actually received. In most all instances of a wraparound, the amortization (G) occurs late in the term of the wrap.

The annual interest rate is found by dividing the interest received by: (1) In the event of 0 amortization as seen in Column G, by the original balance of the difference; (2) In the event of amortization, by the amount of the difference at the start of that year (end of the previous year). You may have a very low annual interest rate when the total cash received in the early years is just above the existing mortgage payments. Therefore, a low annual interest rate is not unusual.

Column (J): *Earned but Not Retained Bonus.* This column need not be filled in completely. Its function is to show the amount of accrual of "extra lending." It represents the amount found in Column E (Difference) less the original balance of the difference. You need only put in this calculation the year the difference peaks out. (The year before amortization begins on Column D, as shown in Column G.) This amount you will show in Column J is the total Bonus for that period. Generally, this is the only bonus you will have for a wraparound.

In the example given in Figure 10-1, you will note that on the line which corresponds to the end of the 15th year under Column E the difference peaks out at $512,289. Further review of the remaining pay-out of the wraparound and the existing financing indicates that the difference amortizes beginning the 16th year. The amount of the amortization (G) is simply found by subtracting the current year's balance from the previous year's balance. The retained interest total (H) is the total cash received (F) less the amount of amortization (G).

Bonus Column (J) is the accrual of the earned but not retained portion of the difference. Of course, it peaks along with the difference. This bonus can be deemed to become a benefit at the time the difference begins to amortize. In essence, the return to the mortgagee can no longer be treated as interest only, as was done as the difference grew. Instead, the annual interest rate must take into account the bonus. While the difference was growing, the annual interest rate was found by dividing the retained interest by the original difference. Now, as the mortgagee is receiving benefit from a new difference, the annual interest rates, for years when there is amortization, are found by dividing the retained interest by the balance of the difference owed at the end of the previous year. For example: At the end of the 15th year the difference was $512,289. During that year the difference had grown and there was no amortization. However, in the 16th year there was a reduction of $62,880 and the balance at the end of that year was $449,409. A total of $115,040.50 was kept by the mortgagee. Of that amount, the $62,880 is principal reduction of the new difference (benefit) and $52,160.50 interest. The annual rate for this interest retained (I) is found by dividing $52,160.50 by $512.289. The result is 10.18%. In essence, for that year the mortgagee earned 10.18% on the mortgage of $512,289.00.

The following year shows a reduction of the new difference by

$69,893.00 and an interest retained of $45,147.50. The annual rate for the 17th year is 10.05% (45,147.50 ÷ 449,409). This calculation is carried out each year until the balance of the wrap is satisfied. By doing these calculations, it is possible to complete the full analysis sheet and to proceed to the final calculation of the overall effective yield for the mortgage.

The first step is to arrive at the primary effective rate which occurs during the early years when the difference is growing. To make this computation easier, I have provided a chart, Figure 10-2, to follow. (This chart shows sections A and B of the necessary calculation.) The use of this chart is not as complicated as it may appear. Once Columns A through J have been filled, in simple math, the use of the sinking fund table provided in this book and a small calculator will make fast work of the primary effective rate.

PRIMARY EFFECTIVE RATE CALCULATIONS
WHEN DIFFERENCE GROWS . . .

SECTION A

(A) Amount of original difference: $ _____
(B) Annual cash retained: $ _____
(C) Annual interest rate (Line B ÷ Line A)   _____
    (state as decimal):
(D) Total new difference: $ _____
(E) Amount of bonus (D less A): $ _____
(F) % of bonus (Line E ÷ A)   _____
    (state as decimal):
(G) Total years for period: _____ # years
(H) Total benefit at period $ _____
    (Line B × Years) + Line E:
(I) Average annual benefit $ _____
    (Line H ÷ Years):
(J) Averate rate (Line I ÷ Line A)   _____
    (state as decimal):

Note: Primary effective rate will lie between average rate (Line J) and
       annual interest rate (Line C).

SECTION B

Formula to Find P.E.R. (Shown Below)
Primary Effective Rate—(% of Bonus* × 1 S_N) = Annual Interest Rate
*Shown as a Decimal

---

1.   Target _____ Annual Int. Rate
2.   Less _____ (A)

3.

4.   ――――――― (B)

INTERPOLATION

$$PER = \underline{\hspace{2cm}} + \frac{.01 \times (A)}{(B)}$$

$$PER = \underline{\hspace{3cm}}$$

Taking the known facts from the Hodges Shopping Center Case study, Figure 10-1, examine how the primary effective rate for the first period was obtained. Note that the first period is the time the difference was still growing.

The question is stated as follows: If $250,000 is invested now and the investor receives $33,259.50 each year for 15 years, and at the end of the 15-year period has a return of his investment plus $262,289, what is the investor's effective rate of return? This data is found in the computations on the Analysis Chart (Figure 10-1). With this information, fill in and compute Section A of the Effective Rate Calculation.

PRIMARY EFFECTIVE RATE CALCULATIONS
WHEN DIFFERENCE GROWS ...

SECTION A

(A) Amount of original difference: $250,000.00

(B) Annual cash retained: $ 33,259.50 (Column F)

(C) Annual interest rate (Line B ÷ Line A)   0.1330 (13.3%)
    (state as decimal):

(D) Total new difference: $512,289.00 (Column E
                                                 at 15th year)

(E) Amount of bonus (D less A): $262,289.00 (Column J
                                                 at 15th year)

(F) % of bonus (Line E ÷ A) (state as   1.0492
    decimal):

(G) Total years for period: 15 years

(H) Total benefit at period $761,181.50
    (Line B × Years) + Line E:

(I) Average annual benefit $ 50,745.43
    (Line H ÷ Years)

(J) Average rate (Line I ÷ Line A)   0.202982 (20.2982%)
    (state as decimal):

To complete the primary effective rate calculation, it is necessary to complete Section B of the chart (Figure 10-4).

Since the following calculation requires an assumption to begin with, examine the relationship of the annual interest rate and the average rate. The annual interest rate shown is 0.1330 (or 13.3%) and the average rate is 0.202982 (or 20.298%). The primary effective rate will lie somewhere between these two.

The formula is: primary effective rate (P.E.R.)—(% of bonus $\times$ 1 S_N) = annual interest rate. The calculation 1 S_N is found in the sinking fund table provided in this book. Because the P.E.R. is unknown, make a guess at a rate slightly less than halfway between the annual interest rate and the average rate. In this case, use 0.16 (16%) as a starting point. In completing the formula you will look in the sinking fund table under the rate you assume to be correct for the period of years which in this example would be 0.16 (16%). Look at the 16% table for the 15th year. The resulting number represents 1 S_N for 16% at 15 years. The number shown in the table is 0.019358. From the previous Section A of this chart on Line F, the percent of the bonus has been found. That number, shown as a decimal, is 1.0492. The annual interest rate, also found in Section A on Line C is 0.1330. Now complete the formula with the first assumed interest rate as shown on Figure 10-4, Line 1.

PRIMARY EFFECTIVE RATE CALCULATIONS
WHEN DIFFERENCE GROWS ...

SECTION B

The Formula to Find P.E.R. (Shown Below)

Primary Effective Rate—(% of Bonus* $\times$ 1 S_N) = Annual Interest Rate

*Shown as a Decimal

---

1. .16 − (1.0492 $\times$ .019358) = 0.139689   Target: 0.13300 Annual
2. .15 − (1.0492 $\times$ .021017) = <u>0.127949</u>   Interest Rate

                                  0.011740 (B)   Less: <u>0.12795</u>

                                                              0.00505 (A)

3.

4.

INTERPOLATION

$$PER = \frac{0.15}{} + \left(\frac{0.01 \times 0.00505 \text{ (A)}}{0.011740 \text{ (B)}} \right)$$

PER = 0.15 + 0.00430, thus PER = 0.1543 (PER = 15.43%)

The resulting annual interest rate on the assumed P.E.R. of 16% exceeds the target rate. The target rate is the actual annual interest rate of 0.1330. Therefore, it is necessary to reduce the assumed rate. Try 0.15 (15%). In the table, locate 15 percent at the 15th year. The corresponding number is 0.2017. Therefore, the second part of the calculation would appear as $0.15 - (1.0492 \times 0.02017) = 0.127949$.

The annual interest rate found with this assumed rate of 15 percent is less than the target rate. By subtracting the annual interest rate on this lower interest from both the *target rate* (actual annual interest rate) and annual interest rate on the higher interest (16%), you can obtain the basis for Interpolation.

(1) $0.16 - (1.0492 \times 0.01968) = 0.13989$ Target: 0.13300

(2) $\underline{0.15 - (1.0492 \times 0.02017) = 0.127949}$ $\underline{0.127949}$

    0.01   0.011740 (B)   0.00505 (A)

$$\text{PRIMARY EFFECTIVE RATE} = \text{Lowest Rate Assumed} + \left(\frac{\text{Spread} \times \text{Difference A}}{\text{Difference B}} \right)$$

therefore

$$\text{PRIMARY EFFECTIVE RATE} = 0.15 + \left(\frac{0.01 \times 0.00505}{0.011740} \right)$$

$$\text{PRIMARY EFFECTIVE RATE} = 0.1543 \text{ (stated as a \% } = 15.43\%)$$

The Interpolation will approximate the effective rate once you have narrowed it down. In the lower tables, you can come very close to the actual rate and will not have to use a full point spread in your assumed rates. The formula for the interpolation is:

PRIMARY EFFECTIVE RATE CALCULATIONS WHEN DIFFERENCE GROWS ...

SECTION A

(A) Amount of original difference: $250,000.00

(B) Annual cash retained: $ 33,259.50 (Column F)

(C) Annual interest rate (Line B ÷ Line A)   0.1330 (13.3%)
      (state as decimal):

(D) Total new difference: $512,289.00 (Column E
                                        at 15th year)

(E) Amount of bonus (D less A): $262,289.00 (Column J
                                        at 15th year)

(F) % of bonus (Line E ÷ A) (state as decimal):   1.0492

(G) Total years for period: 15 years

(H) Total benefit at period (Line B × Years) + Line E: $761,181.50

(I) Average annual benefit (Line H ÷ Years) $ 50,745.43

(J) Average rate (Line I ÷ Line A) (state as decimal):   0.202982 (20.2982%)

The primary effective rate for the case study, as of the end of the 15th year, is 15.43 percent. If the mortgage were to balloon on that date, there would be no further calculations. If the mortgage were to be paid off earlier than the 15 years, the entire process would be computed on the balances and amounts applicable for the specific period of time.

Should the mortgage continue beyond the 15th year, the annual yield for each succeeding year would have to be added to the multiple of the effective rate thus far obtained and the years received. See these calculations on the consolidation section of the effective yield calculation.

CONSOLIDATION OF YIELD

| Period of wraparound analyzed | Effective rate per period | | No. of years rate earned | Rate × yrs. |
	Annual interest rate	Primary effective rate		
1st		15.43	15	231.45
2nd	10.18		1	10.18
3rd	10.05		1	10.05
4th	9.86		1	9.86
5th	9.57		1	9.57
6th	9.18		1	9.18
7th				
8th				
9th				
10th				
11th				
12th				
Combined Totals of Rate × Years: Total				280.29
Divide by Term of Years on Wrap: Effective Rate				14.015%

The foregoing table gives you the effective rate of interest earned by the mortgagee over the term of the mortgage. This sum, 14.015 percent is the result of the leverage obtained over the existing financing. You can see that a balloon on the 15th year would have given an effective yield over those 15 years of 15.43%. The later years of this wraparound gave a higher cash flow return than the early years. However, the benefit or bonus return accounted for the majority of that cash flow. It would have been best to have obtained the full benefit at the 15th year.

HOW TO USE THE EFFECTIVE RATE IN SELLING THE WRAPAROUND CONCEPT TO A MORTGAGEE

Keep in mind that the majority of mortgagees you will deal with will be sellers. The wraparound is a prime tool for increasing return to a seller, and this fact alone can convince many sellers who are reluctant to hold paper to do just that. To see this point clearly, examine the case study again (Figure 10-1). A wraparound in the amount of $2,150,000 was created for 20 years at 9% per annum. The difference held by the seller was $250,000. Over the term of the loan the seller received a total annual yield of 14.015%. What this really means is that in order for the seller to have done as well he would have had to hold a fourth mortgage at the same interest rate or greater. A buyer offered that kind of financing may balk at such a high rate. The leverage shown in the case study was not exceptional for the wraparound, and it is not uncommon for you to have much more dramatic results than that. Nonetheless, a 14.015% per annum return is not readily available and may be enough to motivate the seller. In third-party lending this same advantage will hold true. The third-party lender comes in and uses the same benefit to increase this overall yield on new money lent. The technique you use in convincing a seller of the advantages of holding the wraparound, instead of normal secondary paper, will depend on your fully understanding this leverage. The seller may find it to his advantage to accept a little more or even a lot more paper in order to take this increased yield. Yet, there are also other advantages to the seller in holding a wrap. All of these are discussed in the next section.

ADVANTAGES TO THE SELLER OR OTHER MORTGAGEE AND HOW TO CAPITALIZE ON THEM

1. *Effective yield increases.* This is one of the most important advantages to the wraparound. Great leverages in annual return are commonplace in wraps. No form of secondary financing can be as productive in increasing yield for the lender.

2. *Default notice.* When a seller or other mortgagee holds a wrap-

around mortgage, the owner of the property makes one payment to the mortgagee. From this payment the mortgagee then causes the existing mortgage payments to be made. Because the new owner has no control over this act, his default will come at the level of the wrap. In other words, if the new buyer falls behind in his payments the wrap mortgagee is the first to know. Action to collect, and even foreclosure if necessary, can be made at an early date—well before the existing mortgages themselves become overdue or go far in arrears. Of course, the mortgagee can easily step in and pay down the existing financing with no difficulty in the wrap. This advantage is considerable. If the mortgagor is going into arrears, it is not unusual for the mortgage having the lowest priority to be the last to be paid. It is possible and quite common, for example, for a new owner of multimortgaged property in financial difficulty to let the last mortgage (the third or fourth mortgage held by your seller) to go unpaid. In the meantime, this mortgagor may keep the first mortgage current for a while, then slip into problems. But if the seller-held mortgage is sizable, the mortgagor may keep that one current and let the first mortgages go into default. Even with provisions that lenders are to notify the other mortgagees of any default, this may not occur until a bad situation has advanced into a most impossible default.

The wraparound solves this problem nicely. Point out the priority of a fourth mortgage to your seller and show him the possibility of not knowing about economic problems the new buyer is having until it is too late. With the wraparound he still has the same position against the property, but he gets all the money and makes the payments himself.

3. *The selling tool works for the seller.* When you are marketing a property and have the ability to provide what appears to be an excellent mortgage, at terms under current rates and years longer than those available at local lenders, you have a good advantage in selling the property. This advantage goes to the seller. It is important to remember that you need not offer alternatives. A buyer may well understand the leverage of the interest on the existing mortgages and may not want to have that advantage pass on to the seller or some other party. In this event, he may ask the seller to hold secondary paper at a nominal interest rate and take over or assume the existing mortgages at their lower rate. The fact that the seller will hold a wrap, however, should become the new financing offered. Hence, the comparison that a buyer must make is not between the wrap and normal assumption of the existing mortgages and secondary paper, but between the terms offered on the wrap and the conventional terms available at local lenders. The wrap will compete favorably in almost any market, providing the existing financing can be wrapped around. In marketing a property with the wrap, you will find it easy to make this comparison: "Mr. Buyer, we have provided terms which are far better than those currently available at the local lenders. This fact, the ease in closing on the property due to this mortgage, and no points are to your

advantage." So, while this is a seller's advantage it is a buyer's advantage as well.

4. *Maintain installment sale.* The wraparound mortgage has a most important use that has nothing to do with leverage on rates or even its use as a marketing tool. When a property that has a very low basis is sold, there is a capital gain circumstance that can often be costly. If the owner of the property for sale has mortgages above the basis, simply to receive a sale, with no money down, can cause tax to be due. For example: Barkley owned a sizable office building for nearly twenty years. The current basis is only $50,000 even though the fair market value is over $500,000. He had placed new financing on the property a few years ago and currently owes $300,000 on it. He had a buyer willing to pay $500,000 with $100,000 down. Barkley determined that he would have a $425,000 adjusted gain in the sale and over $140,000 in capital gains tax. To make the sale would require him to come out-of-pocket over $40,000, plus fees, commissions, and other closing costs.

A wraparound mortgage was established in the amount of $400,000, payable over 20 years at a nominal interest rate. As Barkley was still on the mortgage and the buyer did not assume the liability, he was not relieved of that amount of debt. The income that came in over the term of the wraparound allowed Barkley to maintain an installment sale since he did not receive more than 30 percent in any year. The capital gains tax was still there, but now it was payable over the term as though a normal installment sale had taken place.

ADVANTAGES TO A BUYER OF PURCHASING WITH A WRAP

1. *The best terms in town.* The wraparound is so flexible that a high effective yield can be passed on to the mortgagee even though the buyer has a better rate and years than available elsewhere. The buyer saves on points, and when given no alternative of closing with assumption of the existing financing and the seller holding normal secondary paper, he will choose the wrap. Of course, the wrap can also offer better terms than assumption and secondary paper. If the existing financing has a low interest rate, but also a short term to go, the annual payment may be just about as high as the buyer can pay or the property can stand. To place on top of that a second mortgage of even the most modest annual payment may be more than either the buyer or the property will pay. The wrap has the capability of having a very low retained interest on the difference. The build-up of the bonus and its later recoupment and greater yield are most unique to this form of financing. This factor can save many transactions that have a short balloon in one of the existing mortgages by having

that mortgage amortized out of the total wrap and carrying forward the new difference to a later year.

Many buyers are cash flow conscious. They don't really look to the term of the mortgage. A 20-year mortgage is just 10 years less than a 30-year mortgage. When an investor is looking at how much cash he gets now on his down payment, then the wrap can keep the debt service at a more constant level, and often much lower than other forms of mortgages.

2. *Increase cash flow*. Because the wrap can provide a lower total annual payment (even though over a longer term) than a combination of existing financing and secondary financing, the advantage to a buyer in the case of income property can be considerable. A property with a NOI of $20,000 and existing debt service of $15,000 provides a cash flow of $5,000. If the investor demands a 10 percent cash flow yield he can pay $50,000 cash to the existing financing. However, the seller may want $60,000 to the existing financing. If the combined cash down and balance owed is within the fair market value range and the seller is firm on the price, the wrap can provide the answer. The question to answer here is: What total amount of wrap, at what interest rate, for how long, will cover the existing mortgage and its constant annual payment? Assume that the amount is $100,000 at 8 percent for approximately 10 years, and as the annual payment is $15,000 the constant annual payment is 15 percent. Also assume that the investor will pay up to $45,000 cash down.

To find J, refer to annual constant percentage tables. Begin at same rate shown in Line I. Find constant nearest to but no greater than constant rate shown in Line G. Check years and find actual annual payment by multiplying constant rate found in column by amount of wraparound in Line C. Increase interest in increments of less than 1 percent, maintaining the same number of years or more as indicated on Line H, and a constant not more than that shown on Line G.

Any of the possible terms shown would offer a total debt service that would not exceed the maximum amount available for debt service (Line F). With a wraparound on these terms, the minimum cash flow yield demanded by the investor would be met, and at the same time the seller would have obtained the total asking price desired.

The seller would no doubt look to the maximum interest rate which would still offer the annual payment as shown. The 10 percent over 14½ years would give the seller a greater overall effective yield than 8 percent over 12 years. The buyer would look to the smaller amount if he had his choice. When using this method, it is important to make sure that the annual payment on the existing debt service is met for the entire term of that mortgage. In a wraparound with only one existing mortgage, it is only necessary to keep the rate at or above that charged on the existing mortgage to accomplish this. If, however, you have a wrap that encompasses several mortgages, using the highest rate on any existing one and the maximum terms on any other (even if they are not the same mortgage) will also

		(1)	(2)	(3)	(4)
A. Minimum price					$160,000
B. Maximum cash to invest					$ 45,000
C. Amount to be held as wraparound					$115,000
D. NOI					$ 20,000
E. Cash return demanded					$ 4,500
(Line B × rate demanded)					
F. Amount available for debt service					$ 15,500
G. Constant annual payment percentage					13.479%
(Line F ÷ Line C)					
H. Minimum years possible (total years of remaining pay-out on existing mortgage)					10 years
I. Nominal rate on highest existing mortgage					8%
J. Possible terms					

	(1)	(2)	(3)	(4)
Nominal rate	8% (same as I)	8¾%	9½%	10%
Years	12 years	12.5 years	13.5 years	14.5 years
Constant shown	13.270%	13.471%	13.450%	13.353%
Annual payment	$15,260.50	$15,491.65	$15,467.50	$15,355.96

accomplish this. It is possible to use an interest lower than the maximum rate on one of several existing mortgages, providing that the annual payment on the wrap does not fall below the combined annual payment on the existing mortgages and the unpaid balance of the wrap is equal to or larger than the declining balance of the existing financing. This will involve looking at the entire mortgage however, and if the first method (maximum rate and maximum years) is used this will automatically be accommodated.

3. *Ease of payment.* In multimortgaged property, nothing can be more annoying than to have to make several payments to different lenders each month. Keeping track of the amortization of each is a problem. With the wrap however, the buyer has only one payment to make and can look to one amortization schedule. The form of payment is very important, as this is the area where most objections arise. Because the buyer does not directly make the payments on the existing mortgages, he may be most concerned that those payments will in fact be made. There have been

many cases of wraparounds where the buyer faithfully made his monthly payment, but only to find that the seller collecting that payment did not pay any of the existing mortgages. This is a nasty situation, and people that have experienced it have been needlessly hurt.

PAYMENTS SHOULD BE MADE TO AN ESCROW ACCOUNT —ALWAYS

When you set up a wraparound mortgage it is imperative that the payments on it be made to an escrow agency, or collection agency. The agency would then make the existing mortgage payments, collect for taxes and insurance, and disperse the balance to the mortgagee. This makes the maintenance of the wrap relatively easy for all parties concerned, and assures the mortgagor that the existing payments which should go to the existing mortgages are made. This escrow agency, either a commercial bank, savings and loan association, or other third-party service, should be paid by the mortgagee, but it is not unusual that this cost is shared by the mortgagor as well.

HOW TO PROTECT THE MORTGAGOR AND THE MORTGAGEE IN THE ESCROW AGREEMENT

The escrow agent will only do what he is instructed, so it is important that he has complete and comprehensive instructions. The factors that need to be covered in this escrow agreement will be:

1. How the fee is paid for the escrow service. The escrow agent will normally deduct his fee from the amounts collected. If the mortgagor is sharing this cost, his portion of the fee must be added to the total wrap payment.
2. Collections for taxes and escrows covered in the wrap or existing mortgages. A first mortgage may have a constant monthly payment added each year to the amortization which accrues annual taxes, insurance, and other assessments. It is imperative that these provisions be made a part of the wrap document, and that the escrow agent be instructed to make those out payments as well. In the event of a future assessment, or changes in taxes or insurance that would alter this escrow collection, the wrap should provide for those changes and the agent instructed on how to notify the mortgagor of these additions or subtractions to his total payment.
3. Prepayment provisions. Careful analysis of prepayment provisions in existing mortgages should be made and incorporated in the wrap-

around. The holder of the wrap should provide an equal pro-rata reduction of both the existing financing as well as the wrap for all prepayments. For example: If the outstanding balance at the time of the prepayment is shown to be 80% to existing financing and 20 percent to the *difference*, then the prepayment of $20,000 would be divided by that ratio. The 80 percent would then be prepaid to the holder of the existing financing. Of course, the entire 100 percent is reduced from the wrap balance, and new calculations would occur. The prepayment in full is the same as a balloon with regard to the effective yield rate.

4. *Grace Period*. There should be a shorter grace period on the wrap than on the existing financing. This will assist in notification of default ahead of due dates on the existing financing. When there is a very short grace period on any of the existing financing, it may be desirable to allow a build-up on one period to accrue in the escrow account in order to advance the lead time on default on the existing financing. For example: If a second mortgage has a 10-day grace period, the mortgagee may find it to his advantage to allow collections, less dispersements, to build up to an amount equal to one period payment on that second. If it is a monthly payment, then the grace period allowed to the mortgagee is now one month plus 10 days.

5. *Automatic foreclosure by underlying mortgages.* In an multimortgaged property, the first mortgage may have a provision which provides that it will automatically be in default and foreclosable in the event that any secondary lender file foreclosure proceedings. There is no real justification in this, but some lenders have this provision in their loans. It is far more important that the inferior loans have this provision, in the event the existing mortgagee or superior mortgagees file foreclosure. As the mortgagee in the wrap pays the existing mortgages, he knows when a default will occur. However, since he has the ability to make the existing payments on the existing mortgages, he can keep them current even though the wrap goes into default. Should he file foreclosure proceedings against the mortgagor, and should the existing mortgage have this automatic foreclosure provision in their loan, they too may file foreclosure, even though they are current. In this event, the escrow agent must be instructed not to file such proceedings without obtaining an agreement from the existing mortgage lenders that they will not file as long as they keep current. Most lenders, even if they have this provision of automatic foreclosure, will go along with such a request.

6. *Maintain integrated accounts.* The escrow agent should keep one account for the funds. The account should be in the name of the mortgagee. If the agent is a bank or other lending institution with

savings accounts or checking accounts, then all the funds collected should be paid into that account. Then, the agent will pay out the funds required for the existing financing. Have your lawyer draw up this escrow agreement. It is a very important part of the wrap process and is highly recommended. Naturally, this is not a necessity, yet to have a wrap without collections made by a third party can be less than prudent for the mortgagor.

THE WRAPAROUND CAN PRESENT UNIQUE PROBLEMS FOR THE THIRD-PARTY LENDER

When a wraparound mortgage is given to a third-party lender, such as a commercial bank or mortgage company, some unique problems occur. Take this situation as an example: Midwest Central Bank examines a potential lending situation that will involve a wraparound mortgage. They have concluded that by lending new money to a buyer of property and wrapping around the existing mortgage they will leverage their yield to above 12 percent. Assume that the new money they lend is $100,000. At the end of the first year of the loan they will receive their total investment of $100,000 plus $12,000. The mortgage they are wrapping around has a one-time payment (shown as follows).

	Face amount	Rate	Term	Due at end of term
(1) Existing Mortgage	$400,000	7%	1 Year	$428,000
(2) New Money	100,000	?	1 Year	?
(3) Wrap Total	$500,000	8%	1 Year	$540,000

Total principal and interest return on wraparound, End of 1st Yr.	$540,000
Less total pay-out, 1st mortgage	428,000
Total principal and return on new money	112,000
Less original principal on new money.	100,000
Total return on new money	$ 12,000
Effective rate of return on new money at end of 1st year .	12%

The third-party lender has lent only $100,000 in this transaction. He has not had any obligation to pay the original first mortgage of $400,000. If he makes the wraparound loan with the existing owner and original mortgagor on the existing mortgage, or a new owner that has assumed the first mortgage, he is advancing only new money with no liability on the existing financing. Courts have contended that in these situations the return to the lender *is* 12 percent and if the sum is usurious the loan is not valid.

In the wraparound mortgages we have concluded it is possible to leverage a yield much higher than the 12 percent shown in this example. Nonetheless, in many states a 12 percent return may be usurious. Therefore, this examination of return must be considered as a major problem for the third-party lender. The real advantages for a third-party lender are the leverage and the increased yield. If in making these loans the courts determine that usury is present, the loan can be null and void and the lender face loss of the sum lent and have a penalty placed on him as well.

The face rate of the wraparound is only 8 percent, well below usury in most states. But since the lender has no obligation to pay the existing financing, *no risk* as it were, the actual yield can be considered the effective rate of return.

HOW TO AVOID USURY ON WRAPAROUND LOANS BY THIRD PARTIES

The actual answer to this is not clearly defined by the courts. However, it does seem that if the third-party lender can place himself in the same shoes so to speak as a seller holding a wrap, then this problem can be averted. To do this will require the lender to assume the full obligation of the existing financing being wrapped around. When the lender has liability against the existing loans, then he may well be in the same position the seller would be in by holding the wraparound.

It is hoped that in the near future this matter of possible usury on third-party loans will be more clearly defined by the courts. In the meantime, third-party lenders must accept the advice of their legal advisors on this matter. There are numerous cases which have occurred in various states that indicate the above solution is perhaps the answer. But states may vary in this regard, so it is best to take a close look at what has happened in your state.

HOW TO CALCULATE INTEREST EARNED FOR ANNUAL INCOME ACCOUNTING

It is necessary to know how to account for interest earned in the wraparound for income tax purposes. In essence, the interest earned on the wraparound mortgages will be the interest to be reported as income. Deductions of interest to be reported as income and deductions of interest paid against the underlying existing mortgages will offset that total interest as long as the tax laws permit deduction of interest.

Total Interest collected at end of 1st year on a $500,000
    existing wrap at 8% per year $40,000

less

Total Interest paid out on existing mortgage, assuming
    a $400,000 existing mortgage at 7% per year   <u>28,000</u>

                                                   Net difference: $12,000

Income to be reported	$40,000
Interest Deduction	<u>28,000</u>
Taxable	$12,000

Note: Watch tax laws that may limit or remove interest deductions on real estate mortgages.

HOW TO TELL IF A SITUATION IS IDEAL FOR A WRAPAROUND MORTGAGE

There will be definite signs which should indicate to you if a situation is right for the use of the wraparound mortgage. Your ability to recognize these signs will aid you in reaching the conclusion that the wrap will help achieve the goals of your client. Listed below are some of the primary signs that you will encounter. At times they will present themselves alone, while at other times in combination with each other.

Signs That Indicate the Need for a Wraparound

1. *Existing loan constant annual payment percentage relationship to maximum loan potential:* Take a look at the total annual payment of the existing mortgages. Then find the constant payment percentage this represents of the total loan potential. If this constant is *below* a normal loan constant, you have a prime candidate for a wrap. For example: The total loan payment on three existing mortgages is $15,000 per year starting the first year. The property is priced at $225,000, therefore a normal loan may be 80 percent of that amount or $180,000. The $15,000, existing loan payment represents 8.33 percent of the total loan potential. A look at constants available in the market for new money may show as 11 percent annual constant to be reasonable. The spread of 2.67 percent in constants for the first year is tremendous. In fact, a spread of only 0.5 percent would be sufficient to warrant a further look to see if the wrap would be desirable. If you find that the constant annual payment on the existing financing is higher than the present market constant, a wraparound may not be effective.

2. *A forced wraparound:* If you have existing financing that cannot be assumed and a refinancing of the property is not possible due to market conditions or economic cost, then the wraparound sign is very strong.

3. *Reinvestment goal of the seller:* The leverage gained on the yield may be most attractive to the seller, and could be a primary sign that the wrap should be considered. Keep in mind that the constant spread in-

dicated in the first item (above) should be favorable for the leverage to occur.

HOW TO USE THE WRAPAROUND TO MAKE MORE SALES

You should have a good understanding for what the wrap will do, should do, and can do. The ability to take this tool and apply it to the selling of property will depend on whether you can sell the concept to the parties involved. The proficiency with which you accomplish this will therefore depend on how comfortable you feel in dealing with this tool. I suggest that the first step is to take several properties you presently have listed and restructure the existing financing via wraparound to see what happens to their marketability. If you see that you can offer a property with better financing and increase the cash flow, you are on the way to having a better inventory and making more sales.

You will have only relative difficulty in selling this concept to the buyer. After all, this depends on the alternatives offered to him. If he can buy with the wrap, instead of conventional financing, and the wrap offers better terms than the present market, then he will go with it.

The seller must also see the advantages it has to offer him. This chapter has given you all the ammunition to make that part of the sale easier than it might have been otherwise.

The wraparound is a fine tool in the hands of the real estate broker or associate. It is most effective as a selling tool, and while third-party loans may become more frequent in the future, the major lenders will continue to shy away from this format. Do not let that aspect dismay you however, since the third party lender has problems that are unique to the wrap that the seller does not have. Unfortunately, however, the power third parties exert in the lending area has been to hold down wider use of the wrap by sellers and brokers.

Remember: The wraparound is merely a tool. It has limitations and drawbacks. The return to the mortgagee is often postponed until the future, and though the yield is leveraged upward, the funds may not be available for use when they are needed. This factor should be considered as the major disadvantage to the wrap from a seller's point of view.

Figure 10-6 which follows is a blank Wrap Analysis Chart (see Figure 10-1 for one filled out). Have this reproduced along with the other charts shown in this chapter for analyzing the effective rate on the wrap-around.

THE PRIMARY ANALYSIS CHART

The calculation of mortgage amortizations using complicated formulas is no longer the drudgery it once was. The chart used to set down the pertinent data on the wraparounds, enabling you to find the pay off amounts and calculate yields, is shown on p. 206.

The Wrap-Around Principal Balance @

End of Period	Wraparound mtg. Yrs.___ Rate___ Payment (A)	1st Mtg. Yrs.___ Rate___ Payment (B)	2nd Mtg. Yrs.___ Rate___ Payment (C)	3rd Mtg. Yrs.___ Rate___ Payment (D)	Difference Column A less B, C, and D (E)	Total cash received on difference payment A less payments B, C, and D (F)	Difference amortized amount of column "E" paid off (G)	Retained interest (H)	Annual interest rate (I)	Earned but not retained bonus (J)
0										
1										
2										
3										
4										
5 etc.										

Chapter 11

HOW TO USE THE SALE AND LEASE-BACK IN REAL ESTATE

A sale and lease-back is the sale of an interest in realty and the subsequent leasing back of that same realty. The sale and lease-back is one of the best tools to use in generating more useful capital from one realty that can be used by the seller. This form of financing starts as a sale. The seller then agrees to lease-back the property being sold. Sometimes this lease-back can merely be a move to entice the buyer into the transaction. In its most effective form for the seller, however, the lease-back provides continued use of the property by him.

The property being sold can be all the realty, meaning land and buildings, or it may be just the buildings or just the land. Each aspect of the sale and lease-back can have different long-range results, depending on what portion of the realty is sold and then leased back.

HOW TO STRUCTURE THE LAND LEASE-BACK

The most basic of the sale and lease-backs is the land itself. It is very common in many parts of the world to have leased land under many types of buildings. These land leases generally began with a sale to one party, who then leases the land back to the seller. Over the years the owners of the leasehold change, but the lease remains.

In all lease-backs, and more particularly in the land lease, the ultimate title to the realty does not belong to the lessee. All the lessee owns is the leasehold interest. If the leasehold is later sold, the interest passed on is merely the remainder rights in the underlying lease or a portion of that lease. This factor creates many problems in land leases and leasehold interest, as it can cause difficulties in most conventional methods of financing buildings when the land is not owned in fee simple, but in leasehold.

THE SUBORDINATION FACTOR IN LAND LEASE

Because many lenders will not lend on buildings situated on leased land without that lease being subordinated to the mortgage, and because many owners of land are reluctant to lease land to someone who wants to put a huge mortgage over their legal position (due to the subordination), there is a natural reluctance to subordinate. Nonetheless, there are thousands of subordinated land leases in the United States and for the most part they are viable transactions, but not without risk.

Development on leased land requires the lessee to choose one or a combination of these three solutions: (1) use all cash with no lien; (2) obtain an insecured loan; (3) find a lender who will treat the leasehold as a fee simple. Taking the first solution, many builders do just that. They build with their own cash. It may be they have leased the land with options to purchase, and so they build without having to lay out the cash needed to buy the land. They pay the nominal rent during construction, and later, when the building is finished, obtain a mortgage, pay off the land by exercising an option to buy, and move on to another project. This is done in single-family housing where the builder can and does build the house quickly, and then sells it before many of the outstanding bills on it come due. In those cases, the overall cash outlay by the developer is not as great as if he had bought the land for cash.

An unsubordinated lease maintains the owner of the land in the first position. Any loans made subject to the lease are in a secondary position. To find a secondary loan to fund a major development on leased land without subordination is not impossible, but extremely difficult.

There are lenders, however, who approach the leasehold interest as being similar to fee simple. In some areas of the world, a long-term lease of such a time period as to be beyond the normal life span of the building planned, may be accepted as being the same as completed ownership. Each lender will have a different opinion on this topic, and each situation must look to the substance of the lease itself. When the cost of the land lease is not excessive, a lender will often be willing to lend behind the lease.

LEASEHOLD VERSUS FEE SIMPLE VALUES

Unlike the creation of a normal lease, whether it be land or buildings, the sale and lease-back is unique. The previous owner, or fee owner, becomes the leasehold owner. It is this change of ownership which makes the sale and lease-back both dangerous and quite often rewarding.

A lease is accompanied by a rent, and the value of the lease is based on the ability of the lessee to pay the rent or the security he offers to support that ability to pay the rent. If the tenant, or lessee, fails to pay the rent, and the security is not sufficient to support the economic base of the property until another lessee can be found, the lease may then become worthless. Of even more consequence, it may cost the lessor money to get the tenant out of the property.

If the building is a single-purpose structure and the tenant not very strong, then the ultimate ability to pay the lease and the long possible delay in finding another tenant could reflect on the value of the fee simple. An existing lease runs with the land, and a new buyer accepts the tenant on the remaining terms of the lease. The property may be worth $100,000, but if there is a 20-year lease at $3,000 per annum the value is not $100,000, due to the effect of the rent return. Also, if the rent were $10,000, but the tenant is always late with his payment, the value may not be substantiated.

ESTABLISHING THE LEASEHOLD VALUE

The terms and conditions of the lease establish the value of the leasehold. It is clear, for example, that two identical parking lots, side by side on leased land, will have values depending on the terms of the underlying land leases. The parking lot which has an annual rent of $1,000 will be of far more value as a leasehold than the one which has an annual rent of $2,000. In reverse, the owner of the lots will find the lease which returns $1,000 per year is less valuable than the one which returns $2,000 per year. What is shown here is the variable between value of the lease and value of the leasehold. It is important, then, to distinguish these two values in each sale and lease-back situation. The sale and lease-back creates both events: the leasehold and the fee owner, or the lease.

HOW TO DETERMINE WHEN THE LEASE-BACK
IS EFFECTIVE

The sale and lease-back is used in these situations:

1. When the use of the property has more value than owning the property.
2. To substantiate the value of the fee by creating a fixed return.
3. The need for capital makes the lease-back more economical than other forms of financing.

These three situations cover a lot of territory, and from a practical point of view, the latter two will be seen more often in real life. However, a quick look at the three gives some insight as to the use of the two aspects of this form: the value of the fee and the value of the leasehold.

WHEN THE VALUE OF THE USE EXCEEDS THE VALUE
OF OWNING

A case history illustrates this point. Kayser had a small restaurant. He owned the land and building free and clear. He wanted to start another restaurant across town, but found he did not have sufficient capital to do this. Naturally, he looked to the normal forms of financing to raise this capital, so he visited the local banks and savings and loans. Even though his past record was good, he found that new restaurants are not easily financed because they are costly to start up. He did find that he could obtain new financing, up to a point, but the balance must be cash out of his pocket. Kayser counseled with his broker and discovered he could approach an investor to buy his present restaurant to create the new capital. His options on a lease-back showed he could set up a sale and lease-back on the land, or the buildings, or both. The final decision would depend on capital needed, on the value of the property, and the rent he was able to pay.

The value of the land was $135,000. This was based on other similar properties in the area. The buildings had been appraised at a value of $200,000. The new restaurant Kayser was planning was expected to cost about $400,000.

Kayser was sure he could support an overall debt service of $35,000 to $45,000 in annual payments with ease, once the second restaurant was built and operating. At present, he was making a good living from the first restaurant by taking home around $90,000 per year. He expected to make the same, or more, from the second one.

If Kayser were able to sell his first restaurant for $300,000 and lease it back on a net-net lease (he has to pay all maintenance, taxes, insurance, etc., as well as the lease), he should easily be able to borrow the remainder on the new property to finish the construction and provide working capital.

The broker knew that an investor would be inclined to buy the first restaurant since it had a good track record, and Kayser would be, after all, leasing the property back at a good return to the investor. That return, by the way, is subject to good, hard negotiation. There are many factors on which to bargain in sale and lease-backs, and the buyer and seller can find much to negotiate on before the final transaction is signed and closed.

For Kayser, the value of owning has taken second place to the value of use of the property. As long as he has control of the restaurant, it may not make much difference if he owns or leases. His leasehold value becomes more apparent after he leases. In this case the lease-back was $30,000 per year, based on a sale at $300,000 as Kayser was netting $90,000 before the lease. The $60,000 he will net after the lease becomes the factor in establishing the economic value of the leasehold. As restaurants have a demand yield of about 15 to 20 percent, the leasehold value is from $300,000 to $400,000.

The investor has this leasehold value as additional collateral on the lease, as long as the business is good and Kayser can pay the rent.

HOW TO SUBSTANTIATE THE VALUE OF THE FEE BY CREATING A FIXED RETURN

In this event, Kayser might not want to build another restaurant at all. The fact of the matter could be that business is off, and for the past year the best he was able to take home was $40,000. In this situation, he may want to get cash out of the property for other reasons.

To substantiate the value of $300,000 on the sale, he agrees to lease the property back on a long-term lease. That pleases the investor, until the lease becomes worthless and Kayser goes off to another state to run a bar. Of course, the title to the bar is in his wife's name.

HOW TO USE THE SALE AND LEASE-BACK WHEN OTHER FORMS OF FINANCING ARE MORE COSTLY

If the money market will support your financial needs at reasonable rates through more conventional forms of mortgaging, there may be no need to look elsewhere. However, due to any number of circumstances, a reasonable or sufficient loan may not be available.

Specialty types of real estate fall into categories that many lenders will shy away from, or at best they'll quote high interest rates and low loan to value amounts. The combined effect of insufficient restructure of existing debt and high constant payments on the borrowed funds may put the borrower in deeper trouble than that in which he currently finds himself.

During this same time when the money market is tight, interest rates tough, and loans low or nonexistent, there may be a solution via the sale and lease-back. Your ability to determine the effectiveness of the sale and lease-back will require you to examine the effect the two forms available have on the situation.

For example: Lloyd has a used car lot. He makes a good living from this business, but finds he needs cash to expand his inventory. He has approached a local lender and has found he can borrow only 75 percent of what he needs by placing a first mortgage on the property. Besides the insufficient sum of money available, there is a high point cost and interest is set at 5 points above prime.

On the other hand, a sale and lease-back may produce 100 percent or more of the cash needed at an overall interest rate that is lower than that charged by the lender. As Lloyd needs the property and has substantial records to show he can support the rent, he may, out of necessity, move in the direction of the sale and lease-back to solve his problems. He recognized that his ability to earn money on the input of new capital is greater than the cost of the land lease. As long as he has a prudent lease-back from his long-term growth, he will make this move.

Of course, he will be forced to look to some other form of financing, or capital seeking, if he cannot raise the money in the conventional money market. However, Lloyd should seek conventional sources as possible alternatives to his problem, if for no other reason than as a comparison to the sale and lease-back.

There Is a Risk in the Lease-Back

There are valid reasons for the lease-back. But the risk involved, due to the value adjustments, requires buyers to be rather cautious of overstated values of the fee or of the *leasehold*.

It is possible for the seller to substantiate the value of the fee by creating the fixed return with a minimum of risk to the buyer. This can be accomplished with lease insurance. The insurance will cover the rent in default should the seller/tenant get into trouble. What could be a bad deal can become a "Triple A" transaction.

THE VALUE OF ALL LEASES DEPENDS ON THESE SIX FACTORS

1. *The lessee.* Who or what is he? What is his past record, financial backing, and motivation. Will he sign personally? If not, why?

2. *The use.* Has it been successful? Is the operation well run, managed, and staffed? Is there a future for the present use? Does the use present unusual hazards to the property? Does the use limit the function and flexibility of the property?

3. *Lease conditions.* The term of years—too long or too short? Who pays taxes, utilities, assessments, repairs, maintenance, and other property costs? Is there a provision for increasing the rent due to cost of living increases? What other provisions can affect the future return to the owner (options, provisions for cancellations, etc.)?

4. *The performance.* What is the record of the lessee in making his rent payments? In new leases, this is a big unknown and only time will tell.

5. *The property.* Is the economic life of the property beyond that of the term of the lease? If so, the fact that a new tenant must someday be found or the same tenant enticed to stay can cause a problem in the future. Is the location suitable for the present tenant? Is the tenant suffering because of the property or the location?

6. *Fee versus leasehold.* There must be a real value in both. The greater the value in the leasehold, the greater the security for the lessor. In the sale and lease-back, this apparent value in the leasehold should be carefully examined.

The value of the lease depends heavily on the use and the user. Artificial value can be generated in the leasehold by the lessee. This artificial value is, in essence, a burden to the property and results from pushing this form of financing.

THE NEED FOR CAPITAL

Need necessitates action, and a need for capital is generally the reason for the sale and lease-back. There are many more favorable forms of financing, if they can be obtained in the market. For example, there is no real reason why a seller who wants to use the property should take a sale and lease-back transaction, unless the economics of accepting another form are onerous or unavailable.

However, this does not make the sale and lease-back the last resort, and it should not be considered as a step down from something not available or economically unsound. It *can* be highly advantageous to the seller. If the seller cannot borrow the necessary funds and he needs the use of the property for economic reasons, then the sale and lease-back can solve these problems.

ADVANTAGES AND DISADVANTAGES
OF THE SALE AND LEASE-BACK

Here are the advantages and disadvantages as they apply to both the seller and the buyer:

The Seller

Advantages	*Disadvantages*
1. Allows the seller to retain use of the property.	1. Seller gives up many benefits of ownership of improvements and land.
2. Allows the seller to negotiate the amount of the rent by off-setting the sale price.	2. Future appreciation of land usually lost completely.
3. Often, the terms of the lease are more flexible in the lease-back.	3. Leasehold value has a shorter life than the property.
4. Can firm up the price and value.	4. A decline in leasehold value can be a total loss.
5. Gives flexibility to difficult transactions since the land and improvements can be separated.	
6. As the seller is the ultimate tenant, he has great strength in dealing on the lease-back.	
7. Can provide capital when all else fails.	

The Buyer

Advantages	*Disadvantages*
1. Can provide an excellent tenant.	1. Either the price or the rent will be to the seller's advantage; often both.
2. Offers some flexibility in price vs. rent negotiations.	2. Too hard a push on the seller may give you an investment without a tenant.
3. In the case of unsubordinated land: (a) low risk investment, (b) future recoupment of improvements, and (d) appreciation.	3. A lease-back by a nonuser may be a good sign that the income won't support the value.
4. If very carefully examined and secured, can offer an excellent investment potential.	4. May have to step into a large mortgage to protect his interest.

To these advantages and disadvantages you can apply most pro and con aspects of any lease. One thing is definite, however. The sale and lease-back is more complicated than it appears on the surface. It requires good, sound advice and consideration. A seller should never walk into the sale and lease-back unless there is absolute confidence that the transaction is beneficial to both parties. It is far too easy to boost the value with this form of financing and take advantage of some buyer, not aware of the potential danger. Be sure you understand the pros and cons of the lease-back before you establish that transaction.

This form of financing has a place in real estate. It is used in commercial realty and other forms of development, land planning, and, of course, industrial realty. Lenders find it an ideal tool for securing their position in large development loans. Here the lender may take a land lease under a project he is financing. In this way he participates in the overall project to the degree that he will always own the land. In many cases, the developer may buy the land back in the future at an escalated price. Since the lender may not be extending more funds than he would have on just the loan, he has a strong advantage over the seller.

Yet the seller may not fare too badly either, as he can cash out ahead of the project and still own the improvements. The cost of carrying the land and paying the portion of debt service that applies to the land lease will never retire any principal, and the ratio of constant to remaining balance will increase faster than in a mortgage without a land lease.

HOW TO SET UP THE SALE AND LEASE-BACK

When you are sure the sale and lease-back is the proper way to go, carefully examine the two values involved:

1. The fee simple
2. The leasehold value

There will be some flexibility in the adjustment of these two values. This adjustment may have tax-saving results. For example, if the seller has a low base it may be possible to set a price which is near that base, and reduce the rent the seller will pay in the lease-back to offset the reduced price. Remember, the lower the rent paid by the seller the higher the value of the leasehold. Naturally, you cannot reduce the price to a point that is below the market value just to save on taxes. However, there is usually ample room in which to work in order to provide some flexibility in these negotiations.

It may be in the seller's best interest to attempt to establish the lowest value on the sale to reduce gains tax. The rent paid later on the lower base can, over a few years, make up the reduced sales price. On the other hand, if the capital gained from the sale is not sufficient, then the higher price, even with the tax, may be more prudent. Because the sale and lease-back can justify a higher price, the spread in the low to high value will be greater than in a normal sale. This high value is said to be somewhat artificial and warranted only on the basis of the lease-back.

Negotiating a Lower Price

This occurs because the buyer recognizes that he is buying at a good price and can adjust his income accordingly. The buyer should realize that the lower the rent, the higher the value of the leasehold. The higher the value of the leasehold, the more security to the buyer.

A buyer will find that the maximum security he can have on a lease-back is the lease insurance. This type of insurance is obtained by the tenant and insures the lessor in the event the lessee fails to pay his rent. It is not easily obtained, however, and is not used too often in sale and lease-back situations. But if the buyer wants the utmost in security, then this type of insurance will provide it.

If only the land is being leased and there is no subordination, the risk to the buyer is limited. If the price for the land is realistic and not inflated, then the buyer has a sound investment. There would be little reason to consider insurance with this type of transaction. In limited subordination, where the lessee has the right to put on a mortgage of limited proportions, the buyer will find his security waning. The amount of the mortgage, a percentage to the value of the property, will establish the value of the security. Should the lease-back carry full surbordination, the risk to the buyer will be predicated on: (1) the success of the property, and (2) the ability of the lessee to pay the rent.

The buyer should realize that in the sale and lease-back the lessee may have made a profit, but may have no actual equity in the property or the leasehold. In this event, the loss to the lessee in a failure to perform on the lease may be small.

We have seen two values. The feel simple and the leasehold. In fact, there may be three values. The third being the value of the business itself. A retail shop, for example, may have a business value not dependent on the exact location or improvements. If the lessee can move his business with ease and retain its value, the security to the buyer is reduced unless he ties the lessee into the lease more stringently.

The ability of the seller-tenant to move the business does not in itself reduce the buyer's security, however; unless the improvements are single purpose and the new owner were to find it difficult to rerent the space should the lease-back tenant fail on his lease for some reason. The best security for the buyer in the sale and lease-back will always be *extreme caution.*

SALE AND LEASE-BACK HIGHLIGHTS

What it will do:	1. Generate cash. 2. Provide terms on a lease to suit the lessee.
When to use it:	1. When value of use exceeds value of ownership. 2. To substantiate value of fee. 3. When borrowing to raise capital is not economically effective or available.
What to look for:	1. Seller who has successful use of property. 2. A use that is potentially successful, but may need either time or capital or both.
Negotiating points:	1. Term of lease. 2. Sale price. 3. Other options, such as: (a) subordination, (b) recapture of ownership, (c) subdivision of property to separate lease (land or improvements).
Danger to seller:	1. Gives up advantges of ownership. 2. Loses future appreciation of property.

Chapter 12

HOW TO BENEFIT FROM THE REAL ESTATE EXCHANGE

Internal Revenue Code 1031 provides that under specific circumstances a real estate transaction may be closed whereby a capital gain will not be taxable at the time of the closing. In fact, if the deal is handled properly any tax on the gain can be postponed indefinitely.

This indefinite postponement of tax on a gain, gives this kind of transaction the mistaken name *the tax-free exchange*. It is important that you understand that the IRC 1031 provisions can have that end effect if all elements of the transaction are established with that goal. But to be fully free of a tax, it is necessary for the owner to die while he or she stills owns the property.

Later on in this chapter, I will discuss the specifics of the 1031 provisions. For the moment, just keep in mind that this tax-free exchange is a viable tool for many investors to use. It is one of the very best methods of moving equity and building wealth.

However, exchanges are complicated and to use them properly will require care and study on the part of any buyer or seller who finds that his or her benefits are desirable for the situation at hand.

First let's set the record straight. Not all exchanges you may consider or in fact accomplish will qualify for the 1031 provision. For some exchanges that would qualify, it may not be advantageous for you to use the 1031 provision either. It is all a matter of understanding the bottom line and the future you have in mind for that asset, the new asset, or your investment portfolio.

For example: If you have very little or no gain at all in the property you want to dispose of, a 1031 provision has little or no effect on your transaction from your point of view. On the other hand, the other side of the deal may find the 1031 provision of postponing tax on a gain to be absolutely critical to the transaction. In fact, it is so critical that without that benefit there would be no reason to make the deal at all.

In any exchange, you will find that the motives and goals of the two parties can differ. In addition, as exchanges often have more than two parties in the deal, the motives of three or more owners can be very different indeed.

You should look to your goals first as always, and attempt to make the kind of transaction that works best for your situation. Any give and take in the format of the deal becomes negotiation that should be counterbalanced by some other element of the deal.

If you can save money through postponing the tax, then you are ahead of the game by that amount. If you can entice a reluctant seller into a transaction by showing him how he can save money through the 1031 provision, you may make a deal that would escape you otherwise.

A QUICK REVIEW OF WHAT EXCHANGES DO

Because of the nature of exchanges, there will be at least two property owners who are affected. Keep in mind too that as exchanges are generally transacted through brokers there may also be two or more brokers in the transaction.

It is important that you pay close attention to the four key benefits that are the mainstay of exchanges. I will expand on these benefits and get into the fine points, as well as some creative twists to this fine tool later in this chapter.

WHAT EXCHANGES DO

Exchanges usually affect three or four parties—the owners of at least two properties and the broker(s) (although there are rare instances in which two owners exchange properties without broker involvement). Therefore, the results of the exchange itself can be seen from two points of view. It is important that both points of view be analyzed briefly, as this will help establish the proper attitude toward the exchanges attempted.

WHAT THE EXCHANGE CAN DO FOR THE PROPERTY OWNER: FOUR KEY BENEFITS

Any exchange situation should be approached with a simple question: "Will the exchange solve, or move you closer to a solution of, the problem at hand?"

To be able to answer this question, you must have a clear understanding of the problem. It is crucial to know where you want to go when it comes to exchanges. If the answer to the question stated above is "No, it does not solve my problem or move me closer to a solution," then, obviously, the exchange should not be attempted.

Here are the four key ways in which exchanging can benefit property owners:

1. Tax-free benefit. Under the tax changes of 1986, capital gains tax calculations that existed prior to the change were eliminated. As of 1987, the exclusions allowed to reduce the taxable portion of a "capital gain" were removed, and all gain is to be reported as "earned" income. The 1031 provision allows the base to be transferred and thus remove a taxable gain in many circumstances. The present tax laws allow exchanges of like property, to avoid the payment of income tax at the time the transfer takes place. This has been referred to as "tax-free benefit," but this is really a misnomer. The tax is merely *deferred* until ultimate sale of the received property. Should the device of exchange be utilized time after time, the tax on the gain continues to be put off until a final sale. Upon death, of course, other taxes come into play. New tax laws for estates carry forward the old basis, which will have an effect on the later sale. Nonetheless, the tax-law benefit has many applications and is one of the major reasons for exchanges. The law provides for the transfer of basis from the old property to the new property. Some tax may be due at the time of the transfer, but this will depend on a number of factors and will be covered later in this chapter in the discussion on the method of transferring the basis.

An exchange will be considered to be "tax free" when two or more properties are exchanged that are like property. The term "like property" has caused much consternation in real estate circles. Like property is the intent of use more than the physical characteristic. So, to be specific: *like property is any real interest that is held for use in a trade or business or held as an investment and was not acquired for resale.*

To simplify this definition, any property which is owned by a non-dealer can be exchanged for any other kind of property to be used in the same category as the old property. For example, Roland owns several vacant lots which he used for outdoor storage of his equipment. There is no question that an exchange of one of these lots for another lot (to be used for storage) in another town would meet the like for like portion of the law.

Another lot, however, also owned by Roland, has not been used for several years. He did not sell it because he decided it would be a good investment and would increase in value in the future. He exchanges this lot for an apartment building. Because the apartment building can be construed as an investment, the exchange will meet the like property test.

There have been countless combinations of exchange in realty. In every instance, the like property test must be met for the exchange to have the deferment of tax at the time of the transfer. It is important for you to realize that this test need not be met by both parties, nor does it have to be met at all for an exchange to be beneficial. The advantage to the exchange, from a tax angle, will depend greatly on the situation and the individuals.

2. Increased depreciation. Because investment and business property can be depreciated, there are times when exchanging is used with the primary reason being to increase the amount of depreciation the owner is currently obtaining. This advantage is available because of the tax deferment ability, but has special significance to many transactions. The value of the depreciation itself may be taken into consideration if the client needs a tax loss.

For example: Keaster owns 100 acres of land and an old farm building which he has been leasing out along with the land. His base in the entire property is $45,000, since he paid $60,000 nearly ten years earlier and depreciated the building to nearly zero. The value is $250,000 and he has a small $15,000 mortgage balance. Keaster exchanges his equity for a large apartment house worth $900,000 and having a first mortgage of $650,000. Keaster's new base is increased by cash paid plus the difference between the two mortgages. The subsequent depreciation will then be calculated on that base, less an allocation for the land.

What would have happened if Keaster had sold the farm and then bought the apartment house? Look at the two examples of this case study: (1) the exchange as it actually took place; and (2) the results from a sale and later purchase of the apartment house (Figure 1). The amounts shown are net sums, and brokers' fees are not shown at this time.

In comparing the two situations, you will see several important tax consequences. From the depreciation point of view, the new annual depreciation of $22,240 amounts to 148 percent of the cash paid ($15,000). The sale followed by the purchase of the apartment complex required

TABLE 12-1

THE EXCHANGE			A SALE AND THEN A PURCHASE		

THE EXCHANGE

Current
Depreciation:	$	0
Current Equity:		$235,000
Existing Mortgages:		$ 15,000
Net Market Value:		$250,000

Exchange Equity of $235,000 for
Apartment house (shown below):
Net Market Value:	$900,000
Existing Mortgages:	$650,000
Equity (Apt.):	$250,000
Less Equity (Farm):	
Cash to Pay:	$235,000
	$ 15,000

ADJUSTMENT FOR NEW BASE

Old Base in Farm:	$ 45,000
Less Mortgage Amount on Farm:	$ 15,000
Plus New Mortgage on Apt. Bldg.:	+$650,000
Plus Cash Paid at Closing:	+$ 15,000
New Base:	$695,000

Ratio of value: Land vs. Bldg.
(20% Land vs. 80% Bldg.)
New Base:	$695,000
Land:	$139,000
Building:	$556,000

AVERAGE RATE (ESTIMATED) DEPRECIATION

Straight line 25 years:	$ 36,579
Cash Paid in Transaction:	$ 15,000
Equity in Apt. Bldg.:	$250,000

A SALE AND THEN A PURCHASE

Current
Depreciation	$ 0
Current Equity:	$235,000
Existing Mortgages:	$ 15,000
Net Market Value:	$250,000

Assume a sale at this price:
Calculate Tax due at the close of
the transaction.
Sales Price	$250,000
Less Base:	$ 45,000
Gain:	$205,000

(Estimated gains tax based on a
35% maximum rate.)
Tax:	$ 71,750

Total Proceeds from Closing:
Cash Received by Seller:	$235,000
Less Capital Gains Tax:	$ 71,750
Net Cash to Seller:	$163,250

SELLERS NOW WANT TO BUY THE APT. HOUSE

Price of Apt. House:	$900,000
Less Total Mtg.:	$650,000
Cash Required:	$250,000
Cash from Sale of Farm:	$163,250
Additional Cash Needed:	$ 86,750
NEW BASE:	$900,000
Depreciation Base $900,000 × 80% =	$720,000

AVERAGE RATE OF DEPRECIATION

Straight line 25 years:	$ 47,368
Cash Paid in Transaction:	$ 86,750
Equity in Apt. Bldg.:	$250,000

$86,750 cash, and generates $28,800 of new annual depreciation or 33 percent ratio depreciation to cash.

The cash required to end up with the same property differs greatly, the reason being the tax which must be paid in the sale. Keaster had no tax to pay at the time of the exchange, so his adjustments in arriving at new basis did not reflect the addition of taxable gain.

3. *Expansion of the market.* If you have a property which is difficult to move for one reason or another, then exchanging may provide an increased market. The key to this is to determine what you plan to do with the proceeds of the sale. If you intend to reinvest the money, or a major portion of it, in more real estate, then the exchange will not only be the extension of the market, but a tax saver as well. There are many dealers in the exchange market who will take property in trade just to make a move. These people are generally brokers or associates that have taken property from previous exchanges as a part of their fee. This "fee property" becomes barter for these brokers, and exchanges within this area are more on the "I'd-rather-have-that-than-what-I've-got" basis.

The expansion of a market is most important. There are many investors locked into large capital gains who cannot sell their investments without having to pay the tax. These investors will look for exchanges to move their equity or to increase depreciation. It is not important at this point that you may not want what they have. Often, their property is highly marketable for cash—*they* just can't sell. But you can make the trade and then *you* can sell their property.

4. *Cash-out.* This occurs when the owner of a difficult-to-sell-or-finance property exchanges it for another property that is easy to sell or finance. Cash, not the property received in the exchange, is the motivation and the benefit. Ruth owns a vacant lot, the value of which is $100,000. Ruth needs cash, but cannot sell or finance the vacant property. So, she exchanges it for a free and clear home. The home is easily financed, and once she has raised $70,000 on it she puts it on the market at $85,000. The $15,000 down payment and reduced price is apt to produce a buyer, whereas the same reduction on the lot would not.

For a cash-out, the easiest property to exchange is a free and clear home up to $150,000. This home becomes prime cash-out potential for exchangers.

Investing in real estate is best done with some sort of plan. The desire to start here and end there may require more than one step or move. Exchanging should be considered as a part of the steps in a dance. Or would you prefer to sit this one out?

Six Reasons People Avoid Real-Estate Exchanges

1. *Because they don't understand them.* It is human nature to avoid something you don't understand. But remember this about your "comfort zone"—it works both for you and against you. As a real-estate investor, you must strive to expand all those areas that can increase your profit potential, and one such area is that of real-estate exchanges. When you know the techniques of this kind of investing, you no longer can use this excuse. But in dealing with people ignorant of exchanges, you will have to go slowly to avoid giving the "sharpie" look to what you are doing.

   2. Because they believe that one party to an exchange gets the raw end of the deal.   I won't say this doesn't happen from time to time, but it can happen in anything you do. How many sellers feel they got the most they could? How many buyers feel they paid the lowest price possible? The client of mine who tells me that he will make one offer and it will be a take-it-or-leave-it would be most chagrined if the seller said, "Okay, I'll take it." That buyer would forever wonder if he hadn't offered too much.

   The more you know about exchanges, the more you will realize that for some people the exchange is more beneficial than a sale. In fact, some sellers will accept in an exchange a property they would not have purchased (given a wide selection and the cash to make the purchase), because the exchange was offered to them and the cash was not.

   Your use of exchanges will show you that both sides of the exchange can and most often do come out smelling like a rose. The biggest proof of this is that most exchanges occur between members of the real-estate profession—brokers and salesmen exchanging real estate in their own portfolios with other brokers and salesmen. These exchangers form clubs and networks where they deal with one another. The slipshod or shifty dealer is quickly recognized and is "dealt" out.

   3. Because they believe that people who exchange set two prices: one for exchange and a real one for cash (which is much lower).   Now this point is often true and is to me one of the drawbacks of the exchange side of investing, unless you know how to deal with it. The basic reason for setting prices this way is that most people don't understand that since exchanges can save you tax money, the exchange should be at a lower value than what the sale would have to be to end up at par after paying the tax. After all, I'd rather have a $40,000 lot in exchange (if I wanted the lot) than $45,000 in cash with a $90,000 tax to pay. Other people set higher prices on exchanges than on cash sales out of defense. Personally, I like to quote one price and then stick to it like glue to glue. However, you can easily counter the double standard of pricing by never asking someone the value of the exchange, but, instead, always asking what the price is for sale. Work from that evaluation every time.

   4. Because they believe that if you are going to exchange, you must end up with exactly what you want.   This is downright silly. You don't end up with exactly the cash you want when you sell. If you truly understand your goals, you will have an easier time with this negative view of exchanges. A clear view of your end goal will enable you to see when the exchange is taking you closer to that goal. You do not need to make the jump from San Francisco to New York in one exchange. Not mind you that such an exchange isn't possible, only that you are far more likely to get to New York if you take Phoenix, then St. Louis, then Washington, D.C., on your way to New York. When it comes to real-estate exchanges, you have to be willing to give up something that is not doing for you what it should, or what you need to progress toward your goal, in exchange for something that will. Remember: *any exchange that moves you closer to your goal is a good exchange.*

5. Because they can't accept the thought of taking something they don't want at all as an intermediate step.   This is often very difficult to explain, though it appears simple enough. The professional exchanger will frequently take a client through a multileg exchange to end up with a beneficial exchange. For example, if I want to acquire a duplex, I might offer the owner of the duplex cash (which I'll get from refinancing the duplex) and some vacant land out of my Armadello Ranch near Naples, Florida. If the duplex owner doesn't want my vacant land, the deal could die right there. But it probably won't if I explain (and I will) that he doesn't have to keep the vacant land—that we can exchange it for something he does want or is willing to take if he will allow me the time for the extra legwork.

If he agrees to allow the deal to be tied together (binding us both to the exchange if I can dispose of the vacant land for him by bringing in something he will take), then I can work out the rest of the deal. He might say he would take a vacant lot, but only if it were in the Florida Keys. I might find a lot he would take, but that owner doesn't want the vacant land in Naples, Florida. I keep going until I find someone who will fit the slot and make the whole jigsaw go together.

I'm not sure what the world record is of legs to an exchange, but I know of one that had over 25 different steps before it was finally put together. Patience and a determined broker are essential to exchanges.

6. Because people believe you have to own something to make an exchange.   The answer to this is simply that you can exchange property you don't even own. How?

REAL-ESTATE EXCHANGES ARE PRIME OPTIONS FOR BUYERS OR SELLERS

The fortunate thing about real-estate exchanges is that you will have the opportunity to use them as both a buyer and a seller. Your ultimate benefit, of course, is not to be a buyer or seller when using exchanges but to be an exchanger.

As a Buying Tool

When you learn the motivation of the seller, you often realize that the exchange might be your way to do one or both of the following things:

1. *Get rid of something you don't want to keep.* If the seller of what you want is highly motivated, he is apt to be willing to take as part or all of this equity something you have in exchange.

2. *Motivate the seller because of tax benefits.* The seller hanging on the fence might be motivated by the tax savings you can show him through the exchange you are offering.

As a Selling Tool

As a seller, there will be times when you have to dig deep down to the bottom of your soul and come up with some powerful tricks. After all, not all real estate will sell itself; sometimes you have to find a "taker" for your property, as that is often the start of a deal.

Offering your property, or part of your equity, for an exchange will b9oaden your market. There are buyers out there trying to find what you have, only they don't have money. Try to show them how to make a cashless deal that will solve your needs.

In finding "takers" for your property, you generate additional options for yourself. When someone says to me, "I'll take your property and assume the new mortgage I can put on it (giving you 80 percent cash) if you take this lot for your remaining equity," I now have cash and a piece of land, which I can keep, exchange, or offer out on the same basis (I'll hold the mortgage and take something for 20 percent of the lot's equity).

I've made million-dollar exchanges in which only a small portion of the transaction was property taken in exchange while the majority of the deal was cash and mortgage. One such exchange arose out of my desire to sell a large tract of oceanfront land I controlled in the Vero Beach area. My marketing program simply didn't produce a buyer, no matter what I did. Then I decided to open the property up for exchange. The exchange was neither the most desirable nor the most practical thing to do because of the nature of my partners in the ownership of the property. Nonetheless, I knew finding a "taker" was essential.

Shortly after placing the land on exchange, the offers began to come in. A large villa in Spain, an orange grove in Florida, other proposals that didn't get to the writing stage. Then an offer to take some vacant land, free and clear of mortgages, for the equity in the oceanfront land. This offer came from a highly qualified "buyer" who thought of himself as an exchanger. Through heavy and long negotiations over four months (nothing else was happening on the property anyway), the deal was concluded. The exchanger saved face by giving up some vacant land, and we got cash and mortgage for the balance. What started out as an exchange with no cash ended up as a lot of cash and very little exchange.

When you find a taker for your property, you have the choice of moving on your own property or moving off the exchange property. For example, if I offered you a small duplex as part of a deal to buy your motel, you might say: "I'll take the deal if I can find a buyer or other exchange for your duplex, as I don't want it."

If I'm motivated to take your motel, I'll sit still for a while and let you go in two directions. I can't stop you from making a deal without me if someone else comes along to buy or exchange for your property. I'm at the mercy of your intent to try to move off my duplex onto something else. I can, of course, try to find a buyer to take the duplex out of the picture and give you cash.

All sellers should investigate their opportunities and examine the value of an exchange. Even the seller who says "I can't exchange, because I need cash" might find that there are no buyers for what he has to sell and that his only way out is to exchange for something that is sellable.

THE MECHANICS OF MAKING EXCHANGES

There are several essential mechanical aspects of making exchanges. The first is the *balance of equities.* The others relate to *presentation* and the *maximizing of gains.*

Balancing Equities in Exchanges

All exchanges must have a balance of equities. There are three ways to achieve this balance.

The cash balance. Assume that you own a duplex worth $75,000 and owe $50,000 in a first mortgage against it, so your equity is $25,000. You want to exchange for Peter's apartment building, worth (to you) $200,000. Peter has a first mortgage of $130,000 on the building, giving him an equity of $70,000. You want to make the exchange and will balance the equities with cash, as shown in Table 12-2.

In balancing equities with a mortgage, you add an additional mortgage to the property you are to take. In this case, you give Peter a $45,000 mortgage against the property you are taking from him, or some other property you already own.

TABLE 12-2 CASH BALANCE OF EQUITIES

	(You)	(Peter)
Property given up	$75,000	$200,000
Less outstanding mortgages	− 50,000	− 130,000
Equity	25,000	70,000
Cash balance—who gives cash	45,000	0
Balance of equities	70,000	70,000

The mortgage balance. If you don't have enough cash to balance the equities, you might try a mortgage balance, as shown in Table 12-3.

TABLE 12-3 MORTGAGE BALANCE OF EQUITY

	(You)	(Peter)
Property given up	$75,000	$200,000
Less outstanding mortgages	− 50,000	− 130,000
Equity	25,000	70,000
New mortgage owed to		(45,000)
Balance of equities	25,000	25,000

The combination balance. In the combination, you might give Peter $10,000 in cash and $35,000 in the form of a mortgage. Or you would augment your equity by adding other properties. Nothing will keep you from offering Peter the duplex, a gold watch, and seven partridges in a pear tree in addition to some cash and a mortgage.

Presentation

The key to all exchanges is the presentation to the other party. Does this sound familiar? It should, because so much of your success in real-estate investing depends on the tone set at the time the original offer is presented, and how well the pressure of the deal is both maintained and accepted.

If you are dealing with a real-estate broker who has not dealt in exchanges, you are apt to have some problems from the very start. For the same reason, however, it is very difficult for you to make your own exchanges. So your first step is to acquaint yourself with someone knowledgeable in exchanges in your area. I'd suggest a call to the local board of realtors, or a look in a newspaper for a real-estate-exchange column, or just calling several brokers and asking them whom they would recommend you talk to. Since having the best representation won't cost you any more commission than the worst—and the worst can be more expensive in the long run—try to find the best *in your area*. I stress this last part because finding a great buy 1,000 miles away won't do you a dime's worth of good.

In the presentation of any offer, there are seven things that should be avoided.

1. Never ask the other party what the exchange value is of their property. You only want to know the sale value.

2. Never presume the other party will turn down anything. Only soothsayers are good at presumption, and even so, look where they are.

3. Avoid too much talk. Simply say, "I want to buy your property, Mr. Seller, and I'll give you five acres of pine woods and ten thousand dollars as my deal." Sounds much better this way and won't upset a never-before exchanger.

4. Never present an offer without documentation for the other property in the exchange. Have some backup package on what you are offering, too. If you let your broker go off without a package, you will lose the edge.

5. Be persistent with your offers. Make them until you are blue in the face, but don't be too conciliatory too quickly. "Look, Mr. Seller, I'm very interested in your property and will keep coming back to you if I can think of something to make this deal work." No genuine seller will want to turn you down too flatly, as you are demonstrating that you are a taker—and you might come up with something.

6. Never be too set on what you will do. Exchanges are a new, wide-open game for many people. You might be turned on by an offer for an around-the-world cruise on the QE2 as part of a deal, and who in the world would have thought of that? Options that are opening up to you will be exciting. Live with them for a while.

7. Never close doors too hard. It is all right to ease them closed: "I'll say no to this, as it doesn't solve my problem, but I do appreciate your interest and I hope we can work something out."

The Benefits of the 1031 Exchange

The IRS Code 1031 says that if you make a like-for-like exchange, you don't have to pay the gains tax at the time of the exchange. This is true as long as you have done everything properly, have not received any boot, nor had net mortgage relief. Let me explain. "Like for like" simply means "investment for investment." You can't exchange part of your inventory as a builder for an investment, or part of your parking lot for an investment, and have a 1031 exchange. Investment for investment is the major thing for you to remember.

"Gain" on property is the sum of everything you get in a sale (or exchange) less your adjusted cost. Your gain, or profit, is thus the price you get less the price you paid, after the latter has been adjusted for depreciation or improvements.

The basis is like book value. When you buy a property, it has a value. You can add to the value by building something on the property. You can take away from it by certain deductions, such as removing part of the improvements, or depreciating the assets over the years as allowed by the IRS.

In the tax law revision of 1986 the depreciation rules were revised drastically to reduce real estate as a major tax shelter for investors. The law also revised the calculations for adjustment of basis. In essence, when you depreciate a property you artificially reduce its value, and reduce the basis accordingly. In reality, of course, depreciation has little effect on actual value. The IRS allows depreciation to be treated as an actual expense (even though n˙ money was spent) and, as such, in the year-end tax accounting it will reduce actual earnings or profits. As earnings are automatically reduced each year, you pay tax not on actual earnings but the reduced amount.

Real estate losses are generally passive losses and will offset only passive income. An exception would be an investor who owns, say, 10 percent or more of real estate investments and who actively manages that property. He or she could then apply a passive loss against $25,000 of active income. Continually review the IRS revisions as more changes in the treatment of real estate are anticipated.

For example, if I earn $100,000 this year, but I have depreciation of $100,000 from my real estate, my taxable earnings are zero. Of course, in this example, I actually received $100,000 in earnings and I actually didn't spend the depreciation of $100,000, but as far as the IRS is concerned I did, so I won't have to pay any tax.

Along with the new depreciation schedules, there has been a change in the accelerated-depreciation rules. In short, now if you take any form of depreciation faster than straight line (25 years at straight line would be 1/25 each year, or 4 percent of the present value less salvage value each year), that depreciation cannot be used to create capital gain, and the gain equal to the overage will be ordinary gain.

This means that if you had a building worth $250,000 and a $20,000 lot cost and depreciated that building on the straight line over the 25 years allowed, you would have $10,000 of depreciation each year. At the end of five years, your adjusted basis would be $175,000 plus the lot cost of $20,000, or a total basis of $195,000.

If you sold the building and lot for a total price of $295,000, you would have a gain of $100,000 and it would be taxable as income.

Sales price:	$295,000
Adjusted basis:	195,000
Long term capital gain	$100,000

"Boot" is the part of the exchange that will be taxable even in the best-set-up 1031 exchange. Boot is anything other than real estate. If you get $10,000, it is boot. If you get a gold watch, it is boot. A car, boat, airplane, diamond ring—all are boot and are taxable. You can qualify for a 1031 with receipt of boot, but you will still be taxed on the boot portion.

Net mortgage relief is something else to look for. When you exchange one property for another and they are both free and clear of any mortgages throughout the exchange, there is no mortgage relief in that there are no mortgages given up. However, when you deal with properties encumbered with mortgages, you need to look for the situation referred to as "net mortgage relief."

Assume you have a property worth $100,000, and you owe $55,000 against it. If you exchange for a property worth $45,000, making an even swap—your equity for theirs—you will be relieved of $55,000 of mortgage obligation. You now own a $45,000 property without mortgages. You have had an exchange without any boot, but you have a recognized gain of $55,000 (the amount of the mortgage). You will have a taxable exchange if the mortgage relief is greater than your realized gain by the amount of the mortgage relief. If there is any gain at all, and you have net mortgage relief, you will have some tax in this exchange.

The reason for this should be simple to understand. Assume for a moment that today you own the same $100,000 property and it is free and clear. You go down to the local savings-and-loan and borrow $55,000 in cash, which you put into your pocket tax-free. A day later you make the exchange shown above, getting a free-and-clear $45,000 property. As you now have net mortgage relief, you may have a tax because you have already received the $55,000 cash without paying any tax on that revenue.

Calculating the Taxable Gain in Exchanges

Smyth and Greenbalm are our two owners. Smyth owns 100 acres of land. Its value is $200,000. He owns this land free and clear of any mortgages and his basis is the $100,000 he paid for the property. The other $100,000 in value is appreciation over 12 years of ownership. Greenbalm owns a 15-unit apartment house. Its value is also $200,000, and it, too, is free and clear. Greenbalm's basis is $140,000 (he paid $180,000 but has taken $40,000 in depreciation). Smyth and Greenbalm make a trade with no cash paid between them and no mortgages swapped or assumed. It is an even-steven exchange.

In the second exchange, the two parties are Jones and Blackburn.

Jones owns 100 acres of land valued at $200,000 with a first mortgage of $50,000. Jones's basis is $100,000. Blackburn owns a 15-unit apartment house valued at $300,000. His basis in the apartment house is $125,000 and he owes $200,000. Jones has an equity of $150,000, while Blackburn has a $100,000 equity. In order to make the exchange, Blackburn must balance his equity with Jones's. He will do so with a $50,000 cash payment to Jones.

Table 10-4 show the tax calculations in these two exchanges. In examining this table, you will notice that in the Smyth-Greenbalm exchange there will be no resulting tax, as the recognized gain for both Smyth and Greenbalm was zero. But look what happened to Jones and Blackburn.

You can use the numbers of your own exchange in place of those shown in Table 10-4 to see just where you will stand in the case of a potential tax. The tax, of course, will be calculated on the taxable-gain

TABLE 12-4 CALCULATIONS OF TAXABLE GAIN IN EXCHANGES

	Jones	Blackburn	Smythe	Greenbalm
Value of Property Received	$300,000	$200,000	$200,000	$200,000
ADD Cash Received	50,000	0	0	0
Other Boot Received	0	0	0	0
Mortgage Relief	50,000	200,000	0	0
SUBTOTAL	$400,000	$400,000	$200,000	$200,000
SUBTRACT Basis at Time of Exchange	$100,000	$125,000	$100,000	$140,000
Amount of Mortgage Assumed	200,000	50,000	0	0
Amount of Cash Paid	0	50,000	0	0
Amount of Other Boot Given	0	0	0	0
GAIN REALIZED	$100,000	$175,000	$100,000	$ 60,000

TABLE 12-4   (CONT.)

	Jones	Blackburn	Smythe	Greenbalm
TO COMPUTE THE TAXABLE GAIN:				
(1) Total Mortgages Relieved	$ 50,000	$200,000	$ 0	$ 0
(2) Less Total Mortgages Assumed	200,000	50,000	0	0
(If [2] is greater than [1] put 0 Amount)	0	$150,000	$ 0	$ 0
Less cash paid	0	50,000	0	0
Subtotal	$ 0	$100,000	$ 0	$ 0
Plus Other Noncash Boot Received	0	0	0	0
Plus Cash Received	50,000	0	0	0
RECOGNIZED GAIN	$ 50,000	$100,000	$ 0	$ 0
Taxable Gain is the lower of Gain Realized or Recognized Gain. Note below calculation shows the Gain which is not taxed by virtue of the exchange.				
GAIN REALIZED	$100,000	$175,000	$100,000	$ 60,000
Less Taxable Gain (Recognized)	50,000	100,000	0	0
GAIN SAVED:	$ 50,000	$ 75,000	$100,000	$ 60,000

portion by using the current capital-gains calculations. As these are apt to change from year to year, consult your tax accountant for the current method. Under the old 1981 and new tax laws, the maximum capital-gains tax is 20 percent of the gain. Yours, however, may be less than that. The taxable gain is to be added to your income and your total adjusted income applied to the tax tables for your year.

GETTING INTO EXCHANGES

The only way to get into exchanges is to make exchange offers. You don't make exchanges by sitting on your rear waiting for someone to come around and ask you if you want to exchange. The best way, I believe, is to find an exchange-minded salesman and then go through a learning process with him or her. All investors who expect to make profits over a long haul, and to reduce or eliminate as much risk as possible, will be continually learning. I know that I feel slighted if I don't learn something every week I am in business. Fortunately, I never feel slighted, as I usually learn something every day. All that learning doesn't always keep me out of trouble, but it sure keeps me from being bored.

THE PITFALLS OF EXCHANGES

Frustration is the enemy of the exchanger. There is a lot you can get frustrated about when it comes to exchanges. You will be dealing with people who think you are out to take them—or, at best, will pretend they don't understand anything. You will have to deal with double-pricing situations, with hotshot salesmen who will tell you that a five-story building is a seven-story high-rise. You will get turned on only to find that what was described as a beautiful home by the sea just washed out at high tide.

But, as Elbert Hubbard once said, "There is no failure except in no longer trying." When it comes to exchanges, you have to keep trying. Your day and the right deal will come along.

From an economic point of view, you need to watch your tax laws and your own tax situation when it comes to the exchange at hand. It is possible that you will be better off making a sale and then purchasing, accepting the tax liability in that year, rather than allowing your old basis to carry over to the new property. You see, if your old basis in that $200,000 property is only $25,000 you would have a $175,000 gain in that year. Even with a 20 percent maximum tax on capital gains, you would have a $35,000 tax to pay. However, if you also had a major loss in the same year—say $175,000 worth—you might prefer a sale in which your losses would offset the gain. You could then step up your basis in a new property, beginning fresh rather than passing along a $200,000 value with only $25,000 of basis.

My suggestion is that you don't try to be an expert on tax ramifications (unless that is your business of course) and that you hire the services of a professional in tax law and taxes.

When you find a seller who will approach an exchange as a beneficial move on his or her part, or a seller who will take an exchange as a part of the deal, you are on your way to building equity for yourself prior to the deal and making a cashless transaction. You can do this *even if you don't own the property you are going to exchange.* In fact, you can make more exchanges at greater profit if you don't own the property in the first place.

What you are going to do is this: Find out what the seller wants or will take in the form of other property; then go out and locate something that is similar to or exactly meets that requirement and borrow it for a while until you make the deal.

Let's say you are interested in buying a small office building you have located in your town. The property is offered at $300,000 and has an existing first mortgage of $110,000 and second mortgage of $55,000. You know you can refinance the building, generating around $210,000 net after mortgage costs.

The seller started the negotiations saying he wanted all cash to the existing financing, but in end game agreed to take a minimum of $100,000 cash and hold some paper. The seller confided to you (or your agent) that he needed the cash to buy some vacant land on which to build some apartment buildings.

Armed with this knowledge, you now see a possibility of finding some apartment land and making an exchange. You search around for a few days and find a tract of land that is zoned for business and commercial use, but can also be used for apartment sites. The property has not sold as a business site because it is a poor site for that kind of use, but it's ideal for apartment construction. The property owner will sell the land for $75,000 on easy terms.

The fact that the land is not labeled "apartment property" (it's zoned for business) causes many investors to forget that labels in real estate mean very little. It is what you can do with the land that is important, not the specific category of the zoning. Most zoning (get to know yours) comes in grades: business, industrial, commercial, residential, etc., in varying orders of classification. In many parts of the world the building regulations permit a "down use": for example, the right to build apartments on a business-zoned property, but not the right to build a business on apartment land.

Okay, you have an owner of some vacant business land who can't sell it, but wants to sell it. You then offer him a "soft deal" that ties up the land so you can make your exchange on the small office building you wanted in the first place.

You set this up by telling the owner of the land that you will buy the land giving him $5,000 down and a $70,000 second mortgage on the office building across town. You tell the owner that you are about to refinance the office building and it will have a new first mortgage of $215,000. You set the interest on the second mortgage lower than the market rate because the seller of the vacant land would rather have some cash coming in than keep the cash-eating land.

You now go back to the seller of the small office building and tell him that you will do the following:

1. Give him $25,000 cash.
2. Take over his existing financing—subject to your obtaining the new financing mentioned.
3. Give him the apartment land (which can also be used for commercial and business use as a bonus). The value of this land you peg at $100,000.
4. Give him a personal note signed by you in the amount of $100,000.

If he accepts this, you will then apply for the loan you want of $215,000, which, less $5,000 in loan costs, will net you $210,000. You will use this to pay off the existing mortgages on the small office building, a total of $165,000 (a first of $110,000 and a second of $55,000). This will leave you with $45,000.

But wait, you have to pay the seller of the land $5,000, so that also comes out of the $45,000, leaving you with $40,000. You then take another $25,000 from that and give it to the office-building owner. You end up owning the small office building and have $15,000 left over for fix-up— or for further negotiations if this deal didn't fly on the above-described offer. In short, you have another $15,000 to play with to make your cashless deal work.

Even if you had not been able to increase the value of that vacant land, you were putting yourself in a far better economic position than by trying to buy the office building with the usual financing. The landowner, after all, was willing to take soft paper, which enabled you to maximize your leverage of the office building with some mortgage at below-market value.

FINESSE IN THE USE OF THIS TECHNIQUE

Every time you buy real estate, there are four things you should do to ascertain whether the seller can be enticed into this kind of transaction.

1. *Get to know the goals of the seller.* In the previous example, knowing that the seller wanted to build apartments was what started you off on this tangent.

2. *Take a quick look around the marketplace to see if you can help the seller meet the desired goal.* Sometimes the seller has picked out exactly what he wants to buy. If you can find out what it is and then talk to the owner of that property, you might find you can still do the "soft paper" deal shown in the previous example. You do not want to be hunting for pie in the sky, however. Some sellers set unrealistic goals—and since even they won't find them, why should I spend my time looking for them?

3. *Tie up the "borrowed property" before making the offer to the seller of what you want.* You must have control of a property before offering it in an exchange. If you have only a loose deal based on a handshake, it may not survive to the closing. Remember, good intentions are offset by many things, and greed is the number one cause of death of real-estate deals.

4. *Understand that "ideal" doesn't exist, so don't overlook other alternatives.* Perhaps the seller would build office buildings instead of apartments. If there aren't any apartment sites you can tie up to use in an exchange, try something else. Any property owner can and will take *something* in exchange. As long as you can "buy" a property on soft paper and move that paper onto the property you are going to buy, you have something to exchange. In this way you can generate a "cash" equivalent of property equity. You might tie up a North Carolina lot by agreeing to give the owner $20,000 (full price) in a soft mortgage on the $75,000 duplex you are buying. If you can give the seller of the office building the $20,000 lot as your total down payment, then you've just made another cashless deal.

PITFALLS OF THE BORROWED-PROPERTY EXCHANGE

The usual pitfalls—lack of control over the property you are dealing with being the major one. Another is that the opportunity to make this cashless deal can move you into heavier debt than the property will support, but this is less of a danger here than in some of the other techniques we've examined. Using a soft mortgage deal as a part of the total financing structure will aid you in the economics of the buy, but that may not be enough. You must watch your *pro forma* carefully and not kid yourself about what you can do.

SOME FINE POINTS OF EXCHANGING—AND HOW TO IMPROVE YOUR ABILITY IN MAKING MORE AND LARGER TRANSACTIONS

1. *Be on the lookout for exchanges wherever you go.* Any time you talk to owners or prospective buyers of real estate, ask them if they have anything they would like to exchange. Sometimes a buyer will suggest a piece of property you have not been talking about and the seller is always a prime candidate for the tool.

2. *Learn to negotiate with other exchangers.* You will benefit from their experience, or at least will become comfortable in the language they use. It is a good idea to write up several hypothetical deals for self-practice before you sit down with your clients. If there aren't any advanced exchangers around to talk to, don't worry. See your attorney and have him or her go over one of the standard exchange forms with you so you will be able to use it properly. Tell your attorney that you are going to make some big deals (you will if you try), and that as your business improves your attorney's will too.

3. *Don't get hung up on the math of the exchange.* First of all, it is not hard. You only have to follow the sequence, as shown in this chapter, to get at the right answers. Much of the time you will have help. When it comes to calculating the tax on the gain, you will have to pass that task on to the client's accountant anyway. The tax samples shown here are only estimates. You will never be able to arrive at the exact tax unless you have considerable knowledge of the client's other income. Whenever you do show a tax consequence, be sure to point out the assumptions you made. Once you have the client's accountant working with you, he or she will do the rest of the calculations. Keep in mind that in math, there are different ways of arriving at the same solution. Don't be quick to tell the accountant that he or she has figured it out wrong, unless you see the calculations and know what assumptions were used.

4. *Use exchanges in other parts of financing.* This is a tool to be used for finding solutions to your clients' problems. You can and will find ways to mix this form with others. For example, it is possible to take a property and break it up into land and buildings. Once values are set, you can sell part and exchange the other. Sale and lease backs can be intermixed into exchanging. A property can be sold, leased back, and the leasehold later exchanged for some other property. The possibilities are many.

5. *Don't become a professional exchanger.* There are a few people who have made that transition successfully. I am of the opinion, however, that exchanging is just one way to skin the cat. If you rely on this format alone and are unwilling to consider the possibility that you

or your client should not exchange, then you will not be objective in your service. Be flexible.

6. *Take the upper hand.* You can become experienced in exchanging in a very short time. Try to read more about the topic. Articles often appear in some of the major real estate publications. Look for these new ideas used by others. Watch for changes in the law that affect exchanges.

Chapter 13

HOW TO USE
THE PYRAMID FORM
OF FINANCING

In the world of creative financing, one of the best methods of building wealth quickly is through the pyramid form of finance. This method is widely used and works nicely with some of the other techniques outlined in this book. Investment finance forms of pyramids are not to be confused with the old-time sales pyramids. The pyramid to which I shall devote this chapter is simply good sound business psychology.

There is no investment strategy that requires a greater confidence in one's abilities than pyramiding, so if you have doubts about your ability to use this technique properly, don't use it until you have gained more knowledge of your abilities, your goals, and the marketplace in which you are about to invest.

Pyramiding has an element of risk, but the risk is more one of time than of money if you are the buyer. As a seller to another party using the pyramid, you must be overly cautious and follow my guidelines in this chapter to ensure that you are taking prudent care of your investments.

Pyramiding is a financing form that is best suited to a rising economy, but not to the extent that some of the other highly leveraged forms of finance are oriented. To this degree, the safe way to go is in fact pyramiding if your other alternatives are heavy interest, short-term payback, or other terms of a mortgage or financing that hamper your chances of making the transaction work.

As you will see, the dangers in pyramiding are the ease with which the pyramid can be put into place and overextension of investors' financial abilities. However, as long as you take this form of financing for what it is and do not abuse it, you in turn will not be abused.

The basic premise of the pyramid is a steady increase of value in the real estate you put in the pyramid. In an economy that declines or in a specific decline of value of the property you own (even in a rising economy), the pyramid can be put into danger of collapse.

WHAT IS PYRAMIDING AND HOW DOES IT WORK?

Pyramiding is a form of leverage borrowing in which you use equity in other property to support financing to acquire additional property. This is similar to the blanket mortgage, except that for the blanket mortgage it is usual for the new property to be included in the mortgage security. In the pyramid, you will never have any cross-collateralization back to the new property. For example, if I buy your free and clear home and give you $20,000 cash and a first mortgage on a vacant lot I own in Texas as the balance, I have used a simple pyramid. If that same transaction included the home and the lot as security in a mortgage, the financing method is no longer a pyramid but a straight blanket mortgage.

It is possible, however, for you to use a pyramid that incorporates a blanket form as well. Therefore, remember that you can use the advantages of the blanket as a seller to secure the mortgage with additional security. In this situation, I might buy your home, give you $15,000 cash (less cash, but a more secure mortgage) and a first mortgage for the balance with a lot in Texas and a lot in North Carolina as security. The combined effect of more than one property make the pyramid also a blanket.

Review the advantages and disadvantages of the blanket to see how this additional twist might make the pyramid system work even better.

There are several reasons why the pyramid works better for the investor than conventional financing and even better than normal seller-held financing.

Let's look at a case study and take it apart to examine these different attributes.

Assume that Ryan is a typical real estate investor getting started. He owns a small home he bought for $55,000 four years ago. At that time, he obtained a first mortgage for $45,000 and invested $10,000 cash. A rough estimate of the value of this home today might be $75,000. Assume that Ryan has paid down his mortgage to the point where he now owes $42,000. This gives him an overall equity of $33,000 ($75,000 − $42,000 = $33,000).

Ryan now wants to buy an income property. He has found a nice four-unit apartment building that he can buy for $110,000. There is no mortgage on this apartment building, and the seller has indicated that he would hold some financing, assuming he gets a healthy down payment.

Ryan goes to the seller and offers the following:

1. A purchase price of $100,000
2. A cash down payment of $75,000
3. A second mortgage on his own home for the balance of $25,000

This kind of offer will have a very strong chance of success for the following reasons:

1. The amount of cash down is more than the seller thought he was going to get. That is in his favor, and he may drop his price because of that.
2. As the seller will not have to hold the second mortgage on his own property, he will feel relief that he is not financing 100 percent of the transaction. Sellers like the idea of being out of the deal.

Ryan will set the terms on this second mortgage that he will give the apartment building owner. Since this mortgage is private, with no lending institution involved, there will be no closing costs, points, or the like associated with the mortgage—only state stamps on mortgages, recording costs, and preparation fees that will apply.

In the presentation of the transaction, Ryan makes statements such as: "In addition to the $75,000 cash, I will give you a $25,000 mortgage against this home (showing a photo of the home), which is where I live at present." Ryan would continue to explain the nature of the mortgage by easing into the transaction if he sees the seller showing interest to the deal. "I know the $75,000 will be of interest to you, Mr. Seller, and this second mortgage will pay back to you $177 per month for the next 120 months and then balloon in full at $25,000. That would total nearly $60,000 in all if you were to invest the payments to you at 9 percent per annum."

The Grass Looks Greener on the Other Side of the Fence

This statement is true in all forms of investing and financing. People from New York City think prices in Florida are low, people in Florida think prices in South Carolina are low, and so on. The pyramid will thrive on this single syndrome of human nature: We often look at what other people have and wish it were ours. Once Ryan has outlined the basics of the deal and the seller shows his interest by agreeing (at least in principal) to accept the price of $100,000 and the amount of cash down, the rest of the deal is simply formality. The mortgage is presented almost as though it were already in place: "In addition, I'll give you a $25,000 mortgage against this home."

Once the deal seems to be workable between the parties, the details should be discussed. Of course, the method of payment of the mortgage will not work in all situations. If the seller felt a need to cash out the mortgage more quickly, the 120-month payment (ten years) would be a bit long. On the other hand, if the seller had a seven-year-old child (or grandchild) the mortgage would provide a nice annuity to set up an education fund for the child. The $177 per month for 120 months with a $25,000 balloon will indeed total about $59,400 if set in an interest-bearing account at 9 percent per annum. This $25,000 mortgage is really an interest-only payment at 8½ percent per annum and would leave some room for betterment.

The advantage to this pyramid transaction is easy to follow:

1. Assuming the deal is sound, Ryan could go to an institutional lender and borrow the $75,000 without any problem. As long as there is no second mortgage on the property—which in this case there is not as the second mortgage is against another property (Ryan's home)—the lender will not be bound by any rules or limitations on lending with the presence of secondary financing. The advantage here is that Ryan will get a better loan than if he were trying to get the maximum loan on the property, or if he did want to get a maximum loan he could pocket some additional cash if he wanted to.

2. By using the "grass is greener" approach, the second mortgage that is at a lower than market interest rate may be accepted. After all, the seller is out of the property, has pocketed a bundle of cash, and can go about his business collecting from Ryan on the second mortgage.

As you contemplate using the pyramid, you should take into consideration that while this is one of the very best *nothing down* kind of techniques, it is very effective in lowering the overall interest rate or debt service on an investment. The nothing-down guys will show you how you can buy two properties easier than one by taking the equity from one transaction and using it as a "second" to buy the second property. The equity from the second property would be the second mortgage to the first.

For example, suppose Ryan didn't own the home against which he was offering to put the second mortgage of $25,000. He would have said, "This is a property I have tied up [he has a contract pending]. To bind the deal with you on the four-unit complex, I will give you a second mortgage of $25,000, along with my check for $75,000."

To the seller of the home who wants $75,000, he says, "We can make this deal if you accept my check for $50,000 and a second mortgage in the amount of $20,000 on this [shows photo] four-unit apartment house I have tied up."

Note that some of the same arguments apply here as in the first deal: slightly lower price, lots of cash (from a regular mortgage), and the pyramid to lower the overall debt cost—and no cash down.

Add to this some cash, and you have a fantastic financing tool.

Have Your Cake and Eat It Too: The Real Benefit of the Pyramid

The strategy of pyramiding is to move into new real estate transactions without capital outlay, or at least keep the actual dollars spent at a minimum. Because you are able to use apparent equity as a basis for the exchange, you retain ownership of the previous property and at the same time gain another.

Any owner with an equity can go into the marketplace and attempt to find someone who will take that equity as security for the property being sold. The difficulty, of course, is finding "that someone" who will, in fact, take the equity in the form of a second or third mortgage on a property other than that sold.

Generally speaking, there will always be properties available, because there are owners so highly motivated that they will do anything that offers an opportunity to relieve themselves of what they own. While many of these situations would fall into the category of distressed properties, sometimes it is the owner who is distressed and not the property

Pyramiding Is a Risk That Can Be Worthwhile

You should not get the impression that pyramiding is to be avoided, as there are many situations that are acceptable for all parties. It is only necessary for you and other participants in a pyramid to be aware of the risks involved. Without a doubt, pyramiding is one of the highest leverage forms of financing available to the broker or his client. There will be times when the risk is well worth the possible gain.

Because real estate has a special quality, appreciation, and is often very difficult to evaluate in exact terms, apparent equity can be generated in a very short time. This new equity, or surplus over what the owner has invested, becomes the power behind the pyramid. In a rising market, this value may have the promise of rising further, adding to the "security" of the junior mortgage to be used in the pyramid.

HOW TO BUILD A FORTUNE IN A HURRY BY PYRAMIDING EQUITY

The amount of risk the pyramider takes depends on the amount of equity he has to begin with. Because this is the total limit to his loss capability, except for time, pyramiding is obviously weighted in his favor. That is as it should be, of course, since pyramiding is primarily a buyer's tool. There is one exception to this rule, however, and later on we will see how a seller can use pyramiding to his advantage.

The best way to explain pyramiding is to go through an example. I have chosen an extreme example because it points out the many aspects and benefits of this exciting tool.

How One Investor Started His Pyramid with $30,000 and Ended Up with $510,000

Blackburn owned an apartment building worth $90,000. Against this value there was a first mortgage of $60,000 and he had a real equity of $30,000. His desire was to buy more properties, but he was limited by the capital he had to invest—only $30,000 in cash. While he could live without the income from his investments, he could not invest more cash than the $30,000. Blackburn's long-range plan was to build as much equity as possible, sell out, and retire to a ranch in Montana. Everything he had was dedicated to this goal.

In working with his real estate broker, several interesting apartment houses of varying sizes were located. Each needed some improvements to increase the income, but these repairs could and would substantially increase the value. The first property was a ten-unit building for sale at $100,000. The property had a recent first mortgage of $70,000.

Under the advice and counsel of his broker, Blackburn offered to buy the apartment house for the full price of $100,000. However, he did not invest cash, but assumed the first mortgage and gave the seller a second mortgage of $30,000 secured by his first apartment house. To this amount Blackburn added $8,000 in cash from his bank account to improve the property.

With the improvements made, the income was quickly improved and the fair market value of the ten units increased to $130,000. It took Blackburn six months to accomplish this build-up of value, and at the end of of this period the first apartment house had also increased in value by $5,000 due to an overall improvement of the market. Blackburn now had: (1) first apartment house ($95,000 value, against the total mortgages of $90,000 leaving an equity of $5,000); and (2) a ten-unit apartment house worth $140,000 with mortgages of $70,000 (equity in the ten units was $60,000 plus a remaining cash amount of $22,000).

The next step: moving into another transaction. Next, the broker found a 20-unit apartment house also in need of repair. The estimated cost for repairs was $15,000. Although the seller was asking more, the broker knew he would sell for $180,000. There was a mortgage of $100,000 on the property.

Blackburn went to his banker and told him he would like to borrow a net of $140,000 on the twenty-unit complex. (An additional $4,000 was needed for closing costs to cover the lending expense, etc.; so the total loan required was therefore $144,000.) Blackburn explained to the banker that he would spend $15,000 on the property after the closing, and with this improvement the property should be worth over $220,000. He showed the banker a *pro forma* the broker had worked out, indicating the rental potential after the minor improvements and repairs.

The banker agreed. Blackburn then offered the seller $25,000 cash, and a second mortgage on the 10 units of $55,000 to equal the seller's $80,000 equity. The total cash needed in this transaction was: $25,000 to the seller, $100,000 to pay off the existing mortgage, $4,000 for closing costs, and $15,000 for improvements ($25,000 + $100,000 + $4,000 + $15,000 = $144,000). Blackburn had made the transaction totally out of the new loan proceeds, and therefore did not have to touch his remaining cash in the bank.

What the pyramid looked like after twelve months.   At the end of twelve months, the three properties were worth more and the picture looked like this. (The reduced mortgage amount is due to principal payments made).

Property	Present value	Total mortgages	Equity
1st apartment house	$100,000	$ 86,000	$14,000
10-unit complex	$130,000	$125,000	$ 5,000
20-unit complex	$220,000	$144,000	$76,000
Totals	$450,000	$355,000	$95,000
Plus $22,000 in cash.			

In each of the above transactions, Blackburn had to be sure that the income from each property would cover the debt service being placed on it. Because the second mortgages are always from the previous purchase, Blackburn did not move on to other deals until there was income to support the new second to be used as part of his subsequent acquisitions.

Blackburn did not stop here, however, but continued to do the same thing on a larger scale.

Blackburn's broker shows him how to pyramid into a mini-warehouse.   The broker found an old industrial building which would convert nicely into a mini-warehouse and storage facility. He knew Blackburn would have to put all his remaining cash into the renovations, but the deal looked promising. He outlined the plan to Blackburn and here is what happened.

Blackburn offered the owner a second mortgage of $75,000 secured by the twenty-unit apartment house and assumed the existing mortgage on the industrial building of $325,000. He then went to the bank holding the mortgage on the building. He got them to extend the loan by the amount of interest for one year and at the same time put a one-year moratorium on principal payments. He told the bank he was going to put another $22,000 into the property and presented them with a detailed *pro forma* prepared by his broker showing how he expected to double the present revenue within twelve months. Since the bank was concerned about the future of the present loan, they liked Blackburn's idea and decided to work with him.

At the end of another year, Blackburn had increased the value of the warehouse to $550,000—with the promise that in a few years it would exceed $600,000.

If you succeed once, why not try again. Because of his luck in the last venture, Blackburn did the same thing across town. He bought an even larger industrial complex which had been vacant for over two years and put $100,000 into remodeling the buildings.

How did he get the $100,000? The complex was on the market at a rock-bottom price of $1,025,000. Blackburn knew his bankers would lend up to $750,000 since the existing loans on the property were only $225,000.

Blackburn and his broker went to the owners and explained what he wanted to do. He offered them a deal which, after much negotiation, ended up as follows:

$370,000	Cash paid to the owners
255,000	Pay-off of existing mortgage
150,000	Second mortgage secured by the mini-warehouse
$775,000	Total so far

Blackburn then offered the owners a land lease under the complex's property subordinated to a first mortgage not to exceed $750,000. The land could be purchased by Blackburn at any time within the next twenty years, or the lease would continue for a total of forty years. Blackburn and the sellers agreed that any loan proceeds over the amount to be paid on the purchase price must go into improvements on the property. The amount of the lease was to be $24,000 per year. This amount was agreed to as being slightly over 8 1/2 percent of the $275,000 remaining value of the land. The option to buy the land during the twenty years was at a flat $290,000. As an additional kicker for Blackburn, the rent did not start until twelve months after closing. The transaction went as follows:

$ 370,000	Cash paid to the owners
255,000	Pay-off of existing mortgage
100,000	Improvements
15,000	Paid as loan cost
10,000	Legal and other closing costs
$ 750,000	Amount borrowed from Blackburn's bank
275,000	Value of land Blackburn leased
$1,025,000	Full asking price

At the end of twelve months, with the new complex fully rented and doing well, Blackburn's overall financial picture, due to increases in value and principal reductions, looked like this:

Property	Market value	Mortgages	Equity
1st apartment house	$ 105,000	$ 83,000	$ 22,000
10-unit complex	$ 135,000	$ 122,000	$ 13,000
20-unit complex	$ 230,000	$ 215,000	$ 15,000
Mini-warehouse	$ 575,000	$ 475,000	$100,000
Industrial complex	$1,110,000	$ 750,000	$360,000*
Totals	$2,155,000	$1,645,000	$510,000

*Buildings only

In only a few years, Blackburn had built his net worth from $60,000 to $510,000—with only equity and $30,000 in cash to work with. At this point he was generating a cash flow of about $55,000 per year. (All values used were based on the positive cash flow being just over ten percent of the equity.) At this stage in Balckburn's plan, he could retire to Montana to live out his life punching cows—or stay in the pyramiding game a bit longer.

How to Set Up the Most Profitable Pyramid

There are two major factors to keep in mind when you approach pyramiding: (1) Pyramiding is highly risky; (2) The property taken in the pyramid should have the potential to substantiate the risk. Once these cautions are clear in your mind, you are ready to go to work to make use of this high-leverage financing tool.

The six key steps in building a strong pyramid. In keeping with the step-by-step procedure, follow these six steps to pyramiding:

1. Review your goals. Then work toward these ends.
2. Outline your risk equity and/or cash.
3. Substantiate your equity by appraisals or pro formas.
4. Look for property that has not reached peak income potential.
5. Make an offer.
6. Do not move on until the new property will support new pyramiding by carrying a secondary loan.

Suppose you want to build an estate, and you determine that to build this estate quickly you can risk going into the pyramid program. The next step is to establish the value of the equity on which you plan to build. In Blackburn's case, he started with a $30,000 equity plus $30,000 cash. (Cash is not always a requirement, but some may be needed to improve the properties being acquired.)

An appraisal of one sort or another would be desirable to show the real equity in the property with which you plan to start. Appraisals generally work to the owner's advantage since it is rare for a property to sell for a price over the appraisal, and market value often lies somewhere below that appraised value. The appraisal, therefore, will give a value above the actual marketable sales price in the majority of cases. If you know that the market will support a higher price than that given by the appraiser, then be ready to support that price with hard facts.

Armed with this appraisal, the equity for the pyramid will be apparent. This equity will determine the amount of a second mortgage to be secured by it.

One of the best sources for properties that may be available for pyramid buying will be the local exchange group. In essence, the pyramid buyer is exchanging a mortgage in one property for equity in another. If you don't have an exchange group in your area you may find your job more difficult, but not impossible.

In either case, start with what you would like to buy and what you are capable of managing or developing into a winner. It may be possible to work out a transaction that blends the pyramid into a normal transaction. We saw how Blackburn was able to use the pyramid and give the seller cash by refinancing the existing mortgages. *Look to the combination of as many forms of financing as possible to meet the goals you have set.*

HOW TO PRESENT THE PYRAMID OFFER EFFECTIVELY

Once you have located one or more properties that seem to be worth considering, make an offer. Do not contact the owner and ask if he thinks he might be interested in taking a second mortgage on other property as a down payment on his sale. Assume that you will be successful in buying the property.

What Not to Do

"Mr. Owner, I notice you have an apartment house on 2nd Street that has a 'For Sale' sign in the yard."

Owner: "That's right."

"I was wondering, you wouldn't be interested in taking a mortgage back on another property instead of cash down, would you?"

It is obvious that this type of approach is not professional or effective. However, because this *is* the approach that many buyers *do* take, a brief analysis is needed. *First*, very few sellers know what kind of transaction they will accept until they actually accept one. *Second*, a negative approach (you wouldn't be interested, would you?) will invite a negative reply.

How to Present the Offer

Follow these key steps in presenting pyramid offers:

1. *Have all the data about the security on the property being used to leverage up in the pyramid.* A survey, appraisal, income statements (if the property is an income producer), comparable sales values, and photographs are helpful. Be ready to take the seller over to the property if he wants to see it for himself.
2. *Begin the presentation in a positive mood.* If you know you are going to make the deal, you will begin with an edge.
3. *Don't become defensive when the seller rejects the idea.* This is normal. It is a natural reaction to what the seller wants, and most times you will get a first reaction that is negative.
4. *Agree with the seller that the offer does not satisfy his desire to receive cash instead of the mortgages.* But then restate his objection in a softer tone. "Mr. Seller, as you say, it would be better to get cash, but there are some aspects that deserve careful consideration." At this point, you should talk about the property being used as security for the mortgage. Go over some of the material you have brought for this purpose. From time to time, mention what you plan to do with the new property. If cash has to be spent to upgrade it, say: "And I will be investing additional cash too." This may mean more than you think.
5. *Call on your very best closing techniques; the rest is up to you.* When it gets down to this stage, there are no guidelines to follow. You must play it by ear the rest of the way. Some sellers will have to sleep on the offer. Don't get pushy here, since pyramiding may be a very new concept to them. Other sellers may go to the dotted line right away.

HOW TO USE PYRAMIDING AS A SALES TOOL

There are times when a property is difficult to sell because of the low mortgages it carries. A free and clear property may be extremely difficult to sell unless there is some form of financing available, either from the seller or from other sources.

When a combination of the following factors is present, the pyramid can be used to benefit the seller.

The Seller's Checklist to See If Pyramiding Can Aid a Sale

1. The seller's equity presents a problem in the sale. This will occur in many situations where a high equity and minimal existing financing require a high capital investment on the part of the buyer.
2. The seller cannot or will not hold purchase money financing to facilitate the ultimate sale.
3. The conventional financing market does not offer effective refinancing of existing financing. This may be the major stumbling block in the sale of the property in the first place. If the property is an income producer, a high interest rate and a high constant rate may not be absorbed in the net operating income to offer a respectable yield to the investor.
4. The seller wants to reinvest into more real estate. This factor makes the seller a buyer, and the pyramid program can be examined in detail to see how it can be used to satisfy all four of these criteria.

In a situation that involves a seller and where all four of these criteria can be met, you can then move into a pyramid.

The objectives of the pyramid for the seller are to help make the property more salable, and at the same time reinvest the equity into more real estate. To follow this, I am presenting an example that shows a step-by-step application of these principles for the seller.

Bristow was the owner of a retail complex that consisted of seven shops. He is one of many investors that like to build and own with a high equity position. In this case, he had built the complex with his own cash and had no mortgage at all.

Over the years, he realized that his attitude toward real estate investing was not giving him the desired leverage on his capital. Thus, he wanted to sell the retail complex and build a larger one by using the capital from the first.

When I examined the property and his situation, I realized that his conservative approach would make the sale difficult. First, he needed to realize most of his equity to move ahead with his plan. Second, he therefore could not hold much paper, if any, at all. To test the third item on the checklist, calls to the local lenders were made. These indicated that while there was money available for mortgages on the present complex, they would be costly and could hurt the ultimate value since the constant rate was high.

The fourth item on the checklist was already met, as the seller was indeed ready to reinvest. There were numerous options to follow in a marketing plan. The property could be put on the market with new financing, but I felt that the loss of value, due to the cost of the money alone, would make this choice secondary if we could come up with another solution. To be specific, the value of the property was determined to be $250,000, based on the fact that the NOI was $25,000 and a 10 percent capitalization rate was felt to be warranted in this situation.

Commercial money was available at 9¾ percent per annum, over 17 years. This created an constant rate of 12.07 percent, or $22,631 per year (P&I) on the maximum loan of $187,500 (75% of the value). On top of this, the loan cost would be approximately $8,000.

With a NOI of $25,000 and a deduction of the annual debt of $22,631, a cash flow of only $2,369 would remain. If the investor wanted a 10% return, his total capital payment would have to be $23,690. But as $8,000 of that would go to the cost of the loan, the seller would receive the $187,500 plus $15,690, or $203,190. Thus, *with conventional financing the seller would get only $203,190 for a $250,000 value.* A loss of over $46,000 was too much to take without further study.

How the Pyramid Got the Seller the Full $250,000 Value, and Made Another Sale for the Broker at the Same Time

I knew if financing could be put on the property, that would provide a 10% constant, at no cost to the ultimate buyer or seller, the overall value of the complex could be sustained.

In counseling with the seller, I ascertained that he wanted to buy a vacant tract of land where he could build another, larger complex. He did, in fact, have several locations in mind, even though he had not negotiated on any of them. His conservative nature had kept him from buying until he sold. One site was a three-acre tract that was well suited for his needs. It was on the market for $210,000, a very fair price, and was free and clear of any debt.

My first approach was to see if the owner would consider an exchange for the shops. An offer was presented in the normal exchange procedure. He would not exchange. Yet, I learned that he only wanted a secure return and would sell with a very low down payment and hold paper for the balance. However, this would not solve my investor's problem, as he needed the land free and clear to obtain a development loan and had to sell his property.

A pyramid was structured. We presented the seller of the three acres with a contract that would allow Bristow to meet his needs, if all went well. The owner of the three acres was to receive $10,000 cash and a first mortgage in the amount of $190,000 on the shops as the full price for the land. The mortgage was set up on these terms: 8 percent per year, interest only for the first three years, then an amortized pay-out over the remaining twenty-five years with a balloon on the fifteenth anniversary of the closing. The closing was to occur upon the sale of the retail complex, providing this sale could be accomplished within sixty days.

How the Pyramid Helped Sell the Retail Complex

In an instant, the retail property now had a $190,000 first mortgage that offered an investor excellent terms and potential for return. The interest only at 8 percent for the first three years meant that the annual debt service on the $190,000 would be $15,200. This would leave a cash flow of $9,800. If the property were to sell for $250,000, the down payment of $60,000 would show a 16.33% yield. This provided excellent leverage for those three years. At the end of the interest only period, the annual debt service would go to a 9.27 percent constant, or $17,613. If there were no improvement in the NOI (which was projected to go up), the cash flow would be $7,387 or a 12.3 percent yield on the original investment of $60,000. The balloon did not hamper the sale of the property, as the time period allowed ample opportunity for future refinancing of the loan prior to its balloon. On this basis, the sale of the units was rather easy and was accomplished well within the sixty-day period.

The investor came out well as Bristow sold the retail complex for its full value of $250,000. He took $10,000 of the $60,000 he received on the sale and paid that over to the seller of the three acres. Then, the $190,000 mortgage was established to the benefit of all of the parties involved. Bristow now proceeded to develop a larger complex on the three acres that he owned free and clear.

FINE POINTS IN FINALIZING THE PYRAMID

The pyramid can be used in many different ways to produce a foot in the door, as well as "the final close" to a purchase or sale you are trying to accomplish.

Some highly creative aspects of the pyramid come into play when you begin to use it in connection with other techniques that either have been discussed thus far or will be covered in the book later on. To give you an overview of some of these combinations and a preview of things to come, take a look at the following four examples of very creative use of the pyramid.

Remember that the pyramid used value in another property as a security for debt you will place on a property you are trying to buy. This is the natural "grass is greener" aspect that occurs in this technique that makes it so powerful and effective.

THE DISTANT PYRAMID

The distant pyramid is where you double up on the use of the pyramid concept to the extent that two sellers are involved, each taking the other property as security for a second mortgage on the purchase of their property. In this creative look at the pyramid, you will actually buy two properties more easily than one.

For example, Alex wanted to buy a ten-unit apartment building. He had approached the seller with several different techniques, each using a low down payment offer, and each offer was turned down with the same reply from the seller: "Look, son, I'm not going to finance any buyer that doesn't have equity to back up his offer." The seller you are dealing with may not put it that bluntly, but the end result might be the same. The fact of the matter is that many sellers balk at the very idea of holding financing on their own property simply because they remember how much they paid for that property. After all, if they paid $20,000, how can they justify holding $80,000 in secondary financing on that same property, even if they are selling for $300,000.

While Alex was fooling around with this apartment building, he found a strip store complex that he liked and felt would be a good investment. He made several offers on that property and found the same kind of response from that seller.

So Alex decided to offer the apartment seller a second mortgage on the strip store as security for that part of that contract. At the same time, he offered the strip store seller a second mortgage on the apartment building as a part of that purchase offer.

Each owner would be taking a mortgage position against the other property. In each situation, Alex was careful to word the contract as not to be misleading. He made sure that each seller knew that the second mortgage was to be on a property "that I am in the process of buying," and Alex covered himself with an "out" provision that both transactions were to close at the same time or the deal would be voidable at Alex's option.

Another example of a distant pyramid is shown in the following example.

Steve had been working his comfort zone for about six months. He had made a list of all of the properties that he thought would be good deals if he could buy them. Like Alex, Steve made several offers on several properties at the same time, but knowing the power of the pyramid he discovered that he could start right out with the pyramid to his best advantage.

One such deal involved these following two properties:

1. A three-bedroom home that Steve wanted to move into. He felt it would be a great home for his growing family. The seller was asking $125,000, and except for a small $38,000 loan there was no other debt.

2. An older home down the street that was on a lot zoned for multi-family properties. Steve was sure that he could convert this older home and the two-story separate garage that went with it into five

apartments. The price Steve thought would be the "right" price was only slightly less than the seller was asking, $95,000. But Steve anticipated that he would have to spend $25,000 to make the changes he needed to convert the property into apartments.

Here's how the deal progressed.

STEVE BEGAN WITH AN OPTION ON THE OLDER HOME

He went to the seller and offered him $90,000 cash for the home, subject to Steve being able to arrange new financing on the property within 75 days, with a closing to follow that by 30 days. As the deal offered was all cash, the seller accepted the deal.

At this point, Steve had the older home tied up and was free to negotiate from a position of strength on the three-bedroom home he wanted for himself.

He offered that seller a straight pyramid deal:

Price: $125,000
Cash at closing: $90,000
Second mortgage on the to be 5-unit apartment house: $35,000

Steve showed this owner the sketch of how he was going to remodel the older home, and an estimated value of that property once the work was completed of $160,000. Steve agreed to put into the agreement that there would not place a first mortgage greater than $100,000 during the life of the second mortgage. With this provision, the seller accepted.

Steve then went back to the older home seller and said he needed to change the contract slightly. He could pay only $70,000 cash at closing and asked if the seller would take a second mortgage on the beautiful three-bedroom home down the street in the amount of $20,000 to balance out the deal.

The seller balked, and to sweeten the deal Steve agreed to pay an additional $5,000 and increase the price to $95,000. The way that deal now looked was:

Price: $95,000
Cash at closing: $70,000
Second mortgage on the three-bedroom house down the street: $25,000

The next step for Steve was to go to two or more different lenders on each property. He was careful not to present both property deals to the same lenders since he assumed that the loan officers wouldn't understand what he was doing and wouldn't approve it. He wanted to get the best new first mortgage he could on the three-bedroom home and the $100,000 maximum loan that he had agreed he would not exceed on the older home.

In usual circumstances, Steve could obtain a $104,000 loan on the three-bedroom home, and if his figures on value were correct, a total of $100,000 plus on the home to be remodeled.

WHAT STEVE NEEDED TO CLOSE
AND WHAT HE COULD GET

	On the 3-bedroom home		On the older home
Needed:			
Cash down	$ 90,000		$ 70,000
Closing cost	1,700		1,800
Fix up	3,000		25,000
Miscellaneous	1,000		1,000
To carry debt*	5,000		5,000
Totals:	$100,000	PLUS	$112,000 = $212,700
Could get:	$104,000	PLUS	$100,000 = $204,000
Would have to add out of his own pocket			= $ 8,700

I have included extra cash to pay both mortgage payments while repairs are being made on the older home, so that Steve can begin to generate income from the newly remodeled and now rented apartments. If Steve didn't need that income, he could buy the two properties without any cash down out of his own pocket.

WHAT WORKS WELL TWICE MIGHT BE BETTER THRICE

It would stand to reason, thought Brad, that if you could buy two properties with a pyramid without using any of your own cash, then three properties would be even easier.

He tied up three separate properties using the pyramid.

1. Property *A* was a vacant lot on which he was going to build. It was offered at $50,000, and Brad offered $5,000 cash and a $45,000 second mortgage on property *B*:

2. Property *B* was a strip store that Brad wanted to fix up and remodel. He was going to turn it into a medical complex to complement the demand for such services in the area. The price was $470,000. He

felt that he would need another $35,000 for remodeling of the center. His offer was a new first mortgage of $350,000, a third on property C for $50,000, and a land-lease set at a value of $70,000, which Brad could buy anytime over the next twelve years at that same amount. The annual rent was to be $6,300.

3. Property C was an apartment building that consisted of 15 units near the beach. The owner was operating it as an annual apartment building, but Brad knew that if he converted it to seasonal units, putting into the building a hot-shot young couple he knew could take care of the property, he could increase the income substantially. The price was $400,000, and he offered the sellers a $300,000 wraparound mortgage (to wrap the existing financing of a first mortgage of $265,000 and a second mortgage of $35,000). In addition, he offered the sellers a first mortgage on property A of $30,000 and $65,000 cash.

To accomplish this, $105,000 cash was required to close on all three properties. If Brad could show that property B would be worth $575,000 due to the new income projection, he might be able to borrow up to 80 percent of that amount, or $460,000 (an increase of $110,000 over his original mortgage on that property of $350,000). Even with some added expenses for that mortgage, Brad could buy these three properties without using any of his own cash.

Brad could have extended this concept even farther by bringing in another property and so on, but the more properties you have in any transaction, the greater the difficulty in closing the whole transaction. Therefore, even though it might be tempting to bring in additional properties in pyramid transactions, it is best to keep the new deals to a minimum. However, it wouldn't matter how many second or third mortgages you offered on properties you already owned as part of the package.

PYRAMID TRANSACTIONS OFFERING LAND LEASES

Bryan owned several different properties, all of which were producing more income than was needed to support the expenses and current debt service that was on the property. This gave Bryan a positive cash flow that increased the value of the property substantially over his original cost. He wanted to remove some of this equity, but wanted to keep the cost of the new debt at a minimum.

One way to do that is to deal with land leases created on other property you own. This is a form of pyramid, only instead of dealing with a mortgage secured by that asset, you establish a land lease and offer it as an income source to the seller of the other property you are trying to buy.

UNDER EVERYTHING IS LAND

There are many people who believe that ownership of the land is the best, and that better than a mortgage is actual title to the land.

There is no argument to that from me, and as long as the lease is favorable to my needs I will take a land lease just as I would cash—in fact, sometimes quicker, for reasons that I will explain.

Bryan got to a point in a negotiation on a small office building where he needed to move some of the seller-held debt to another property so he could over mortgage the property he wanted to buy to generate the cash to make the transaction. He looked over his inventory of real estate and discovered that in several situations he could create extra debt without hurting himself or the property.

BRYAN CREATES A LAND LEASE

He had a twelve-unit apartment building. It was throwing off a net operating income of $46,000. From this, he had existing debt service of $31,000 (which represented annual payments on $305,000 of mortgages). The office building he was trying to buy was offered at $275,000 and was free and clear. The seller demanded a minimum of $150,000 cash down and said he would hold a first mortgage for the balance. That wouldn't work for Bryan, so he "created" a land lease on his apartment building. He sat down with his lawyer and had a simple, but effective lease drawn up. It had provisions that I will show you later on in this chapter, and an annual rent of $11,250 per year. In addition, it had an option to buy the underlying land for $125,000 anytime within the first twelve years of the lease, which was a forty-year lease.

Bryan then offered the seller the $175,000 cash he wanted and the land under his twelve-unit apartment building subject to lease. In essence, Bryan was offering to give the seller of the office building the twelve units at the end of the forty-year lease if Bryan had not bought out the land prior to that time. In the meantime, the seller would have full ownership of the land. Bryan put in several other provisions that we will discuss now.

THE LAND LEASE CHECKLIST

1. *Do* provide for an option to buy back the land. Try to keep it at the same set price you have established as the value of the land at the start.
2. *Do* have the land lease extend more than thirty-five years . . . or at least ten years plus the option term past the longest term of an existing mortgage. Assume that the longest mortgage was fifteen years,

and your option to buy back was twelve years. You would then have a total of 10 + 15 + 12, or 37 years. The reason for this is you may want to refinance the mortgages that are on the property prior to the termination of your option to buy. You would need a minimum of ten years beyond that new mortgage term to have a lease in effect for most lenders to approve the loan. As you might wait until the end of the first option to buy the land back to decide if you want to keep the land lease instead of buying it back (twelve years), you would need that term plus a similar term for a new mortgage, or an additional 12 + 15 years. Longer would be good, but you anticipate buying back the land within your first refinance term or letting someone else worry about that as you may sell the property within a short time.

3. *Do* allow for a refinance during the term. If your land lease is subordinated to the existing financing only, you would not be in a position to refinance the property once the existing financing has been paid off. So provide for additional refinancing, but be ready to limit the amount to some percentage of the value of the land and buildings—say, 80 percent of the lender's appraisal of the land and improvements.

4. *Do* make sure the document is a land lease and not a mortgage. Your lawyer should make sure that this is the case. If you are using this technique to take advantage of the tax laws that fit your circumstance, and the document that says "land lease" is deemed by the IRS to be a mortgage, it could be a costly mistake.

5. *Do not* have a "required" pay-back agreement, where you must buy back the land. That is one of the first keys that the tool is really a mortgage.

6. *Do not* have your rent payment increases tied to a cost-of-living index, or any other index that has no known future value, unless you: (a) can time the increases to come into effect following a date which you believe you could exercise an option to buy the property; (b) can limit the effect of any future index by obtaining credit for payments of rent against the purchase price, or by having only a percentage of the increase of the index apply; or (c) have no other choice and are ready to take the risk that the cost-of-living increases will not decrease the lease's benefit to you.

7. *Do not* make your offer with the idea that the land lease is something that will be "established" or negotiated. You might flex a bit on its ultimate value, but never on the terms of the lease.

Bryan had created a lease that had an annual payment of 9 percent, which at the time was better than he could do with a second mortgage or in any institutional first-mortgage situations. The seller took the land lease because there is that feeling that some people have about that sort of thing.

THERE ARE PROBLEMS, OF COURSE

Land leases can cause lots of problems for both sides of a deal. Generally, the problems come from three major areas.

1. *The carelessness of one or more of the parties to leave something important out of the lease.* Remember that memories are meaningless when it comes to what was intended to be included in a contract that looks bad to one side later on. If the contract isn't absolutely clear, you will absolutely have problems.

2. *The subordination dilemma.* If you are on the receiving side of this deal, you should know that for this to work for the investor the land lease would have to be subordinated to the existing and possibly future financing. This means that the "position of lien" has been subordinated (given up) to allow the mortgages to come ahead of the actual ownership of the land in the event of a default on the mortgages. Should such a default occur later on, the owner of the land may find him- or herself having to take over a mortgage to get his or her own property. If the investor has run the property into the ground, there may not be income available to support the mortgage . . . and value may have eroded as well. Keep in mind that this problem would be similar to that of a junior mortgage holder.

3. *The time problem.* I have seen investors actually let a land-lease option to buy slip past and expire because they "forgot" when it was coming up. You cannot rely on your lawyer, your banker, or your accountant either.

Despite these kinds of problems, there remains a world of flexibility in land leases and pyramids.

In a general summary of the pros and cons of pyramids, there are a number of elements that I have covered that should be repeated and remembered.

PYRAMIDS WORK ON THE GREENER GRASS THEORY.

PYRAMIDS CAN BE THE BOX BEHIND THE SILVER CURTAIN.

SELLERS WILL HOLD SOMETHING THEY "SEE" AS VALUABLE THAT ISN'T THEIRS.

YOU CAN PYRAMID OFF REAL ESTATE YOU OWN OR DON'T OWN.

In going into a pyramid program, you should review some of the general advantages and disadvantages.

There are two factors that create a risk in pyramids that can bring a swift end to your economic house of cards.

1. The ability to pay the increased debt service.
2. The danger of having greater debt than value.

As you can see, both of these factors are related. If the client extends his or her value-to-equity ratio to the point where there is no real equity at all, the over-leverage may cause all of the cards to come tumbling down. We've seen this effect in other improperly used techniques.

What are the advantages and disadvantages? First, remember that there are two different parties involved. The buyer's goals and motivations will generally be greatly different from those of the seller. Each party should look at the end result of the transaction from his or her own position and needs.

The Buyer: The Person Who Generally Instigates The Pyramid

Advantages	*Disadvantages*
1. Expands holdings	1. Possibility of overleverage
2. A low-cost financing tool for reinvestment	2. One failure and the whole pyramid can fall
3. Establishes good "selling" terms	3. Buyer limited to fewer sellers
4. Fantastic estate builder	
5. As the interest paid is apt to be on an "exchanged" mortgage, the interest would be deductible.	

The Seller: The One Who Feeds the Pyramid

Advantages	*Disadvantages*
1. Creates a sale	1. Sale generates paper, not cash
2. Tax advantages, due to spread of gain on the sale to the terms of the mortgage taken	2. Paper may not be secure
3. Provides long-term income	3. Another remote transaction could have a great effect on this security
4. Secured by other property with visible results	4. Paper is flexible in terms

The seller in the pyramid is generally a person highly motivated to sell. He considers and later accepts the offer for paper because it is the best deal offered. If you were to compare the pyramid offer to an all-cash offer of the same value, there could be no question as to the better, less risky transaction. However, this is not a proper comparison. The seller wants to sell and has a plausible offer. Hence, it may be worthy of acceptance and better than holding onto the property.

HOW TO MAKE THE TRANSACTION WORK

The pyramid can be a very safe and profitable way to finance new acquisitions if used conservatively. This means the amount of real equity transferred via a mortgage should be kept at a low to moderate amount. In most cases, the total debt service on the property should not exceed 80% of the net operating income of that property. In very stable income properties this percentage may be extended to 90 percent. There should be a 10 percent or greater buffer between income and expenses. In taking over a new property, the buyer should consider out-of-pocket expenses to bring the income up, and this out-of-pocket must be taken into account *before* the transaction is completed. It should be figured into the total price or at least accounted for in later expenditures. If the buyer is able to generate this needed out-of-pocket cash from additional financing on the acquired property, then the total debt should be reasonable and not overleveraged.

The market conditions themselves will provide some limitation to this overleverage, as it will be difficult for the buyer to obtain excessive financing on marginal properties. But the domino effect of the total pyramid can build up quickly if you are not careful.

The seller should exercise caution in any transaction that does not involve cash. However, that caution should not mean a pyramid transaction is not worth considering. To the contrary, the property being sold may not be saleable by any other method.

Chapter 14

HOW TO APPROACH A DISCOUNT SALE

A discount sale, as it applies to real estate, is a sale at a drastically reduced price in relation to the supposed value. This reduction must be for sound reasons, and not simply a ploy to save on capital gains or other taxes.

The Internal Revenue Service will review a discount sale with a careful eye to see if it has been contrived as a method of cutting the possible tax consequences or not. Of course, the sale may never come to their attention, but don't count on that because they may very easily examine such a transaction at some time in the future. The three-year statute of limitations on audits of past income tax returns will not hold if there is reason to believe that fraud was committed. If the discount sale was accomplished to evade tax, fraud may be claimed. You should be very cautious in the use of the discount sale and should follow the simple checklist shown below. If you can answer "no" to all of the questions, then you should be able to justify the use of a discount sale. In using this checklist, however, it is wise to check with your tax advisor to see whether he has any special problems with the use of the discount sale.

CHECKLIST TO DETERMINE WHETHER A DISCOUNT SALE CAN BE USED

All questions must be answered "no." Even one "yes" answer may raise doubt as to the acceptability of using a discount sale as a method of selling a property.

1. Is the buyer a relative of the seller?
2. Is the buyer a close business partner or associate of the seller?
3. Does the seller owe the buyer money or any special favors?
4. Is the sale price below the assessed value of the property?
5. Is the sale tied to other terms or conditions involving other property?
6. In the event of a lease-back by the seller are the terms of the lease unreasonable for either party based on the market area.
7. Is there a mandatory recapture provision where the seller must become a buyer at a future date?
8. Is there reason to believe that the seller does not need immediate cash or other financial relief?
9. Are there buyers at a higher price, with reasonable terms?
10. Have similar properties been sold above the sale price within a reasonable time-span?
11. Has the seller taken a large (for him) long-term capital gain in the same year?
12. As a broker or salesman and listing agent are you the buyer?

Assuming you have answered "no" to all the above questions you can now proceed with the discount sale as a method of helping your seller accomplish his goals.

The discount sale has a real function. It can often be the only solution, short of financial disaster, for some clients and some properties.

A DISCOUNT SALE GENERALLY MEANS CASH

A sale at half the value may, after all, be the only cash price you can get due to market conditions. Because the reason for a discount sale is usually the need to produce immediate cash, it is generally associated with the "cash sale."

If you have a client in need of immediate cash who is not in a position or is not willing to borrow the required sum of money, and the sale of a real property becomes the only suitable solution, you may find yourself looking to the discount sale to satisfy his needs.

From the buyer's point of view, a purchase at a bargain price is more appealing than buying at a market price. Of course, the all-cash requirement may limit some buyers. But for the most part, the number of possible buyers will be increased when a "steal" is being offered.

As for the seller, it depends on what problems he is trying to solve. If his most critical need is for cash, then you can raise cash with more ease by utilizing the discount sale. Often, his need for cash is over-shadowed by the necessity to "get out" or to be released from financial burdens he is unable to support.

Roscoe owned an apartment lot suitable for ten units. In a good rental market the lot might bring $25,000. In fact, a few years ago this price may have been attainable. However, times are now tough and rental properties are over-built and have high vacancy factors. Roscoe has been hurt by the decline in the economy and is in need of some ready cash. The property cannot be sold at its past value. Some prospective buyers have indicated a willingness to pay $20,000, but only with a very low down payment and long terms on seller-held paper. Since Roscoe needs cash immediately the broker recommends the discount sale as a method of solving the problem.

Roscoe sells the lot for $10,000 cash. Because of the obvious "steal" at this price, a buyer was found almost overnight. But the discount sale has a buy-back option, so Roscoe retains the right to re-purchase the lot within the next thirty-six months for $16,000. If he fails to do so the option is lost forever.

The discount sale solved the immediate cash need Roscoe had, and at the same time offered him an opportunity to buy back the property in the near future if the market reversed itself. Should the value return to the lot within the thirty-six months, or increased values make the lot worth more than the supposed $25,000, then Roscoe will profit.

The buyer of the lot will have a limited gain should Roscoe recapture the lot within the thirty-six months. Yet, his gain will still be substantial. Hence, the bottom line for the buyer is the recapture. He may gain much more if Roscoe cannot or will not recapture within the thirty-six months.

LEASE-BACK, RECAPTURE OR OPTION: A NECESSARY PART OF THE DISCOUNT SALE

Lease-back, recapture, or option—one of these methods is almost always used in conjunction with the discount sale to provide for future gain to the seller.

How can these methods be useful? First, accept the fact that the discount sale offers the most potential when the market for the type of property being offered is not at a peak. After all, when there is a demand for what you are offering you need not offer a discount. When the sale of apartment lots is down and not many buyers are around, it may be nec-essary to seek drastic measures in order to sell. Of course, the poorer the market the greater the discount required to make the buy a "steal."

At times, the discount by itself is still not enough to entice a buyer. You may have a floor under which you cannot go. The seller may have financial obligations to pay off or may simply be unwilling to sell below a fixed price. Many sellers have lost all rather than drop the price to a level at which the property would sell.

The lease-back can be brought into the terms of the deal to make the property saleable. In such a situation the seller will arrange to lease the property from the new buyer for a period of time. This is the same as a sale and lease-back, but with a discount on the sale.

If the seller has a use for the property and can produce income to pay the lease, the reasons may be sound. With the discount and additional income (in the form of rent), the transaction may proceed. The amount of the lease can usually be lower than an economic return on the price, as the buyer is looking at the discount as the major incentive for buying. This is another flexible aspect of this form of financing. You can negotiate different time periods of the lease, amount of the lease, and discounted prices. The variance on any one could alter the others in the market place.

The Recapture Allows the Seller to Recoup Value

With a recapture clause in the lease, the seller may, at a later date, buy back the land at a price fixed in the contract or at a price adjusted by other agreements.

The most common *extra* provision used with the discount sale is the option to buy back. Because the seller is taking a reduced price, he may want to buy back at a future date. This future price may be considerably higher than the price the property was sold for in the first transaction. Consider this case:

Astoff owns 200 acres of farmland outside the city in a growing area. Land nearby has sold for $500 per acre. Based on this information, the current value of the land should be $100,000. Astoff wants to get some cash to buy a yacht and spend a year or two at leisure. He paid $50 per acre twenty years ago and presently has no use for the farm site. The current market conditions indicate that there are not many buyers ready, willing, or able to buy this land today, or in the very near future.

DISCOUNT SALE EQUALS A STEAL

At what price then do the 200 acres become a "steal"? When you can answer that question to the highest dollar amount you have the probable discount price. In this case it was $300 per acre. Remember, the discount sale may require all cash to suit the client's needs. If the $60,000 which can be generated by the discount sale is more than Astoff needs, then you may back off and sell only a portion of the property at a discount and hold onto the rest. However, we found that Astoff needed the $60,000 and we proceeded to market the property with this in mind.

In the future, Astoff's 200 acres may skyrocket in value due to a new subdivision nearby or for some other reason. If the value should go to $2,000 per acre, some of the new value of $400,000 could be recouped if Astoff had taken an option to buy back the land at the time he sold it.

An option to buy back, however, is normally not granted for a long period of time, except in lease-back and recapture situations. The reason is simply that the option is one sided, and the new owner does not want to be locked into the property for a lengthy period of time without being able to sell. As Astoff felt the land would appreciate greatly within a few years, he negotiated for a short option at a lower recapture price rather than a long option at a high price.

He settled for a four-year option at a $110,000 recapture price. This would give the new owner a $50,000 profit, less his carrying cost, for four years—should Astoff buy the land back at the end of that time. If the land went to $400,000, Astoff could buy it back at $110,000 with a profit of $290,000—plus the original $60,000 he received from the first sale. Had Astoff made the decision to sell the property for its top value of $100,000, that would have been the maximum top dollar he would have received —less the tax.

RECAP OF THE TRANSACTION

Astoff had land similar to that which had sold for $100,000. To get a quick sale, he took a discount and sold it for $60,000, but with an option to buy back within four years at $110,000.

Three years later, Astoff realized that a new subdivision nearby had opened up this farmland and that it could be sold for as high as $400,000. So, with time on his side (he had 12 months before the option came due), we put the land on the market. He knew that he could exercise his option to recapture the land if he got a buyer.

A year later a buyer came along, and Astoff sold his option to him for $260,000. The new buyer exercised the option for $100,000. Astoff sold the option rather than exercise it for capital gains reasons. He had held the option long enough to take a long-term gain; whereas, had he recaptured the land then sold it, he may have found he had a short-term gain.

It should be obvious that Astoff made more money with this form of financing than if he had sold the property for the $100,000.

ADVANTAGES OF A DISCOUNT SALE

There are four basic advantages of the discount sale:

1. Cash in a hurry
2. Fast closing

3. Action in a bad market
4. Very flexible

The Discount Sale Can Be Used Effectively in These Situations:

1. The seller needs cash in a short time
2. The market is difficult
3. The property is difficult to sell
4. The seller needs a fast transaction
5. A fast cash-out for an exchange is needed

The discount sale is a seller's and a broker's tool, but can be used by an astute buyer as well. The buyer can go into a transaction offering a reduced price. The later buy-back can become a negotiating point. It can follow many avenues and can be very flexible.

The discount sale and buy-back option offer the seller more possibilities for return when the property has the promise of fast appreciation. In the event of a property valuation decline, the seller simply does not use the option and walks away from the property.

DISADVANTAGES OF A DISCOUNT SALE

Many things can go awry in planning a discount sale. It may be that the price is reduced too low, or the terms of the buy-back are too high or for too short a period of time. The value in appreciation may not warrant the buy-back and the seller may have lost out on part of the gain. Many things can and do go wrong, but this is more often a fault of the planners and not of events. We cannot fit the discount sale format into all situations. In those cases where there is a threefold increase in the value of the property the year after the option is dropped, the planning was obviously wrong.

Because the discount sale is highly effective, the broker should not recommend its use unless he is sure that the seller has no other option available which can solve the problem. An overzealous broker can sell a lot of property with the discount method, but not always to the benefit of the seller.

A discount sale holds considerable risk for the seller if the market value of the property does not appreciate to cover the pick-up cost, or if his situation changes and he cannot exercise the option when the time comes. The amount of risk the seller is taking depends on the amount of the discount and the probability of appreciation. A reduction from $100,000 to $60,000 with a likelihood that the value will go to $200,000 in three years, is less risky than a reduction from $100,000 to $75,000 with little hope of an appreciation in value to $150,000 within four years.

Because of this risk factor, the discount sale can be used by the buyer with a certain degree of effectiveness. It is normally the seller who is telling the buyer how great the value of this property will be in a few years. In essence, the buyer turns that around and says: "I'll give you part of your price now, and if you are right about the future, a lot more later."

The following guide will be helpful in reviewing the discount sale from the seller's point of view.

1. Keep in mind that the discount sale is effective when:
   a. Fast cash is needed.
   b. The seller has no other acceptable way to get the cash.
   c. A fast closing is needed.
   d. The property is very difficult to sell.
   e. A cash-out for an exchange is needed.
   f. The seller knows the value will increase substantially.
2. If one or more of the six preceding factors is not present, the discount sale will probably not be the best form to use.

FINE POINTS IN THE DISCOUNT SALE

Since the seller is in a give-and-take situation by virtue of the discount on the price, he is able to negotiate terms not normally possible on the later buy-back, or lease-back and recapture. However, the buyer knows that the longer the time period of the option the less value the discount has, unless there is another counterbalance. It is possible to structure these counterbalances to provide some protection to the seller for a longer time, without unduly burdening the buyer.

The seller, for example, wants a ten-year option to buy back, a very long time for the discount sale. In this event, a number of factors can be brought into play to make it feasible.

1. The future price to be set at a predetermined base price, with an appraisal to be made at the tenth year, a future percent of which value shall be the buy-back price or the predetermined base price, whichever is greater. (The amount of the future percent will be another negotiating point, and should be no greater than 75% nor less than 50%. This limits the amount of profit the seller can take on the recapture.)
2. Give the buyer the right to "buy out" the option with a payment to the seller. This provision will allow the buyer, for a sum of money, to null and void the option. It is possible that the buyer may want to sell or even develop the property, and with the option over his head that may not be practical. The sum of the buy-out is normally at least the balance to the discount plus some profit. If the value was

$100,000 and the discount sale was at $60,000, the buy-out may be at $45,000. However, this is a highly negotiable point.

3. First right of refusal. This may be all the seller can get, or may run with the property for a period of time after the option to buy back has expired.

4. Escalating option or lease price. The seller may agree to a series of higher prices in future options to buy back. The same may occur in the lease payments. This and other long-term options or provisions are used in vacant and other nonincome-producing properties more often than in income-producing property. The reason is the new owner may not properly maintain the structure if the option price prevents him from a recapture of his invested capital.

Most any other provisions which could be coupled to a normal sale, or option, can be used with some effect on the total overall discount sale. Keep in mind that the discount sale is more than just a lowered price.

Chapter 15

WHEN, WHY, AND HOW TO DISCOUNT A MORTGAGE

The ability to increase the yield on a mortgage by selling it below face value can be utilized in many ways. The concept of mortgage discounting is widely used in the government loan programs and has applicability to the private sector as well. The *discounting of a mortgage* is when the holder of the mortgage sells the note to either the maker or a third party at an amount less than the principal plus interest owed. The result is that you would, upon satisfaction of the note at its contract rate and terms, receive a greater yield than the original holder.

WHEN A MORTGAGE SHOULD BE DISCOUNTED FOR CASH

A mortgage should be discounted whenever the need for cash, or the yield which can be obtained with the cash, exceeds the return on the mortgage. Naturally, there are other alternatives, such as obtaining a loan against the mortgage or seeking the funds elsewhere. These alternatives, which may be highly desirable solutions in normal circumstances, may not work quickly enough or produce the desired results as effectively as a discounting of the mortgage.

The cash discount is a sale of the paper at a reduced price to enable you to have an overall yield greater than the contract rate on the mortgage. This cash sale of the paper can occur at any time after the mortgage is written and up until the date it is satisfied. A mortgage which has some maturity is considered to have a performance record, and hence may be discounted less than if it had no record of payment. Mortgages discounted in the early years will generally have an additional penalty for this lack of seasoning. This will depend on the type of mortgage and the position in rank. It is obvious that a second mortgage will not be as saleable as a first mortgage on the same property. Therefore, it may require a greater discount. Yet, a third mortgage on one property may be more marketable than a first mortgage on another property. The loan to value ratio is important throughout this ranking process. If a property is valued at $100,000 and there is a first mortgage of $40,000, the loan ratio is 40 percent and the equity ratio is 60 percent. That same property with an additional loan (second) of $20,000 would have a loan ratio of 60 percent to value and the equity ratio of 40 percent. Therefore, the loan to value ratio is crucial and the remaining equity ratio essential to determine the "risk" factor to the mortgage.

For example: Castelle had taken back a third mortgage when he sold his home nearly two years earlier. The mortgage now had ten years to go and the unpaid balance was $10,500. The contract rate was 8 percent and the monthly payment to amortize the balance was $152.88. Castelle felt that he would be able to sell the mortgage if he could discount it to show an investor 10 percent on the invested capital. This meant that the investor could not pay more than $9,639 for it to have that yield. The first investor looked at the discounted price and was interested. He asked Castelle what were the loan percentages and equity percentage ratios. Castelle wasn't sure what the investor meant, so they figured them out together. The estimated value on the property was $60,000.

The mortgage represented 17.5 percent of the total value and the superior financing totalled $42,500 or 70.8 percent of the value. This meant there was a total of 88.3 percent financing and 11.7 percent equity. The investor decided that with only 11.7 percent equity between the mortgage and foreclosure, he needed a 12 percent return. The mortgage would have to sell for $6,993 to show a 12 percent yield. Castelle decided to keep the mortgage, since his need for cash would not generate a 12 percent return.

However, later in the same year Castelle found a small apartment building he could buy if he had cash to the mortgages. The apartment building should throw off nearly 13 percent cash. He tried to get the owner of the building to take the mortgage as part of the transaction. Failing in that, he went back to the investor and discounted the mortgage to come up with the cash to buy the apartments. Castelle now had a greater use for the cash than the present return generated from the yield on paper.

WHEN SHOULD A MORTGAGE BE DISCOUNTED IN EXCHANGE?

In the previous example, Castelle attempted to get the owner of a property he wanted to buy to take paper he held. This was a step to exchange the paper at its face amount. Later in the negotiations Castelle tried to make the paper more attractive by discounting the face amount, but the apartment owner had a need for cash that overshadowed the yield any reasonable discount could generate. While Castelle failed in the exchange of the paper, he was at least on the right track in trying to better the buying power of the paper by using it as a part of a transaction rather than discounting it.

When an investor attempts to buy a property it is wise to offer as a part of the total transaction any paper being held, especially if the paper has a yield less than the expected return on the property being purchased. Yet, even though the yield on the paper is greater than the overall yield, the leverage gained in the purchase terms may make the use of the paper desirable.

Redding, an investor, offered to buy a strip store. He had $75,000 in cash and $50,000 in paper he was holding on a vacant piece of land he had sold the year before. The strip store had a first mortgage of $300,000 and an annual debt service of $33,000. The NOI of the store was $45,500, or a cash flow of $12,500 on a total offering of $125,000 cash to the mortgages. The $50,000 in mortgages Redding was offering would yield nearly 12 percent. Nonetheless, Redding was most interested in the strip store because of yields other than just the cash flow. In the first place, the tax shelter boosted the yield as did the principal build-up. Appreciation was that added bonus that he was not getting in the mortgage.

There are two ways to discount a mortgage in an exchange. The first is in adjusting the total price offered, still showing the mortgage at its face amount. The second is adjusting the price and showing the mortgage at a discounted value.

Here's an actual example. Rosenbloom wanted to acquire a vacant parcel of land to build on. The asking price was $100,000. Rosenbloom had cash and, in addition, a $15,000 mortgage he was holding from the sale of another property. He decided he would not pay more than $80,000 cash plus his mortgage.

FIRST OFFER: ADJUSTED PRICE WITH FIRM FACE VALUE ON PAPER

Price	$95,000
Cash	$80,000
Mortgage in exchange	15,000
Total	$95,000

SECOND OFFER: ADJUSTED
PRICE AND DISCOUNTED
VALUE OF PAPER

Price	$90,000
Cash	80,000
Mortgage in exchange	10,000
Total	$90,000

It would appear that the proper method would be the first offer. After all, it is argued, the higher price is the best way to go. This may be true in many circumstances. However, if this is the maximum which can be offered, that is $80,000 in cash and the balance in the paper, and the face amount of the paper is $15,000, then there is little room for negotiation.

Therefore, I suggest that in the offering of paper in exchange for a part of the transaction that the paper be generously discounted right at the start. If the above $15,000 paper yields 8 percent at its face amount, and assume that if discounted to $10,000 it will yield 16 percent, you have removed the primary argument of the value of the paper before the seller can settle in on that portion of the negotiations. If he were to counter at a higher price, you could merely remind him that in fact there was another $5,000 in face value in the paper anyway.

In Rosenbloom's situation, he knew the maximum he wanted to pay for the property and that he wanted to use the paper as a part of the transaction. Generally, sellers will absorb part of a bigger deal in old paper, thereby removing the paper from the buyer's portfolio.

HOW TO DETERMINE THE AMOUNT OF A DISCOUNT

This is a two-part problem. The first is the market condition. What amount of discount is necessary to make the paper saleable? The second part of the problem is the actual computations to arrive at the discount.

HOW TO ANALYZE THE MARKET
FOR A DISCOUNTED MORTGAGE

To some degree, it is the old story of how long must your legs be. The answer of course is long enough to reach the floor. In the discounting of mortgages the amount of the discount must be sufficient to market the paper. Investors dealing with the purchase of paper look to a demand rate that is generally greater than the yields on the property securing the paper.

If the mortgage is a first mortgage and there is a low loan to value ratio, the discount will be reduced as the risk is lessened. On the other hand, if the mortgage is a second or third mortgage and the total loan to value ratio is high, equity is therefore low and the discount must be increased.

The motivation of the seller of the paper must be considered as the most important factor. If the seller must have cash, then he has little choice but to increase the discount until the paper sells. But if his need for cash is limited to a portion of the mortgage, he may be able to borrow the needed funds by placing the mortgage up as security for the loan. The interest paid on such a loan can be greater than the yield offered in the discount, and yet the total cost is less than if the mortgage were discounted.

When you deal in the discount mortgage market it is a good idea to establish a few buyers for such paper. You need to have a list of such investors on hand in case you need one. It seems that the need arises when time is short, and an attempt to find a buyer then can be difficult. The investors will dictate the amount of discount needed from their point of view. Unless you are able to dispose of the paper through other means, the general market will be your only hope—and they set the terms.

HOW TO FIND THE DISCOUNT

Constant annual percent tables are provided in this book. These tables have many uses, one of which is an easy way to arrive at the discount amounts for mortgages. The method of finding the discount is explained in the example below.

Williams needed cash and had a mortgage to sell. The principal amount was $50,000 over fifteen years at 8 percent annum. The monthly payment was $478. Once the pertinent data is given, the next step is to find the current constant annual percentage of the mortgage. The monthly payment is $478, therefore twelve times that would give the annual sum of $5,736. The annual sum is then divided by the face amount of the mortgage (that amount still unpaid) and this gives the current constant annual percentage ($5,736 ÷ $50,000 = 0.1147). This should be stated as a percentage (in this case 11.47 percent). This represents the percent of the total annual payment in relation to the outstanding balance for the years remaining. With the constant annual percent known, the remaining calculation is quite simple. In this example, assume the yield the investor demands is 12 percent. We know the mortgage has 15 years to go. Find the constant annual percentage which corresponds to 12 percent for 15 years.

In the table of constant annual percentages you would look in the 12 percent interest column for the 15 years. The answer would be 14.40

percent (some tables may vary based on the full calculations made*). Now complete this formula:

$$\frac{\text{Constant Annual Percent}}{\text{Demand Rate Constant}} = \text{Discounted percentage}$$

$$\frac{11.47}{14.40} = 79.65\%$$

To apply these results multiply the face amount of the mortgage by the discounted percentage ($50,000 × 79.65% = $39,326). The $39,326 is the value of the mortgage to an investor demanding a 12 percent yield. To find the percentage of the discount, subtract the discounted percentage from 100 percent (100% − 79.65% = 20.35% discount).

MORTGAGE DISCOUNT SHEET WHEN DEMAND RATE IS KNOWN

1. Face Amount of Mortgage
   (Present Balance Owed) . . . . . $_____

2. Contract Rate . . . .   _____ %

3. Payment (Monthly __, Quarterly __,
   Semi-Annual __, Annual __; check
   one) . . . . $_____

4. Constant Annual Percent
   Annual Adjustment of Line 3
   Divided by Line 1. . . . .   _____%

5. Demand Rate . . . .   _____%

6. Term of Years of Mortgage . . . .   _____ years

7. Constant at Demand Rate.
   Find by Looking in Demand Rate
   Column for Number of Years . . .   _____%

8. A. $\dfrac{\text{Line 4}}{\text{Line 7}}$ = Discounted Value %
   . . . .   _____%

9. Discount Percent (Subtract Line 8 from
   100) . . . .   _____%

10. Amount of Discount
    (Line 9 × Line 1) . . . . $_____

*Use Table A. Note that examples shown are rounded off so that 11.817 would become 11.82 in the table.

11. Amount to be Paid at Discount. . . $_____
    A. Line 1 less Line 10
        or as check
    B. Line 1 × Line 9
        or as check

When you are computing a mortgage that has payments which are other than monthly or does not have equal payments over the term, this method of arriving at the discount will cause errors. However, when the payments are equal but not monthly you can still compute the constant percent for that mortgage by using the table for payment at a given rate.

For example, assume a mortgage is paid semiannually at 8 percent over 15 years. To find the constant annual percentage, look in a table for semi-annual mortgages at 8 percent for 15 years. The semi-annual payment is $57.83 for each $1000 of the mortgage, or $2,891.50 twice a year for a $50,000 mortgage. This totals $5,783 per year or a constant semi-annual percent (per annum) of 11.57 percent, whereas the monthly constant was 11.47 percent. To find the constant rate, take the payment ($57.83), multiply it by 2, and move the decimal to the left one place. Since this mortgage is payable semiannually, you need to take the demand rate from the same table. As the demand rate is 12%, look under 12% for 15 years. This indicates a $72.65 semiannual payment per $1,000. Multiply the payment by 2 (72.65 × 2 = 145.3) then move the decimal to the left one place (14.5). The end result is the constant annual percent of the demand rate based on a semiannual payment. The formula can now be completed as in the first instance. However, remember that different payment schedules at the same contract rate and term of years will have different constants.

Mortgages with unequal payments require rather complicated calculations. However, it will be possible to obtain an estimate for such mortgages by totaling the payments received on a mortgage with equal principal plus interest. This will provide an average constant. The following calculations are for a $10,000 mortgage.

Estimate Constant Annual Percent for Mortgages with Constant Principal plus Interest on the Unpaid Balance

Assume $10,000 mortgage, $1,000 per year and interest at 8% per annum. 10-year payment.

    Step 1: Compute total interest for term of loan.
            FORMULA: Principal Amount × (Term + 1) × Rate ÷ 2.
            $10,000 × (10 + 1) × .08 ÷ 2 = $4,400
            TOTAL INTEREST PAID: $4,400

Step 2: Add Principal Amount

Interest:	$ 4,400
Principal:	$10,000
TOTAL:	$14,400

Step 3: Divide by years (term of loan). This gives the average annual payment.

$14,400 ÷ 10 = $1,440

Step 4: Divide average annual payment by original principal amount of loan and convert to a percentage.

$1,440 ÷ 10,000 = .1440

Converted to % = 14.40%

This results in the Constant Annual Percent for the Mortgage: 14.40%.

In this example, assume the demand rate is 12 percent as in the other examples. Because we have adjusted the payment of the mortgage to show an annual average payment of $1,440, you can use the annual payment table for 12 percent to find the demand constant. Using the table you will find $176.98 is the annual payment for $1,000 for 10 years at 12 percent. It is not necessary to multiply this by 2 as with the semi-annual payment—merely move the decimal one place to the left: 17.7 percent (rounded off). Complete the formula:

$$\frac{14.4}{17.7} = 81.35$$

The 81.35 percent is the discounted price of the mortgage in this estimate (81.35% × $10,000 = $8,135). Remember that this is just an *estimate.* It is not accurate because the constant annual percent is based on averages only.

HOW TO FIND THE INTEREST YIELD ON A MORTGAGE WHICH IS DISCOUNTED

It will be necessary from time to time to know how to calculate the yield on a mortgage that is offered at a discount. For example: Sterling has a $50,000 mortgage with 15 years remaining at 8 percent. The payment is $478 per month (same as Williams' mortgage mentioned earlier). Sterling is offering this mortgage for sale at a 20 percent discount. The purchase price of the mortgage is therefore 80 percent of the face amount ($50,000 × 80% = $40,000). What is the yield to an investor?

The following chart will assist in this calculation. Note that it is very similar to the previous discount chart but with one important difference—we do not know the demand rate. The formula in this computation is:

$$\frac{\text{Constant annual percent}}{\text{Discounted value percent}} = \frac{\text{Constant at}}{\text{yield rate}}$$

The chart has been worked out below. Review it and make your own by using it as a guide.

Yield on a Discounted Mortgage

1. Face Amount of Mortgage (Present Balance Owed) $50,000

2. Contract Rate   8   %

3. Payment (Monthly √, Quarterly ___, Semiannual ___, Annual ___; check one) $478

4. Constant Annual Percent
   Annual Adjustment of Line 3
   Divided by Line 1   11.47   %

5. Discount Rate (known factor)   20   %

6. Discounted amount ratio
   100 Less Line 5   80   %

7. A.   Constant Annual Percent
   $$\frac{\text{(Line 4)}}{\begin{array}{c}\text{Discounted Amount Ratio}\\ \text{(Line 6)}\end{array}} = \text{At Constant Yield R}$$

   $$\frac{11.47}{80} = 14.33\%$$

   B.

8. Find Yield from Tables:
   Locate Closest Constant Rate at 15 Years.

Constant Rate Found:	Corresponding Yield:
A. 13.64	11%
B. 14.40	12%
C. _____	

9. Estimate yield at nearly 12%

HOW SELLERS CAN USE DISCOUNTED MORTGAGES TO HELP THEM SELL THEIR PROPERTY

Given a standard set of circumstances, any buyer will pay more for a property on terms than he will pay if he must invest 100 percent of the price in cash. This conclusion is based on two major assumptions: (1) the buyer can earn a greater yield on his capital from the income of the property or from other sources than the cost of the financing; and (2) the buyer has the alternative of paying cash, such as obtaining financing from the seller.

The seller now has the opportunity to use this factor to his best advantage. If the buyer wants to pay cash, there is no problem and the discounted mortgage aspect does not enter into the picture. However, to broaden the market, or to create a market for a property that is difficult to sell, the seller may offer reasonable financing.

Robinson owns a 50-acre tract of land. It has been on the market for $20,000 per acre ($1,000,000) for nearly six months. His broker suggests that the terms he wants (50% down and short pay-out) are the major drawback. Robinson, however, needs cash for another venture and agrees to reduce the price to $18,000 per acre to move the property ($900,000), but he still needs 50 percent down. His broker examines the situation and proposes that Robinson keep the price at $20,000 per acre since it is reasonable for the market, but that he be willing to accept only 10 percent down. The balance of 90 percent will be broken into two mortgages: a first mortgage in the amount of $500,000 and a second in the amount of $400,000.

The terms are to run concurrently for fifteen years at 6 percent on the first at normal amortization with monthly payments and 8 percent interest only due on the second for the fifteen years. The broker then suggests that Robinson look to a discount of the first mortgage to generate the cash required.

The first mortgage will pay out at the rate of $4220 per month over the fifteen years. The mortgage is saleable if it will yield 10 percent in the general market, as it is only 50 percent of the total value and represents low risk. The broker calculates the sale price to be $392,600, so Robinson would clear this amount on the sale of the mortgage. He would also receive $100,000 down on the property and then have a total of $492,600 (before he pays his broker his fee). Also, he still is owed $400,000 which is earning interest at 8 percent per annum.

Had Robinson offered the property at $900,000, it is unlikely that it would have moved. Instead, the broker used creative financing to convert a difficult property into a more easily marketable one. The buyer needed only $100,000 down, and had a low interest first mortgage and an interest-only second mortgage—both highly acceptable forms of financing for a buyer. Also, since the seller was offering the property with 90 percent financing, little room was left for negotiations by the buyer to reduce the price.

The buyer of the mortgage obtained a good yield at a fairly safe risk. In Robinson's case, the land was at a fair value so the risk was slight. Robinson came out better than he had thought in that the package produced a sale. Had he received 50 percent down at a price of $900,000 he would have had $450,000 in cash, whereas with the $100,000 price and the discount he had $492,000.

The trade-off of a discounted mortgage, instead of lowering the price, will work in many areas of real estate. A free and clear property where the seller can use a first mortgage for the discount, as did Robinson, is best for such a transaction, but the secondary mortgages can be discounted as well.

HOW TO FIND INVESTORS WHO WILL BUY DISCOUNTED MORTGAGES

There are several markets for mortgages. The most organized is that consisting of mortgage brokers. These professional people make their living by placing and making mortgages. They deal with private investors as well as institutional funds and will act on their own behalf or as broker-agents. Because they have daily contact with this field, they are a prime source for discounted mortgages.

Locating these sources is relatively easy. Most will be listed in your phone book. You can also obtain the names of others who are outside your area from your banking sources. The contact you make with them is important.

It should be noted that not all the mortgage brokers you may contact will be viable. Some don't have the contacts that others may have, or may find dealing with you uncomfortable. I presume that you will not be dealing as a mortgage broker and as a real estate broker at the same time. You should make your situation clear to the mortgage broker right away. Your interest in dealing with discounted mortgages is merely to help your client reach a desired goal. Unless you are licensed as a mortgage broker, you may not be entitled to receive a fee. The mortgage broker knows this and will be relieved that you also understand the situation. Those of you who may have both types of licenses already know how to get the co-operation of your fellow mortgage brokers. Therefore, I shall leave that topic alone.

Mortgage brokers are but one source. Trust departments and pension funds that may be located in your area are also candidates for good mortgages, and they like the idea of leveraging up on a discounted mortgage. These sources are found in your local commercial banks and insurance companies. The commercial bank is the best place to start and you might as well go right to the top—the secretary of the president. This astute lady will direct you to all the right people. Often, a recommendation from her to the person you want to deal with is more important than if the president himself called the trust officer and said you were on your way. How so? Follow this suggestion: meet and establish good rapport with the bank's president. This is essential to other dealings you will have in the community anyway. Go over some of the services that the bank offers. Do they have a trust department? If so, what type of trust services do they give?

Once you have had two or three meetings with this bank president, you will have made contact with his secretary. Be sure she knows who you are and that you are on friendly terms with her boss.

The day you want to sit down with the trust officer, give the president's secretary a call and ask her the name of the trust officer in charge: "Is it a Mr. Rankin?" you might ask. Then ask her if she would mind giving Mr. Rankin a call as an introduction for your appointment that day. She usually will and will also have something nice to say about you.

Once you are with the trust officer ask him about his services. He will become a salesman, giving you data about his department. Do not rush in to a trust officer you have never seen and confront him with a discounted mortgage you must sell by that afternoon or else blow a big deal.

Question him about the mortgage brokers he must deal with in buying private mortgages for the trust account or pension fund they represent. If he gives you some names remember them, but the important thing you have learned is that the bank does buy such mortgages. Ask the trust officer who approves such private mortgage purchases how you would go about presenting a package to them.

Private investors are numerous, although very difficult to cultivate. Earlier chapters have dealt with this private investor in mortgages. But to be somewhat repetitive, remember the private investor in mortgages is not greatly unlike the investor in real estate. They both recognize the advantage of realty as a security. However, the mortgage investor is willing to take a lower yield at a reduced risk than the real estate investor.

Some of your realty buyers may like to sink some of their portfolio into mortgages, so don't overlook your own buyers of real estate as possible investors. To some degree, this source comes out of your back pocket because you will not receive a fee for placing such an investment. But the sale of the mortgage may close another deal. Besides, passing a good mortgage at a high yield on to a past investor will be appreciated and the favor will be returned.

Look in the mirror. The person looking back at you may be a prime discounted mortgage buyer. It is not impossible that you may look to the mortgage as the total commission or at least a part of your fee. Sellers will often ask you to take part or all of a mortgage as your fee. Your ability to plan for this possibility and to have the mortgage discounted will depend on your willingness to take the paper.

If you approach the possibility of discounting a mortgage as part of a cash-out program for the seller, you should speak to him early and tell him that at times your firm will buy mortgages as an investment or take the paper as all or part of the fee. Do this only if you are prepared or if your firm is willing to do it. The opposite is also necessary. Tell the seller that your firm is not in a position to take paper on such a discount, but you will do all you can to help him dispose of the mortgage.

To avoid mention of one of these two possibilities will leave the suggestion up to the seller. Refusing to take the paper at that moment in time may cast doubts in the seller's mind about your earlier suggestions that he make such a transaction and hold such paper in the first place.

Don't forget the mortgagor. He may be a prime buyer for a discounted mortgage. Naturally, in these situations the seller of the mortgage is the mortgagee. He may be holding paper from a previous sale or may be investor who bought a mortgage from you or someone else. Before you run off and seek out other investors, offer the discount to the guy who makes the monthly payment. By giving him a break in the pay-off, he may become a good client later on. In any event, the buyer of the mortgage makes little difference to the mortgagee selling the paper—it is the cash that is important.

A Review of the Sources That Will Buy Discounted Mortgages

1. *Mortgage brokers:* For the broker who will not deal frequently with discounted mortgages, this source can be consistent and easy to approach.
2. *Trust funds and pension funds:* A little harder to approach, but one of the prime sources used by the mortgage broker. These sources are found at your commercial banks and insurance companies.
3. *Private investors:* Look first at your own realty investors. Some of these clients may like a good discounted mortgage. Other private investors will advertise in local papers or can be found through your bank or savings and loan.
4. *You:* Take a discounted mortgage as part of your fee. However, be careful you don't have to give a discount yourself to buy the mortgage. Early disclosure of your firm's attitude to mortgages as part of your fee will help in dealing with the seller.
5. *The mortgagor:* Never overlook the person who writes out the monthly check that pays off the loan.

A PARTIAL DISCOUNT TO THE MORTGAGOR

It may be possible to raise some quick cash by going to the mortgagor and suggesting a discount on the future payments if he will prepay some of the outstanding principal. I was involved in such a case some time ago. Emory was holding a $45,000 second mortgage on a business he had sold several years earlier. The mortgage had fifteen years remaining at 8½ percent interest per annum. The annual payment was based on monthly payments of $443.25. The constant annual percent on this mortgage is 11.82 (found in constant table under 8½ percent at fifteen years). Emory needed a quick $15,000 and found that if he were to discount the mortgage the yield necessary would be 12 percent. This meant the sale price would be $36,936 (11.82 ÷ 14.40 × 45,000). Emory felt this was too great a discount to take in order to obtain the $15,000 needed.

He approached one of the local mortgage brokers to see whether he could borrow against the mortgage, but that did not produce any positive results. By the time Emory called me, he was at his wits end. "I need the cash by the end of the week," he said, "and it seems that the more I need it, the tougher it becomes to get it." Sounds very familiar, I know.

After counseling with Emory, I suggested we make the following proposal to the mortgagor. The mortgagor would prepay $15,000 on the outstanding mortgage. This would bring the unpaid principal balance down to $30,000. Based on this balance, the monthly amortization would be reduced to $295.50. As an inducement or bonus to the mortgagor, Emory agreed to reduce the interest rate on the mortgage to 6½ percent rather than the 8½ percent for its remaining term. This gave a new constant of 10.45 and a monthly payment of $261.25 instead of the $295.50. What this meant was that the mortgagor was obtaining a discount for the remaining balance by the prepayment of the $15,000. Over the balance of the term the mortgagor would save $6,165. The cost to Emory was not really the $6,165 however, as the reduction of the interest lowered his pretax income and converted future pay-back (the mortgage) into ready cash. A discounting of the mortgage would have caused a greater reduction of total earnings, and hence all parties benefited.

There were many other ways to approach the benefit Emory had given the mortgagor, but this solution seemed to be the best for Emory. The mortgage, as it turned out, was paid off four years later when the property was sold by the mortgagor. No doubt the low interest on the second was somewhat instrumental in attracting a buyer, even though the property was refinanced anyway. The gamble Emory took in reducing the interest rate was well calculated. Had he reduced the principal amount in the discount, that sum would have been a lost item regardless of when the mortgage was paid back. The reduced interest was an expense to Emory only as long as the mortgage was in force. Emory knew that most mortgages have a maximum life span of seven to ten years in the type of business he had. The life span of mortgages is important in discounting. The early retirement of a mortgage will boost the yield to the holder when the face amount is discounted.

The bonus yield that comes when a discounted mortgage is paid off cannot be calculated except by experience in the loan market for the area. Some savings and loans and commercial banks will give you the statistics on their type of loan history, but many feel this is confidential information. Here's why:

Assume that Emory had sold his $45,000 mortgage at a discount which would have yielded 12 percent. As we saw in the example the price would have been $36,936. Remember, the face amount on the mortgage is $45,000. If the loan were paid off at the end of the first year the new mortgagee (the investor who bought the mortgage from Emory) would have been paid approximately $48,800. As the investor paid only $36,936 for the paper, his return on his investment for one year would be $11,864, or a yield of 32.12 percent. Each year this bonus will decline, and by the fifteenth year the yield is down to the 12 percent discounted yield. The incredible bonus interest that comes with this early prepayment is one of the real advantages of the discounted mortgage and should never be taken lightly.

Examination of the total financing on the property may disclose a potential necessity for refinancing in which a mandatory prepayment of a mortgage may be imminent. For example: A first mortgage is offered for discount. It is a twenty-year mortgage at a moderate interest rate. Because of the term of years, the discount will be rather high. The mortgage broker examines the underlying mortgages and finds a large second mortgage which is interest only for three years with a balloon payment. The combined financing is less than 60 percent of the value and the second mortgage is nearly half that total. The mortgage broker concludes that the owner of the property will refinance all of the mortgages into one new first mortgage before the end of the three years when the second mortgage balloons. Not only is such a mortgage a good risk, but the discount and probable bonus will give an exceedingly high yield.

Another situation would be when the discounted mortgage is a second mortgage behind a low interest rate first mortgage that is nearly paid off. Such mortgages have a high constant rate and become prime candidates for refinancing even though the new interest rate would be higher. The constant rate for income property is often more important than the interest rate. Once the mortgage is refinanced, the second mortgage would automatically be paid off.

The combinations are endless. The motivation of the mortgagor is also important. Some mortgagors have a history of early prepayment. If you have this information, it's worth its weight in discounted mortgages.

Chapter 16

TWO PROFESSIONAL TECHNIQUES THAT BUILD WEALTH

One of the primary rules of smart investing is: Reduce your risk. I have referred to this concept several times. You reduce your risk in a variety of ways, and risk is relative to your knowledge and ability. One man's risk is another man's fun.

"I'll pay your price if you accept my terms." This works for any savvy buyer as long as the buyer knows the alternatives available to make the terms fit the price he is willing to pay. What happens is this: I find a property I want to buy and then approach the seller with the news that I'm interested in buying and will pay a reasonable price. The seller views reasonable price in different terms than I do, but let's not argue at this stage of the game. "Tell me your price, Mr. Seller. As long as I can work it out, I'm interested in buying."

The proper avenue to take when dealing through a broker is to tell the broker of your intent and begin there. As long as you're not buying for all cash, you know that whatever the price offered, there will be some terms that you can work out to bring the price in line with what you can afford. This chapter will give you two good and creative techniques that can be used by themselves or in combination, and there are many different and highly creative formats of offers you can devise using these two techniques.

The two techniques to be covered in this chapter are the preferred purchase deal and the option.

PREFERRED PURCHASE

One of my early clients taught me about this deal. It is a magnificent way to get down to the nitty-gritty in a deal where the seller is telling you, "I'd love to keep this property but I need some cash." Mind you, this kind of transaction is based on a sizable amount of cash coming into the deal and is usually not an option available to the low-cash-down buyer. Of course, frequently the "cash" can be obtained from other sources, but from the seller's point of view cash is what is going to talk.

Let me set the stage for a preferred purchase deal.

Charles owns a beautiful office building in downtown San Francisco. It is fully rented, or nearly so, and Charles has a nice suite of offices in the building. He has a pro forma showing the income and expenses, and projects that within a year or so, when he can increase the rents in the building, the investment will provide a very good return to a prospective buyer.

"I need some cash," Charles says, and your broker has conveyed this to you.

Now, buying an office building is one thing, but assume that you aren't in the business of managing office buildings. You like the idea of the rent and the income and the tax shelter, but the idea of management isn't to your liking. Besides, you live in Chicago.

In this deal, Charles reports the following:

Price	$1,500,000
Mortgages	750,000
Cash to buy	$ 750,000

The debt service on the existing $750,000 mortgage is $94,000 per year. On top of that Charles reports that the operating expenses and taxes and the like total another $50,000 per year. Gross revenue at the moment is $220,000.

If these figures were correct and you paid $750,000 cash for this deal, you would be making the cash flow shown below:

Gross revenue	$220,000
Operating expenses	50,000
Net operating income	$170,000
Debt service	94,000
Cash flow	$ 76,000

This is slightly more than 10 percent on your invested capital. This is not bad, because you have lots of other benefits going along with this deal. There is ample tax shelter and lots of future equity buildup. If the rents can be increased and costs held down, there is even appreciation. Not a bad deal at all.

Except that Charles has overestimated on the pro forma a little. The expenses are probably low by $10,000 or more, and there is no vacancy factor accounted for. There is about $25,000 in income at risk here, although that's being conservative from the buyer's point of view. But the property is a very nice building and you would like to own it.

Offer a preferred purchase deal.

You offer to buy 50 percent of the building and will pay $400,000 cash for that opportunity. All you want is the following:

- To be preferred (to receive from the top of the cash flow), 10 percent on your cash invested. The seller takes the next equal amount, and everything else is split 50/50.
- All or most of the depreciation. This is a negotiating point; depending on the deal and the motivation of the seller, you might end up with the building and the seller with the land (land is not depreciable).
- When the property is sold or refinanced, you will share in the proceeds on a 50/50 basis.

   There are other points you could have asked for, such as the right to buy out the seller's interest at a time in the future at a formula to be offered in this deal, or just a first right of refusal down the road. You might find that as the loan is paid off and the value increases you would be able to buy out the partner through the funds obtained in refinancing the property.

You could also have asked for the deficit (if any) of your preferred interest to build up and add to your investment. For example, say there is a bad year and the total cash flow is only $30,000. As you would get the first 10 percent of your invested capital, which was $400,000, you would get the entire $30,000. Yet you are $10,000 short. If you have a buildup on deficit, then your invested capital for next year's calculations is now $410,000. This would go on until some defined point where the partner would see his share eaten up and would drop out of the picture.

Why would a seller accept a deal like this? Well, look at it from his point of view. He is getting $400,000 in cash and still has 50 percent of the deal. He will be given a management contract as a part of the deal, so he will be allowed to take a mangement fee off the top. If he has confidence in the deal, he will quickly see that within a few years he is going to profit far more than if he had sold the property and taken the $750,000 cash to the mortgage. But note one very important aspect here: Charles isn't being given the choice of $750,000 or the preferred deal. He must choose between this preferred deal or his best offer (if any).

The buyer's advantage is easy to see. You as the investor in this deal have bought sound management with motivation to stay in and do a good job. You would offer a preferred deal, by the way, on the condition that the seller to do exactly that—manage the property. If you were concerned about that ability, then you had best stay away from the deal unless it was so good that outside management could be found easily and quickly.

In making this kind of deal you might well find the seller suddenly changing his tune about how good the project is. "Well, I don't think the income will be *that* good" is the aftermath of some preferred presentations.

Big smart money uses the preferred deal to nail down solid projects with good management and a motivated seller who needs some cash. In the development business there are often good managers and developers who get cash-short on a new project and for construction overages or whatever. These deals make for the mainstay of the preferred deals, but they aren't necessarily limited to that kind of project.

You can buy a business or any small venture on this preferred plan. Whatever you buy that is income-producing has the potential of being financed in this way. If you are looking at a business, don't buy 100 percent of the deal, but instead keep the current owner in at a percentage of the deal. That way you can move into many varied deals without losing your flexibility.

THE OPTION

Buying with an option is an ideal way to put time on your side for a change. The option contract gives you the opportunity to put up some money that can build into a sizable equity in a hurry if you are right about the trends. If you are wrong, then you have kept your risk at a minimum.

There are several kinds of option agreements, but for the most part they fall into two categories, the straight option and the conditioned option.

The straight option is, as the name would suggest, a standard type of agreement that simply provides for the would-be buyer to pay to the seller a sum of money for the right to buy the property at a set date in the future at a price agreed to in the present.

Nearly all aspects of the contract are flexible and open to negotiation up until the contract is signed. For example, you can have a price that is tied to some third element, such as the price of gold, or income. You can have a date for the ultimate purchase that is flexible. Whatever those items are, they should be spelled out in detail at the time the option is given and the money is paid. A contract to buy and sell is part of the option agreement.

In the straight option there is no guarantee of sale, of course, and the seller is being compensated by the option price for the time the property is taken off the market. Also, the seller is fixed to the terms of the sale agreed on in the option, and if the value goes up well above the set price, it is the buyer who has profited.

At the signing of the straight option the money goes to the property owner, and there is no possibility of a return of that money to the buyer unless the seller cannot deliver the kind of title called for. The inability of a seller to deliver a clear title doesn't occur often, but it is a possibility. Because of this, it is advisable for the option buyer to check the title early in the period. If the idea is to hold the option and sell the contract, the whole plan can be ruined if the seller can't deliver good title.

The Conditioned Option

Here the optionee has included in the contract some conditions that can cancel or change the contract. These conditions might be such that the price will change, or the time to buy will be increased or decreased; most important, the conditions may call for a full return of the option money if something doesn't occur (or does occur, as the case may be).

From the buyer's point of view the conditioned option is the least risky of deals. If you have an option agreement and can tie up a tract of land for a period of time, and because of some condition in the agreement (which you may control) you can get your option money back, you haven't risked anything.

Conditions frequently used in conditional options include:

1. *Soil test.* Your right to test and approve the subsoil conditions.
2. *Survey certification.* Your approval of the exact dimensions, etc.
3. *Bering test.* A more detailed subsoil examination.
4. *Site plan approval.* Government approval of your planned development.
5. *Issuance of building permit.* Actual and final stage before building.
6. *Partner's approval.* A clear out if your partner nixes the deal.
7. *Corporate ratification.* Similar to the above.
8. *Obtaining satisfactory financing.* Necessary in many deals.
9. *Government approval.* This covers a wide range of sins.
10. *Prior sale of a third property.* When you need to sell something else.
11. *Prior development of a section 1031 exchange.* You have to develop an exchange before you can close.
12. *Preleasing of to-be-developed space.* Many lenders will demand this.

Of these twelve items, you can see that some can be simply accomplished and would not normally take a long time, while others can take months or in some cases, such as government approval, years. In all cases you (the buyer) have control over these items and can make sure the condition fails to be met.

The seller in the conditioned option contract will naturally object to tying up his land with the buyer having a full right to a refund of option money in situations where the buyer can back out of the deal. In essence, what has been created is a free option, with the money being not much more than good-faith deposit. Yet despite the fact that many sellers will object to such contractual agreements, many conditional agreements are made each day. Sellers try to limit the time for these conditions, realizing that the option is "free," and to provide for other safeguards to counterbalance the lack of security in the refundable deposit. Such counterbalances are in strict timetables, elements of past performance being a main criterion in the decision to go along with the condition if it is time-consuming. In essence, if the optionee is genuine and can give the impression he is going to buy, his chances are improved in using a conditioned option agreement.

All twelve items used in the option contract can be conditions in the actual sales agreement as well, and when they are used in that form of purchase they convert the buy-and-sell agreement into a conditional option agreement.

USING OPTION AGREEMENTS

The scenario is as follows: A tight money market, high interest rates, and unrest in the real estate market. It is a growing buyer's market, and while the trends indicate that there is a turnaround somewhere down the road, you aren't sure when that is going to be. You have found a property that you want to buy. You know that the more you reduce your risk, the more profit potential you have in the future.

The price you feel you can get the property for is $100,000. The seller has been asking more, but that's what you want to pay. You find that current interest rates are around 15 percent in the prime market, around 12 percent in land sales.

Your first offer is a conditioned option agreement. You offer $10,000 option money for the right to buy the property for $100,000. You agree to give the seller $10,000 right away. As a condition to the deal you call for your unqualified approval of a subsoil test. You want to make sure that there are no subterranean conditions which will make building on this site very expensive. You allow for ninety days for this to be made. If you disapprove of the results, you get your money back and the deal is off.

If you approve the test, you have nine months in which to exercise the option to buy. All you have to do to exercise the deal is to sign the buy-and-sell agreement attached to the option and return it to the seller. You have sixty days to close on the deal after that. (By the way, when you close on the property the option money you paid is to be applied to the sales price.)

The soil test condition gives you three months to examine the property and decide if you want to go through with the deal. If you go ahead, you have another nine months to exercise the option to buy, and then another sixty days to close on the purchase. In all, you have one year and two months to make the deal. You paid $10,000 at the beginning, which is counted as a part of the purchase price. Even if the seller had insisted that the $10,000 not be counted at closing, you would have tied up the property for under 10 percent interest for those fourteen months.

When You Know You Are Going to Buy, Use the Option

You can see that when you aren't sure about buying, the option gives you some time to make the final decision. It locks up the price and terms so that you know exactly what to base the decision on. But when you *know* you are going to buy, the option gives you added appreciation and reduces your carrying cost for the first year or so.

In the deal described above, you would have tied up a $100,000 property for fourteen months at no real cost in the long run. You would have gotten fourteen months during which time you didn't have to pay the real estate taxes on that property and you got all the appreciation. As long as you don't need immediate title to the property, the option-to-buy deal is a great way to get a head start on appreciation.

Using the Option to Sell

The seller likes the option because he is a gambler. If you were a seller and you didn't have a buyer for your property and someone came along and said, "I'll give you money just to let me decide if I'll buy the property," you might be inclined to take the deal. After all, if the option fails to be exercised, you still have the property. In the meantime, the investor has paid you for the time which passed, during which you might not have sold the property anyway.

Options work because people like to gamble and options are a safe way to risk little from the seller's point of view.

As a seller you can use the option to help entice a buyer into your hard-to-sell property. If a buyer will pay your price if you accept his terms, then you should be able to get a better price by offering better terms. In the case of a tough-to-sell property, you may have to resort to some very creative selling techniques. There is nothing wrong with being creative, and moving a dog in a tough market may call for all the creativity you can generate.

One of the problems of the real estate market is that there are times when value has little to do with the ability to sell something. The inability to finance a deal might cause a builder to shy away from your kind of land, or a potential user to decide not to buy your vacant building. Use the option to get their interest, then sink the hook.

It's like anything else. If you can get someone's attention, then you can often create an environment that didn't exist before. In dealing with builders and developers, getting them involved is often the first step in making the deal.

A tough deal may need lots of good ideas and some hard work running around getting tenants, getting sites rezoned, etc. The builder won't do that if he has to lay out heavy bucks to tie up the land. So offer him an option.

When the potential buyer has an option, he will start thinking how he can make a profit. Once the would-be buyer starts thinking about making a profit, then his creative mind is working in your favor as well as his. He will have to buy your land or building to make his profit.

The idea is to find a probable buyer for your property and establish some rapport with him. You can't walk into his office and say, "How do you do; by the way, I'll give you an option on my land." Sure this sounds fresh and creative, but also a little nuts.

A better approach is to have your broker make a presentation to the buyer. ("How would you like to buy Jack's land?") You will get feedback when you do that and you will see if there is any interest. One of the first signs of interest comes with the statement, "The price is too high." There is no reason to knock your price unless there is some interest (or he is just one of those guys who likes to knock everything).

Your broker can take this approach:

"Mr. Prospective Buyer, I understand your reasons for saying the price might be too high. But I feel that someone with your experience could put this site to its best use. The owner is so conscious of your ability that he'll give you a sixty-day option to buy this land. I know that if you truly become interested in this land you will profit by it."

Yet options are more of a tool than just this. In fact, over the past dozen years the option has evolved into one of the best methods of building a great amount of wealth. Move on through the remainder of this chapter to see just how attractive the option can be when used in the right circumstance by a knowledgeable investor.

USING THE OPTION TO FINANCE YOUR WAY TO A FORTUNE

As you have discovered thus far, there are many ways to use the option in real estate investing and financing. The creative ways in which you use this tool will depend only on your full understanding of four elements of the option.

THE FOUR KEY ELEMENTS TO THE OPTION

1. The option is a one-sided event that gives you control over some future event that the owner of the property does not have.
2. The option has a psychological effect on sellers and buyers alike depending on the circumstance and use of the tool.
3. Options can be used successfully by both the buyer and the seller.
4. Options are a promise of a future event, a box behind the curtain that holds is a lure to the other party that can be more attractive than the known offer.

Using the option to your best benefit will depend on its placement in the right situation. Look at several examples of how you might use the option and win.

THE PRIMARY OPTION

The primary option transaction is a basic study in greed. In this technique, the buyer uses the option to keep the cost of the total financing at a minimum, while tying up the property for a period of time in which the buyer can back out of the deal without excess cost. As in all option transactions, the buyer holds the cards and all the aces.

The significance of this specific kind of option is the buyer knows ahead of the game that he is absolutely going to buy.

The advantage of the option in this case is purely as a delaying tactic to the usual costs of a closing: down payment, interest, costs, and so on.

The transaction follows this scenario: A seller is asking, say, $800,000 for the tract of land on which you want to build a shopping center. You know that you will buy the land and are attempting to (1) lessen the interest cost between now and the exact date you have to fund the construction project, and (2) reduce your immediate cash outlay.

To accomplish these ends, you make the following offer:

You'll pay the seller $30,000 cash within 90 days as option money to allow you to make a feasibility study of the specific site for commercial use. For this payment, you will be allowed 240 days in which to complete the study. If you are satisfied with the study, you can proceed to a closing, within a 60-day period or you can obtain an extension of the option period for an additional 180 days by paying to the seller another $50,000. If you determine at the end of that time that the commercial venture is not feasible for any reason, the seller keeps the option money paid and you are released from any further obligation to that party. On the other hand, the contract indicates that if you determine that you want to purchase the property, you can proceed with the closing. At the closing, you will receive full credit against the purchase price for any and all option money thus far paid to the seller. The end result of this transaction is ideal for the buyer. He has tied up the property for 390 days for only $30,000. He can extend this time if he wants or can close. The $30,000 paid, as well as any additional option money, is applied toward the purchase price. Best of all, the actual closing, and interest that might have been otherwise due on any mortgages, is postponed during this same time. This interest would have exceeded the total option money paid.

OPTION TO BUY IN A LEASE

In a sale lease, one of the most critical elements to the transaction is the option to buy the property, and if possible all sale leasebacks should contain the option to buy back.

Remember, options are absolutely one-sided. The best time to establish them is when you have control in the transaction. If you are leasing, insert a simple option provision in the lease if you can. If you are selling your own property and leasing it back, even the most hard-hearted buyer is apt to grant an option for you to buy back your own property at a more than generous profit to the buyer down the road. Keep in mind, this option may end up having no value to you if you overestimate the future growth of the area or that specific property. On the other hand, if things go as they have in the past, you might find that the sale of your option in the future is far more profitable than the sale of the property the first time.

Whenever you have a sale leaseback, the option to recapture the property is a benefit that you should attempt to negotiate into the deal. You may have no interest at the moment of ever owning the property, but times change and property values can skyrocket when future events create demands not deemed possible at the present.

HOW TO WRITE THE OPTION

"The lessee herein has the option to purchase the subject property anytime during the lease or its extensions for $1,000,000." It might be as simple as that, but most likely it will be far more complex. As in all contracts, it is important that you get it right, and that means get it done with a good real estate lawyer.

The following list should be reviewed by you and your lawyer when it comes time to draft the option agreement into the lease or sale-leaseback portions of the contract. Many of these items are business decisions you or the other party will have to make a judgment on. Since you should know more about the property and what you can do with it than your lawyer, that decision should be solely yours.

THE FIVE KEY ELEMENTS TO THE OPTION CONTRACT

1. Think Beyond What You Think You Need.   This is where most people overlook the option in the first place. "Well, for goodness' sake, I never thought about asking for an option." Well, now you will, right? You should attempt to put the options in every agreement you can whenever you buy or lease real estate. Remember, the worst that can happen is that the other party will want to remove it, giving you the opportunity to counteract by putting in another benefit to you.

2. Use the Option as a Negotiating Tool.   Assume that you are trying to lease a home. The property owner is telling you that you can have a two-year lease. The price is okay, but you want to push for additional leverage or benefits in the deal. You say something like this: "Mr. Property Owner, as my wife and I plan to improve this property by living here, we would like to have the option to buy the home at the end of the lease. If we can establish a fair price to you at this time, we will put that amount in the lease. That will give us incentive to improve the property. Naturally, if I get transferred to California and we are unable to take advantage of the option, you will keep the improvements we do to the home."

There are several subtle elements here to help the property owner make up his mind to give you the option: improved property, fair price, incentive for the lessee to improve (and stay and pay rent on time), and best of all, the lessee might be transferred to California and lessor keeps all.

If you are leasing an office within an office building, ask for an option to buy the building. "Mr. Office Building Owner, as we may have to expand over the years, it is possible that we may need the whole building some time in the future. If that were to occur, I think it would be the time for us to own the building. We will sign your lease right now if you could give us an option to buy the building within the first ten years of our lease."

3. Watch Out for Sellers or Landlords Who Try to Entice You with the Option.   There is a program called Shared Equity Transactions, which I describe in more detail in the chapter entitled "Fifteen Creative Deal-Making Techniques." This is a wealth building plan that works on buyers' or tenants' motivation to own their own property.

The way the plan works is this: A real estate investor will buy a property for $40,000 and then advertise that he will sell 50 percent of the equity for *nothing down.* When someone comes along, the deal is described as follows: The prospective buyer, who has nothing to put down, will move into the home (or apartment) and pay all actual costs. These costs might include (1) payments on a $55,000 mortgage, and (2) taxes, insurance, and upkeep of the house. The deal is that if the prospective buyer will stay in the house for five years, the house will then be sold, and the prospective buyer will get 50 percent of the net proceeds of the sale that exceed $60,000.

The actual numbers may differ, but the plan works by enticing the prospective buyer to believe there is equity in the home and that entering into a lease with this kind of option has value. It may have, but you should always know values prior to making that kind of contract. The people who teach the courses that instruct the real estate investor how to use the shared equity plans stress the "profit" that comes up front in the deal through increased value from the day the property was bought to the day it is leased under the kind of option explained (even if that was day two of the transaction).

Options offered to tenants that have unrealistic prices or formulas to arrive at a price have no value to the deal and should be viewed as the bait to the deal. Of course, you can keep the option in, but be sure you recognize what might be nothing more than an attempt to get you in the property. Make sure that you are not taking the lease for that reason alone.

4. Know Your Options in the Negotiations.   Many people ask for an option, and when the sharp property owner puts in a paragraph that looks like an option they are satisfied. Here are some elements you can ask for in option provisions.

   a. *Option to extend your lease.* If your lease was for one year, ask for options to extend for additional years by doing something each year on the eleventh month. That something might be a notice to the owner, or payment of $50 or whatever you can put into the lease. If your lease provides an option to buy during the term of the lease that provision should also include extensions of the lease, so that your "option to buy" would not terminate simply because you extended the term of the lease.
   b. *Option to buy during the lease.* You can ask for, and some owners will agree, to give you credit for some or even all of the rent paid. This will be determined by the need of that property owner to get the place rented in the first place.
   c. *Options should have a specific price, or clear formula at establishing prices for new rent or purchase prices.* There are many different ways to approach this. A percentage of the cost of living, or the entire increase of a cost of living index can be used. However, there are several different indexes, so ask your lawyer about this format. I recommend that you remember the term "All Items Index" as that averages out the specific items index that can rise quicker than the average.
   d. *If all else fails, get a "first right of refusal."* This is an option only triggered when the owner has a bonafide contract from another party which is acceptable to that owner. You would have a period of time

to accept the same terms. This is the weakest of all options, but none
the gives you some control over the property.

e. *Remember, when it comes time to take advantage of the option to
renew your rent or buy the building, you don't have to do it as the
contract says.* The option only binds the other party to those terms.
"Mr. Property Owner, my option to buy is at $150,000. However, as
conditions are not as attractive now as I had thought they might be,
I don't feel the property is worth more than $125,000. I'll pay that
now, or wait a couple of more years to see if I could afford the full
price covered in my option."

5. *Use Options as an Asset When Buying Other Property.* As a
part of the deal, you can offer the seller of a property the same option you
have with the office building owner. If you own property, you can use
the option as a future benefit bonus in any transaction you want to move
forward.

Chapter 17

FOUR ADDITIONAL METHODS OF FINANCING REAL ESTATE

In the writing of this book, there were several forms of financing that did not seem to constitute a complete chapter. Nonetheless, they are all very important and have some special use either as a complete form of financing in themselves or when used in combination with other forms. They can often mean the difference between making or not making a deal. Therefore, I have put these four forms into this chapter. They are not placed in order of importance. Each is equally important.

These four methods of financing are:

1. Leasehold financing
2. Percent of income
3. Land lease
4. Co-ventures and syndicates

The purpose of this chapter is to cover these five methods of financing—to enable you to see how they are used, what they do to help you make more transactions, and when to bring them into play.

LEASEHOLD FINANCING

A leasehold is the ownership of a right to use a specific property for a term of years for which the lessee pays rent. The tenant has a leasehold interest in the property or space, and as long as the terms of the lease are met that interest is real and can be pledged as security on loans. Some types of leasehold interests are more valuable than others, and this value depends on the following factors:

1. The type of property leased. It should be obvious that different properties will have different values. If all other aspects are equal, lease on an office building should be more valuable than a lease on vacant land. A lender looking at the possibility of making a loan on a leasehold will look very strongly to the value of the space or property. If the leasehold loan is for improvements in a boutique in a shopping center, the usefulness of that space for other types of businesses will be important. The economics of the property will be most important in the evaluation of real equity.

2. The annual rent of the lease. The lease is the document which will create the actual value. The leasehold equity will become the security for the unsubordinated loan, and leasehold equity is found by appraising the space or property and deducting a capitalized value of the rent from that amount. For example: FPA Corp. has a 60-unit hotel on the beach. It is located on leased land. FPA Corp. owns the right to use the property —for which they pay an annual rent of $26,500. Assume they had no financing and built the hotel with cash. The finished value of the building was $1,050,000 and the land is worth $875,000. Therefore, the total combined value is $1,925,000. As FPA Corp. pays $26,500 in rent, this amount can be said to represent a cost of a capital investment. Setting a cap rate of 10 percent on this cost would make the investment $265,000. An 8 percent cap rate would increase the investment to $331,250. See the computations below to determine the leasehold equity at 10 percent and 8 percent cap rates with a leasehold mortgage of $800,000. It should be clear that the cost of the lease, in terms of annual rent, must be capitalized to give an adjustment in the equity. The rate which is used may vary from property to property and from lender to lender. It is a good idea to show the leasehold equity at two different rates and then take the lower rate in your loan package. In any event, the fact that FPA Corp. is leasing the land at $26,500 per year, and the land has a current value of $875,000, is some indication that you will have excellent leasehold appreciation and equity. Yet, the leasehold equity must consider the improvements and their existing financing.

3. The period of time remaining on the lease. If the lease expires in one year, the leasehold equity will be that equity which can be substantiated economically over the remaining term of the lease. The hotel

	10%	8%
1. Annual rent on lease of land	$ 26,500	26,500
2. Capital investment of cap rate to provide rent	265,000	331,250
3. Combined value of land and buildings	1,925,000	1,925,000
4. Less existing financing	800,000	800,000
5. Gross equity before adjustment for land lease	$1,125,000	1,125,000
6. Less amount from Line 2	265,000	331,250
7. Total leasehold equity	$ 860,000	793,750
8. Less capital investment	100,000	100,000
9. Leasehold equity appreciation	$ 760,000	693,750

owned by FPA Corp. on leased land will continue to have value, as will the land. FPA's leasehold value, however, will begin to decline at a point in time when the remaining term of the lease does not allow return of capital at a reasonable rate of return for that remaining period. For example: The hotel has a value based on the economic return. In most income properties this economic value is the more important of all value approaches, and should be close to or below the replacement cost evaluation. If the replacement value were lower than the economic value, it might be more prudent to build a new hotel. Nonetheless, this economic return may continue for twenty years in a reasonable projection. However, FPA Corp. may have only ten years in which to enjoy the benefit of their leasehold if their lease expires at the end of that time. An investor interested in purchasing the leasehold from FPA Corp. would analyze the yield only for the remaining term, giving little credit to the actual value of the property. A lender would look at the leasehold equity in the same way.

4. The conditions and provisions of the lease. Each lease is a new ball game. There are many provisions or conditions which can make it desirable or undesirable. Rights to sublet, diversity of use, high maintenance costs and the like will be examined carefully by any lender prior to a loan. Because these terms are so important in possible financing, a lessee should make every effort to create a lease that will offer a good basis for leasehold financing.

5. The use of the property. Is the building a single-purpose structure or is it easily adaptable to other uses? Is the use economically sound or not? These are important factors to the lender, not only because he may end up with the building, but for the tenant to survive and the leasehold equity to be maintained the economics of the operation must be in the tenant's favor.

6. The tenant. Of course, the lender will always take a good long look at the tenant. After all, it is the tenant that wants to borrow the money. All lenders are very interested in the person they lend money to.

These six factors will be the main criteria which will create leasehold financing. Each factor is important on its own, but it is the combined effect of all six that will provide a package that is financeable.

Leasehold financing comes in two forms: *subordinated fee* and *unsubordinated fee*. There is a considerable amount of money lent in both types, but the majority of the larger loans are on leasehold interests with subordinated fee. The situation of FPA Corp. with their hotel on leased land is a good example. The land lease had a provision which enabled FPA to obtain a first mortgage that would be secured by the improvements as well as the land. The owners of the land subordinated their interest to the lender on the first mortgage and took a second position. The lender could foreclose on both the improvements and the land if FPA Corp. defaulted on the mortgage and the land owners did not step in to take it over.

This adds to the land owner's risk of course, and increases the value of the lease as less equity is needed to build the hotel. Any increase in appreciation in the combined package will be leveraged upward due to this financing. The lender generally looks to the subordinated land lease as secondary financing behind his loan.

Many owners do not want to subordinate their land or other interests so that the leasehold owner can use their equity to obtain a loan. After all, when the land is subordinated, the lender will look to the real value of land and buildings without deducting the capitalized rent cost to arrive at a leasehold equity. If the owner does not subordinate the fee to the lender, then the financing must be made with unsubordinated fee.

The terms of the lease become most important here. If the lease is for a very long term (usually the term of the loan plus a sufficient remaining term to allow the investor to benefit from a build-up of equity, say 150 percent of the mortgage life) and the payments on it are not onerous, then the lender will look to these leasehold interests as a pseudo-fee. This fee or ownership of the land is seen as a clear use of the land, and if all other factors work out a loan can be made without the subordination.

There are some areas in the world where almost all the land is leased and most all real estate financing is leasehold. Hong Kong and Hawaii are good examples of places where leasehold financing is rather prominent.

How Leasehold Financing Can Be a Deal Maker

The ability to pull apart a property to a fee equity and a lease-hold equity can be used in many different forms. A sale and lease-back, for example, is generally the sale of a property and then the leasing back of it by the seller. It may be feasible to sell the land to one party and lease that back and sell the building to another investor and lease it back. These two separate types of leases each have different values. First, the land lease could have excellent terms for the new owner of the land, thereby giving him a secure return for which he will accept the lower rate you want. The investor looking for tax shelter, and not much cash flow, may like the idea of owning a building. The fact that it is on leased land may add rather than subtract from his desire to buy. He cannot depreciate the land, but can deduct the rent on it.

The ability to obtain new financing on leased land or on leasehold space in other buildings will depend on your contacts in the money market. It will also depend on the total combined effect of the six factors shown in the earlier part of this section.

The rise and decline of the leasehold equity is, of course, the most important aspect of leasehold financing. The security offered by this equity, along with other risk reducers such as personal signature and guarantee on the note and pledge of other collateral or security, makes the leasehold mortgage a most interesting form of financing.

The sources for such finance monies are commercial banks and mortgage bankers and brokers. These sources do most of the lending in this form of financing, yet the savings and loans associations and insurance companies are effective in leasehold financing on a larger scale. All loan sources have dealt with one form of leasehold money at one time or another and continue to do so.

If you are financing on subordinated fee to a leasehold, then the lender will approach the loan as though the property is owned in fee simple rather than a leasehold. In that event, seek the normal lender for the type of property you have.

PERCENT OF INCOME

This form of percent taking is far more frequent than the sharing of actual ownership. In this form of financing the lender will receive his normal payment of interest and principal. But in addition to those payments, he will also receive a bonus of all or part of the income above a set standard. For example: Insurance Company A loans all the money needed to build a major shopping center. Their loan provisions indicate that they will receive a bonus of 20 percent of all income above a gross revenue of $2,500,000. Another lender, REIT B., has just financed a ten-story office building. Their loan states they get a bonus of 3 percent of the gross income above $200,000.

Both of these situations required the borrower to pay a percent of the income on the project to the lender. These types of loans are very similar to rents under leases that require the tenant to pay a bonus or percent of the gross income. Sometimes the lender will look to these leases as a source of the bonus on the mortgage. If the tenants in a center average 3 percent overages on their leases (that is to say, the leases are set at 3 percent of gross income against a minimum rent), then once the base rent is reached by the calculation of the 3 percent of gross income, all income above that will earn the bonus of 3 percent to the landlord. If the lender is participating in the income with the developer, then one method may be to split or in some way divide the over-ride of gross income on the leases.

Lenders usually have a cutoff on this revenue to assure that they do not exceed the usury for the area. For example, if the maximum interest which could be charged was 12 percent, then the total interest earned by the lender for that year could not exceed 12 percent. In most areas there is a difference in usury between private parties and corporations, with the corporation having the highest chargeable interest. Because of this, most lenders wishing to participate in ownership or percent of income will require the borrower to be a corporation. This will give them a higher amount of interest that they can receive and an additional buffer between earning and potential earning.

Offering a percent of the income on a property as an incentive to the lender to give good terms has its merit. If the base income passes through without any bonus to the lender, then only that income that may come because of improvement or appreciation in the property will go to him. And since the investment and cash flow are improved for the buyer, he also benefits from the transaction.

Using this same principle, it is possible to entice a seller to hold a good second mortgage on the sale of an income property. For example: Wilton wants to buy a small shopping center that Miles owns. Miles is asking $650,000 with $225,000 cash to his existing $425,000 mortgage. The existing cash flow based on the current debt service is $24,000. However, Miles is sure that the income will increase, as there are several vacant stores and rents will undoubtedly go up with new tenants. Wilton, however, demands at least a 12 percent return on his invested cash and can't quite see how to get it out of this center.

I took a look at the situation nearly four weeks after Wilton had given up on the Miles center. Wilton had come to me to see if I had anything else he might like to buy. During the several visits we made to other centers, he kept talking about Miles's center. I asked him why he was unable to put it together. "Miles won't take paper" was the reply. I spoke with the broker that had shown Wilton the Miles center and we agreed that if I could get Wilton back there and show Miles how a deal could be made, we would split the fee.

The first step was to go visit Miles with the other broker. I wanted to see how strongly Miles felt about the future of the center, and what was his motivation to sell. It turned out that Miles was motivated to sell because of an inability to cope with the problems of the center. He was not management oriented, and the tenants had quickly found that they could get what they wanted by bugging Miles to death. Yet, he did feel strongly about the future of the center and knew that if someone had the knowledge to manage it properly it would show a greater return than it presently did.

Based on this information, Wilton and I went over the income statement of the center. Wilton agreed that the income could be increased, but he had to be sure of a 12 percent return.

Here is what Wilton did: He offered the full price of $650,000 since it was a fair price. He was to pay $150,000 cash at closing and give Miles a $75,000 second mortgage to make up the balance. The pay-out of the second mortgage was as follows: ten-year interest only at 7 percent per annum. At the end of the ten years the total outstanding balance would be paid (Wilton would refinance the first mortgage at that time). As an inducement, Wilton added the provision that Miles would receive an additional bonus of 25 percent of all cash flow above $24,000.

Aside from some minor changes added by Miles to clarify the term "cash flow," we were able to sell him on the contract. Wilton could not prepay the second mortgage without a stiff penalty so Miles is still collecting on it. The income is over the original estimate and the property is throwing off better than a $33,500 cash flow. Miles is receiving an annual bonus of $2,375 along with his interest only payment of $5,250, giving him a total yield of 10.17 percent. In addition, the income is apt to increase before the mortgage is paid off.

The use of percent ownership or percent of income as negotiating points will depend on their introduction at the right time. At times, the adversary in the negotiations brings these factors into the picture when you don't want them. A lender, for example, may want a piece of the action, but your client has not anticipated this possibility and has not allowed for such an eventuality. Many brokers do not know how to handle this type of situation and become confused by the lender's suggestion. Many lenders will look you right in the eye and tell you that they all want this kind of action. That may be true, of course. They may want it, but not all lenders demand it. Stick to your guns when you are unwilling to give up a piece of the action, but don't close the door. See what the lender is willing to do to get it.

LAND LEASES

The creation of a land lease is often one of the best methods of generating cash. This tool, when used properly, can be better than a mortgage and have a longer lasting effect. For example, Victor owned a large hotel with over 100 rooms. He had a good first mortgage and a satisfactory second mortgage. The total loan to value ratio was only 60 percent financing, as the property had appreciated greatly since Victor had financed it originally. He needed to generate some ready cash for improvements to the hotel.

In counseling with Victor, I asked him how much cash he needed to generate and what return he felt it would create for him in the improvement of the hotel. He said he needed $240,000 and that most of that would go into a complete refurnishing of the building. He expected the increased income from these improvements to be in the neighborhood of $50,000 to $60,000 per year.

We ruled out the possibility of refinancing the hotel, as the existing financing was at very low rates and the cost of new money was excessive. Points would have to be paid on the funds just to pay off the first and second, plus the extra money. Victor ruled out financing or leasing the furniture as too costly. And anyway, that would not cover the other work that needed to be done.

I suggested that Victor consider selling the land under the hotel and then leasing it back. After several conversations with him and his lawyer, it appeared that this was the best way to go.

A document was drawn up and the land was offered at $310,000 with an annual lease of $31,000 net, net, net. Victor had an option to recapture the land any time after the sixth year and before the fourteenth year for $31,000 plus $500 for each year after the sixth.

An investor bought the land and entered into the lease. The lease was subordinated to both the first and the second mortgages, but then these mortgages did represent a low percentage of the total value since the land value alone was in excess of $500,000. Victor could have obtained more for the land lease, but his payment would have been greater. The lease suited his needs and in fact generated more cash than required for the improvements.

Owning Land or Leasing—How to Determine Which Is Best

The question of leasing instead of owning (or the other way around) has caused many brokers to pull their hair out by its roots. There is no clear-cut answer unless you have a multitude of facts about the situation. In an attempt to shed some light on this matter, I have provided the following guidelines as a method of giving economic justification to either the ownership or leasing of land. If we assume that a buyer of an income property can either buy the land under the improvements or lease that land, we can see the need for the buyer to make this determination.

First, let's look at the economic factors that affect the land:

1. Land has no depreciation. In some types of land, mainly mineral or organic producing land, there is a depletion allowance which has a similar affect as depreciation. However, in land under income property, the land itself will produce no tax shelter.

2. The capital investment in land does not produce income. It is the use of the land that produces the income. If there is a medical complex on top of the land, or a parking lot or a hotel, it is the improvements and the use that produce income. The use of the land is not dependent on ownership. All value will ultimately depend on the use. Even when land is rented or leased, it is not the land that produces the income. It is the use that gives it value and warrants a lease, which in turn throws off income to the owner even though he may not be the user.

3. A capital investment in land must be offset by the economic rent that can be allocated to that investment. This economic rent is the income which that capital investment would earn if invested at the maximum or nominal rate which the investor could obtain elsewhere. If an investor buys land under an office building at the same time he buys the office building, he has both the use of the land and the ownership of the land. The cost of the land, or his capital investment which can be allocated to the land, must carry this economic rent expense for the ownership to be feasible. If the investor is able to earn 9 percent on his investments outside the investment in the land, this rate of 9 percent would be his economic rent expense.

4. Ownership and leasing must be considered on the life of the economic use and the value at the end of that use to be comparable. It should be obvious that ownership is infinite whereas a lease terminates. However, if the lease is for a sufficient time period to encompass the economic use of the improvements and has a value at the end of that time, there will be economic justification in the lease.

5. Use extends beyond the physical manipulation of the site. The right to mortgage, develop, sell, transfer, and so on, are all values which must be considered in the analysis of a lease. Ownership generally has these provisions, whereas a lease is usually limited in some degree. This limitation will deduct from the value of the lease.

6. The continued cost of the lease over its term will no doubt fluctuate in most cases. The economic rent of land in ownership also fluctuates and must be considered. For example: Ownership costs the economic rent based on the reinvestment rate. As this increases, the capital tied up in the land also increases in cost. The appreciation of the land by normal processes increases the amount of capital tied up and therefore pushes the economic rent even higher. If Liggett paid $100,000 for land ten years ago, and the economic rent was 11 percent then, his cost was $11,000 per year. If the land has a present value of $150,000 and the reinvestment rate is now 12 percent, the cost of the land is $18,000 per year.

7. Because ownership of land requires a major capital investment, whereas the lease is generally limited to a fraction of that capital cost, the initial economics will often depend on the initial capability of the investor. If the investor is capable of buying the land, he may still choose to lease it for economic reasons. On the other hand, if the land cannot be purchased and is available for lease only, then the investor must weigh the value of the lease in connection with the cost of the improvements.

For each situation there will be a point at which the lease becomes economically feasible. This may, of course, require adjustments in the one factor that is flexible—the price of the improvements.

For example: Heathcote was negotiating on a hotel and found that the improvements were on leased land. The lease did not provide for a recapture of the land so he could not buy it. He could only buy the improvements on the leasehold. The NOI of the hotel before land lease was $100,000 and the land was $20,000 per year. The price asked on the hotel (subject to the lease) was $700,000. The cash flow on this free and clear property was 11.42 percent per year. There was no question about buying the land, but had it been available it would have been worth nearly $300,000. In adjusting the investment then, if Heathcote had been able to buy both the land and the improvements at the price of $1,000,000, he would have had a NOI of $100,000 or a yield of 10 percent per year. This would place the economic rent at 10 percent of the reinvestment capital of $300,000. The economic rent would therefore be $30,000, whereas the actual rent on lease was only $20,000. This produces one of the economic criteria in determining the value of leasing over owning. If the economic rent is higher than the actual cost, the lease may be more desirable than if the leasehold will sustain its value through the economic life of the hotel and retain value beyond that time.

This of course raises the question: How do you determine the economic life of a property and the value thereafter? This will call for a projection based on known facts. You must find out how quickly the investor wants to have the return of his capital investment, what yield he wants in the meanwhile, and what appreciation he feels he should obtain on his investment. If Heathcote invests $700,000 in obtaining the hotel on the leased land, and then demands an 11.42% cash flow, wants to see a complete return of his capital within 15 years, and also wants an annual appreciation simple of 3%—these would be the factors to analyze.

Heathcote has set a 15-year economic life on his investment. Therefore, he knows that a buyer must be able to pay a price at that time which would give him his capital investment plus, and that the property would have to have remaining life to warrant an investor paying the required purchase price. Heathcote's price in 15 years is easily calculated since he has purchased the property free and clear. Three percent per year appreciation times 15 years would give a simple interest appreciation of 45%. The price at the end of 15 years would therefore have to be $1,015,000. This would mean that the cash flow would have to increase by the same 3% for a buyer to reap the same yield on his investment as Heathcote has. The feasibility of this will depend on the property and the economic condition of the location 15 years from now. This is a most difficult factor to project—but possible based on past trends.

However, 15 years from now, a new buyer will look at the property at $1,015,000 and make a similar analysis. The economic value of the property must project a higher return in future years to enable this new investor to recoup his investment plus some appreciation. If the original lease was for 30 years at the time Heathcote purchased the property, the new investor must obtain all his return and recoup capital plus appreciation out of the income from the property, as there would be no possibility of selling the leasehold once it has terminated. If the remaining life cannot support this estimated value, even with optimistic projections, then the original lease-hold purchased by Heathcote was excessive, or his projections on yield demanded and appreciation anticipated were too high.

Therefore, it is important that all situations which provide the opportunity to lease instead of purchase land, or when the land is leased and ownership is not available, be analyzed with the total return capability over the economic life with sufficient time to provide return of capital and appreciation. To make this analysis as easy as possible, I have provided two checklists which can be filled out to determine if the economic situation favors leasing or ownership. Keep in mind that the economics alone will not be sufficient to determine the acceptability of the lease; the other factors mentioned must be considered as well. Nonetheless, if the economic value does not favor the lease, there must be adjustments in the price of the improvements to bring about a change to make the lease acceptable. If these changes are not possible, then either the buyer must accept the lease as it is, often due to the inability to raise sufficient capital to buy the land, or the investor must pass on the transaction.

Checklist 1. This list of calculations would be used when the land is offered either as a part of the purchase price or with an option to lease instead. To understand the use of this list, look at the facts of this case study and then see the checklist below.

Ambrose is looking at an office building which can be purchased for $700,000 with a $20,000 per year land lease, or for $1,000,000 including the land. The property has a NOI of $77,000 and an existing mortgage of $400,000 payable at $40,000 per year. Ambrose must find the cash flow yield for both situations and establish the economic rent expense of the land.

CHECKLIST FOR WHEN THE LAND CAN BE LEASED OR PURCHASED

NOI: $77,000 Debt service: $40,000	Purchase on terms	Purchase with 100% equity
1. The total purchase price of land and improvements	$700,000	$700,000
2. Less total financing available	400,000	0
3. Total cash down	300,000	700,000

CHECKLIST FOR WHEN THE LAND CAN BE LEASED
OR PURCHASED (CONT.)

NOI: $77,000 Debt service: $40,000	Purchase on terms	Purchase with 100% equity
4. Less reduction of cash down if land is leased	200,000	200,000
5. Cash down if land is leased	100,000	500,000
6. Annual lease payments on land	(A) 20,000	20,000
7. Cash flow before land lease (NOI less debt service)	37,000	77,000
8. Cash flow after land lease (line 7 less line 6)	17,000	57,000
9. Cash flow yield (no land lease) (line 7 ÷ line 3)	(B) 12.33%	11%
10. Cash flow yield with land lease (line 8 ÷ line 5)	(C) 17%	11.4%
11. Economic rent expense of land if owned (line 4 × line 9)	(D) 24,660	22,000

In reviewing the checklist, notice lines A, B, C, and D. Line A is the annual lease payment or the rent cost of the lease. Line D represents the economic rent expense of the land if the land is owned. Whenever A is lower than D the primary indication would be that the lease is economically more feasible than ownership, all other things being equal. Lines B and C show the cash flow yields on the investment without the lease and with the lease respectively. The greater the percent in C, the more desirable the lease.

You will note that the analysis was done in two stages—first with the terms offered and then as though the price were 100 percent down. It is necessary to show both these calculations, since the debt service on the existing financing may be excessive during the early years of the purchase and the premise shown above would reverse itself. For example: If the annual debt service were $56,000, lines 6 through 11 would show the following:

6. 20,000 (A)

7. 21,000

8. 1,000

9. 7%   (B)

10. 1%   (C)
11. 14,000 (D)

This would cause A to be greater than D, and B to be greater than C. If the 100 percent calculation also showed the same status, this would mean that even though the amounts would be different, the lease was not more favorable than ownership from an economic point of view. If the 100 percent investment varies from the purchase with terms, this indicates there is a negative leverage present, and it is the terms of the financing that have caused the lease vs. ownership calculations to be misread. Naturally, if the terms on the financing cause the cash flow on line 7 to be less than the land lease payments, then the economic structure of the lease is not possible without greater capital investment or a restructuring of the financing terms.

Once a determination has been made as to the favorability of the lease over ownership, the full criteria of the lease can be analyzed. Does the lease provide transferability or mortgagability and will the economic life allow for a recoupment of capital? If not, the original economic favorability must give way to the overall analysis of the lease and its effect on the future return of capital plus appreciation. Sometimes, the buyer has no option except to buy with the land lease. It is not uncommon to have property with existing land leases. In these situations there may not be an option to buy land. The calculations are centered around the need to know if the total price for the improvements needs adjustment to make the land lease economically feasible.

This case study involves these facts: A motel is listed at $600,000 and is on leased land. There is an existing land lease of $24,000 per year and an existing mortgage of $450,000 (75% of the price of the improvements) payable at $45,000 per year. The NOI is $87,000 per year and shows a cash flow after debt service and land lease of $18,000.

Checklist 2. This list (Figure 17-2) is also computed with the purchase on the terms stated, and again with 100% equity. This will provide a check against a misread check if the debt service is the culprit in the land lease showing up as unfavorable to ownership of the land.

In the first analysis (Figure 17-1), we can see that under the terms offered with the land lease the economic rent expense (Line D) is far less than the actual cost of the land lease. Also, the cash flow for the project without the land lease is greater than with it, based on the hypothetical purchase of the land and the estimated financing which would be available. Of course, it is important that this estimated financing be real to the market conditions. To determine if the financing is creating this disfavor of the land lease, the computations are done again with 100 percent equity. The same result is seen; however, not as dramatically as before. The result clearly indicates that the land lease is not desirable under the price and terms of the purchase.

CHECKLIST 2 FOR WHEN THE LAND CAN ONLY BE LEASED

NOI: $87,000* Debt service: $45,000 New mtg. debt service: $62,000†		Purchase on terms	Purchase with 100% equity
1. Total purchase price of improvements		600,000	$600,000
2. Less total financing available		450,000	0
3. Cash down		150,000	600,000
4. Annual payment of land lease	(A)	24,000	24,000
5. Current cash flow (or projected)		18,000	63,000
6. Cash flow yield with land lease (line 5 ÷ line 3)	(C)	12%	10.50%
7. Estimated value of *land* alone		225,000	225,000
8. *Total* purchase price of land and improvements (est.)		825,000	825,000
9. Less estimated total financing available if land could be purchased (75% of new value)		618,750	0
10. Cash down (which would include land) (line 9 less line 10)		206,250	825,000
11. Cash down allocated to land (line 10 less line 3)		56,250	225,000
12. Cash flow adjustment to estimated financing (NOI less new debt service (B))		25,000	87,000
13. Cash flow yield (no land lease) (line 12 ÷ line 10)	(B)	12.12%	10.54%
14. Economic rent expense of the land (line 11 × line 13)	(D)	681.75	23,715

*Before land lease cost has been deducted.
†In calculation with buyout of land.

CO-VENTURES AND SYNDICATES

These two forms of financing will be discussed together since they both involve some similar techniques. To some degree they can be the same thing, depending on your point of view.

A *co-venture* is a joint effort by two or more people who combine abilities or capabilities. In real estate, the co-venture can take many forms. It may be a land owner who joins up with a developer. The land owner puts up the land and the builder his knowledge of building, and together they develop the land. Or, it could be two doctors who join forces to buy a lot to build a medical complex.

A *syndicate*, on the other hand, is generally thought of as a group of people who combine their monetary ability to buy land or other property for a mutually profitable end result. As you can see, the syndicate is a form of joint venture, even though not all co-ventures take the syndication route.

There are numerous legal forms of ownership for both types of investing and financing. Limited partnerships have been used for both co-ventures and syndicates and have special tax privileges which, to some degree, still hold up under the new tax laws. Investment trusts, corporations, professional associations, and partnerships all are legal forms of ownership which can be used in both of these creative forms of financing.

The purpose of this section of this chapter is not to make you an expert in co-venture enterprises or syndications. This takes considerable study and knowledge. Instead, the brief passages on these topics are meant to spark your interest in these exciting fields.

What Co-Ventures and Syndicates Can Do for You and Your Clients

There will be times when the price or size of a property you represent is beyond the capability of the average investor. When this situation presents itself, the solution may be to divide the ownership interest among several buyers. This division of ownership could take the form of a syndication and you would become the syndicator.

Remember, no matter which form of financing you use, your goals are the first factor to consider. If all parties are suited for a co-venture, then this tool can be used satisfactorily. However, the co-venture transaction will keep the seller in (if the seller is a co-venture partner, of course) and this fact may not provide the desired results, but remember, any form of financing which will give reasonable results should be attempted.

Where Do You Find Partners for Co-Ventures?

They are almost everywhere. The first step is to determine the probable use of the property. Once you know, or at least have some idea of, the use which would be economically feasible, you will know where to go to find a partner for the transaction. For example, if you represent the owner of a tract of land that is suitable for construction of a shopping center, you would look to developers of shopping centers as possible partners.

Your build-up of contracts in other areas will help. Mortgage bankers, mortgage brokers, architects, and general contractors all have leads that can direct you to someone actively looking for such a transaction.

What You Can Do to Make the Transaction More Appealing to the Possible Co-Venture Partner

This is the most important part of the process. Once you have a property and feel that the co-venture is best suited for your seller, the move you make to entice the developer into the transaction may mean the difference between a deal that will work and one that will not.

There are many ways to structure a co-venture deal, and the actual transaction itself can vary from the original plan with just minor changes. Most sellers are not aware of the special clauses which are often inserted in such transactions. Many make the deal workable, others just complicate it. All are important, however. Some of the more important fine points are the following:

Five Important Features in Co-Ventures

1. The preferred return.   Often, one of the partners will demand a preferred return on his investment. Either the seller or the other partners can request this, but it is generally the money partner who will prevail. The seller may offer this as an inducement to get big money investors. The preferred return, in essence, is a condition that allows the first percent of the income to go to this investor. The percent can be a set percentage, such as 12 percent, or some other percentage based on income gross. For example: Reynolds invests $100,000 into a co-venture deal and is preferred 12 percent on his investment. This means he will get the first $12,000 of income. The other partners then get the next $12,000 and the overage is split based on other provisions of the agreement.

2. The guaranteed return.   This is much stronger than the preferred return and is not used too often. The same occurs as in the above situation, except that Reynolds will be *guaranteed* the return of 12 percent. What would happen if the income did not total enough to pay his return would depend on the balance of the terms of the agreement. However, a guaranteed return may constitute a security and should be used only in situations where the sellers can sell securities under the laws of the state in which they act and meet Federal Security Laws as well. It is best to seek the advice of a lawyer on this matter. This type of agreement is widely used outside the United States, and is seen in international real estate transactions frequently.

3. Accrual of unpaid but earned return.   This can be used with both the preferred return and the guaranteed return. Here, the investor will not be paid the amount of the preference or guarantee, either because of a lack of income from the project or his desire not to receive the funds.

The amount of his investment is then increased by the amount not paid, thus increasing his later return. For example: Reynolds was not paid $12,000 this year because the income and expenses broke even. His total investment is now calculated at $112,000 and his preference or guaranteed income will be based on that amount, instead of the original investment of $100,000.

4. Subordinate interest. While either party can subordinate its interest, it is generally the seller who is called on to do this. The seller puts up all or a part of his equity in the transaction behind financing to be obtained. This will allow the co-venture to benefit from the full equity and obtain the maximum mortgage available. This requires the party giving the subordination to accept higher risk, but may be warranted if the transaction is economically feasible.

5. Land bank. At times, the owner of a tract of land may be willing to carry the cost of the land while the co-venture partner gets the development ready. In essence, the cost of carrying the land will become an additional expense for the owner, but land banking is sometimes essential for obtaining the other partner. It is usually used when the time needed to bring the property to development cannot be determined, or is already known to be such that immediate development will not be possible, and when the co-venture partner does not want to hold land.

Your ability to use these features to make the co-venture attractive for developers or investors will depend on your understanding of the area's and the investors' needs. For example, it would not be productive to look for a developer for a hotel if hotels cannot be financed or are in disfavor in your area for some reason. Also, the use of the property must be almost immediate. However, remember that the time it takes to develop a shopping center is much longer than the time it takes to build a strip store. Because of this, the time needed to begin construction will vary. A major center will take at least two years from the word "go" to the word "open."

What You Can Do to Become Involved with Syndications and Co-Venture Deals

The first step may be this book. It contains most of the tools used by both the syndicator and the broker to put together co-ventures. Study these tools and see how they can be used in these forms of financing. The application of all the aspects of financing will be no more difficult when dealing with a group of buyers for a syndication or a builder for a co-venture than when dealing one-to-one with a buyer. The only difference may be the size of the commission, which might be greater in the syndication or co-venture.

Ask your lawyer to help you with the syndication or to give you some information about the co-venture deals he has put together. If you can read over some actual co-venture and syndication prospectuses you will learn a great deal.

Be careful of the legal requirements in syndication. There are many laws which control the sale of securities and most syndications will fall within one or more of these laws.

Do not become a professional syndicator.   This is the guy who does nothing but syndications. He is generally not highly regarded in the industry since he will syndicate anything to make a deal. However, this certainly does not hold true for all professional syndicators. The best syndicators are those knowledgeable brokers and associates who use syndications as a tool to build their own wealth. Remember, you should want to invest in real estate yourself if this is your profession. And what better way to do this than to bring in other investors to help you.

Look around your market area and see who is involved in syndicating. If you can locate several brokers, talk to them and see what they feel you could do to get started. Some will be candid and offer you help in this direction while others won't encourage competition.

Chapter 18

EIGHT CREATIVE WAYS TO FINANCE REAL ESTATE

In this chapter, I will cover the following list of financing techniques.

Sliding mortgage
Double finance
Glue transaction
Discounted paper
Other people's property
Shared equity
Stock options
Zero coupon bonds

Each of these techniques has its own niche in real estate financing, as well as its own specific kind of problems. While I don't intend to spend as much time on these techniques as I have other forms of financing in this book, by now you should have a good understanding of how to take a creative concept and apply it to your own specific problem using, as a model, some of the other techniques thus far discussed.

I will follow the same pattern in each of the eight methods in this chapter and the five techniques in the following chapter to make it easier for you to assimilate the form of the technique and its problems. This form will (1) give a brief description of the technique, (2) give an example, (3) show several fine points to the method, and (4) show the pitfalls to the technique.

THE SLIDING MORTGAGE

The sliding mortgage technique occurs when you slide a mortgage from one property to another, removing that specific debt from a property you are buying or exchanging and replacing the security with some other form of asset or promise.

Donald has contracted to buy a small home for $65,000. The seller has agreed to the following:

1. A down payment of $25,000.
2. Donald to assume the existing debt, which consisted of a first mortgage of $28,000 payable over four remaining years at 10 percent interest, and a second mortgage of $12,000 payable over ten years interest only at 8 percent. This second mortgage is held by the previous seller and was initially a fifteen-year mortgage.

Donald's plans are to tie up the property, give himself an "out" in case his plan fails, then go to the former owner of the property who is now holding this below-market second mortgage and offer to slide it to another property. If he were successful, Donald would then anticipate some minor fix-up of the home, refinance the transaction at closing putting a new first mortgage on the home at maximum percent loan to value, pay off the existing first, give the seller his $25,000 cash, cover the cost of the transaction, and if all goes well pocket some cash at the same time.

THE END RESULT OF DONALD'S DEAL

The small home appraises out at $74,500. Donald gets 80 percent financing, or a total of $59,600. The former owner of the home agrees to slide the mortgage over to a free and clear lot Donald owns, which he will sell, or build on, and that has a real, fair value of $30,500. To give the mortgagee a bonus, Donald pays him $500 principal against the amount owed on that loan. The former owner is no longer in a second position, has gotten some cash, and has strong value behind his loan so he has improved his situation.

The cash from the loan then goes as follows:

$25,000 To the seller
 28,000 To pay off the first mortgage
    500 To the former owner, now mortgagee on the lot
  1,800 Loan and closing costs
  4,300 To Donald's pocket (tax-free, too)
$59,600

Donald has improved his position in several ways. He took a good mortgage with good terms and put it on a vacant lot that will help him sell the lot if he so desired. He has pulled out some of his equity from the lot without having to go to a lender and take out a mortgage. Many lenders don't like to make vacant lot loans either, so the deal worked several benefits other than getting Donald the home and cash in his pocket.

The lender came into the deal and made a usual 80 percent loan. From their point of view it was a good deal. Everyone is happy.

To fine tune this deal might be tough. But other deals might not be as clear as this and need some finesse. Getting the mortgagee to want to move to another security is not always easy. If they think they can block the deal by sitting put and require you to pay them off, they sometimes will do exactly that.

Setting up a purchase to allow your mortgages to be slid to another security is one way of helping a prospective buyer to come along and take you out of a property when it is time for you to sell. After all, the seller in this example got what he wanted—cash.

To establish slidable mortgages is not too difficult if you have the mortgage drafted in such a way that you or any future mortgagor can replace the security to the note and mortgage with another property. Any smart mortgagee will insist on protction, and it is apt to follow any or all of the below:

1. Move from a second or junior position to a first position.
2. Have a more favorable value-to-loan ratio.
3. Have an improvement in the terms of the loan.
4. Have an increase in payment.
5. Have personal signatures on the note.

PITFALLS IN SLIDING MORTGAGES

Not many pitfalls will occur for the investor other than the risk that he has overextended the capability of the property to carry the new debt. If Donald is able to unload his lot quickly, however, now that he has some attractive financing to assist that purchase, Donald will have made a very satisfactory transaction.

The big risk comes to the mortgagee that is allowing his mortgage security to be shifted from something he knows to something he doesn't know. Yet by being careful in this matter that problem can be safely covered. Donald by the way, as will you, knows of many other ways to entice the mortgagee to slide.

DOUBLE FINANCE

Double finance is the application of two or more techniques of finance to allow the buyer to maximize the financing and minimize the capital invested.

In many situations, much like Donald by using the Sliding Mortgage technique, he also refinanced with a conventional lender, obtaining more than 100 percent financing. The surplus went into his pocket, or to be used as a down payment for another property.

Frank needed $800,000 to purchase a strip store complex that consisted of 25,000 square feet of shops. He wanted to upgrade the center at an estimated cost of $100,000 and hoped to be able to buy the property and do the fix up with no more than a total cash outlay of $75,000.

To accomplish this, Frank used several creative tools to meet his objectives.

1. Frank knew that as in all financing techniques he had to have control of the property, so he went to contract with the seller giving himself a period of 90 days in which to establish all the financing required to close on the transaction.
2. Have a clear understanding with the seller on the terms. Those terms were the following:
   a. Price of $800,000
   b. Price broken into two segments:
      1. The improvements (at $600,000)
      2. The land (at $200,000)
   c. The land would be optioned at $200,000 and for the time being, up to 40 years, Frank would lease the land for $18,500 per year with increases in the rent as per a cost-of-living index every three years. The land lease would be subordinated to a new first mortgage not to exceed 80 percent of the appraised value of land and improvements.
   d. The improvements would be paid: $425,000 cash at closing, and the remainder of $175,000 in an exchange for some land Frank owns in a growing area west of town.
3. Have details on the improvements to be made prior to talking to any lenders about the new financing.
4. Present the total package to the lenders. Frank knew that if he showed the improvements and how that would allow him to increase the

rents substantially and there by increase the value, the loan to Frank should be more than enough to take care of the cash requirements.

If Frank would be able to show an appraised value of $1,000,000 based on the improvements he plans, he would be able to obtain a new loan of $800,000. A quick review of Frank's cash flow would show that he would need $425,000 to pay off the seller and $100,000 to fix up the property. This would leave Frank with $275,000 cash in his pocket. Even after paying for the loan, he would have sufficient money to buy the land if he wanted. On the other hand, if the property could support the debt service, Frank might be better off taking the cash (which as in all borrowed cash is tax-free) and buying more real estate.

The pitfalls of double financing are the same as any over leveraged property. Frank might be correct in his assessment that once the center is fixed up he can get more rent, and afford a greater debt service. However if he was cutting things short, and there were a delay in construction, or some unforeseen problem came up that caused the plan to go awry, then Frank might have to dig into his own pocket and meet the heavy debt payments. If he had already spent his bank roll then his house of cards may be on the way down.

The solution to this kind of problem sounds more simple than it is.

1. Know and understand your own goals. Do they allow risk of other property and cash based on projections that require elements to happen over which you may have little control?
2. Have a long-range plan. Are you keeping to that plan? Does the plan have safe guards?
3. Learn money management. Start by watching each dollar spent and don't let your income drop below your cash outlay without knowing full well the reasons for it, and have some plan to reverse that situation.

THE GLUE TRANSACTION

A glue transaction occurs when the seller, or partners come to you and ask you to do the transaction, generally at no cost to you, because of your reputation or knowledge.

As you develop your knowledge of your comfort zone area, you will begin to recognize opportunities for investment. As you add to that knowledge, the techniques of investing and financing found in this book and in other sources such as seminars, books, tapes, college courses, night adult courses, you will begin to demonstrate that you are confident in your abilities in real estate investing. Each time you find some area in which you are weak, act to improve in that area and remove that weakness. All of this can and will happen if you want it to, and if you understand that it is not an overnight process and that there is no single source, no key that can unlock your future without your direct and continual growth and action.

Alex has done all of those things. He has learned his comfort zone like the back of his hand, and has bought several properties in the area and turned them into gold mines. Alex's specialty and strength is in finding properties that are under used. He discovered early in his real estate investing that if he could buy a home that was on a lot that would permit multifamily living, he would be able to convert the home into apartments, increasing the income potential, and increase the value by a greater ratio.

The single most fastest way to increase value is by income enhancement. This can be easy to do if you follow a plan like Alex had. But first, review Jack's seven rules of value.

THE SEVEN RULES OF VALUE

Rule 1   All real estate value is related to the actual or potential income* from a specific property.

Rule 2   Value goes up when the actual or potential income goes up; conversely, value goes down when the actual or potential income decreases.

Rule 3   If you can buy knowing ahead of time that the actual or potential income can be increased, you ensure that there will be increases of value.

Rule 4   *Value* is based on a capitalization rate to income. That is, if the anticipated yield is 10 percent on cash invested and the net operating income is $10,000, the value would be $100,000.

Rule 5   Every dollar of increase in net operating income will increase *value* by the multiple of the capitalization rate. Then if the cap rate were 10 percent and income went up $2,000, value would go up $20,000.

Rule 6   *Profit* is the increase of equity above your investment. If you put $25,000 down on a property worth $125,000 that had a net operating income of $12,500 and you increased that income to $14,500, your value increases to $145,000 ($125,000 plus the $20,000 value increase as described in rule 5). In the beginning, your equity was $25,000. You increased income by 16 percent (16% of $12,500 equals $2,000). Your value went up the same percentage. How-

---

*Income and all other benefits derived from the specific property.

ever, your equity increased from $25,000 to $45,000. That
is an increase of 80 percent.

Rule 7   Learn this kind of math. It works wonders to the pocket-
book.

Alex knows that each time he converts from one use to another and
the conversion improves the income potential—and in time the actual
income follows the potential—he is making the best of his investments
and is building profits along the way.

All of Alex's success was going unnoticed by his friends and others
in the neighborhood. Some of them had gone to some of those high-priced
seminars that promised overnight success, but they ended up having to
look in awe at Alex's success. One day one of them got a terrific idea.
Why not let Alex help them make money?

This is the first step to a glue deal. Someone out there recognizes
your ability. He comes to you. You don't go to him. If you do go to them
first, it isn't a glue deal. It might be a syndication, or a joint venture, or
whatever.

THE GLUE CONTRACT

When this person contacts you, you will want to enter into an
agreement—that is, of course, if you plan to go ahead with the deal. There
are some specific elements that you will want to know and understand
about the other people involved and the property in question. Most importantly, you have to decide who is going to be in control of the deal.
You or them? Each answer will have different specifics to consider, and
you will have to examine the total deal to make that judgment. To help
you in coming to this decision and to set up the contract between you
and the other people, follow this checklist.

THE GLUE TRANSACTION CHECKLIST OF DO'S
AND DON'TS

1. *Do* get to know *all* the other people involved, including wives and
   husbands alike. When you are in a joint venture of any kind, it can
   be the hidden partners (the spouses you didn't meet) who can make
   your life miserable.
2. *Do* try to get a feel for their objectives and goals. Keep in mind that
   one single property may not fill each person's objectives or goals the
   same, if at all. Will that cause in-fighting later on? Or will everyone
   be happy no matter what?
3. Do let it be known the moment you feel you want to do the deal that

you expect to be compensated handsomely. Keep in mind that they are going to be more demanding later on than now, so if you don't get your piece of the action tied down up front, you may find it slipping away into that dark abyss called poor memory.

4. *Do* have the option to buy them out. Set a fair formula so they will always have a profit, then never take advantage of that agreement unless there is an absolute break up of the group. Even then, you may want to pass any additional profits (if any) on to them.

5. *Don't* let people use your name in some deal over which you have no control. They will ruin your name far more easily than their own.

6. *Don't* stick with a sinking ship. If the deal is going sour and they won't get out, make sure you have had the foresight to build in an escape provision for yourself.

7. *Don't* help people obtain objectives or goals that are against your own principals. You don't need that kind of money, those headaches, and those sleepless nights.

8. *Don't* sign your name to a mortgage unless you have a majority control and interest in the property, have absolute confidence in your abilities, and the full understanding and potential of the property, and have an agreement that if any short fall occurs in the income to meet the debt service, and the other people don't pay that short fall that you can take their interest and sell their interest to cover that short fall. In hard times, if you are the only one with money in your pocket you may have a hard time getting your partners on the phone.

9. *Don't* hesitate to enforce any penalties on your partners. That is only sound business, and if you try to struggle through it may put the whole project in trouble and your future as well.

10. *Don't* let this keep you from doing a glue transaction. They can be great, and if you approach each deal with the knowledge that you can make a profit doing something you know and love to do, and help others too then why not. You will find that by taking on some partners you may be able to buy a larger property than you would have by your self. This can allow you to grow in confidence and ability and take you to more and greater opportunities.

Pitfalls in glue transactions are generally the simple lack of knowledge of your partners and of the property in question. As long as you follow the checklist and avoid overextending your own abilities or fail to get compensated properly for your time and effort, you should be okay.

DISCOUNTED PAPER

Discounted paper is notes or mortgages which you buy or create and use in a transaction at a discount.

This kind of transaction often serves two purposes at the same time:

1. Allowing you to buy one property
2. Helping you set up future financing on something you want to sell

Lou is interested in buying a condo so that he and his wife, and their little dog, can live close to his business a few blocks away. At the same time, Lou has decided he would like to sell a motel he owns on the beach. If Lou were to use the discounted paper as a technique in this deal, he would place a mortgage on the motel (it would be a third mortgage, as he already has a first and a second) at reasonable interest and payback terms, and then offer the mortgage to the seller of the condo as part of the contract. To make the mortgage more attractive, Lou would be quick to discount the mortgage so that it would give a better yield to the seller.

Lou would want to keep the terms and payback of the mortgage as light as possible because he has to make the payments until he sells the motel. If the terms are attractive, the mortgage may make the motel more saleable, and at a higher price too.

Since debt payments distract from the ultimate cash return of any investor, whoever buys the motel will want to keep the debt payments as low as possible, thereby increasing the cash return.

For example, if Lou creates a $75,000 mortgage that is payable over 15 years at 9 percent interest, the mortgage payment would be $760.69 per month, or $9,128.25 per year.

Lou makes his deal on the condo using this mortgage as part of that transaction, as though it were cash, but had to offer the seller of the condo an improved yield of 10 percent. In this case, the actual face value of the mortgage would be $75,000, but because of the discount Lou would only get credit for $70,788.75. You may want to review the chapter on mortgage discounts to learn the math to use in obtaining this discount. A quick review of what happened follows.

The mortgage Lou creates is for $75,000, 15 years, with monthly payments of $750.69 (see the mortgage rate Table A: under 9 percent for 15 years—12.171; multiply this times $75,000 to get the annual total of the 12 monthly payments or $9,128.25; divide by 12 to get the monthly payment of $750.69).

The condo seller wants a 10 percent yield. To find the discount, you take the constant rate at the face amount (12.171 from the foregoing calculations), and divide it by the constant rate for the yield wanted. To find the constant at 10 percent, look at Table A under 10 percent for 15 years to find 12.895. Divide 12.171 by 12.895 to get the discount of 0.94385, which means that 94.385 percent of the face amount of the mortgage will be the discount needed to give a yield of 10 percent. Multiply the original mortgage of $75,000 by 0.94385 to get $70,788.75, which is the discount amount that Lou would get credit for at the closing on the condo.

WHY WOULD LOU DO THIS?

One reason is to make the deal without having to add that much cash to the condo deal. It might also have been that Lou was using this technique to be able to take cash out of the condo through new financing. However, one additional benefit occurs with the financing on the motel.

In the marketplace, Lou might find that a third mortgage on the motel would not be available through normal sources. If Lou leaves the mortgage off the motel, all that does is increase his equity and gives a prospective buyer additional areas to negotiate with. In the end, it might reduce Lou's ultimate profit or price in the transaction. Also, to make the deal Lou might have to end up holding a mortgage like that himself, and that would put him back into the position of having to pay cash for the condo now. After all, the condo seller wants to satisfy his primary goal, the sale of the condo. If he is willing to take the paper at a discount, then let him.

Lou knows that a realistic third mortgage on the motel might be at a rate closer to 12.5 percent or higher. A $75,000 mortgage for 15 years at 12.5 percent would have an annual payment of $11,092.50, which is $1,964.25 more than the payment on the mortgage Lou has set up. Let's go back to the value rules for a second. Remember, if the cap rate the buyer wants when he buys the motel is (say) 10 percent, the added cash in the investor's pocket due to Lou's smart move with the condo seller would be $1,964.25, which is worth $19,642.50 in value. Lou traded the mortgage at a discount for less than $4,300 and gets back an extra $19,642.50 or so from the motel sale. He has accomplished this with no expense to himself in the long run. Since the seller of the condo is happy and Lou is happy, so would the buyer of the motel who now has to invest less cash to make the motel profitable.

This is just one example of mortgage discounts as a transaction maker. You will have to examine all other potentials that may present themselves. By rereading the chapter on mortgage discounting and by applying these concepts to other techniques, you will come up with many different methods of using this highly creative tool. You should always remember that the tradeoff (Lou's first discount to the condo owner) between the discount and the benefit of the good terms (the sale of the motel) should be designed to work in your favor.

PITFALLS IN DISCOUNTS OF MORTGAGES

Remember the baker who thought a dozen was 13? Well, when it comes to finance and the mathematics of finance, you have to be sure you are using proper math. When you calculate yields in mortgages, you will find that due to the multiples of cap rates or the kind of amortization schedule you are using a small error in the formula is exaggerated with the end result you may get. I discovered just recently that a calculator I had been using was rounding off its built-in formula on amortization schedules to the point that in a sizable mortgage discount the end result could be economic despair in comparison to a more comprehensive table. For that reason, I suggest that you use the following step to check your calculator if it has built-in finance programs to see if you are getting correct answers to your math problems.

Solve this following problem using your calculator: Calculate the monthly payment on a $150,000 mortgage payable over 30 years (360 months) at 12 percent per annum (1 percent per month). Now, go to table A in the back of this book. Look for the constant rate that corresponds to 12 percent interest for 30 years. That constant rate is 12.343. Convert the constant percentage to a mathematical number by moving the decimal left so that you now have 0.12343. Multiply that times the mortgage amount ($150,000 × .12343 = $18,514.50). The result, $18,514.50, is the annual total of the 12 monthly payments. Now divide the annual total by 12 to get $1,542.87 as the monthly payment.

Compare this last answer with the answer on your calculator. If your calculator gave you anything more than a couple of dollars less than $1,542.87, then it is rounding off decimals to the extent that you are obtaining improper and potentially damaging information.

Take the calculator back to the shop where you bought it and get your money back. Or use it just to add, multiply, divide, and subtract. You can use the tables in this book to obtain more accurate information. Keep in mind that if you get an answer that is very close to the $1,542.87 it could be that you have a calculator that is carrying the problem to more decimal places than the table, in which case you are in good shape. You can find out by taking the monthly payment you get and working back to the constant rate. Assume you got $1,543.13 as your monthly payment from your calculator. Multiply that by 12 to get the annual amount, which is $18,517.56. Divide that by the amount of the mortgage ($150,000) to get your constant rate in a mathematical form, which would be 0.1234504 more or less. If your calculator shows 0.1234 or 0.12345, you have a good financial calculator and can work with it to obtain accurate calculations.

Using discounts properly will depend on your use of this kind of math. Do not rely on a banker or mortgage broker to come up with these calculations for you may be getting wrong information if they have an old calculator that is rounding everything off.

OTHER PEOPLE'S PROPERTY

Buying real estate using other people's property is a technique where you use an asset that isn't yours as a vehicle to acquire something of your own. This can be accomplished through mortgages, exchange, or barter.

Unlike the concept of buying with OPM, which is other people's money, you can use other people's property as a method of acquiring the real estate you want to own. This works if you remember that it is benefits that count, and any benefit can have the same weight as the money equivalency. In fact, sometimes the benefit is more acceptable because it hits the hot button.

Dominic wanted to buy a vacant lot on which he planned to build a small apartment building. The price of the lot was $25,000. Dominic offered to pay $10,000 cash out of the construction loan's final draw and to settle the balance with a $15,000 lot in the Florida Keys. The Florida Keys lot was not owned by Dominic, but he knew the owner and had made a side deal with that owner to "sell" him one of the condo apartments when the building was finished using the $15,000 as the down payment on the apartment.

James wanted to buy a home in Charleston. As a part of his deal, he offered the seller a second mortgage on a mountain home in the Beech Mountain area of North Carolina. James didn't own that home, his father did. He had made a deal with his father to take a piece of the action on the Charleston home when it was sold.

Roger offered a holiday at an ocean side resort in the Bahamas to the seller of the duplex he wanted to buy. Roger didn't own the resort, but he knew someone who owned several time-share weeks there and cut a side deal with that person, bartering some of Roger's time as a carpenter for the value of the time-share week.

In each of these examples, the buyer knew of someone who had something that could be offered as a part of another transaction. It is likely that you will have no problem finding someone who you could use, if the opportunity came up, as an OPP part of the deal.

Of course, you can go out and find a few people right now and have them ready and willing when the time comes. For example, meet some rental apartment owners in your area that own and operate tourist types of rentals. They will have units that are vacant during specific times of the year as a natural course to their business. Those people will make deals with you just to have someone in the apartment if they can get a reasonable value for that effort.

Parents and relatives may not be the best place to go unless you are ready to give up a piece of the action on the property you are trying to buy. I say this because the best way to make an enemy out of a relative is to use that person or their assets to the point where you profit at their expense. If you deal with a relative, give him or her some added benefit. It might be the depreciation, it might be a percent of a sale down the road. But those are the kicker prices to pay when dealing with relatives.

PITFALLS IN THE OPP DEALS

The biggest pitfall is not getting it straight with the other property owner. Have it up front, and have it in writing. Working on good faith, you are apt to go out and cut a deal with a seller only to find that your brother-in-law says, "Hey now, Charlie, I don't remember saying you could *have* that lot of mine up in Maine to use in buying that run down fish cannery."

Make sure that the plus and down sides are covered. Never make a OPP deal without the other property owner understanding his or her risk. If it is slight or limited to some time use in the other property, be sure you spell it out.

SHARED EQUITY

In this program, you "sell" your property to a tenant, who will get a percentage of the equity at the time of a sale and in turn will make all payments to maintain and carry the property until that time.

This is a very hot item that has been getting a lot of coverage on television and in seminars. It works on the "dumber than I am" concept, which sounds great on paper but can be filled with many problems. Nonetheless, let's first discuss the concept and later deal with the problems.

Saul is going out and tying up properties that he wants to buy. He has been doing his homework and has found properties owned by motivated sellers on which he has negotiated excellent prices. One such property is a home that he can buy for $45,000. It needs a little work, and Saul plans to spend $500 on the property.

Thus far, the deal is that Saul is buying the property. Assume that he is able to spend the $500 to paint and fix up the property, get the seller to hold an unsecured note for $10,000, and get cash for the balance. Now Saul goes to the local savings and loan and gets a new first mortgage for $40,000. Based on an appraisal of $50,000, this loan would be approved. This gives Saul the cash to close with the seller, the money for the new mortgage, and the cash to fix up the property, with about $3,000 left in his pocket.

He advertises for a "nothing down deal", the buy-your-own-home-for-nothing-down kind of deal. Along comes a prospective buyer, who has no cash, and Saul says: "Move in now, pay everything in the way of debt service, and we will split the profit at a sale within four to five years away."

The "buyer" gets a contract that is much like a lease with option that says that at the end of the agreed term the property will be sold or that the "buyer" can take Saul out of the deal. Each party will get half of the equity of the sale or some formula that is established at the time of the lease transaction.

Saul might consider his equity to be only $500. "After all," he might say, "I just bought the home and I have a first mortgage of $40,000 and a seller-held note of $10,000." In this deal, the "buyer" would pay the debt on those two loans and get a percent of any sale above $50,500 less the mortgage reductions.

On the other hand, Francisco owned a small condo for a couple of years and learned of the shared equity kind of transaction. He put a maximum mortgage on the property to pull out tax-free cash and then proceeded to find a "buyer" who would come in with a price of $60,000. As Francisco had placed a $45,000 new mortgage on the property, and as the "shared equity" was based on the value of $60,000, the "partner" in the deal with Francisco would benefit only above the equity of $15,000 ($60,000 value less the $45,000 mortgage equals $15,000 equity). In essence, Francisco would be paid the first $15,000 above the mortgage at the time of the sale and then both Francisco and the "partner" would split the balance as would be agreed.

The motivation in these transactions seems to be the ability to entice "buyers" through the nothing down concept. Property owners feel that a tenant who thinks he is building up equity will be a better tenant and that the long-range profit will be greater for both parties than if the comparison is to "rent only."

In Francisco's deal, he has already taken out the majority of the equity tax-free, and he likes the thought of keeping the tax shelter for a couple of years longer. In addition, and the real plus factor for Francisco, it would be unlikely that he could sell this condo for $50,000 in the current marketplace anyway.

PROBLEMS WITH SHARED EQUITY DEALS

Whenever you approach a technique with the idea of pulling the wool over someone's eyes, you are apt to have problems. In this type of transaction, the temptation to "boost" the current values is a bit more than in the common marketplace, where competition takes care of overpriced homes or condominiums.

Because the seller is looking for a tenant and not a buyer, the motives are not set for a good transaction.

Once the tenant moves in and begins to realize that he is paying more rent than everyone else in the building, or if there is a decline in the market and he sees values dropping or people offering to sell similar apartments at lower prices than his "base equity for participation," this "buyer" becomes very disgruntled.

Disgruntled tenants have been known to move to Texas in the middle of the night, taking with them refrigerators, carpets, drapes, sinks, ranges, and light fixtures, nailed down or otherwise.

Of course, you and Saul and the rest of the people doing shared equity deals might be giving your "buyers" the best deal in town. And if that is the case, your problems will be small ones.

My own approach to this kind of transaction is: Since it is relatively easy for a buyer to buy real estate without using any of his own cash anyway, why would that same person get into a deal with you or anyone else that was not a truly beneficial deal? The answer would seem to be that he wouldn't unless he didn't know any better.

STOCK OPTIONS

Buying real estate through a corporation you own or form using stock or stock options as a part of the transactions is a form of finance the big boys use, but is available to the small investor as well.

Financing by giving up stock in your corporation can be a tricky business because your transaction may fall within the security and exchange laws of your state or of the Federal Security and Exchange Commission. However, because this technique can be very successful in many kinds of transactions, I want to cover some of the fine points to dealing in this form. As with any contract, I recommend you seek a qualified lawyer to advise you in the specific laws of your area and to assist you in the preparation of any documents that you may have with respect to any offers you make.

In general, however, you will find that as long as you limit any discussion about stock or stock options to the specific party with which you are dealing—namely, the seller of the property you want to buy—you will find that you can proceed to a business transaction without potential problems with the legal authorities. Do not publicly advertise in any way that you are a "buyer" seeking to make deals using stock.

Wayne wanted to build a hotel on an ocean-front site in Atlantic City. He offered the owner of the land 20 percent of the outstanding stock in his development company that was going to build and own the hotel as full payment for the land.

Lenard wanted to buy 1,000 acres of farm land to convert to a cattle ranch. As the down payment for the land, he offered the owner stock options in his corporation. The options gave the owner of the land the right to (1) buy the stock in the company at a major discount, or (2) turn the options back to the company for a cash payment. Lenard coupled the stock option with a personal note that would be due and payable at the same time the options were exercised. The amount of the note was equal to the price of the stock. If the owner didn't exercise the stock options, the note ran for another four years accruing interest along the way.

Lenard's deal used several creative concepts in stock option transactions. First, he gave the seller of the land a note for the full amount of the down payment. To back up the note, he added the stock options as a bonus. If the seller of the farm land decided to buy the stock, all he had to do was turn the note over to Lenard as full payment for the stock. The price of the stock took into account the interest that had been adding to the amount "owed" on the note at that option time. On the other hand, if the stock price was not attractive even at the price offered in the option, the seller of the farm could elect to keep the note and cash back the options at a price that would pay up interest on the note to that date.

In all, this form of the deal is most attractive to all parties depending on the quality of the stock in the first instance, and the potential of the stock value in the future. You should be able to see that there are many elements that can be negotiated within this transaction, and additional fine points that could be added.

Richard was attempting to buy a major hotel in San Juan. He met with the owner in New York and offered $2,000,000 worth of stock in his company as down payment. The stock would be delivered over a period of time, much like an installment sale, and was tied to the dollar amount at the market rate rather than to a specific number of shares. As a bonus, Richard gave the seller the "option" to buy additional shares of stock at specific dollar amounts using credits against the mortgage, which the seller took back in the deal. In this way, if the stock went up or down in value it didn't effect the dollar amount of the first $2,000,000, which was the down payment. However, if the stock went up in value and the seller of the hotel realized he could buy more stock at a lower value simply by converting into stock some of the mortgage owed him, he would. This was a very strong incentive to sell, since Richard's stock looked very strong and could very well have taken off.

Raul had a fast-food restaurant that he was thinking of franchising. He wanted to buy several sites for new locations and offered the owners stock and stock options in much the same way as did Richard. In addition, Raul offered each seller the right to become a franchisee as well, reserving some geographic area for a short time.

If things went well, the sellers could make out nicely by having their stock go up in value, as well as taking advantage of having locked in a franchise if they wanted it.

PITFALLS IN USING STOCK OPTIONS

Remember what I said about possible violations of security and exchange laws. Check with a good corporate law attorney prior to offering stock or stock options to anyone.

Second, the biggest problem is the overdilution of a corporation using this method. You should limit the amount of stock you "spend" this way. Keep it to the down payment or a part of the down payment, if you can. No need to be developing too many partners.

Third, make sure the other party has had good legal advice. If your stock goes down, it is possible that you will find yourself in a legal battle over the propriety of the transaction. If both parties are properly represented by legal counsel at the start, the likelihood of the seller claiming he was "taken advantage of" is reduced. Remember, people can sue for any reason, right or wrong.

ZERO COUPON BONDS

You offer the seller a zero coupon bond as security for a note or as part of the payment at the future value of the bond.

Brad had negotiated with Francis to buy her home, and they were very close to making a deal. Francis didn't need any cash, but didn't want to do a deal that wasn't secure for her.

The price was agreeable to both parties—$300,000.

The property had a first mortgage that Brad could assume in the amount of $150,000. What was in question was the balance. Brad offered to give Francis a note that had a single payment at the end of fifteen years of $150,000. In addition, he would give her right now a zero coupon bond that would pay another $150,000 at the end of fifteen years. Francis didn't need the cash, so she took the deal by putting the note and the bond in the names of her three grandchildren for their college fund.

Brad closed on the deal by putting a new first mortgage on the home for $189,000. He paid off the existing $150,000, bought a fifteen-year zero coupon bond that would pay $150,000 for $35,000, and paid for the mortgage with the balance. Brad had no thought of keeping the house for fifteen years, so wasn't concerned about the other payment of $150,000 down the road fifteen years from now.

WHAT IS A ZERO COUPON BOND?

Zero coupon bonds are negotiable instruments that are sold by the United States Government, corporations, utilities, municipalities, and the like. They have no coupon, which means that from the day you buy them until the day they mature there is no payment of interest, only the single lump payment at the end.

Since municipalities sell these kinds of bonds, they are often free of state or federal tax. Not all are, so if you are dealing with someone such as Francis, it might be helpful to know which kind of bond would be attractive to her. It is always good to argue that the interest in the zero coupon bond would not be taxable.

Because there is no payment of interest along the way, the original cost is much less than the usual interest-paying bond. For this reason, you can buy a fifteen-year bond for between 3 to 5 percent of its final value depending on the interest rate it earns.

The best way to check on the cost of bonds is to call your commercial bank or stock broker and get a quote on current prices for different kinds of bonds. Remember, the higher the interest earned, the lower the initial cost to buy the bond.

FINE POINTS USING ZERO COUPON BONDS

The first step is to learn everything you can about what the bond is and how it increases in value. To do this, you need to understand compound interest. This is interest that is added to the principal. The two factors that govern compound interest are time and interest rate. Time falls into two segments. How often does the interest get added to the principal so that the principal being larger and more interest can be added. If it is annual, the interest is added at the end of each year and the next year would earn interest on the original principal plus interest on the previous interest added. Obviously, monthly is better than annual, and daily is better than monthly. The other time factor to consider is the total duration of the bond. If it is a ten-year bond, it doesn't get paid off until that time; a thirty-year bond pays off thirty years down the road, and so on. However, you can sell these bonds prior to that time and take the price someone is willing to pay at that time.

Bond prices fluctuate due to market demands as to the yield that investors demand to earn at the time they pay for the bond. If there are other higher paying forms of investments than the yield on the bond you want to sell, you may find that you have to take a discount on your bond. If it is a long-term bond that you haven't held for too long, it is possible to lose money selling bonds over what you paid for them. On the other hand, if the yield is better than other investments, you can make money in the bond market.

Interest rates can be lower in tax-free bonds and still be more attractive investments if the buyer is in a high tax bracket. For that matter, tax-free bonds have some edge in any tax bracket, all things being equal in other circumstances.

PITFALLS

The biggest pitfall is and end up taking a zero coupon bond as part of a sale without realizing what its actual "cash out" value is good only as of that very moment. Don't fool yourself by taking a thirty-year bond that will pay $200,000 and think it is currently worth that. If you had to sell it right now, you would be shocked at what you would receive.

On the other hand, if you view the bond as additional security and don't mind sitting back and not getting any return for a while, there are situations in which this form of financing can be attractive.

Also, under the 1986 income tax revisions, changes in installment sales reporting eliminate the advantages for most sellers in holding long-term mortgages. Review your circumstance with an accountant prior to accepting any mortgage when you sell a property. You may discover you have a tax to pay that is greater than your cash down.

The buyer has little to worry about as long as he or she understands what is going on. Too many people get caught up in the use of a technique without really understanding what is going on. Don't let that happen to you by using zero coupons incorrectly.

Chapter 19

SPECIAL TECHNIQUES TO CLOSE A DEAL

In this chapter, I will cover four creative techniques that provide you with methods to lock up deals you might miss otherwise.

Split Funding
Landscape deals
Keep the plus, sell the negative
Private time shares

Each of these techniques allows you to obtain the maximum the benefit through 100% or more financing. Each technique is easy to use, and each has built-in flexibility to allow you to combine the technique with other methods of financing.

336

SPLIT FUNDING—THE PSYCHOLOGICAL EDGE

With the split funding technique, you agree to pay the requested down payment, but you don't pay it all at once. In reality, all you do is establish a payment plan in which you make two or more payments. The down payment then is viewed as a separate event from the payment of the rest of the purchase price. This technique often seems to work simply because of its psychological affect on the seller.

For example, you have offered to Bob, a seller of a small office building you want to buy, a purchase price of $250,000. The terms of your offer consist of $25,000 down with your assumption of the existing first mortgage of $150,000. Bob will hold a second mortgage for the balance of $75,000 for seven years at 9¾ percent interest.

He, as would many sellers, objects to the low down payment and the high second mortgage. He insists on a $50,000 down payment.

Using the split funding method, you would meet his objection with a positive statement: "Okay, Bob, I'll pay the $250,000 price, I'll give you a $50,000 second mortgage for nine years at 9½ percent instead of the $75,000 mortgage, and we'll set up the down payment at $50,000. Okay?"

While he is beaming, you go on to explain the full details of your counteroffer. "Here's how we'll handle the down payment. We will 'split fund' the payment as follows: At closing, I'll give you $25,000 and at the end of eighteen months the second $25,000. Naturally I will be making payments on the second mortgage each month in addition to this split funding of the down payment."

What you did, of course, was agree to the $50,000 down payment— only you won't pay it all at once. The net effect of this split fund is it will give you an opportunity to obtain some other financing during that eighteen-month period, or at least collect some income on the building to help make the payment. For Bob, it took that additional $25,000 out of the mortgage and got it into his pocket earlier.

There are several fine points to this example that you should look at now. First, I show no interest on the second $25,000 payment. This is a matter subject to negotiation between you and Bob. If you can get away with no interest, great. There is no law that says you have to show or provide interest on this kind of payment. From Bob's point of view, the IRS will assume that he received interest in that second payment and that the principal amount was less than $25,000 and the difference was an interest imputed into the deal.

Another factor that generally comes to play whenever you "give in" to the other side's demands is a counteroffer to even out the deal. In your split-fund counter, you have reduced the second mortgage to $50,000 but at the same time have extended the term to 9 years and reduced the interest to 9½ percent. This tactic may do nothing but move Bob's attention to that factor and cause him to say: "Okay, but the mortgage has to be the same term and interest rate as before." On the other hand, you might end up with some compromise that is more in your favor.

SPLIT FUNDING NEAR THE END OF THE YEAR

The split fund often tactic works to the seller's advantage when it allows him to split funds over two taxable years. In this example, you show the seller that by taking the down payment in two different taxable years he can reduce the tax to be paid. An advantage to you as buyer can also work to the seller's benefit too. Of course, the seller may be aware that this form of installment selling would be available through holding a mortgage, but we are not talking about a long-term payout, but a short time to allow you, as the buyer, to get into the property to establish your new credit value so that you can either refinance or pay off the amount owed in the near future.

It is helpful to know when the taxable year end is for the seller, as the IRS allows you to take a fiscal year rather than a calendar year. This of course is a matter that you should be aware of when it comes time for you to sell your own property. Paying tax to Uncle Sam is not something you should look forward to doing if you can properly avoid those payments through sound investment strategy.

MIXING THE SPLIT FUND WITH OTHER CREATIVE TECHNIQUES

If the assumption is that you will meet the obligation of this split-funded down payment from the property itself, you need to plan the purchase accordingly.

The following are two methods of getting cash out of a property you just bought. Each of these methods is described in more detail in other chapters in the book and is shown here only to illustrate the need for you to be as creative as possible in combining techniques.

SPLIT FUND–SPLIT DEAL

You have just contracted to buy a twenty-acre tract of land. The purchase price is $250,000. The down payment is $50,000 split into two payments. A payment of $20,000 is due at closing and the balance of $30,000 is due in 18 months. The balance is a first $200,000 mortgage held by the seller for 15 years at 9 percent per annum.

Your plan is to sell off some of the twenty acres so that you can generate sufficient cash to cover the balance owed on the down payment. You know from your homework that by breaking this twenty acres into smaller tracts you can increase the value of the sites on a per-acre basis and profit greatly.

However, you must be sure that you have set up the purchase money mortgage to allow you to obtain *releases* from the first mortgage to permit you to sell off some property. Keep in mind that when you have a mortgage secured by property you now won, that mortgage creates a lien on all of that property. When you establish the mortgage, you must install a provision that allows you releases from the mortgage. The following statement will give you an idea of what I mean. However, be sure to have your lawyer draft the actual mortgage document, and don't just try to insert this following paragraph into a standard mortgage. There may be conflicting wording in a standard mortgage that will destroy your ultimate plan.

PARTIAL RELEASE FROM MORTGAGE STATEMENT

The Mortgagor may obtain releases of portions of the property which secures this debt by payment of principal sums owed in the following manor. For each $12,500 reduction of the principal owed, the mortgagor may obtain a release of one acre. The releases may be accumulated and taken in amounts greater than one acre provided those releases:

1. Are shown on a certified survey indicating the actual acreage and location of the release.
2. Follow the release pattern attached.
3. Are not less than one acre increments.

There are many other provisions that could be put into a mortgage release statement, and many different forms of releases could be devised. The $12,500 payment in the foregoing example is what would be termed an *above par* payment and would obviously pay off the mortgage prior to the separate release of each of the twenty acres. The mortgage of $200,000 relates to $10,000 per acre. This release of $12,500 is a 125 percent release. If the seller called for a 150 percent release, the release price would be 150 percent of the allocated value per acre of the face amount of the mortgage, or $15,000 per acre. Keep in mind that some lawyers would word a release to say 150 percent of the purchase price per acre. The purchase price per acre is $12,500 per acre so the release as just worded would be $18,750. That could mess up some great plans if you were counting on a $15,000 release payment.

Armed with the release provision, you could then anticipate that to meet your split fund and pay the release you would have to sell sufficient land to pay the $25,000 balance on the down payment, and (at 125%) a release of $12,500 per acre.

If you could sell off small tracts at $22,500 per acre, you would need to sell three acres.

Proceeds from 3 acres		$ 67,500
To release from the mortgage		
(minimum of one acre increments)	$ 37,500	
To pay the split fund down payment	25,000	
Cash balance in your pocket	5,000	
Balance	$ 67,500	$ 67,500

By using the split fund with the split deal, you would have the flexibility to spin off some of the land to meet your other obligations as well. It is important to remember that whenever you buy a property that can be divided, you should attempt to allow for releases within the mortgages. If financing already exists on the property, you may not have the opportunity to change those mortgages, but you *can* ask for that as a condition to the transaction. Previous mortgages can be altered, and the prospect of an early payment or advance payment through releases may be attractive to mortgagees of mature mortgages.

Certain provisions that are critical in these circumstances would be:

1. *The release pattern.* You must allow flexibility to suit your needs or development plans. Sellers or mortgagees will want to ensure that the remaining property more than secures the mortgage balance owed. For this reason, sellers or mortgagees will want to keep the prime portions of the property under the mortgage umbrella.

2. *Where advance payments apply.* If you stated "any advance payment of principal will apply toward releases as well as the next scheduled payment" you will have ideal method of payment for a buyer. In this format, you may take care of three years of scheduled payments with one release, and not have a principal payment for three years in so doing. The other side of this coin is the statement "and any advance payment in excess of the normal scheduled principal payments will be applied to the last payments due on the mortgage." This statement is the usual provision in mortgages, which simply means that if you make an advance payment you don't effect the mortgagee's schedule for regular payments except by accelerating the ultimate payoff of the mortgage.

3. *Penalty if the mortgagee doesn't give the release.* You might have a sale and not be able to deliver because the mortgagee decides that he isn't going to give you the release no matter what the mortgage says. A paragraph added by your lawyer could give you some protection in this event by allowing you to provide some incentive for the mortgagee to act according to the original agreement.

SPLIT FUND–PLANT DEAL

The split fund used in connection with the plant deal is very creative and will work in certain unique situations. The plan is to sell off crops or timber or plants on the property for sufficient cash to meet the obligations of the down payment owed.

This concept works well in farm or timber lands as you might visualize, but also in areas where the property may have an overgrowth of "landscape quality" plants.

The deal is simple to set up provided you do your homework in advance. If the investment is farmland, you have to have a good understanding of the marketing of that type of produce. Buying farms that have groves or crops in the field is a very special kind of investing and generally not for the novice. Nonetheless, it is possible that you are buying the land for some other reason and that the land just happens to be an old farm or grove. Why not capitalize on its potential to spin off some additional income one last time before you turn it into a subdivision?

Selling standing timber is relatively easy to set up if there is a market in the area. There should be timber brokers, mills, and the like who could give you some help in this area. The state agricultural agent, who can be found through your state's Department of Agriculture, or another similar agency within your state or county government, would be a good source for information on where to sell your crops or timber.

A landscape deal requires a bit more finesse, since you might have a gold mine under your nose and not recognize it. Landscapers will pay a lot of money for the right kind of plants. If there is a lot of "large style" development going on in your area—such as clubhouses, banks, shopping plazas, airports, hospitals, and so on—mature plants will be in demand.

SEVEN TIPS ON SETTING UP THE LANDSCAPE DEAL

1. *Get to know two or more landscapers in your area is part of developing your comfort zone.* It is important that you obtain some basic information early about the cost in landscaping. You will find that maintaining shrubs and plants is one of the best ways to improve the value of a property. However, the larger and more mature the plant, the more costly it is. You can buy a small plant for $2.50 that will be worth $150 in a few years. Many landscapers have pricelists that they provide to real estate developers and contractors.

2. *Become a landscape wholesaler.* It is easy for you to become a "qualified" buyer of wholesale products by incorporating or taking out a city occupational license as a "decorator" or "home repairer." Usually nothing more than a municipal fee of $25 or so is required for that title. Then if your state has a sales tax, contact the local sales tax office and get

the forms and a tax identification number. This is required for businesses that will buy wholesale and sell retail. At that point in time (depending on your state), the sales tax may be applied. That tax number is the key to the wholesaler that you have done the required steps to be able to buy from him at the below-retail price.

3. *Buy a book on landscaping.* Get one that has photographs or illustrations of plants and check the values of those plants with the price-lists. Always use the wholesale price since that is the maximum price you will get from a landscaper.

4. *When you find a property loaded with valuable plants, do a thorough examination and list the plants along with their sizes.* Go to a couple of landscapers to see if they are interested and at what price. It is possible that that information alone could entice you to buy the property.

5. *Never close on a property based on the verbal promise from the landscaper.* Tie up the property first, give yourself an out or two in the contract, and then get firm quotes from two or more landscapers. Make sure the prices are "in-the-ground" prices and that when the plants are removed and any holes left will be filled in.

6. *If you need plants for that or other jobs, consider taking some of the deal with the landscaper in trade for young plants.*

7. *Don't overlook the fact that many older homes look better once the landscape has been cleaned out and new smaller plants are put in their place.* It could be that a complete change in the landscape around an older property can give it such an uplifting look that values can be increased overnight. By using your contacts with the landscapers, you will find that you will be able to buy as well as sell plants profitably.

Dealing successfully in landscape doesn't mean only tropical items or crops. Keep in mind that beautiful green grass can be turned into green cash too. Sod may be expensive, but if that five acres of yard is just sitting there waiting for the right person to sell it, why shouldn't you be that person?

HOW TO KEEP THE POSITIVE AND SELL THE NEGATIVE

Now that you are thinking benefits and not money, you can see that in each property there are going to be negatives that do nothing for you and are not part of your benefits. In fact, these negatives "cost you" and take away from the full realization of the positive side of ownership. Let me give you several examples of this.

Assume you purchased a home on a lake or river or canal because you wanted a view of the boats and the water. If one of the physical attributes of the property is dock facilities, but you don't own or plan to own a boat, the maximum "benefit" has not been obtained.

An obvious solution is to sell or rent this benefit to someone who wants a dock for their boat. The loss then becomes a productive benefit and the negative has been turned into a positive.

Along with the positive may occur a negative, the loss of privacy, but that is a factor you have to decide upon. Can that be cut to a minimum, or is the income worth the slight loss of privacy?

When people own something for part-time use, there is a lot of wasted benefit. This lost benefit is expensive to maintain and can be a bonus to the investor who knows how to sell it.

SELLING THE NEGATIVE CAN BE THE ANSWER

"For Sale: 50% interest in a Mountain Cabin." This is not a bad idea, and if you have a nice property there shouldn't be a problem in making this kind of sale. In fact, you might want to sell 25 percent to three people so that you keep the remaining 25 percent. This percentage can be divided by specific time during the year, much like a time-share apartment or resort, only with the major difference, the facility will get less use than the time share and will provide much more flexibility to the investor.

SELL THEM THEIR POSITIVE AND KEEP YOUR POSITIVE

Some investors have discovered that they can add to their wealth quickly by looking for a property that is all positive to someone. When the investor locates this kind of property, he can then divide up the positives, keeping the benefit he wanted in the first place and selling off the other positives. One of the best ways to sell them their positives while you keep your positive is by creating your own private time share.

PRIVATE TIME-SHARE PROPERTIES

By constantly looking for the positive property, the investor will discover that if he sets up the transaction properly he can establish many such time-share facilities. These do not have to be limited to real estate either—boats and airplanes can do nicely in this kind of transaction.

Setting up your own private time-share property can be easy, fun, and profitable. It may be the very best way to increase your real estate benefits without having to spend any of your own cash. The method I shall describe is one of the best uses of *other people's money* I know of. If you try it, you will find that there are many potential problems that my checklist will help you avoid.

HOW TO DO A PRIVATE TIME SHARE

1. Look for positive properties. As I have mentioned earlier, these are properties that have benefits that are extended throughout the year. These benefits might not appeal to everyone, but you will only sell that segmental benefit to the person who wants that specific use, so there will be no negative time for sale.

2. Anticipate the kind of market you will be selling to before you tie up the property. If the property is in the mountains and one of the benefits to sell is ski time, you will want a property that is well located to ski areas. Even though you want the place for the cool summer nights and don't care about the proximity to the lifts, you need to consider the needs of the other owners.

3. Make offers that tie up the property but give you an out. When buying a property for a syndication or private time-share ownership, you will want to make sure that you don't get locked into a deal that you can't handle by yourself. One of the best ways to give yourself this out would be to make your offer subject to the full 100 percent subscription to the joint venture you are forming. Give yourself ninety days or more which begin after you have approved the inspection of the property. Don't forget to also allow yourself time to make the inspections without being rushed. Nothing beats honesty in this kind of transaction, and if the seller is anxious to make a deal he or she is apt to go along with you. After all, you are trying to buy his or her property.

4. Have a good joint ownership agreement drafted by a lawyer. Explain to the lawyer that you are going to do a joint venture form of private time share. Have the lawyer go over the specific kinds of forms of ownership you can use and make sure that the laws of the state where the property is located. In setting up the documentation, there are several important factors that you must attend to, as shown below.

KEY ELEMENTS TO PUT IN YOUR PRIVATE
TIME-SHARE AGREEMENT

1. A copy of the purchase agreement. Don't try to hide any of these details from the others. They'll find out anyway.

2. Detailed information on the obligations of all parties with respect to the mortgage (if any), and all costs which relate to the up keep of the property.

3. Have very strict penalties for those members who do not meet their obligations. One way is to prohibit their use. Another would be to rent their time to help cover any unpaid bills. The ultimate penalty would be the sale of their interest to cover the amounts due.

4. Make sure you are in the driver's seat: This is your deal, your prop-

erty, your contract. You are "allowing" other investors to buy a part of your deal. One form of ownership you might consider would be a general partnership. Here you would be the general partner and all other investors would be limited partners. Another form available in some states would be a land or investment trust. Here you are the trustee and the other investors are beneficiaries of the trust.

5. Get *paid for your work*. This means that you are in charge for the control over the property, and that you should get paid for your time. Don't try to be magnanimous about this because there will be things to do and times you don't want to do it. If you provide for payment you can hire others to help, but get paid and have it as a part of the deal from the very start.

6. Provide for a fund for the replacement of furniture and furnishings. This might be a small sum per person deposited into a money market account, but have it because you will need it sooner or later. On this same subject, be sure that all members know that if they break something they have to replace it. On the other hand, if something mechanical stops working, then that is the responsibility of the whole group.

7. Have a reserve fund in the check book. A good idea is to keep ahead three to six months of any expenses. This gives you a better night's sleep.

8. Have an option to buy back the other's interest. This keeps you in control, and if they want to sell at any given time you could either buy then, or let them sell to someone else and retain that option. However, be flexible enough to let the option rise in value or to revert to a first right to buy so that the investor can participate in the appreciation of the property.

9. Make sure you have full and ample insurance to cover any potential casualty or liability.

10. Have a do's and don'ts list that serves as the rules and regulations for all the owners to abide by. The list should include the responsibility for nonowners who may use the facility.

11. Do your homework on the property, the area, and benefits of ownership for all times of the year.

PITFALLS TO THE TIME SHARES

Time shares are filled with traps that can attract even the smartest of all developers and will then cause them to lose their investment capital promptly.

The reason for this is the fantastic profit potential that the winner can take home if he or she hits the time share market right. The kind of time share I am talking about is the one you see that advertises itself as the "best resort in the Rockies," or "Orlando's Finest Time-Share Resort." It is the "hotel"-minded kind of place that caters to you during your week. These places are hard-sell, expensive properties that the developer sells for one week or more at a price of from $3,000 up to $20,000 per week depending on the place and the week.

In Orlando, Florida, the most "populated-by-time-shares" place in the world, a two-bedroom time-share apartment could easily cost $8,000 per week during prime summer months. In addition to that initial cost, the upkeep and taxes for that same week could cost the owner as much as $220 each year (just for that one week).

If the developer sells his week fifty-two times, and the average price is around $7,000 per week, the gross price for the apartment is $360,000. I can assure you that the apartment would not have that resale value if you owned all fifty-two weeks.

This fantastic price is buffered by the incredible cost to market. Time-share developers will admit to as high as a 55% marketing cost and in many more cases. When you consider that the developer will "blow out" his inventory when he gets down to his remaining 100 weeks, the actual cost to market could be as high as 60 percent on an average project. But that still leaves lots of room for unbelievable profits.

This is where the pitfalls begin. Those profits are all in the minds of the projectionist, and in reality the cost to develop and the cost to "create ups," "carry the line," and "buy back bad paper" can eat up the best project and the developer with the deepest pockets.

The "up" is the person who comes in to buy the time share. The former president of the Florida Time Share Council once said, "No one ever woke up and looked in a mirror and said to themselves that today was the day they were going to buy a time share." And he was so very right. To counteract this problem and to provide the salespeople (the "line" all prospects must "run") with fresh minds they can sell, the developers have to spend a lot of money in upfront advertising, direct mail, and prizes that get the "ups" in the door. The cost to "carry the line" is very high. The best "line" will close one out of nine ups that walk in the door no matter what.

Most developers have lenders that finance these overpriced products so that the average buyer can get his or her holiday week for as little as $500 down (which the salesperson might lend him or her) and with payments as low as $49 per month. The problem for the developer is that most lenders require the developer to ensure the paper they are holding. This insurance takes the form of a "buy back of bad paper" agreement. Here, the developer promises to take back any units that the buyer defaults on, and then repays the lender for the balance of the mortgage. Sometimes this buyback is only for the first few years of the total mortgage term, while other lenders force the developer to hang onto the deal until the final payments are made.

Developers often take this risk because they feel they are making sufficient profit to warrant some buy back. However, this most precarious domino will topple the soonest. If a project goes sour, sales fall off, salesmen leave, sales get worse, those who have bought stop making payments, bad paper comes back to the developer, and the whole house of cards comes tumbling down.

The Resort Time Share Is the Best of Two Worlds

The time share concept is best when the project is designed to provide the best possible comfort, benefits, and accommodations for the least possible cost. No one minds a reasonable profit goiing to the developer or to the general partner, but when greed enters into the picture, watch out.

The best way to avoid this pitfall is to examine the benefits you are looking for when you comment to a private time share. If your goal is to add to your real estate ownership, to provide yourself with second home benefits, to have added equity build up, and to do that through the private time-share program, you will succeed.

If you want to profit by selling units in private time shares and don't care about the other aspects of the deal, then you may succeed; but most likely you will fall into the same pit that gets half of the developers who think time shares are gold mines.

KEEP IT SIMPLE

The best way to do anything that involves other people is to consider their benefits as your own. Buy the property because you want the property. Let them in because they too can benefit from the property. No one will ever correctly say you asked too much or took too much and gave too little if you approach things that way.

Chapter 20

HOW TO USE HIDDEN BENEFITS TO FINANCE REAL ESTATE

Real estate investing is a simple matter of transferring benefits from one pocket to another. Most people who deal are never able to relate to this concept. One reason for this lack of comprehension is that there is nothing more personal or valuable than the benefit that you obtain from what you own. You've heard the saying "They think they own gold"? Well, that's exactly what many people think about what they own. The unfortunate aspect of this is that they have this opinion often without considering what the actual value of the "benefits" are.

It is possible to equate a benefit value to everything you own. Your car gives you certain benefits that may include transportation to and from work. Your television set provides entertainment or occupies the children while you do something else. Real estate also provides benefits and these benefits vary from property to property and from person to person.

For example, take a person who owns a home. As long as the person lives in that home, the benefit derived by the investment centers around the basic use of the facility and the long-range appreciation of the asset. This example illustrates that benefits fall into two categories: (1) the living space benefit, and (2) the ultimate appreciation of the asset. This secondary benefit often is more psychological than real, as most investors feel that all real estate is going up in value.

The home owner who sells his or her house transfers his or her benefit to another person. This new property owner may view the benefits differently, depending on the goals of the original owner. The seller takes his or her new benefit and moves on to some other position.

You must think of everything in terms of benefits. The circle of investing to your goals constantly comes home to this single element of success. If you know what you want and strive to get it, you succeed. However, knowing what you want is not a dollar goal, but a benefit-oriented goal.

You seek to get the benefits you want, and in so doing you get rid of the assets that do not provide the benefits you either want or need. To this end, it is critical that you recognize the benefits that you are deriving from your property. Are the benefits part of your goals, or are they lost, such as that sailboat that just sits at the dock going unused or the vacation cabin you haven't seen in four years?

With this concept in mind, you will be able to relate to your ultimate goals and to ascertain far more quickly which of your properties is not providing the goals or benefits you want or need. In making this determination, you can then decide to get rid of a particular property in exchange for or as an alternative to some other property that provides the desired benefits and sought-after goals.

BARTER THINGS YOU OWN THAT YOU DON'T NEED

Bartering is neither new or unique—it is one of the oldest forms of commercial enterprise. The exchange of goods, products, services, and promises for similar items has been going on for hundreds of years and will continue as long as people realize that there are others who want what they have or have what they want.

My reference to barter in this book shall include just about everything from your services as a bartender, CPA, lawyer, doctor or gardener, any item you have around the house, office, or backyard, use of real estate you own as well as ownership of real estate you own or expect to get. Keep in mind that the chapter on real estate exchanges will go into the 1031 type of exchange and to get a full understanding of barter and exchanges that chapter would be worth rereading. Look at some examples of barter.

BARTER OF PRODUCTS YOU OWN OR CAN GET

Phillip wants to buy a condo from Ocean Development Company in Miami Beach, Florida. The drawback is he doesn't have the sufficient cash to make the down payment.

However, he does have barter . . . if he'll only make a proper inventory of what he does in fact own.

Assume for a moment that Phillip is a CPA. That ability has value, and that value is an item he could consider to exchange or barter to Ocean Development Company. If he had to offer his time, off hours, for a year or two, as the down payment on the condo of his dreams, and it was acceptable to the seller, another barter transaction will have succeeded.

On the other hand, Phillip may be a mechanic working for the local gas station. It could be that his hobby is gardening and that the backyard of his father-in-law's house, where he and his wife live, is filled with rare and unique plants, the kind of plants that developers look for when they decorate their condominiums.

If Phillip is lucky, he might find that his plants were more than enough to be his down payment. Chalk up a second barter deal that just succeeded.

Most investors find that the biggest problem in buying is to find someone who will extend credit. However, you often can make a deal if you can give a down payment—then you have equity. The more equity you have, the simpler your task is of getting a mortgage, or other needed financing. Therefore, one of the foundations of creative financing is the transfer of equity. Barter can help you create equity and make deals. Look at the following example.

I own a vacant lot, free and clear of all debt, which is worth $15,000. My intrinsic benefit is a banking of $15,000, yet this benefit is not the same as a realized benefit. The lot does little for me unless I look at it either as an investment that I hope will increase in value or as a future building site. On one hand, if the area was booming and property values were going up each week, I would look to appreciation as the benefit. But it is important for me to make some judgment on this lot. Why do I own it? What do I want to get out of it? What are the benefits I hope to obtain from owning this lot? *Can I swap it for that immediate benefit or another benefit closer to my goal?*

Along comes Charlie, who offers me $11,000 cash. This now creates a scale to which I must weigh the benefit of the lot. Would $11,000 cash provide more benefit than the vacant lot? Or should I hold out for something else? Whatever the answer is, I should review my goals once again.

Then along comes Alex. In exchange for the lot, he offers me a 48-foot sailboat that has a mortgage of $60,000 against it. This presents another dilemma, another opportunity to examine the benefits I want versus the benefits offered.

You need to look at your assets as a route to your goals. Through barter and exchange, you can frequently go directly to GO and collect that desired benefit. That three-year-old car sitting in your driveway might be the down payment to get you into that duplex across town that in turn will help you attain a part of your desired goals.

Real estate investors need to open their eyes to the potential of barter.

It may be that barter will only be a clincher to a deal and not the total transaction itself. Professional dealmakers know the value of some final benefit to lock up a hard-to-close transaction.

An example of this is what I often call the "vacation on me" barter transaction. The goal of this type of closing technique is to be in a position to offer the seller something that guarantees your deal. The item here would be a vacation for the seller and his wife:

"Mr. Seller, you will notice that I have adjusted your counteroffer only slightly, giving in to the majority of your needs. To compromise those areas that were not possible, I want to offer you and your wife accommodations for seven nights, space available of course, in any resort in the world affiliated with the RCI organization. I have here a catalog of the hundreds of such resorts located around the world."

RCI is the primary time-share exchange network in the world. Time-share properties are usually a condominium form of ownership that is divided into "week" segments. For example, the 23rd week of the year at Orlando International Resort Club would relate to my actual ownership and fixed use during my ownership of that week at that location. However, through RCI I can "bank" my week's use and swap it to another location at another time vis à vis other time-share owners banking their weeks in the same manor. If I owned only one time share that was approved by RCI and I was a member of the organization, I could select to exchange my week for any other location for any time of the year and I could give you or another person that week's vacation. This simple act might be enough to close the deal.

But what about those thousands of you who don't own a time-share week that you could so simply offer as a dealmaker? Don't worry, you can either obtain your own time-share week, or at least obtain use of a week through barter. The key here is to know someone who has a time-share week that you can borrow for a year.

Assume that you know me and that you feel that if you offered the seller a week's vacation somewhere you could tie down the deal. You could come to me and say: "Jack, I'll . . .

a. paint your car."
b. supply carpets for your rental units . . ."
c. do your income tax calculations for two years."
d. recover your living room sofas."
e. give you 20 hours of tennis lessons."

and so on, so that you could obtain the use of one of my time-share weeks to use it as a clincher to one of your deals. I might find that one of (a) through (e) was more of a benefit to me than the time-share week. If so, I would make the deal with you, and you in turn could use that week as a dealmaker. This naturally is just a hint of the hundreds of such potential transactions you could do for yourself with other kinds of benefits. It might be that the "dealmaker" for your transaction would be a seven-day cruise to Jamaica, a mink coat, or a sapphire and diamond ring. Each of these "things" can be obtained through barter.

WHAT IS A BARTER CLUB, AND SHOULD YOU JOIN ONE?

In most cities, there exist what are called "barter clubs." They have names such as Barter Center, Exchange Club, or Interchange. These organizations act as clearinghouses for barter of all kinds by giving their members "credits" or barter dollars for the exchange made between members. In this way, I could get from you barter dollars for an item or service I trade to you. Later on, I could "pay" to someone else those barter dollars for an item or service I was to get in exchange.

The concept is very sound and works out great on paper. In fact, in some real situations barter clubs serve a good purpose and actually give their members a fair value for the cost, which usually is a cash payment to the club based on a percent of the trade dollars you spend or receive (or both).

The benefit to owning barter dollars is the freedom to make one deal and to spend the credits in several places.

For example, one club I belong to has members that offer every kind of service you can think of from acupuncture to yoga classes. There are doctors, dentists, accountants, massage clinics, schools, auto repair, advertising, professional consultations of different needs, carpet sales, restaurants, vacations of various kinds and location, and so on. Each business barters their service or product for the barter dollars they will get, which they can then spend on other services or products available.

If you accumulated a bankroll of barter dollars, which you could very easily do by offering a service to the barter club members in your part time, you could use these "dollars" as part or all of a down payment on real estate you want to buy.

For example: Assume that you join one of the local barter clubs that you find listed in your Yellow Pages under Barter, or Exchanges, or Trades. Whether you have a professional service or hobby you could offer, or just some hard work, such as cleaning offices or waxing cars, put a top price on the service.

As you collect barter dollars, you are on your way to accumulating equity that you may be able to use in your real estate investing.

However, there is a drawback to these barter clubs. The people who offer their services often have double standards. I'll wax your car or do your books or paint your car for this cash price, but for barter dollars you have to pay more. While this might be realistic, in the long run it cheapens the value of the barter dollar. Also, some people in the barter clubs get barter dollar heavy from one or two large transactions and then "dump" their dollars by buying anything they can get their hands on. This too cheapens the value of the barter dollar.

HOW TO TELL IF A BARTER CLUB IS OKAY

1. If they have been in business for more than five years, that is a plus.
2. Will they give you a list of members prior to your joining? If not, forget about that organization.
3. Talk to some of the members. What do they tell you? Are they happy with the barter exchanges? If not, avoid the club.
4. Will the owner of the club give you references? If not, forget the club. If he does, check them out by calling the person directly. Ask questions such as: "How do you know this person?" "Have you dealt with the barter club?" "How so?" "Do you think my joining the club is a good idea?" Keep the person on the phone for a while. Even the best reference will start to tell you the nitty gritty after a while. Play it by ear, but if you are not comfortable with what you hear then forget that club.
5. Ask the Better Business Bureau if they know anything about the club. If they do, it is apt to be through complaints. Get as much information on that aspect as possible.

SWEAT EQUITY AS A BARTER CONCEPT

Your own sweat can be one of the very best of the barter elements. Since this form of barter is actually a separate technique, I will treat it as such.

Make Deals with Your Promise to Perform as a Valued Service

The first-time investor can look to the sweat equity kind of transaction as one of the very best to enable that first transaction to be made with a minimum amount of cash passing hands.

In essence, sweat equity is your own work or labor that will be used to transform a property or provide value to the seller, or both. You will use this future or promised value as the down payment (all or part) in the transaction.

Why Sweat Equity Transactions Work

Sweat equity deals sometimes work because the seller is enticed to believe that if the intended work is not completed on time, or if the buyer cannot then get the financing needed to complete the transaction, the seller will end up keeping his property that has now been improved.

Other sweat equity transactions work because the sellers are very willing to sell on easy terms and need only be convinced that the transaction proposed by the buyer is "safe." The equity the buyer brings to the transaction is in fact real. It is work, time, and effort—all of which are expensive and have value. Of course, the key is to find the right transaction.

Look at the guides on the following pages that outline the steps in looking for a property that will fit the profile for a sweat equity deal.

Property Profiles for Sweat Equity Deals

You will want to look for properties that fit as many of these criteria as possible. While it is possible to find properties outside of this list, as this may be your first investment stick to the guide if possible.

1. Look for properties that are:
   a. not more than one hour drive from where you now live.
   b. in need of some repair or fix up.
   c. in an area that has properties of greater value.
   d. the kind of property you would want to own.
   e. properties that you feel you can handle.
2. The first property you buy should be:
   a. an income-producing property.
   b. have at least three separate rental units, or be convertible into three such units or more.
   c. well constructed.
   d. not have any serious defects.
3. For you to get the best deal, find an owner who is:
   a. a successful and busy professional person (doctors make ideal sellers).
   b. unable to manage his own property.
   c. owner of other real estate.
   d. local or not, but lives far away.
   e. not in need of immediate cash.
4. Make sure you know what your sweat equity abilities are by:
   a. being honest with yourself as to what you can do.
   b. trying to learn sweat equity abilities if you have none.
5. You will find this property by:
   a. developing your comfort zone.
   b. looking for "For Rent" signs on neglected property.
   c. finding a real estate broker you can relate to.
   d. making offers.
6. Before you buy you should:
   a. visit the property during all hours of the day and night.
   b. get a good understanding of the rental market in the area. Know

what is for rent, what is not rented, and the prices and comparisons of rentals.

c. know and understand the zoning restrictions.

d. know and understand the subdivision restrictions if any.

e. make sure that you can deliver your sweat equity offered.

f. have a good real estate lawyer.

The Johnson Sweat Equity Case

Robert Johnson worked as a manager of a super market. His wife was a secretary for a real estate office. They lived in a small one-bedroom apartment that was about twenty minutes from both their jobs. They had a little cash saved. Mr. Johnson could work different shifts at the supermarket he was more flexible with his free time. They took stock of their sweat equity abilities. Those abilities were:

Robert's Sweat Equity Abilities:

1. good at painting.
2. a green thumb so good at gardening.
3. can do very minor carpentry.
4. strong.
5. can be flexible with his time by working night or weekend shifts at the super market.
6. willing to learn other tasks that will help own real estate.

Robert's Wife's Sweat Equity Abilities:

1. good at color selections.
2. can sew.
3. also good at gardening.
4. knows where and how to buy things right.
5. willing to learn other jobs.
6. free weekends and evenings.
7. very supportive of her husband's ideals.

You can see that the Johnsons are moderately equipped in the sweat equity department. If it isn't on their list, we will assume that they are going to have to seek outside help. Therefore, if it requires plumbing or electrical or beyond simple carpentry, extra help will be needed. That means added expense so when the Johnson's look for a property they want to avoid properties that require work outside their major advantages. If you are an expert in electrical wiring of homes and other kinds of real estate improvements or are a plumber, you would look for those properties that could be improved with those specific talents.

THE SEARCH FOR A PROPERTY

The Johnsons had been studying a geographic zone that was near where they lived. It was a nice residential area that had a mix of different kinds of real estate. They were looking for a small apartment building or a large, older home that was in an area that was properly zoned to allow multi-family residences that they could convert to apartments.

They searched by using two methods. They had taken up riding bicycles as a form of exercise, so whenever they could they would ride through this area. They didn't just ride their bikes in a haphazard route, however, it was always carefully planned out, and a small map of the area and note pad accompanied them on their nearly daily trips in the area.

What they wanted to do was to become so familiar with this section of town that they would have a mental picture of each property, street, and opportunity when it came up. This process took time. As they would ride through the area and locate for-sale signs or any change in the status quo, they would make note of it.

If the for-sale sign was by a broker, they would have Phillis, a real estate saleswoman they had met and liked, check it out. Phillis was their second method of searching for their future investment. They had met Phillis after talking to several salespeople at several different offices and felt comfortable that she understood their needs.

They soon began to understand the area. They started to get a feel for the streets and the neighborhood. They began to make value assessments based on elements that often go missed by the people who live in the area. Why is this street nicer to live on than another? Or what makes this building a better investment because of what is going to happen in the near future?

That last bit of news was the result of going to the monthly city council meetings where they learned that two blocks away a new government center was to be built that would employ nearly 300 people. The impact to the area would include demand for rentals and increased traffic. The opportunity might not last too long as sooner or later the information would sift down to all property owners.

THEY FOUND THE IDEAL PROPERTY

The sign said, "For rent." It was on a property that they had noticed was going down hill for several months. An old beat-up pickup truck had been left in the front yard, the lawn was in bad shape, and in general the house was showing a lot of wear and little loving care.

When they called the number, they were told they had reached "Doctor Funt's office."

As it turned out, Dr. Funt had owned this property for nearly five years, renting it out for most of that time. The last tenant had turned out to be a dead beat, however, and left in the middle of the night, taking with him anything of value that wasn't nailed down.

The Johnsons simply wanted to see the inside of the home and did not get into any negotiations with the doctor at this time. They didn't even ask if the property was for sale.

After spending about an hour looking through the home, Robert and his wife realized that all that was needed was cleaning, paint, new carpets, new drapes, a new lawn, and attendance to the shrubs. The home would be well worth their effort if they could buy the property on terms that worked for them. The real ace for them was the separate garage which, due to the zoning, could be converted to an apartment and rented out.

The Sweat Equity Proposal

The Johnsons did their homework. They made a long list of all the items that needed repair, cleaning, paint, and so on. The list was very complete, and along side each item was an estimate of the time needed to repair, clean, paint, and so on.

Next, there was a separate list of material needed. This list was equally as complete and the prices for the material were estimated with the help of a salesman at one of the local builder supply stores in the area.

The Offer to the Owner

Armed with this proposal, the Johnsons met with Dr. Funt and proposed that he sell the home to them on the following terms:

1. A purchase price that was reasonable. Johnson suggested $70,000. This was nearly $15,000 more than Dr. Funt had paid for the property five years earlier according to the records down at the county records office.
2. That the Johnsons would repair, clean, paint, and fix up the house according to the detailed proposal that Robert Johnson had prepared.
3. All Dr. Funt had to pay for were the materials, which would cost around $4,000.
4. At the end of the fix-up period, the Johnsons would have 120 days to obtain a new first mortgage on the property of at least $60,000.
5. Dr. Funt would hold a second mortgage for $10,000, plus the material cost of $4,000 ($14,000 total mortgage).
6. The mortgage would be interest only for 7 years at 9 percent interest per annum, payable annually.

Dr. Funt thought about this for a while and then rejected the proposal. The Johnsons let it rest for a few days and then got back in touch with Dr. Funt, asking him to meet them at the house. There they went over each repair that they would make to the property. They stressed the condition of the home, and the time needed to put it into shape.

Robert Johnson reminded Dr. Funt that in the proposal to buy the home the transaction was conditioned on the Johnsons finishing all of the work. If they didn't do so within 90 days, Funt could keep the house with the work done thus far. To show additional good faith, Johnson also agreed to pay half of the material cost up front.

Johnson also reminded Dr. Funt that the property would need most of the work done anyway just to get it rented again, so the doctor couldn't lose. He would get a fair value for the home, or he would get a lot of work done at little or no cost to him.

A couple of days later, the doctor signed the deal that was drafted by Johnson's lawyer. The Johnsons went to work, and by the time they had finished the home looked like a million dollars.

A savings and loan appraised the property for $110,000 and agreed to lend up to $88,000. To soften the terms of the loan, Robert Johnson took only $75,000. He gave $60,000 to Dr. Funt, paid off the $2,000 he owed the building supply house, paid $750 to his lawyer for the work and closing costs, and paid $2,250 back to the savings and loan for their points and costs. This left him with $10,000 in his pocket and a beautiful home.

His equity was his sweat . . . and his brains.

THERE ARE FIVE CRITICAL ELEMENTS TO REMEMBER

1. Put everything down in the contract—exactly what you are expected to do and what you will get because of it.
2. The "option" for you to buy the property must be very specific.
3. Be sure to give yourself ample time to complete the work and to get the financing. Check with your local lenders to know how long the financing may take. Double that time.
4. Start looking to improve your position right away with your new property. Can you sell it or exchange it prior to having to close on it, making a profit along the way? Keep your options open.
5. Perform on the deal. A thousand things can come up that you didn't count on. But do everything you can to fulfill your deal. Future deals will count on it.

Sweat equity has many faces and can be used in many different kinds of transactions. Your sweat equity can come via a three-way deal. You might barter your future work to me for something I'll give you now that you exchange with Dr. Funt. Also, as in all kinds of exchanges and barter you can swap your sweat equity for a note or mortgage. In this way, you can then exchange or swap the mortgage to the seller instead of your sweat equity. This technique would be useful if your specific ability was not needed for the property, but you still needed to create equity from some source other than money.

Of course, you might just as well learn how to print your own money, called scrip. In fact, this method of adding to the deal is used all the time and can be very helpful to you in closing many kinds of transactions.

SCRIP—YOUR OWN FORM OF CASH

Scrip comes in whatever shape, color, and form you print it. It can look like Monopoly money or play cash or it might resemble the currency from some foreign government—just as long as it doesn't look like U.S. currency. Scrip can be for specific values as you decide, and it is good for whatever specific item or service you can provide.

For example, if you own a fried-chicken restaurant, you could print up a couple of thousand dollars' worth of your own money in $10 increments and use this cash as part of your down payment on your next real estate investment.

Or, if you own a fishing boat you could print up scrip in $200 increments to be applied to fishing trips. Or, if you could borrow your father's Cadillac from time to time (paying for gas, oil, and a small rental, of course), you could print up scrip in $100 increments to be applied against your nightly limo service.

The opportunities to create your own scrip are endless as you will discover. In each instance, the concept of dealing with scrip is as a deal closer and not necessarily as the total deal. Nonetheless, there will be transactions that can be made with your using scrip as your total payment to the seller.

AN EXAMPLE OF A SCRIP TRANSACTION

The owner of the fried-chicken restaurant, Charles, printed up $5,000 of his own scrip in $10 bills. He indicates on the scrip that it must be redeemed by a specific date and that it cannot be used to pay tips or tax and that no change will be given against the scrip. To ward against counterfeiting, Charles signs each bill with his fountain pen and marks each bill with an invisible pen (visible only with ultraviolet light).

Charles did all of this because he had seen a small duplex that he wanted to buy. He had made an offer several weeks earlier, but was turned down because he didn't have enough cash down.

The seller of the duplex was asking $55,000 for the property. He had a small mortgage of $25,000 and wanted $30,000 cash above the mortgage.

Armed with his scrip, Charles went back and offered to buy the duplex for $50,000 with $45,000 cash and $5,000 in scrip at his restaurant.

After a couple of days, the seller countered: $52,500 cash, and $2,500 in scrip. Charles knew that he could swing this deal now by putting up $2,500 cash and an equal amount of scrip with the local savings and loan financing the balance. Let's move on to another example.

Ellis owned a kitchen appliance store. He too wanted to use scrip to buy real estate. So he printed up scrip in $250 denominations and indicated on the scrip that it had to be redeemed within twelve months, and that it was not good on any red-tagged sales items during that time.

Ellis had found a property he wanted to buy. It turned out to be owned by a local real estate investor who owned a lot of different kinds of properties. Some of these properties included rental apartments. Ellis knew that this seller would have use of kitchen appliances sooner or later, so this seller fit nicely into Ellis' plans.

This points out the advantage of knowing something about the seller prior to making the offer. Once you know the seller can use the kind of scrip you have, you have the edge in making this type of transaction. Ellis' offer would be a simple $10,000 in kitchen appliance scrip as the down payment on the desired property. The deal may require other techniques to be used in addition, such as outside financing or additional seller-held financing, or some other highly creative technique provided for you in this book.

WHAT TO DO IF YOU DON'T OWN A RESTAURANT OR APPLIANCE STORE

There are several ways to create scrip. Having your own business helps, but it is not the only way to use this very effective tool. In essence, there are two basic methods of generating your own scrip from outside sources. In my book *$1,000 Down Can Make You Rich*, I discuss these two methods as "Watered Scrip," and "Commissioned Scrip."

WATERED SCRIP COMES FROM OTHERS AT A DISCOUNT

The basic element to understand here is that you will acquire from other people credits against their services or products. You will print up the scrip that they agree to honor, and you will buy it from them, either at a discount or by using paper you create against things you now own or are about to buy.

The people who own the businesses must be shown that the scrip you are going to create will bring them business they don't already have, which in turn will generate more business that will be on a cash basis. Scrip business then has an advertising value that accounts for the discount to you. Also, by offering to buy future business now you can frequently get a substantial discount for that fact alone. Couple these factors with the idea that you aren't going to pay money for the scrip, and the idea becomes very attractive for you. Best of all, since you are going to tailor the scrip to the transaction, you will have a higher success rate in real estate transactions. You can go out and get the kind of scrip that will fit the deal.

BUYING SCRIP ON YOUR TERMS

"Mr. Furniture Store Owner, I'll give you a $10,000 second mortgage against a five-unit apartment building I'm buying if you will sell me $12,000 in scrip good only in your store."

Or . . . "Mr. Schultz, I'll give you an option to buy my five-unit apartment building, good for one year, for $5,000 worth of hotel scrip in New York City."

Or . . . "Mr. Marks, I'll give you a two-year lease in the garage apartment for you or one of your clients if you will give me $12,000 in scrip good for meals in your chain of restaurants."

Or . . . "Mr. Hennington, I'll give you $12,000 in scrip for meals in Mark's restaurant chain if you'll give me $14,000 in scrip good for cars on your used car lots."

In each case, you want to offer something of value for scrip at a greater face value. The difference between the two is your profit for doing the transaction, but it comes to you at no real cost to the other side of the scrip transaction. The furniture store owner has a mark up of his products and may want to move off some furniture. He would want to make sure the scrip didn't apply to sale merchandise, so the $2,000 profit you make in the scrip versus second mortgage trade is warranted. By the way, it is possible that he would take your second mortgage and use it as a down payment on something himself if he was unable to swap furniture for the property he wanted to buy.

COMMISSIONED SCRIP

Unlike the watered scrip that you "buy" at a discount, the commissioned scrip is scrip that you establish through some third party and then redeem as it is used for cash . . . less your commission.

This kind of scrip doesn't have the benefit of allowing you to exchange a long-term payback as you can if obtaining watered scrip by giving a three-year mortgage on the five-unit property you are going to buy. However, it does have a very strong impact on a transaction and can help you close transactions that need this kind of kicker. You will get a discount nonetheless and frequently get up to a year or so to pay for the scrip.

Assume for a moment that you are attempting to buy a vacant tract on which you will build a small strip store. The owner of the site is asking $200,000 for the site and you have offered $175,000.

The negotiations have gone on for a week or so and the seller is agreeing to the following terms in his most recent counteroffer to you:

Price: $185,000

Cash down: $50,000

Terms on the balance: Cash within 18 months with interest at 12 percent per annum. If you want to build right away, the mortgage would have to be paid off at the time you took out a construction loan.

Most of this is acceptable to you as you are going to build right away, only you hate to put up the $50,000 now as you are going to mortgage 100 percent on the project. In dealing with the seller, you discover that the seller likes to travel—so you come back with this following proposal:

Price: $185,000

Down payment: $50,000, made up of $20,000 cash and a ticket on Q.E.2 Around the World Cruise that leaves in 14 months with a double deluxe outside cabin for two that has a value of $30,000.

The balance is as the seller wants.

If the seller takes this transaction, you will have made a good deal as you have met the seller's terms but you only have to put up $20,000 cash plus a deposit on the cruise of around $1,500. In around 10 months, when the cruise has to be paid off in full, you will not have to pay the full $30,000 price because you will have made an arrangement with a travel agent to become one of their "salesmen." In essence, you get a commission on the cruise.

Back up a moment. There are certain things you can buy that you wouldn't get until some time in the future. Cruises and other vacations of almost any kind are prime examples of closing kickers that you can offer any seller. If the seller likes to travel, he or she is apt to bite at that offer, *even though they may not have spent that much money on themselves.*

You can see that you didn't have to own the travel agency to make the deal work.

Whenever you acquire scrip that you will redeem in the future, you will have a discount built in through the commission. However, if you follow the tips in this chapter, there are other discounts you have to take into account that add to your profit in the transaction. All of these profits require that you set up the scrip transaction properly, so look at the checklist that will aid you in commission scrip deals.

YOUR CHECKLIST TO MAKING PROFITABLE COMMISSION SCRIP DEALS

1. Never enter into a commission scrip deal until you know exactly how much scrip you will need and for what specific product.
2. Do, however, look for the kinds of products that will generally be useful and begin to make contacts in those areas. Meet the owners of these prime scrip products and services.
   a. Travel agencies
   b. Kitchen and other building and home appliances and products
   c. Lumber yards
   d. Jewelry stores
   e. Restaurants
   f. Resorts (best through time-share resorts)
   g. Legal services
   h. Accounting services
   i. Used car lots
   j. New car agencies
   k. Auto repair shops
3. Have a firm agreement with the owners of the businesses that you are doing business with. Make sure the agreement covers these following items.
   a. The name and address of the business or businesses honoring the scrip
   b. The term for which the scrip shall be good (ample time)
   c. What the scrip includes and excludes
   d. A statement that if the business is sold the liability of the scrip shall continue, or the scrip will be bought back for cash
   e. A penalty if the scrip is not honored. If you have to then redeem the scrip for cash yourself, you won't get the commission, so you should be owed that commission from the original party
   f. How and when you are to redeem the scrip and for what price, less what commission
4. Check on the transaction from time to time to see if any scrip you may have traded is being turned down.

No matter what you do, there is apt to be a problem or two if you try to cut your deals too tight. Remember, the dealer in the product or service has to see a benefit. They are dealing in business for a profit and if you hit them for too much commission or don't redeem the scrip on time, the rest of your deal can fall apart. Also, remember that scrip and barter transactions work best when they are offered later on in the transaction and not right up front. They are kickers that close deals that you are getting close to, but just can't seem to nail down.

You will find sellers who are willing to take scrip as the total down payment or outright purchase, but those transactions are far more difficult to find and make.

KICKERS OF ANOTHER KIND

Other kinds of kickers that you can use as dealmakers often are overlooked because you don't spend the time or homework needed to find out what might turn the seller on.

Take a look at your potential kickers, keeping in mind that a kicker is any form of benefit that you can give or lend to the seller as part of the deal or as a bonus to entice him to make your deal.

Assume your assets consisted of the following:

1. You have your home.
2. You own a cabin in North Carolina.
3. You are an excellent tennis player.

Just looking at those assets you could offer a prospective seller some or all of the following:

a. A holiday in North Carolina for two weeks
b. A holiday in North Carolina for two weeks for the next three years
c. A quantity of tennis lessons

Each of these assets has a flexibility, and each has value that doesn't cost you anything other than some time or some inconvenience. Keep in mind that as you could offer the holiday in North Carolina to the owner of the sailboat, who could in turn provide sailing lessons to the seller you are dealing with—the opportunities are endless.

KICKERS USING THE TAX LAWS

There frequently are kickers that are of little or no benefit to you, but are cash in the pocket of the other party. For example, take the tax laws that you can work to your profit.

If you want to buy a property and are very close to making the deal, but no matter how much you try to close the transaction you are still a few thousand dollars apart, the depreciation kicker often works wonders.

Let me set the stage of a transaction that is already filled with several different creative tools but still hasn't closed.

Frank is the seller, and the property is a duplex that you want to buy. The price you and Frank have finally agreed on is $75,000. The terms that are agreeable to both parties are:

Price: $75,000

Cash to Frank from a mortgage to be obtained by the buyer: $40,000

Part of the deal: $5,000 in scrip at Mark's Restaurant chain

Part of the deal: $15,000 in the form of a second mortgage on a property you are buying down the street.

Part of the deal: $5,000 cabin on a two-week cruise for two to Alaska.

We are still $10,000 short. Frank wants that in cash, and you want to give him a second mortgage on the duplex in that same amount.

To close the deal, you go back to Frank and suggest that he take the scrip, the second mortgage, the cruise, but not deed you the property for one year. In the meantime, he can get the new mortgage to which you will be a co-signer, with an agreement from the bank that when the property is transferred to you Frank's name will be taken off the mortgage. In this way, Frank has everything in the deal and still has the property, only it's still $10,000 short.

You agree to rent the property for the exact cost of the mortgage and other fixed costs just as though you owned the property. At the end of the year, you will give Frank $2,500 cash and a second mortgage for the remainder of $7,500.

The benefit is you get the property. You save interest on the mortgage for one year (that might have been $1,000), and you therefore have a net cash payout of $1,500 at the end of one year. The balance owed to Frank is as you had originally wanted.

Frank gets the depreciation for twelve months plus the potential that at the end of the year something will have happened to you and he'll keep the house as well as the scrip, the cruise, and the second mortgage. Most importantly, however, you are able to offer to Frank something that doesn't cost you anything. In fact, if you had to add the interest back into the deal that you had saved on the mortgage, you still benefit.

SUMMARY OF BARTER, SWEAT EQUITY, SCRIP AND KICKERS

In general, all of these techniques are sound financing tools that can be used from time to time in making deals work for you. As I've mentioned several times, do your homework to try to fit the transaction to the seller, but don't worry if you make a cold offer when time or circumstances don't allow any homework. The worst anyone can ever do is turn you down. And one thing all real estate investors know if they are ever to succeed in the game is if you aren't turned down from time to time you aren't making enough offers.

BEWARE OF THE PITFALLS

The biggest pitfalls in barter, sweat equity, scrip, or kickers is knowing who you are dealing with, and then backing up everything with good sound contracts. This means that you will have to be sure you have good legal representation in this area.

People get into trouble in barter by not checking values carefully or—if the barter is through a barter club—by getting in too deep and building up too large a bank account. Barter dollars can be difficult to spend, and if the club folds they are impossible to get rid of.

Sweat equity is most likely the best single tool for the investor who has a strong back, good business mind, but little cash. It is hard to make too many errors if you are careful with your fix-up expenses. The worst area that gets sweat equitors into trouble is not having enough time to do the work promised. They start out thinking that they can do everything in 90 days, only they get the flu or get transferred or a million other things come up. Be very careful of these kinds of problems.

Scrip has a mountain of problems if you are careless or don't document the deal properly. If you are dealing with a restuarant that is sold or goes out of business, your scrip is like bad checks. The people you gave scrip to will come back looking to you for redemption (some might even look for vengeance).

Kickers have few problems as long as you can deliver and as long as you don't tie yourself up with a commitment that you don't want to have to honor later on. For this reason, it is a good idea to have a "cash" value on all kickers that you can pay off if you want to or have to.

Chapter 21

HOW TO PUT A FINISHING TOUCH ON AN ILLUSIVE DEAL THROUGH THE USE OF ONE OF THESE FIVE CREATIVE TOOLS

In this chapter, I will get into some of the fine points of movements of benefits to and from other people. There will be five very creative examples of techniques that will enable you to put finishing touches to transactions. There will be times when all seems to fail to nail down the transaction and that something else has to be added. One of the following items might be the special element that pulls everything together. In each technique, you will offer the seller of a property you want something of specific benefit to him.

FUTURE RENT; MANAGEMENT INTEREST; THREE-PARTY BLANKET; JEWELS AND STAMPS; SUBDIVIDE AND EXCHANGE

If you pledge two years' free rent in one of your apartments to the seller of that building, you are giving up something you have not gotten yet—future rent.

There are many ways to use future rent as part of a real estate transaction. It might be to pledge the rent of another property as security for a note or mortgage on the property you want to buy. Or you might offer the seller the right to stay on for a period of time as a tenant without paying any rent.

It is important for you to think again in the area of benefits and not money. If you have something you have not been able to rent, or even thought about renting, why not offer that on your next deal. If one of those things you own is a mountain cabin, you could offer "free rent" in that facility for some period of time.

Nonetheless, the usual method of using this technique is to take rent you are getting as a security against a note or loan you want to obtain or offer to another party. In this way the seller of the property you want to buy doesn't have to have a need for the property for rent, only recognize that its rent is a value that can secure another note or mortgage.

Brownie got right down to the last straw in trying to make a deal with Roco. The only thing that was holding them apart was that Roco wouldn't take Brownie's unsecured note for $5,000 as part of the down payment. Brownie countered with the same $5,000 note, but added as a security all rents above the first $800 each month from a four-unit apartment building Brownie owned. Each apartment rented for $425 and so had a gross monthly rent of $1,700. Roco saw that his note would be secure providing that Brownie agreed not to put any additional financing on the apartment until the note was paid off. Brownie countered that he would agree not to put any additional debt that could not be covered (along with all normal expenses) for $800 per month. Roco felt that that was reasonable and a deal was made.

In another kind of future rent deal, Oscar offered the owner of a small home the right to stay in the home until Oscar's building plans were completed for the rental apartment building he wanted to build. Then, as the total price for the transaction, Oscar offered the sellers a lifetime right to rent one of the new apartments for $1 per month.

Oscar knew what he was doing, as he had calculated his yield on the amount of money it would have taken to buy the house just to get the lot. He also knew from the ages of the participants that it was a good investment to offer the life estate for $1 per month as on the actuarial calculation the apartment would be vacant within ten years.

Oscar calculated that even if he had to give up the use of that apartment for twenty years, he was making a good decision.

The seller loved the idea, and told Oscar, "What a wonderful incentive to live another 100 years."

Pitfalls in Future Rent Deals

If Oscar had miscalculated his cost and if the people live for forty years in the apartment (or rent out the apartment and live elsewhere for 40 years), then obviously a mistake was made through the actuarial table on life expectancy. Insurance companies can do this because they average out to their favor, and since many people cancel their insurance years before their death that gives an added edge to the insurance company. After all, only those people actually insured at the time of their death are paid benefits.

Of course, Oscar could have limited the "free rent" to a specific term of years, but that may not have gotten him the apartment site.

Future rent is similar to offering future hours of work. The ultimate value may be far greater than you anticipated.

Nonetheless, this technique can be very good in certain situations when you anticipate that you will have a certain amount of vacant space in the best circumstances. If you own or can "get" from others, rent in holiday resorts or seasonal apartments, that might be a "future" worth offering. In that way, you risk very little.

The biggest problem in dealing with future rent is the contract itself. The recipient of such benefits will be very cautious that you will be able to provide that future value. If you were a recipient you would want to make sure that there was a clause in the agreement that kept your value intact if the building burned down or foreclosed on, or some other event occurred that put your "free" use at risk.

A lease might do the trick if it is carefully worded. Get a good real estate lawyer to assist in that part of the transaction.

In any event, it is a good idea not to let the future rent get strung out to a long term. Rents go up, and what started out as a good deal can get very expensive if rents double or triple or more. It is not unusual for this to occur given sufficient time and improving property areas.

Management Interest

Obtaining real estate through a management interest is where you agree to manage a property on the basis that you will receive an ownership interest in the property as part of the remuneration for your efforts.

Mike knew a couple of real estate investors who needed a tax shelter. He found a small ten-unit apartment building and tied it up on a contract. He then told these investors that if they took over his contract he would manage the building and take for that effort a 20 percent ownership in the building.

They went along with the deal, and for a while it worked out for all until some problems set in. Before we look at Mike's problems, let's look at another example.

David was an expert at hotel management. He was asked to manage a property in the Bahama Islands by some offshore investors. He said he would if they gave him a 10 percent ownership in the property with an additional 5 percent for every year that he increases the net operating income by 5 percent or more. David also added that when and if his interest reached 50 percent he would have the right to buy out the other partners on a formula based on the income average for the past three years.

The owners calculated that for David to reach 50 percent ownership he would have to have eight years of growth and that the new operating income would have to increase by 80 percent or more. Based on that, they could afford to sell at the formula offered.

The key to this scenario was David was an expert in hotel management. He knew that the property was currently poorly managed and that he could slowly build the business so that by the time he reached the end of eight years the place would just be ready for even bigger things.

Some property owners go out and try to find good employees by offering this same kind of incentive. The same basic idea works here.

Five Key Factors to Have in a Management Interest Agreement

1. *Specific terms as to the duration of the agreement and how it can be terminated.* This is the toughest part of any such agreement. How does the current owner lock in the "employee" but not to the extent that if it is a bad relationship it can't be ended? On the other hand, the "employee" doesn't want to be doing everything according to the agreement, succeeding to the terms of the management interest pay outs, only to find that the owners want to eliminate him now that the property is running smoothly. These will be terms that will be discussed in such agreements:
   a. *"Golden Parachute" provisions.* What happens if the company or property is sold? The new owner is not going to honor any such agreement that gives away interest to some other party. If you were that other party, you would want protection over and above your actual interest at that moment to the proceeds of the sale.
   b. *Limitation of employment or competition trade areas.* If you leave or are fired for reason, the owners will want some kind of protection that you won't take all the clientele and go into business for yourself down the street. This is difficult to establish, but it is apt to come up.
   c. *Calculations of interest, profits, and dividends.* If you don't have control and have a formula on which all your interest, share of profits, or dividends are calculated, make sure that you have a clear understanding of the accounting. Normal business expenses can also include salary to key people, and the other partners could legally be entitled to salaries that could eat up any profit and take away any bonus you thought you were going to get. Also, to arrive at a net operating income requires deductions from the gross income of all such operating expenses. You might find that unless you had set up things very clearly that gross goes way up, but net drops each year.

2. *Get copies of past years' income and expense statements.* Base your future growth and formulas on known factors. Take into account that things are going to go up, that rent won't be the same, and that the phone bill will increase five years down the road. However, establish those patterns and follow them if you are on a formula percentage basis.

3. *Know the goals of your partners.* If your partners are happy with a small operation, they might be frightened when you turn it into a big operation. Scared partners do things you can't anticipate.

4. *Build a periodic review into your agreement.* This allows you to stop any problems you might have with your partners before they get out of hand. It is good for them, too, but a series of constantly positive reports makes it difficult for anyone to suddenly claim that he or she suspected that you were taking petty cash for the past six years.

5. *Don't play around with what you are due.* If you meet the objectives of the contract, demand what you have coming. When it comes time to exercise your option to buy, remember that you can offer less, that the option is one-sided for you, and that you can take it or leave it or offer less.

PITFALLS IN MANAGEMENT INTEREST TRANSACTIONS

There are several:
1. Getting in over your head with a project you can't handle.
2. Not having everything in writing.
3. Not living up to the spirit of the agreement.
4. Giving cause to be fired when you are really doing a good job.
5. Getting tied down to a job you hate and people you don't like.

Each of these five pitfalls has its obvious counterpart. Use caution and good legal advice prior to entering into the agreement, and do your homework as to the people, the plan, and the future potential.

Three-Party Blankets

A three-party blanket occurs when you add additional property to a mortgage that you don't own. This provides additional security to the lender, who is usually the seller of a property you are buying.

Mark wanted to buy a home in Tulsa. He offered the seller $168,000, which was slightly less than the $175,000 he was asking. The terms offered were:

$25,000 cash down

$110,000 assume the existing mortgage

$33,000 second mortgage on a duplex that Mark owned

The seller agreed to the price, but balked at the second mortgage on the duplex. "Not enough equity," he said.

Mark tried several other tacks, but nothing worked. Then he asked his father if he could "borrow" some land that the family owned for a couple of years. What Mark wanted to do was to add the land to the security of the second mortgage. Mark offered his father a kicker of a percentage of the ultimate sale, and pledged his own equity in the house to his father should anything go wrong.

Mark's plan was to move into the house and fix it up, refinancing the improved home and selling it for about $230,000. If all worked out as he hoped, there would be room for the kicker percentage that he offered his father, and little risk for everyone.

The three-party blanket is a method of bringing in a partner who gets a small part of the deal, or some other kicker because he doesn't have to invest any cash. The advantage is to the seller as he is being appeased with additional equity in any paper he may hold.

Since the value or quality of the paper has been improved, other terms in the deal often can be counterbalanced to offset the kickers that Mark and you may have to pay to get the "use" of the other property.

Notice that the end result is similar to what might happen with the OPP techniques (other people's property) also discussed in this chapter. The technique here is the use of the blanket mortgage in this method. You may wish to review the chapter on blanket mortgages also provided for you in this book.

This technique often is used with first-time buyers who need additional security to make their transactions work. Sellers being asked to hold paper are naturally reluctant to extend credit to "fresh" investors who are still wet behind the ears. In those situations, the buyer has to dig deep into his bag of tricks to find a technique that is acceptable to both the seller and to any third party he is going to find to help.

Remember, the blanket mortgage is a form of mortgage that has more than one property as security to the note. The holder of the mortgage can "go after" or foreclose on any of the properties or all of the properties in the event of a default on that mortgage. This therein is the basis for the pitfalls in this technique.

Pitfalls in Three-Party Blankets

If you were the third party and you allowed Mark to use your land as additional security on his mortgage, and Mark defaulted on his mortgage, you could be at risk for the mortgage in a foreclosure or risk action against your land to recover the amount owed on the mortgage.

Be very careful if you are the third party. Obviously, the solution is to weigh the risk against the kicker being offered. If you are to become a partner in the deal, have not put up any cash, have little risk in losing your security, and the gain potential is good, the whole transaction is sound.

This points up the prime benefit of using the third-party blanket as an investment tool. The person who comes out best often is in fact the person who put up the security in the transaction.

Like co-signers, which will be covered later, the one who helps someone else put a deal together often is the one who profits the most.

Keeping this in mind, as the investor you have to make sure that bringing in a partner, even in the form of a third-party blanket, is worth the effort. Ask yourself this question: "Have I tried everything I could to buy that property without a partner . . . or do I need someone to share my lack of confidence in that property?" The answer to that question might surprise you if you are fully honest with yourself.

TRADING JEWELS AND STAMPS

Two highly "marked up" items that can be traded for real estate are jewels and stamps. An investor uses these items as all or part of the payment in a real estate deal.

Orlando was a gem dealer in Brazil who had the gems right from the ground so to speak. He opened an office in Miami, where he displayed the stones in a beautiful shop in a fashionable area. He made offers for real estate, giving the sellers the right to select anything from the stock in the showroom.

Some of these transactions were quite large, totaling millions of dollars. The sellers had the freedom of taking the gems to a gemologist and having them appraised, and if not satisfied within a reasonable time, the deal would be called off.

Christina had a stamp shop in London and was considered an expert in stamps. She had a major collection that was worth millions. She too made offers on real estate offering her stamps as payment to the seller.

In both Orlando's and Christina's situations, they were offering items at or near face value based on the prices in the shop or in the catalog. Their negotiations allowed them to "overpay" by giving a discount off the sticker price on the items, or to balance part of the deal with cash or mortgages.

These two dealers were honest and made no effort to hide any values from the sellers. However, each was an expert in his or her field and knew that the final value on the gem or stamp was well above "cost."

There is no question, however, that other people have used these two commodities to great wrong to many sellers who have been "taken" in by fast-talking, hard-sale dealers who have traded gems that were worthless and stamps that were counterfeit. In fact, one of the news exposé television shows did an segment on a company that had traded jewels for real estate and that had supposedly taken many sellers of all their equity in real estate a few years ago. This was a good job of bringing the problem to forefront, but the program did nothing to show investors and sellers how to examine the opportunities that do present themselves in honest transactions where these items can be used with good value intended.

Where the Problems Lay in Jewels and Stamps

First, you have to look at the basic foundation of transactions. What benefit are you looking for as a seller, and what benefit do you want to give up as a buyer? If the major benefit for the seller is to get rid of the property or to have someone take over debt, then taking anything in exchange may well suit that goal. If the item taken in exchange turns out to be worthless, the primary goal may still have been met. In other words, for some sellers anything you offer them is better than their current circumstance. If the seller's alternative to your transaction is foreclosure, your deal may be very acceptable.

Many buyers know this and approach those sellers who are looking to get rid of the property, stop paying the debt service required, avoid foreclosure.

However, some investors approach this task looking to better their position by offering a value that is grossly overstated. One such scam occurred around the United States with several investors who packaged several gems of the same category in a nice plastic box; on the back side, one specific gem, presumably selected at random from the collection, was appraised and the value of that gem quoted. The appraisal was on the up and up, and the statement that followed was certainly true. It read something like this: "As the appraised gem as shown has an estimated retail replacement value of $500.00 per carat, and as the total gems within this package weigh 50 carats, then based on the value of the appraised gem, and assuming that all the gems contained within the package are of equal value or more, then the minimum value for retail replacement of these gems would be $2,500."

The problem with this statement is that none of the unappraised gems were worth more than $5.00 or so per carat. They were real stones of the category in question (rubies, sapphires, etc.), but they were worthless stones.

Property owners who would take a package or several packages like this without having each stone appraised would run the risk of being taken advantage of. Many such transactions occurred, and many such property owners were taken advantage of.

Since value is a very relative thing in stamp investing, stamps are highly suspect to value. Some people can make a lot of money with stamps, but the item has no real use except for collection. You can't wear it as a beautiful gem, you can't effectively display it as you might a Miró or Rembrandt as the light will blanch its colors, so it sits within a book, maintaining its value based on some opinion rather than a need or a specific use.

Taking Gems or Stamps

I have, as a seller, taken gems and have learned some lessons in those experiences. I discovered that one does not take gems at their "replacement value," as that is a quirk term used by appraisers to set often unrealistically high values for insurance companies. The concept is that as each stone is unique (despite the fact that you may not know that by normal eye sight, or even with a jeweler's loupe), the replacement of a piece of jewelry with such an exact stone may be much more expensive. The simple replacement of the piece of jewelry with similar quality and value stones would be much less expensive of course. Therefore if you deal with gems, be aware that "real value" and "replacement value" of gems are greatly different.

Finished gems set in jewelry pieces have far more retail value than the separate values of the stones themselves. The "work" needed to custom-make a ring or broach is also greatly overstated. A visit to a jewelry supply area will convince you that you can buy standard settings and have stones mounted quite inexpensively.

The question of time then becomes the real unknown element of value in the formation of jewelry. Obviously, there are specific gems that are so unique and valuable, and custom work that is so unique and valuable that those pieces are best left for the ultra rich. The Hope Diamond is an extreme example to prove that point.

The best lesson in gem dealing is, take jewelry only to the extent that you might buy it if you had the money to do so. Never take it as an investment unless you have a way to convert gems into jewelry or to sell jewelry in a retail market.

As for stamps, my advice is to either become an expert in stamps and know what you are doing, or to avoid stamps altogether.

Subdivide and Exchange

You acquire a tract of land or other divisible property, and in dividing it up you exchange the separated elements for other property or benefits.

Suppose you bought a ten-acre tract of land using a technique that allowed you to divide the land into twenty half-acre lots. Your gross price for the ten acres when you bought it was $25,000. You paid $5,000 cash down and gave the seller a first mortgage on the balance with a provision that you could convert the mortgage into twenty separate mortgages covering each of the twenty lots. Each lot would then have a mortgage of $1,000 against it.

You are now free to sell or exchange each lot to someone else without having to pay off the mortgage first. In this technique, you would use your new equity to exchange.

After all, you have formed a subdivision and have created new use out of old use. No longer is this tract a one-owner ten-acre piece of land. It is now twenty lots, available for twenty separate owners. Its new value might be $5,000 per lot. If that were the case you have an equity of $4,000 per lot. You could take five such lots and offer the equity of $20,000 as a down payment on that apartment building you want to buy or the condo you just looked at.

The exchange of these lots can allow you to move quickly into other property. There is an appeal to a recently subdivided property (like getting in on the ground floor so to speak).

In a situation such as a lot with a low loan-to-value ratio, you have the advantage of paying off or counterbalancing the effect of the mortgage. This would be useful in those circumstances where the other property owner is reluctant to take vacant property that has mortgage payments he would then be required to meet.

If you could exchange ten lots at a gross price of $50,000 against which there was $10,000 in mortgages, and the $40,000 equity allowed you to refinance the new property to the extent that you could pay off the $10,000, then you could give the other party the option of taking the lots with the mortgage and the $10,000 cash, or taking the lots free and clear of any debt.

A counterbalancing mortgage would null out the effect that the other party would have of taking the lots with the debt service on the $10,000 mortgage. In this case, you would exchange the ten lots and give the other party a $10,000 mortgage on the property you are getting with payments that equal those combined payments on the ten lots.

After all, if you make a payment of $150 per month to the other party, and he has the same total payment on the ten lots, the net result is that he doesn't have any cash out of his pocket each month.

The subdivision of the ten-acre tract would give you the added flexibility to deal in more transactions using this newly increased asset value. If you kept the property as a ten-acre tract, its value is dependent on the benefit it can provide to a single investor. Twenty lots can provide more benefits to more people.

Jay contracted to buy a sixteen-unit apartment building. His contract provided that by the end of 120 days Jay would close and:

1. The purchase price would be $650,000.
2. The seller would get $150,000 cash at the closing.
3. A vacant tract in Marathon, Florida, would be deeded to the seller. Its value was established at $100,000.
4. Jay would obtain new financing to retire the existing $400,000.

To meet this objective, Jay started the legal work to convert the apartment building into a condominium. He estimated that as a condo he would have gross sales of $1,120,000 (an average of $70,000 per condominium unit). His estimated cost of sales, including fix-up costs, loan costs, and interest during his anticipated twelve months to sell out would be $220,000. At this, he would see a net profit of $900,000. Jay had already spoken to an owner of land in Marathon and had set up the "exchange" of two units at $65,000 for the $100,000 land to go to the seller of the apartment, with the balance of $30,000 in cash to Jay to balance that out. By going to a local savings and loan, Jay knew that he could obtain a new mortgage of $740,000 based on his anticipated repairs and sell-out projections. That money plus the $30,000 overage in the Marathon exchange would go to:

1. Retire the existing mortgage $400,000
2. Pay off the seller   150,000
3. Provide remodeling and carrying costs   220,000

At this point, Jay has made his deal without any cash out of his own pocket other than his time and effort and initial up-front legal work.

TWO KEY POINTS TO REMEMBER ABOUT EXCHANGING

Many of the different techniques covered in this book use exchanges from one person to another. You should remember that I stress the single element—benefit. All exchanges, money, scrip, barter, sweat equity, paper, subdivided property, or whatever work best when the investor remembers and follows these two key points.

1. People want to feel that they have made a profit in their transaction. No one wants to be told "You sold that too cheap" or "You idiot, that property was worth twice what you got." Yet, that kind of talk comes easy from the very person who would not have offered you even that much. When you offer something of value to a person who can't sell his property, no matter how much that item might have cost you, no matter if it is your spare time waxing his cars or being his CPA for a year or doing five gold inlays, the element you offer has value.

Best of all, that value allows the seller to say, "Boy, did I get my price" or "I got every penny I asked for."

Sellers will do almost anything to avoid loss of face. Therefore, when you come along and don't knock the price, but instead examine the benefits you are willing to give up for the benefits you will get, people will take bags of gems or envelopes full of stamps.

2. Always strive to be honest, but at the same time remember that memories are short and people will believe what they want, think what they find convenient, and want more than they have. You will sleep better

at night if you know you did your best to present anything you offer in an exchange at a realistic value. Now that doesn't mean you have to offer a bargain or give away any secrets, but it does mean that you must allow the other side time to check values, to seek legal advice, to back out of the deal if they feel wronged.

The Pitfalls of Subdividing and Exchanging

What happens if you are counting on getting rid of the property through exchanges and the market falls to pot? Or you overestimate your ability and underestimate the cost to subdivide? Or the city or the county impose moratoriums on such things as subdividing? These are some of the pitfalls that lie in the darkness for the developer.

Be careful of the laws in your state with respect to land sales. Florida and other states have very specific ideas of what a subdivision should consist of and what you have to do in order to meet the requirements of the state. These often can be very expensive requirements if you fall under the control of those government bodies.

Fortunately, even the most strict state will have a cut-off point at which you would not fall into their full or even partial control. Know exactly what that is before you get started.

Chapter 22

THE STAGES OF EVERY PURCHASE

There are four stages that transpire from the start of your quest to invest in real estate to the moment you sign a contract to buy. They are:

1. Laying the foundation to buy.
2. Selecting a property to buy.
3. Negotiating to win.
4. Offering/contracting to buy.

These stages have moments when all seems to be going according to plan. Everything is smooth and no hitches appear. Then the storm can come crashing in and in a second the whole thing seems to fall apart. It is in those moments you see your dream purchase disappear.

Each of these stages has people involved: you, of course, your real estate broker and salesman, the other party to the contract, your lawyer, the other party's lawyer, the CPA, the closing agent, the escrow agent. Each one takes time and adds to the complexity of the transaction.

Buying and selling real estate for a profit is not a one-man job. There is no highly successful investor who has ever done it all on his own. There simply isn't enough time, and once the money begins to build up, the time it would take for some of the simpler tasks will best be left to others you can hire. It becomes a matter of priority as your wealth grows, not a matter of your not being able to do the job yourself. Wealth does have its rewards.

LAYING THE FOUNDATION TO BUY

Without the proper foundation you will have a hit-or-miss chance at success. Granted, there are people who do have success at things they do and they have no foundation at all. You can read about them or you've known people like that. And what did you say when you learned about the guy down the street who sold his house for twice its value because he was the key piece to a redevelopment of that block? "That lucky son of a gun."

That's right, he was lucky, and there are many other investors who will be just as lucky due to no act of their own. They just happened to make a buy that turned into a small pot of gold.

Unfortunately, for every one of these lucked-out investments, there are dozens of not so lucky ones. Buying real estate just is not an absolute guaranteed deal. Not everything you buy is going to go up in value fast enough (if at all) to cover the cost of holding on to it. Not every property will produce a profit; not every apartment building will be fully occupied and become a money machine. It is possible for you to lose your shirt investing in real estate no matter how much you know.

In fact, some of the smart boys lose their shirts. Not every investment I've made has turned out the way I wanted it to. I've taken a few high flyers that could have turned out like a diamond mine, but instead developed into a latrine. The risk in these investments was higher than you might be able to absorb; I thought I'd be able to overcome it. But the best-laid plans of men can be thwarted by men—or time.

So the occasional high flyer (risky deal) should be left to the big boys who can anticipate and afford the potential loss. Building your wealth in real estate won't always be an uphill ride. There will be times in even the most conservative investment when you may have to pull in the belt a notch or two to counteract temporary setbacks, such as high unemployment in your area (which does nasty things to rental projects), or city projects such as new roads that will have a future benefit, but in the meantime can cause you to lose tenants in your strip store because of the torn-up pavement for twelve months.

Being able to bend with these elements of the game is all part of the road to success. If it were easy, it wouldn't be so rewarding when you got there. Success is simply attained. Not easily, just simply. It requires only your dedication and persistence.

The development of your foundation is, of course, up to you. Some of you will get it in the school of hard knocks. That is, you will experience a bit more failure early in your learning, and if you hang in the success will come later. Hard knocks, by the way, is really a misnomer. If you succeed, you will look back on all your failures as important stages in your success. You simply cannot have success without failure. This is the most important part of your total foundation for success.

People who are failures in life find a reason why each failure was not their fault. People who succeed found out what they did to cause each failure, and did not do it again. The successful embrace failure, as it is essential to advancement and success. Into every real estate investor's life a little rain must fall.

I've given you all the basics you need to know to get ready. Applying them is up to you. The six elements of success—knowledge, enthusiasm, motivation, perseverance, clear goals, and no fear of failure—are within you if you pull it together and make them work for you. You can be a little success or a big success depending on your balance of elements. You will find the balance, or you simply will find that real estate isn't your thing.

There's nothing wrong with that. I have many tenants who feel exactly that way.

Finding a Salesperson

There are two categories of real estate brokers and salespeople. There are realtors, and brokers who are not realtors. Let me explain it this way. The National Association of Realtors is a nationwide professional organization, the largest of its kind. The members of the realtors' association, in order to join, must agree to be bound by a series of rules which govern their activities in many ways. They have their own internal professional standard code, and a strict self-policing of that code as well as its enforcement. The realtors make up the majority of the brokers dealing in real estate. But not all brokers are in fact realtors. No state law requires the holder of a real estate license to be a realtor.

As a realtor I feel the major benefit to an investor in dealing with a fellow realtor would be simply that the realtor has a wider access to the product than the nonrealtor. There may be other reasons to choose realtors, and the National Association of Realtors would be quick to point out that realtors adhere to a more strict code of ethics, but while that may be true, I've known many fine and qualified brokers and salespeople who didn't want to bother to become realtors.

Yet, because your interest is in finding the best selection of property for your invested capital, look first among the realtors in your neighborhood to see if you can find the person with whom you can develop rapport; someone who will put his (or her) total knowledge at your disposal so that you will profit. It is your interest that you want this person to have at the top of his list.

The best way to find this ideal salesman is to look for him. Ask around in your own circle of friends to see if a name will be recommended. The good salesman usually has a wide range of satisfied clients who are that salesman's best source of new clients. Let your friends know you are looking for a good real estate salesman and pretty soon you will have several names to choose from.

Of course, that may not produce a person you feel you can work with. The importance of your having rapport with this person cannot be overestimated. He might be the best salesman in town, but if you can't get along with him, then seek out someone else.

Visit some real estate offices and ask to speak with a broker. Tell the broker that you are planning to invest in real estate and you feel you need to meet several salesmen so you can find one you can work with over the years. If the broker is smart, he will discuss your needs with you and introduce you to one or two of his salesmen he feels would be right for you. If he was wrong, then try another office.

It is a good idea for you to explain to the salesman that you want to find a salesman you can work with and you don't want him or her to spend any time on your behalf until you are ready. The salesman will appreciate the fact that you want to find one salesman to deal with and will respect that. There is nothing worse for a real estate salesman than to be working with a client who hasn't told him about the other salesman from a competitor's office that he is currently working with. A lot of time and effort are wasted in the real estate business because of this.

Ask questions and expect answers that demonstrate to you that the salesman is knowledgeable about the area and can be of help to you. If you don't get a good feel for the setup, then don't waste your time or the salesman's—move on. The time you spend in searching out a salesman to work with will pay off benefits later on, and you will be glad you were cautious.

The Kind of Real Estate Salesperson You Don't Want

- The salesperson who doesn't ask you questions. This shows this salesperson doesn't know enough to find out what your goals, your needs, and your time requirements are. If the salesperson does ask questions but they are disjointed and unrelated to your goals, the time you have spent was for nothing. Move on.

- The salesperson who talks and doesn't listen. (The worst thing any salesperson can do!) Some do it because they feel they must impress you. It is okay for the salesperson to give you a brief history of him- or herself and/or his or her office, but you are there to have your problems solved, your goals met. He or she has got to listen to do it effectively.

- A salesperson who is in a rush to make a sale. The first sign of this is when he or she wants to take you out to see a property before he or she has found out sufficient data about your needs. This is a common trait with real estate salespeople and may be a sign of lack of confidence. Understanding your needs is important, so he or she will save time by showing you property that is closer to your needs.
- The salesperson you are uncomfortable with. It doesn't matter why—she smokes and you can't stand smoke, or the accent of his voice, or his hairstyle, or the funny mole on the side of her nose. If you are uncomfortable and can't get rapport, move on.

8 Traits of Top Real Estate Salespeople

1. They listen.
2. They are prompt.
3. They ask pointed and direct questions aimed to help you shape your goals so that they will understand what they are.
4. They are constantly learning. Real estate is a profession that demands constant update and learning.
5. They are enthusiastic about their ability to solve your problem.
6. They demonstrate self-confidence.
7. They look successful.
8. They know the techniques of the trade that will enable you to make more deals.

Once you have a real estate salesperson on your side and you have been candid with him or her about your financial position, you are ready to move on to the second stage of the transaction.

SELECTING A PROPERTY TO BUY

Much has been said already about this stage. You know that the selection of real estate is very important because it sets the theme of the kind of real estate investing you are going to do.

If this is to be your first buy, then you will seek a living investment, that is, one you can live in yourself. That might be a single-family property or an apartment complex. Whatever it is, you will make the proper selection by following the many suggestions I've given you in this book.

10 Key Factors in Finding the Property You Will Ultimately Buy

1. Stick close to your backyard.

2. Don't get beyond the scope of your ability, but know what that ability is.

3. Be willing to stretch yourself to the maximum limit of your economic capability.

4. Remember that risk is relative, and you can ease, reduce, or even remove risk by knowing as much as possible about the area, the market, and the property.

5. In building wealth you must look for property you can improve. The top of the heap has no place to go but down.

6. Have property inspected for problems by qualified people. The cost is nothing in comparison to the benefit of knowing the real condition of the property.

7. Recognize that if you like it and can afford it, this is one of the most important parts of buying real estate.

8. Don't overanalyze a deal. If it is really good, by the time you have made up your mind to buy it someone else will have bought it. Besides, the likelihood is your long-range projections won't be accurate anyway.

9. Trends are generally clearly visible if you know where to look for them.

10. History repeats itself in real estate, so to know what is going on, look back to the past.

In reality you don't select the property you are going to buy, but instead you select property you would like to own. The time between wanting to own it and actually owning it has yet to come. It is highly possible that once you begin negotiating to buy, you will change your mind about the property in the first place. Price and terms the seller is willing to take can be the deciding factors. Or, as you continue to progress in the selection process you might start negotiating on one parcel of land or one building only to find another which suits your goals better than the first. In that event, simply break off negotiations and go on to the second property.

Sellers should recognize that a savvy buyer will not be bound to a deal until the deposit is placed and the contract fully executed on all sides. The highly motivated seller, then, should keep in mind that a bird in the hand is worth a whole flock in the bush (in real estate that's the way it goes).

Naturally, it depends on the status of the real estate marketplace. If it is a sellers' market, that is, if the demand to buy is greater than the supply to meet that demand, then the sellers sit in a good position. They usually will have several potential buyers out there, so the prices are firm and terms not as easy as in other markets. There is a danger here, however. If you are a seller and it seems to be a sellers' market, it could well be that your property isn't in that market at all. Real estate isn't one market-place; it is many. There is the single-family-homes market, but even that is divided into different strata, then vacant lots, acreage, office buildings, hotels, and so on. Not all markets are up at the same time, and fortunately not all are down at the same time either.

When you enter the market to buy, the condition of that market will affect the method in which you negotiate. Obviously, if it is a sellers' market for the kind of property you want to buy and you can't be detoured to buy another kind of property, then you can't be too standoffish in your attempts to bring the price down or to get better terms in the negotiations. If you do, you are apt to lose the deal to a less finicky buyer.

In a buyers' market, the conditions are such that there are more sellers than there are ready and willing buyers. This is more often the case in vacant land and acreage, as there is a lot of that kind of property. However, even this can become a hot item in a local area and then switch overnight from a buyers' market to a sellers' market.

A buyers' market might seem to be the ideal time to buy a property, but this is not always the case. You have to look to your own reason for buying and decide based on your own goal. If you want to utilize the property right away, or you anticipate the need for immediate income, a sellers' market could be your best market. The buyers' market might have been created because of a recession or a slowdown in the growth of the area. These conditions might work against your goals, and buying at this time might not suit your needs. Price is a function of the use of a property, so as the need for the use (in the marketplace) goes down, so will the price.

Hotel sites in an overbuilt area will be a buyers' market. However, unless the buyer can find another use for the site or wait out the overbuilt condition, the purchase of that site at this time may not be prudent. To wait until the time is right to build and pay more might be wiser. Builders and developers have long since recognized the fact that in a developmental program the cost of the land is only a fraction of the total picture anyway. It makes no economic sense to buy cheap and have the risk of holding for a long time when only a slightly increased price (when compared to the total picture) will produce a ready and set property. You should re-member this as well.

Now it's time to move into the third stage of the deal.

NEGOTIATING TO WIN

There are six key factors in negotiating and winning. These are:

1. Avoid personal confrontation during the actual offer. This is ab-solutely essential to successful negotiating. The buyer will do far better if he has a mediator, a broker or salesman, in between him and the seller,

at least at that crucial moment when the offer is presented. Every professional arbitrator, negotiator, politician, salesman, broker, lawyer, and judge knows that placing the two parties (buyer and seller) face to face is not in the best interest of the best deal.

Here's why. A buyer attempting to make the best deal for himself is going to press the transaction. If that pressure is direct and face-to-face the seller can and generally will react in a defensive way.

Buyer: "Mr. Seller, I realize you want $150,000 for this property, but the most I am prepared to offer is $95,000, and that's a good price."

Seller: "Well, you can take that $95,000 offer and stick it."

As you can see, negotiations have broken down. Another example of the same kind of thing happening:

Buyer: "Mr. Seller, if it weren't for the blue and pink drapes in this house, which I'll have to replace, I'd be offering more, but whoever picked those colors out had to be nuts."

Seller: "My wife picked them out, and if you don't like those colors then you don't have to buy this house. In fact, I don't think I want to sell to you."

And so on. I could continue giving you examples of what can happen. Now, granted, there are those rare people who can sit down and make a deal face-to-face with the seller. However, it is too risky in my opinion. It is far too easy to say the wrong thing in such an encounter and end up with a seller who doesn't like you, and who will not be reasonable from that moment on.

Good salespeople who know the art of negotiation can deal with a difficult seller (or when things are turned around with a difficult buyer) without compromising your interest in the deal. The salesperson can absorb (as he or she should) the heat of the negotiations so the other side of the deal can vent his or her frustrations at the broker and not at you.

2. Review your goals prior to making the offer to be sure the property fits in the scheme of things. There is no sense in starting out on a negotiation that will end up with a property not suited for your goals. A simple review of those goals will put you back on the right track. You will find on occasion that what has happened is that emotion has become an insider to the deal and has, at least temporarily, replaced your goals or at best clouded those goals from a clear sight. Watch for that, because once you get away from the goals and let emotion run wild with the deal, you will find yourself rationalizing away the best part of your plan.

3. Try to learn something about the other party's goals. If you know what the seller (or buyer) is really attempting to accomplish, then you might have a better way to help him reach his goal and at the same time benefit yourself. One example that comes to mind involved a client of mine interested in selling a lot he owned in a subdivision west of Fort Lauderdale. A prospective buyer made an offer through another office. My client rejected the offer and countered $5,000 higher. The would-be buyer balked and said he'd think about it. As he and the other broker

were about to leave my office, he asked me what the seller was going to do with the money. "He wants to get a summer home in North Carolina," I said.

"Hell," the buyer said. "I'm a builder in Asheville. I have several homes I'll trade."

The story didn't end there. The owner of the lot never ended up with a home this client had, but an exchange was made in which the builder from North Carolina did participate, and he did get the lot he wanted. The seller of the lot got what he wanted because of the North Carolina builder.

Learning the true reasons for a sale or the real use to which the money is going to be put can be next to impossible sometimes. Your broker or salesman will have to dig a little to find out what he can, and sometimes you are well into the negotiations before you find even anything that resembles the truth.

Yet it is simple and should be clear to you that the more you know about the other party to the deal the better you will be able to come out on top of the negotiation.

In fact, it is more important for the seller to know more about the buyer than the other way around. And best of all, the seller is in a better position to find out information about the buyer once the negotiations start. Sellers being asked to hold secondary financing, for example, can rationally and logically ask for and usually receive financial information on the buyer. References and the like are a good source of data on the buyer, and most buyers attempting to buy hard will be forced to give up some of this information. You should be careful about relying on such references, however, as a buyer wouldn't give you the name of someone who would badmouth him. But you can get leads from a reference on where else to go to get more information about a person, so they are highly useful in that sense.

4. Be flexible in the negotiations, but firm at the same time. Does this sound like a contradiction? It's not. The idea is to decide where you want to be flexible and where you want to be firm. If the deal is all cash, then you are closing the options you are giving the other party and the only place where there is any flex left is in the price. This is, in my opinion, a bad stand for a seller, as it places him in the tightest of all boxes to make a deal. Naturally, this stand must be taken at times when cash is the only way out, and there is no way to generate that cash from some outside source. But the fact of the matter is there are so many options open to buyers to give a seller cash and yet keep their own out-of-pocket cash investment at a minimum that it is folly to assume that all cash to one party means all cash paid by the other.

Financing from a third party can usually be found in one form or other to help the deal along.

Remember "I'll pay your price if you accept my terms." Or, said another way, "I can't budge on the cash down, but I can work out the terms," or "I know I can get the best terms to suit my deal if I'm flexible in the price."

You will see a clearer path in the decision on where you want or need to be firm by having a good understanding of your goals, of course, but it is more than just that. The property and its ability to sustain a profit while it produces income is very important. You don't want to overburden the transaction with heavy debt that can't be sustained unless a miracle happens, just because you are getting the price you were willing to pay.

5. Remember there are other fish in the sea. I've seen buyers go into deep depression because they lost out on a property they wanted to buy. Losing deals will happen to you if you plan to buy and sell real estate. There will be other investors who have snookered you out of a great deal, and other times it will be turned around. Yet, crying over spilled milk won't get you anything. Move on to the next deal. Be careful, however— you might act a little quicker the next time out of fear of losing the next deal, so watch out for this overreaction.

6. Sellers should be careful about holding out too long. There is a time and place for holding out for a better offer. In typical hindsight I'll tell you that the time and place is only when you get a higher offer. Unfortunately, many sellers turn down offers that are never bettered. It might be possible that the seller will get a higher price sometime in the future by holding out longer, but you must consider the time element. If you are a tough seller and yet you really want to sell, keep in mind that as you hold on to a property you are losing the potential from the reinvestment of that capital. Not selling at $100,000 because you are sure you will get $110,000 is okay if you get the $110,000 within a reasonable time. If you had to hold on to the property for twelve months or more, the chances are you have lost ground rather than come out ahead. This depends somewhat on your motivation, of course, and what you might have done with the money from a sale. Remember, time is the key factor to profit.

These six factors will help give you some edge in the negotiation of the contract. You win, however, in every transaction that takes you closer to your goal. Naturally, the real win is viewed from the nineteenth hole. The fifth-quarter viewpoint of the game is always the easiest, and most investors look back at every transaction to decide if they have won or lost.

While this might give the investor a more satisfactory view of his analysis of winning or losing, it does provide the investor with the rationalization of that win or loss. This is natural, however, even though it will distort the true win or loss. The seller says, "You should have negotiated a little harder, because I would have taken much less than you paid."

In retort the buyer says, "That's okay, because if you would have held out for more I was ready to give you double what I actually paid."

Your viewpoint on winning should be tied to what it is you want to accomplish. Your flexibility in the negotiations will be very important to keep alive all possibilities to achieve what you wanted in the first instance. Try to keep personalities out of the picture by avoiding direct confrontation with the other party. If you have a broker or salesman, let him become the buffer, as he should, in nailing down the best deal for you. Remember, of course, that this salesman or broker will have to see the transaction from three vantage points—yours, the other party's, and his own. As long as you keep track of your own interest and help point the salesman in that same direction, you won't have to press the deal; the enthusiastic and knowledgeable salesman will do that for you.

You have progressed well along in the buying or selling process if you have a contract. As a buyer you haven't made up your mind sufficiently unless you are at that stage, and as a seller nothing happens until there is an offer which can generate a contract. Thus, on to the next stage.

OFFERING/CONTRACTING TO BUY

How you present your offers is an essential part of the negotiation process. There are four basic forms of offers—verbal; letter of intent; standard-form agreement; lawyer-drafted agreement. Not all are effective for each situation. Some may not be useful at all.

Verbal

It should be noted that in the transfer of real estate the contract must be executed in writing to be legally enforceable. This doesn't negate the use of the verbal offer, however, as with some people their word is as good as their bond. I've seen many deals hammered out in verbal terms with nothing written down until everything had been agreed to. This is not unusual or uncommon. However, for each deal worked out in such methods I've seen a hundred fall into one hassle or other as one of the parties lapses into forgetfulness as to what was exactly said, and the closing never occurs.

Frequently a buyer will instruct his salesman, "See what the seller will take." This is generally followed by the salesman asking the seller what is the lowest price the seller will take. These tactics generally don't produce any beneficial results and the salesman won't find out the real facts in this maneuver. Most sellers don't know what they will take until a plan is presented to them that suits their goals (at that moment).

For the buyer to tell the seller (directly or through the salesman) that he would like to buy the property and would the seller take, say, $100,000 is equally unproductive. If the seller was foolish enough to answer the question "Yes," the likelihood is that the offer will be $90,000 or less.

Thus, while there is a time and place for verbal offers, most sellers won't respond as effectively to a verbal offer as they would to a cash deposit and written contract. "Here's my offer, Mr. Seller, and here's a big check to show I'm real."

The Letter of Intent: A Written Verbal Offer

What happens in the letter of intent is that the broker or the buyer himself will write a letter to the seller. This letter states that the client (buyer) is interested in buying the seller's property on the basis of terms outlined in detail or in some loose form in the letter. The basics only are discussed, and the buyer leaves out much of the detail that would constitute a contract. One such letter of intent is shown below:

Mr. Bradford J. Williams
President
Westmoreland National Insurance Companies
New York, New York

Dear Mr. Williams:

This letter is to indicate to you the intent of our prospective purchaser THE WORLD DEVELOPMENT COMPANIES N.V. from Aruba, Netherland Antilles, to enter into an agreement for the purchase of the apartment complex your company owns known as OCEAN SIDE APARTMENTS which is located in Hollywood, Florida. We have been informed by THE WORLD DEVELOPMENT COMPANIES N.V. that their legal representatives in Miami will draft the purchase offer and have it in your offices within five days from the date of your acceptance of this Letter of Intent. They are prepared to place $200,000 deposit with the offer.

The terms which would be acceptable to THE WORLD DEVELOPMENT COMPANIES N.V. are as follows:

1. A purchase price of: $5,750,000.
2. A cash down payment (of which the deposit is a part) of $2,000,000.
3. The balance of the purchase price would be held by the sellers as a first mortgage over 27 years term at a variable interest rate to be 2 points below prime as of the first of each month.
4. Closing to occur within 45 days of approval of the various inspections to be made. These inspections will include:
   (a) Structural of the buildings.
   (b) Electrical of the buildings.
   (c) Mechanical of the buildings.
   (d) Plumbing of the buildings.
   (e) Examination of the leases.
   (f) Examination of payment records.
   (g) Inspection of the maintenance records of the buildings.

5. In the event there is no approval given of these items within 15 days from the date the agreement of sale is completed, the sales agreement will be null and void and each party released from further obligations to the other.

6. Each party understands and agrees that there will be other terms and conditions in the final purchase agreement, but the first five terms outlined herein are the basic terms being agreed herein.

It is understood that the prospective purchasers will proceed immediately with the legal document if you agree to the basic terms in this Letter of Intent. It is understood also that this Letter is not to be construed as a contract and only in the approval and execution of the final document of sale will there be a bona fide contract.

Your approval of this Letter in the proper place indicated below will demonstrate your interest to proceed on this matter and your approval in principle of the price and sale terms indicated herein. Furthermore your approval will acknowledge that as seller your firm would be obliged to pay our fee at closing of title; said fee is Three Hundred and Fifty Thousand Dollars.

I have enclosed a packet of information on THE WORLD DEVELOPMENT COMPANIES N.V. which I'm sure you will find highly informative. You will find ample references to check on, and I'm confident you will be impressed with the credentials of these prospective buyers.
Very truly yours,

Jack Cummings, President
Cummings Realty Inc.

I HAVE READ THE LETTER OF INTENT AND DO HEREBY ACCEPT THE TERMS OF THE SALE AS OUTLINED. THIS ACCEPTANCE SHALL NOT CONSTITUTE A CONTRACT, BUT MERELY AN AGREEMENT TO ACCEPT THE PRICE AND TERMS BASED ON THE SATISFACTORY APPROVAL OF A FULL AND BONA FIDE CONTRACT CONTAINING THOSE TERMS. OTHERWISE, THIS APPROVAL SHALL AUTOMATICALLY BE WITHDRAWN WITHIN _____ DAYS FROM THE DATE BELOW.

Date: _____

_____
Bradford J. Williams

There are many items in this letter of intent which could be altered or made less specific, of course, and each letter of intent will be different. The idea is to simply indicate what you want to do and to proceed from there. These letters of intent aren't much more than verbal offers, but they do start things rolling. A more impressive way to present a letter of intent and at the same time make sure you have the attention of the seller is to put a deposit with the broker and have him mention that deposit in the letter: ". . . and the prospective buyer has placed a deposit of $10,000 in an escrow account as a statement of good faith. This deposit will become a part of the total cash down at closing."

Many large transactions use the letter of intent format to get moving, as it enables the buyer and seller to negotiate without having the considerable cost of having their lawyers draw full contracts. However, this shortcut works only in some instances, usually in cases where the broker has a good standing with the seller.

As a realtor I never hesitate to use the letter of intent if I know the buyer is sincere. In fact, I recommend using the letter of intent in many situations. But in cases where I know the seller will react more positively to the more formalized and customary form of offer, I shy away from the letter of intent.

The Standard Form of Agreement

There are many forms of "standard" deposit receipt contracts or buy and sell agreements used by the real estate profession. These agreements are easy to spot, as they will have a notice of who the printer is and in many cases a statement showing the forms are approved by the local lawyers' association and/or were formulated by local realtors' associations. These forms will differ slightly around the country and may vary with the kind of real estate being bought and sold. Condominiums, for example, generally require some different terminology to take care of the special items of interest in that kind of real estate. There will be the usual attention to the condo association, the recreation lease (if any), and the percentages of ownership of the common area. Vacant land also differs in the contractual needs as compared to improved real estate. A contract dealing with vacant land often can be far simpler than one dealing with the sale of a residence.

To see how the standard form works to your advantage, you need to understand some of the selling philosophy that surrounds its use. The form is simple and covers nearly every aspect of the transaction in common, easy-to-understand verbiage. If you are dealing with a board-of-realtors-approved standard form, you will have a form which is up-to-date on the needs of the area. It should have conditions which protect both the buyer and the seller and spell out in detail the important aspects of the deposits and defaults and the like. The magic that works for you as buyer or seller is the simplicity of the form. Nothing will frighten a buyer or seller faster than a twenty-page lawyer-prepared contract, even though the lawyer's agreement might be exactly the same, only spread out over more pages and in a different kind of type.

As a buyer you want the salesperson presenting your offer to be able to concentrate on the deal and not on the form of the agreement. As a seller you want your salesperson to be able to get the buyer in the heat of the moment to make the offer that might solve your problem and generate a sale.

To give you an idea of what one of these standard forms looks like, I've provided a copy of the Fort Lauderdale Board of Realtors' Deposit Receipt Contract. This form is used for any sale, although it does have some provisions which are superfluous to transactions involving vacant land. There is ample room for the buyer or seller to add additional terms or provisions, and you can, of course, alter any of the standard provisions.

The form shown on the next pages has been filled out as though I were buying a $100,000 waterfront home. The property has existing financing of $50,000, and I am asking the seller to hold some additional paper. See what other "buyer" techniques you can spot.

Deposit Receipt and Contract for Sale and Purchase

*Jack Cummings et al*_____, of *2671 E. Commercial Blvd., Fort Lauderdale, Florida 33308*_____ (PH ___*771-6300*___) hereinafter called the Buyer, and ___*Hank Bigdeal*___ of ___*Boca Raton, Florida*___ _____ (PH ___*n/p*___) hereinafter called the Seller, hereby agree that the Seller shall sell and the Buyer shall buy the following described property UPON THE TERMS AND CONDITIONS HEREAFTER SET FORTH AND CONTINUED ON REVERSE SIDE OF THIS CONTRACT.

1. LEGAL DESCRIPTION of real estate located in ___*Broward*___ County, Florida. Tax Folio No. ___*14-869-2770*___
   Lot 11 plus East ½ Lot 12, Block H, Rio Mar Sub. Plat Book 1, page 105, Broward County.
   STREET ADDRESS: ___*1235 South East 15 Street*___
   PERSONAL PROPERTY INCLUDED: *Carpets, drapes, kitchen appliances. The built-in bar. The pool table in den. Master bedroom furniture.*
   Seller represents that the property can be used for the following purposes: *Single-family residence.*

2. PURCHASE PRICE IS: . . . . $ 100,000.0

   METHOD OF PAYMENT:
   Deposit herewith . . . . $ 5,000.00
   Additional deposit to be paid upon acceptance of Contract by both parties
   on or before _____ 19_____ $ 5,000.00
   All deposits to be held in trust by *Cummings Realty Inc.*
   Time is of the essence as to additional deposit.
   Principal balance of first mortgage which Buyer shall
   take subject to $ 50,000.00
   Interest 9½%; Method of payment *monthly*
   Other: *Seller to hold a Second Mortgage in the amount of* $ 25,000.00

   > *for a term of 10 years. Payments to be interest only for the first 3 years, annual payments.*
   > *Beginning the 4th year, monthly amortization.*
   > *Interest to be 10%.*

   U.S. Currency, certified or cashier's check on closing and delivery of deed (or such greater or lesser amount as may be necessary toc omplete payment of purchase price after credits, adjustments and prorations). Said funds to be held in escrow pursuant to provisions of Paragraph R on reverse side of this Contract . . . . $ 15,000.00
   TOTAL . . . . $ 100,000.00

3. SPECIAL CLAUSES: (See page 4 or addendum attached, if any) *This offer is subject to the Buyer's unqualified approval of a Subsoil Test to be completed at his expense. Said*

test to be made within 10 days of acceptance of this offer and approval made (or not) within 10 days after that. If not approved for any reason this contract shall be null and void.

4. This offer shall be null and void unless accepted, in writing, on or before March 1 , 19 .

5. CLOSING DATE: This Contract shall be closed and the deed and possession shall be delivered on or before the 1st day of June , 19 , unless extended by other provisions of this Contract or separate agreement.

WITNESS: Executed by Buyer on 19 Time:
X   /S/ Jack Cummings   (SEAL)
X   (SEAL)
                                              Buyer

ACCEPTANCE OF CONTRACT & PROFESSIONAL SERVICE FEE: The Seller hereby approves and accepts the offer contained herein and recognizes Cummings Realty Inc. as Broker(s) in this transaction, and agrees to pay, as a fee 7 % of the purchase price, of the sum of Seven thousand Dollars ($7,000) or one half of the deposit in case same is forfeited by the Buyer through failure to perform, as a compensation for service rendered, provided the same does not exceed the full amount of the agreed fee.

WITNESS: Executed by Seller on 19 Time:
                                                                      (SEAL)
                                                                      (SEAL)

Deposit received on 19 to be held subject to this Contract; if check, subject to clearance.
By: Cummings Realty Inc. By:
        Broker or Attorney

BE ADVISED: When this agreement has been completely executed, it becomes a legally binding instrument. The form of this "Deposit Receipt and Contract for Sale and Purchase" has been approved by the Broward County Bar Association and the Ford Lauderdale Area Board of Realtors, Inc.

Standards for Real Estate Transactions

A. EVIDENCE OF TITLE: The Seller shall, within days (17 banking days if this blank is not filled in), order for Buyer a complete abstract of title prepared by a reputable abstract firm purporting to be an accurate synopsis of the instruments affecting the title to the real property recorded in the Public Records of that county to the date of this Contract, showing in the Seller a marketable title in accordance with title standards adopted from time to time by the Florida Bar subject only to liens, encumbrances, exceptions or qualifications set forth in this contract and those which shall be discharged by Seller at or before closing. The abstract shall be delivered at least 15 days prior to closing. Buyer shall have fifteen (15) days from the date of receiving said abstract of title to examine same. If title is found to be defective, Buyer shall, within said period, notify the Seller in writing, specifying the defects. If the said defects render the title unmarketable, the Seller shall have ninety (90) days from receipt of such notice to cure the defects, and if after said period Seller shall not have cured the defects, Buyer shall have the option of (1) accepting title as it then is, or (2) demanding a refund of all monies paid hereunder which shall forthwith be returned to the Buyer, and thereupon the Buyer and Seller shall be released of all further obligations to each other under this Contract.

B. CONVEYANCE: Seller shall convey title to the subject property to Buyer by Statutory Warranty Deed subject to: (1) zoning and/or restrictions and prohibitions imposed by governmental authority; (2) restrictions, easements and other matters appearing on the plat and/

or common to the subdivision; (3) taxes for the year of closing; (4) other matter specified in this Contract, if any.

C. EXISTING MORTGAGES: The Seller shall obtain and furnish a statement from the mortgagee setting forth the principal balance, method of payment, interest rate, and whether the mortgage is in good standing. If there is a charge for the change of ownership records by the mortgagee, it shall be borne equally by the parties to the transaction. In the event mortgagee does not permit the Buyer to assume the existing mortgage without a change in the interest rate, terms of payment or other material change, the Buyer at his option may cancel the Contract and all monies paid on the purchase price shall be refunded to him and the parties shall be released from all further obligations. Any variance in the amount of a mortgage to be assumed from the amount stated in the Contract shall be added to or deducted from the cash payment or the purchase money mortgage, as the Buyer may elect. In the event such mortgage balance is more than three percent (3%) less than the amount indicated in the Contract, the Seller shall be deemed to be in default under the Contract. Buyer shall execute all documents required by mortgagee for the assumption of said mortgage.

D. NEW MORTGAGES: Any purchase money note and mortgage shall follow the forms generally accepted and used in the county where the land is located. A purchase money mortgage shall provide for insurance against loss by fire with extended coverage in an amount not less than the full insurable value of the improvements. In a first mortgage, the note and mortgage shall provide for acceleration, at the option of the holder, after thirty (30) days default and in a junior mortgage after ten (10) days default. Junior mortgages shall require the owner of the property encumbered by said mortgage to keep all prior liens and encumbrances in good standing and forbid the owner of the property from accepting modifications, or future advances, under a prior mortgage. Buyer shall have the right to prepay all or any part of the principal at any time or times with interest to date of payment without penalty and said payments shall apply against the principal amounts next maturing. In the event Buyer executes a mortgage to one other than the Seller, all costs and charges incidental thereto shall be paid by the Buyer. If this Contract provides for Buyer to obtain a new mortgage, then Buyer's performance under this Contract shall be contingent upon Buyer's obtaining said mortgage financing upon the terms stated, or if none are stated, then upon the terms generally prevailing at such time in the county where the property is located. Buyer agrees diligently to pursue said mortgage financing, but if a commitment for said financing is not obtained within _____ days (15 banking days if this blank is not filled in) from the date of this Contract, and the Buyer does not waive this contingency, then either Buyer or Seller may terminate this Contract, in which event all deposits made by Buyer pursuant hereto shall be returned to him and all parties relieved of all obligations hereunder.

E. SURVEY: The Buyer, within the time allowed for delivery of evidence of title and examination thereof, may have said property surveyed at his expense. If the survey shows any encroachment on said property or that the improvements located on the subject property in fact encroach on the lands of others, or violate any of the covenants herein, the same shall be treated as a title defect.

F. INSPECTIONS: 1. THE Buyer shall have the right to make the following inspections at Buyer's expense, subject to the provisions of paragraph 4 below:

a) Termite: The Buyer shall have the right to have the property inspected by a licensed exterminating company to determine whether there is any active termite or wood-destroying organism present in any improvements on said property, or any damage from prior termite or wood-destroying organism to said improvements. If there is any such infestation or damage, the Seller shall pay all costs of treatment and repairing and/or replacing all portions of said improvements which are infested or have been damaged.

b) General: The Buyer shall have the right to have a roof, seawall, pool, electric and plumbing inspection made by persons or companies qualified and licensed to perform such services. If such inspection reveals functional defects (as differentiated from aesthetic defects), Seller shall pay all costs of repairing said defects.

c) Personal Property: The Seller represents and warrants that all appliances and machinery included in the sale shall be in working order as of the date of closing. Buyer may, at his sole expense and on reasonable notice, inspect or cause an inspection to be made of the appliances and equipment involved prior to closing. Any necessary repairs shall be made at the cost of the Seller and, unless otherwise agreed by the parties, the Buyer shall by closing be deemed to have accepted the property as is.

2. Escrow for Repairs: If treatment, replacement or repair called for in subparagraphs a, b, and c hereof are not completed prior to closing, sufficient funds shall be escrowed at time of closing to effect same.

3. Reinspection: In the event the Seller disagrees with Buyer's inspection reports, Seller shall have the right to have inspections made at his cost. In the event Buyer's and Seller's inspection reports do not agree, the parties shall agree on a third inspector, whose report shall be binding upon the parties. The cost of the third inspector shall be borne equally between the Buyer and Seller.

4. Limitation and Option Clause: Seller shall be responsible for all costs of the above treatment, replacement or repairs up to ___4___% (or 3% if this blank is not filled in) of the purchase price. In the event the total costs of items to be accomplished under subparagraphs a, b, and c exceed this amount, then either party shall have the option of paying any amount in excess and this Contract shall then remain in full force and effect. However, if neither party agrees to pay the additional amount above the applicable percentage of the purchase price, then, at the Seller's or Buyer's option, this Contract may be cancelled by delivery of written notice to the other party or his agent, and the deposit shall be returned to the Buyer.

5. Time for Inspections: All inspections described in Paragraphs 1 (a) and (b) above shall be completed on or before five days prior to closing.

G. INSURANCE: The premium on any hazard insurance policy in force covering improvements on the subject property, shall be prorated between the parties, or the policy may be cancelled as the Buyer may elect. If insurance is to be prorated, the Seller shall, on or before the closing date, furnish to the Buyer all insurance policies or copies thereof.

H. LEASES: The Seller shall, prior to closing, furnish to Buyer copies of all written leases and estoppel letters from each tenant specifying the nature and duration of said tenant's occupancy, rental rate, advance rents or security deposits paid by tenant. In the event Seller is unable to obtain said estoppel letters from tenants, the same information may be furnished by Seller to Buyer in the form of a Seller's Affidavit.

I. MECHANICS LIENS: Seller shall furnish to the Buyer at time of closing an Affidavit attesting to the absence of any claims or liens or potential lienors known to the Seller and further attesting that there have been no improvements to the subject property for 90 days immediately preceding the date of closing. If the property has been improved within said time, the Seller shall deliver releases or waiver of all mechanics liens, executed by general contractors, subcontractors, suppliers or materialmen and in addition a Seller's mechanics lien Affidavit setting forth the names of all such general contractors, sub-contractors, suppliers and materialmen and further reciting that in fact all bills for work to the subject property which could serve as the basis for a mechanic's lien have been paid.

J. PLACE OF CLOSING: Closing shall be held at the office of the Buyer's attorney or closing agent, if located within Broward County; if not, then at the office of Seller's attorney, if located within Broward County.

K. DOCUMENTS FOR CLOSING: Seller's attorney shall prepare deed, mortgage, mortgage note, bill of sale, affidavit regarding liens, and any corrective instruments that may be required in connection with perfecting the title. Buyer's attorney or closing agent will prepare closing statement.

L. EXPENSES: Abstracting prior to closing, State documentary stamps which are required to be affixed to the instrument of conveyance, the cost of recording any corrective instruments, intangible personal property taxes and the cost of recording the purchase money mortgage, if any, shall be paid by the Seller. Documentary stamps to be affixed to the note or notes secured by the purchase money mortgage, if any, or required on any mortgage modification and the cost of recording the deed shall be paid by the Buyer.

M.   PRORATION OF TAXES (REAL AND PERSONAL): Taxes shall be prorated based on the current year's tax, if known. If the closing occurs at a date when the current year's taxes are not fixed, and the current year's assessment is available, taxes will be prorated based upon such assessment and the prior year's millage. If the current year's assessment is not available, then taxes will be prorated on the prior year's tax; provided, however, if there are completed improvements on the subject premises by January 1st of the year of closing, which improvements were not in existence on January 1st of the prior year, then the taxes shall be prorated to the date of closing based upon the prior year's millage and at an equitable assessment to be agreed upon between the parties, failing which, requests will be made to the county tax assessor for an informal assessment taking into consideration homestead exemption, if any. However, any tax proration based on an estimate may, at the request of either party to the transaction, be subsequently readjusted upon receipt of tax bill and a statement to that effect is to be set forth in the closing statement. All such prorations whether based on actual tax or estimated tax will make appropriate allowance for the maximum allowable discount and for homestead or other exemptions if allowed for the current year.

N.   PRORATIONS AND ESCROW BALANCE: Taxes, hazard insurance, interest, utilities, rents, and other expenses and revenue of said property shall be prorated as of date of closing. Seller shall receive as credit at closing an amount equal to the escrow funds held by the mortgagee, which funds shall thereupon be transferred to the Buyer.

O.   SPECIAL ASSESSMENT LIENS: Certified, confirmed and ratified special assessment liens as of the date of closing (and not as of the date of this Contract) are to be paid by the Seller. Pending liens as of the date of closing shall be assumed by the Buyer.

P.   RISK OF LOSS: If the improvements are damaged by fire or other casualty before delivery of the deed and can be restored to substantially the same condition as now existing within a period of sixty (60) days thereafter, Seller may restore the improvements and the closing date and date of delivery of possession hereinunder provided shall be extended accordingly. If Seller fails to do so, the Buyer shall have the option of (1) taking the property as is together with insurance proceeds, if any, or (2) cancelling the Contract and all deposits will be forthwith returned to the Buyer and the parties released of any further liability hereunder.

Q.   MAINTENANCE: Between the date of the Contract and the date of closing, the property, including lawn, shrubbery and pool, if any, shall be maintained by the Seller in the condition as it existed as of the date of the Contract, ordinary wear and tear excepted.

R.   ESCROW OF PROCEEDS OF SALE AND CLOSING PROCEDURE: The deed shall be recorded and evidence of the title continued at Buyer's expense, to show title in Buyer, without any encumbrances or changes which would render Seller's title unmarketable, from the date of the last evidence and the cash proceeds of sale shall be held in escrow by Seller's attorney or by such other escrow agent as may be mutually agreed upon for a period of not longer than ten (10) days. If Seller's title is rendered unmarketable, Buyer's attorney shall, within said ten (10) day period, notify Seller or Seller's attorney in writing of the defect, and Seller shall have thirty (30) days from date of receipt of such notice to cure such defect. In the event Seller fails to timely cure said defect, all monies paid hereunder by Buyer shall, upon written demand therefor, and within five (5) days thereafter, be returned to Buyer and, simultaneously with such repayment, Buyer shall vacate the premises and reconvey the property in question to the Seller by Special Warranty Deed. In the event Buyer fails to make timely demand for refund, he shall take title as is, waiving all rights against Seller as to such intervening defect except such rights as may be available to Buyer by virtue of warranties contained in deed. In the event the transaction is not consummated because of an uncorrected or unwaived defect in title, the Seller will be deemed to have defaulted under this Contract. Possession and occupancy will be delivered to Buyer at time of closing.

If Seller provided Escrow Disbursement insurance or if Buyer executes a Disclosure and Consent Statement, then disbursement of closing proceeds shall be made to Seller immediately upon closing. The broker's professional service fee shall be disbursed simultaneously with disbursement of Seller's closing proceeds. Payment shall be made in the form of U.S. currency, cashier's check, certified check, unless in the event a portion of the purchase price is to be derived from institutional financing or refinancing, the requirements of the lending institution as to place, time, and procedures for closing and for disbursement of mortgage proceeds shall control, anything in this Contract to the contrary notwithstanding.

S. ESCROW: The party receiving the deposit agrees by the acceptance thereof to hold same in escrow and to disburse it in accordance with the terms and conditions of this Contract. Provided, however, that in the event that a dispute shall arise between any of the parties to this Contract as to the proper disbursement of the deposit, the party holding the deposit may at his option: (1) take no action and hold all funds (and documents, if any) until agreement is reached between the disputing parties, or until a judgment has been entered by a court of competent jurisdiction and the appeal period has expired thereon, or if appealed then until the matter has been finally concluded, and then to act in accordance with such final judgment; or (2) institute an action for declaratory judgment, interpleader or otherwise joining all affected parties and thereafter complying with the ultimate judgment of the court with regard to the disbursement of the deposit and disposition of documents, if any. In the event of any suit between Buyer and Seller wherein the escrow agent is made a party by virtue of acting as such escrow agent hereunder, or in the event of any suit wherein escrow agent interpleads the subject matter of this escrow, the escrow agent shall be entitled to recover a reasonable attorney's fee and costs incurred, including costs and attorney's fees for appellate proceedings, if any, said fees and costs to be charged and assessed as court costs in favor of the prevailing party.

T. ATTORNEY FEES AND COSTS: In connection with any litigation arising out of this Contract, the prevailing party whether Buyer, Seller or Broker, shall be entitled to recover all costs incurred including reasonable attorney's fees for services rendered in connection with such litigation, including appellate proceedings and postjudgment proceedings.

U. DEFAULT: In the event of default of either party, the rights of the non-defaulting party and the Broker shall be as provided herein and such rights shall be deemed to be the sole and exclusive rights in such event; (a) If Buyer fails to perform any of the covenants of this Contract, all money paid or deposited pursuant to this Contract by the Buyer shall be retained by or for the account of the Seller as consideration for the execution of this Contract as agreed and liquidated damages and in full settlement of any claims for damages by the Seller against the Buyer. (b) If Seller fails to perform any of the convenants of this Contract, all money paid or deposited pursuant to this Contract by the Buyer shall be returned to the Buyer upon demand, or the Buyer shall have the right of specific performance. In addition, Seller shall pay forthwith to Broker the full professional service fee provided for on the reverse side of this Contract.

V. PERSONS BOUND: The benefits and obligations of the covenants herein shall inure to and bind the respective heirs, personal representatives, successors, and assigns (where assignment is permitted) of the parties hereto. Whenever used, the singular number shall include the plural, the plural the singular, and the use of any gender shall include all genders.

W. SURVIVAL OF COVENANTS AND SPECIAL COVENANTS: Seller covenants and warrants that there is ingress and egress to subject property over public or private roads or easements, which covenants shall survive delivery of deed. No other provision, covenant, or warranty of this Contract shall survive the delivery of the deed except as expressly provided herein.

X. FINAL AGREEMENT: This Contract represents the final agreement of the parties and no agreements or representations, unless incorporated into this Contract, shall be binding on any of the parties. Typewritten provisions shall supersede printed provisions and handwritten provisions shall supersede typewritten and/or printed provisions. Such handwritten or typewritten provisions as are appropriate may be inserted on the face of this form or attached hereto as an addendum. The date of this Contract shall be the day upon which it becomes fully executed by all parties.

The form of this "Deposit Receipt and Contract for Sale and Purchase"
has been approved by the Broward County Bar Association and
the Fort Lauderdale Area Board of REALTORS®, Inc.

Notice:
   Jack Cummings is a Registered Real Estate Broker and is dealing as a principal, and any profit or loss from a subsequent disposition of the Real Estate in this agreement is of no consequence to the Seller herein. This does not waive the rights of Cummings Realty Inc. to collect a commission herein.

This agreement is shown simply as a sample of what is used in my part of the country. Not all brokers here use this agreement, some opting for simpler agreements. Personally, I find the Fort Lauderdale standard form to be adequate for almost all improved-property deals, although I prefer to see sellers use a form which has the real estate being sold in an "as is" condition rather than have repair conditions for damage and the like. However, to a buyer the provision of repairs is attractive.

If you are the seller in the transaction you must take a very special look at any contract that has a condition that you repair items not working or any damage. I've seen many arguments over this lead to the filing of legal actions. The buyer wants anything and everything that might be determined to be in need of repair fixed by the seller, while the seller will have a different point of view. Inspections are important, but often there is a narrow line on many items. Sure the roof isn't new, but just because it is old doesn't mean it needs to be replaced, or even repaired, for that matter.

My suggestion to sellers is to either remove the repair-or-replacement part of the agreement, or count on having to spend up to the total maximum percentage of the price for that repair or replacement and take that into consideration on the counteroffer.

Buyers should realize, too, that sellers will look at the offer this way and should anticipate the removal of these provisions; see the sample agreement provisions F(1–5). A good way to counteract this is to play the removal.

When you make an offer to buy a property you should anticipate the seller making a counter to you. It is rare that sellers accept the first offer. This will, of course, depend a great deal on the market and your salesman, but in the majority of instances anticipate a counter.

To focus the attention of the seller on one item that you are flexible on (but he doesn't know that), then, will be wise. You do this by anticipating what factors of the deal are crucial to him or difficult in his situation. The inspections might be one area which you might be willing to bend on. If the total maximum exposure the seller would have in the deal due to the percent of price applicable to repairs was $5,000, then you might reduce your offer by that amount and be ready to drop that entire section as long as you had the right to make the inspections and approve of them. In that way you could firm up a deal and if you found the suspected problem was nonexistent then you won. If the needed repairs were extensive, then you could opt to negate the deal and renegotiate for better terms—or walk away from the deal.

You win by letting the other side win too. A smart buyer will put in some term or other that can be taken out of the offer as a face-saver for the seller. One good way to accomplish this is in the terms. The buyer offers a deal which calls for the seller to hold a second mortgage at 10% for eighteen years. The salesman presents the offer that way and the seller balks at the terms. A counter which the salesman feels would be acceptable is returned to you. The price is the same, the interest rate the same, only now the second mortgage has a ten-year balloon. You win because you anticipate paying off the mortgage within that time anyway, through a refinance of the total mortgage structure.

Sometimes it can be simple things like asking the seller to include some furniture, or to close within three months, when you didn't want the furniture or were ready to close much sooner.

As a seller you don't want to play around with the offers and counter-offers that much. That is the advantage of being a buyer. However, because you might be the seller, keep in mind that the way in which you offer the property for sale is in essence your first offer. It is here that you can provide your "room to play," and can anticipate the first offer to be less than your offer for sale.

You will keep your negotiations as a seller to a minimum by offering good terms that have some flexibility for that buyer who wants to dicker with you to win a point.

The Lawyer-Drafted Agreement

Important deals might require this agreement, but there's a good argument against its use. I've successfully sold to happy sellers and buyers properties in the millions-of-dollars price range with the simplest of standard forms. On the other hand, I've had twenty-page lawyer-drafted documents on some of the simplest deals that caused nothing but problems. Why?

If you are a seller and along comes a buyer with a high-priced lawyer and he presents you with twenty pages of legal language, what are you going to do? Go to your lawyer, if you see any merit—or throw the thing into the wastebasket.

Let's assume you go to your lawyer. What happens now?

Your lawyer has to spend time reading each and every word, looking for deviations from the standard form he's familiar with. Also, to show that he's looking out for your interests, he will want to change a word or two, or a page or two, or rewrite the agreement.

Now you have a situation that can get out of hand. The two lawyers start to tear apart each other's agreement, and time seems to go on and on, with the heat of the moment cooling down and the deal lost.

Salespeople know and understand well the emotions of the buy-and-sell situation. As a buyer or seller I want my salesperson to have everything going for the deal. I know enough about what I want to look out for my interest as long as the legal aspect is taken care of. So in those events when I feel I need a lawyer's advice, or a client of mine wants to have her lawyer draft an agreement, I suggest the use of the standard form with changes or additions to protect where needed.

Most lawyers will go along with that when the contract can accommodate the deal. This will be the majority of the transactions, if the lawyer will acquiesce in allowing the standard form to be used. Some lawyers, however, wouldn't use a standard form under any circumstances.

My advice from the realtor's point of view and as a buyer and seller of real estate is to keep it as simple as you can. If you have the best lawyer in town and you are comfortable with his advice, then you should listen to his advice and act based on that. It is rare, however, to find a lawyer ready and willing to come out in the middle of the night to draft an agreement and then stand by to work on the counter, as your salesperson is doing, to nail down the deal.

Every buyer or seller should have the opportunity to seek out legal counsel if the deal warrants it or he feels it is needed. The buyer has more time to do that before the negotiations get to the point of the offer; the seller should know where he is going once the property is offered on the market, before the first offer rolls in.

Make the deal subject to your lawyer's approval. This is a salesperson's touch to nail down the deal even though there is an out. It is important to keep the emotions hot. You are the buyer and you make an offer the seller might be inclined to go along with. "I'll go along," he tells the salesperson. "But while the price and terms seem okay, I don't know how this part in the offer about my holding a wraparound mortgage will affect me. I want my attorney to review this before I sign."

The salesperson, knowing that you, the buyer, might have a change of heart the next day or the seller might have a different point of view after taking the unaccepted offer to his lawyer (as well he might), will opt to get an acceptance subject to the approval of the lawyer the following day.

Two things take place in this kind of situation that are important. First, the seller relaxes in the deal. He does want to sell, and so far everything seems okay. He only wants the lawyer to check it over to see if it is a proper and correct deal. So he accepts the deal subject to the lawyer's review of the contract and approval thereof. The second and most important aspect is the mental release of the property. Sellers frequently hold on to property in their minds, not wanting to let go. If a salesman can get this mental release to take place, then the problems seem to melt away.

As both of these events benefit the buyer and now there is a contract that has been approved by both the buyer and the seller, all that must occur is the approval by the lawyer. Of course, the lawyer can still nix the deal, and sometimes that is exactly what happens. However, it won't occur often, and when it does usually it is for good reasons.

Keep in mind as a buyer or seller that there are times when you will need a lawyer-drafted contract. It is always a good idea for you to have a lawyer you can relate to who understands your goals, to use as a sounding board and adviser for any transaction. Do keep in mind the psychology of the deal and try to keep it simple. Smart lawyers know this and will often use the simplest form possible to get across the most complicated transaction.

CONTRACTS IN GENERAL

Throughout this book, I've mentioned several items about contracts that I want to repeat as a general caution.

1. Watch out for verbal offers. Talk is cheap and memories as convenient as the other party wants them to be.
2. Beware of returned drafts of offers that have been fully retyped except for a slight change that zings you hard—a neat technique whereby your offer appears to be accepted, but what has happened is the offer was changed.
3. Shy away from the standard form that isn't standard at all. Some brokers, lawyers, and investors have developed their own contracts. They look exactly like the standard form I've included in this book except they won't have the name of the authority (Board of Realtors, etc.). Also, they might have some standard-looking phrases that are very one-sided and don't work to your benefit. A protection to you is to deal with a broker or salesperson who will give you a copy of his or her standard form, which you can have your lawyer check over in advance of a deal. If the form is approved, you don't have to worry about the little things and can concentrate on the importance of the sale.
4. Never be insulted by an offer or a counteroffer. Too many deals are lost by sellers who are insulted at a low offer. As a salesman, I tell my sellers that buyers often want to test the market. Making low offers isn't an insult, it is simply a buyer, interested in the property, looking to be educated. Don't feel that as a seller you have to counter on an offer that is very low. The best counter to a very low offer is often no counter at all other than a "Thank you, Mr. Buyer, but you had best check around. You'll find the price we are offering *is a good* price as it is."

Chapter 23

HOW TO DEAL WITH FORECLOSURE

Like "bankruptcy," the word "foreclosure" has a ring of failure about it. In financing, foreclosure is the one thing that investors and borrowers alike seem to fear. The fact of that matter is, however, that foreclosure is not the evil monster that most borrowers believe it to be. Lenders, on the other hand, have good reason to be fearful of its consequences.

WHAT IS FORECLOSURE?

In essence, the act of foreclosure is the legal process which is begun by a mortgage or lien creditor to gain title to property owned by the mortgagor. The foreclosure of the interest of the mortgagor is to defeat that interest or redemption of equity so that the mortgagee may have title to the property without any obligations to or interference from the mortgagor. The reasoning behind the law is usually to protect both the mortgagee and the mortgagor.

We all remember the stories of the banker calling on the widow who was two days behind in the monthly mortgage payment. The sinister banker would twirl his waxed mustache and then boot the widow out onto the dusty front steps. To many, this is foreclosure at its finest hour. Yet, this is not foreclosure at all. How about the widow? She pledged the equity in her ranch on a moderate percentage loan to value, and now just because she is behind in the payment is she to lose everything? I think not, and the courts would agree. Today, even with all the inequities and problems in the foreclosure laws, they are still much more protective of the mortgagor's rights than is generally believed.

In essence, no mortgagor, by right of most foreclosure laws, can be deprived of interest or equity redemption which may exceed the amount of the debt (plus cost and interest outstanding of course) without due process of law. The laws, while different for many states, generally agree that the right of this possible redeemable equity should be retained by the mortgagor. The purpose of this chapter is to take a close look at foreclosure—to see if it is such a terrible animal, and if so, whom does it bite the hardest. An in-depth look at how to avoid foreclosure will be examined, and some sure-fire steps for moving from possible foreclosure to positive cash flow for income properties will be provided.

BEFORE FORECLOSURE THERE MUST BE A DEFAULT IN THE MORTGAGE

The language used in mortgages to describe default and to pinpoint when default occurs will vary. Some mortgages will provide a grace period for payments. This allows the mortgage to enter a period during which the payment is due but actual default has not occurred. These grace periods can be long or short, or there may be none at all for that matter. Even without a grace period, a mortgagee will generally allow a reasonable time for default since notice and legal action to precede foreclosure would take time, and if the mortgage were brought current prior to a foreclosure being filed, the matter could be mute.

Everyone who seeks to borrow money should understand that the lender expects the funds to be repaid. The absence of personal liability on the note or mortgage does not lessen the lender's desire to be repaid, even though it may reduce the obligation for repayment from a legal point of view. In a loan where security is pledged and the borrower gives a mortgage to the lender to evidence the security, the lender will look to the mortgagee's loss of the security as the primary basis for the loan to be repaid. If the loan is not repaid, the security may or may not compensate the lender for the problems he must go through to collect his due. The lenders rights, or ability to collect beyond the security, are seriously hampered, even when there are personal signatures guaranteeing the note.

Lenders often find it difficult to collect beyond the security, as there are numerous ways a borrower can isolate himself from this further action. Courts sometimes do not look favorably on deficiency judgments against borrowers on primary loans, and almost never on purchase money financing held by sellers. There are both pro and con arguments to the controversy, but I prefer to simply state the status quo rather than enter into the battle for or against deficiency judgments.

Therefore, when there has been a breach in the contract between the lender and the mortgagor, the mortgagee has the right to seek foreclosure as a means of collecting his funds. Or, he can sue in a court of law on the debt (the note), attempt to attain a judgment against the mortgagor, and then execute the judgment on property owned by the mortgagor.

Foreclosure then is a process that must be preceded by a default. It is not the only process of remedy the mortgagee can seek to collect on the unpaid mortgage. Because default must come first, the simplest way to avoid a foreclosure is to never go into default. This may sound obvious, but isn't. It is possible to obtain many concessions from the mortgagee for allowing the mortgage to slip into actual default under the terms of the contract (note and mortgage) without default being claimed. These concessions will be discussed in detail later on in this chapter, but you should know that most mortgagees will do almost anything to stop a property from going into foreclosure. Highly institutionalized lenders will generally work with the average borrower. Private lenders, on the other hand, have a tendency of acting quicker to foreclose, as they either want to take over the property or to protect the possible advance of loss should the payments continue to go unpaid.

Once a default occurs, and the lender does not agree to an extension of the grace period, the mortgagee is in a position to call on his rights to foreclose. Prior to the actual foreclosure, however, there is generally a period of foreclosure assertions. That is, the mortgagee threatens to foreclose unless the mortgage payment is made. This pre-foreclosure period is a maze of typical first, second, and final notices, then letters from the lawyer, and so on—all steps lenders take to avoid having to file foreclosure. Finally, there's the nice phone call from the executive vice-president in charge of collections at the bank to ask if you are having problems.

It is during this time that deals can often be made that would curl your hair. But never count on that last ditch transaction to save the whole ball of wax. Foreclosure proceedings have a tendency of being drawn-out affairs that can be most unpleasant. Dealing with the respective parties during this period of actual foreclosure is often far more difficult than when the property was only on the verge of going into foreclosure. The pre-foreclosure period is when the mortgagee hopes or believes that the mortgagor will still make the payments. But when the mortgagor does not make the payments, the mortgagee realizes he must now make good the threats to foreclose.

FORECLOSURE AS SEEN BY THE LENDER

The attitudes taken by lenders, of course, will vary. The majority of all foreclosures are made by institutional lenders, so let's look at foreclosure from their point of view. Once the mortgagor knows how the lender looks at this final stage is of the lending cycle, he will have some understanding of what to expect. Most institutional lenders (as well as many noninstitutional lenders) divide the foreclosure action into four periods:

1. The collection period
2. The pre-foreclosure period
3. The foreclosure
4. The post-foreclosure period

Depending on the size of the lender and the staff available, a standard operating procedure is designed to take care of these four periods. (An outline of this procedure follows.) Note that the institutionalized approach to this very critical event is impersonal. The people involved have very little actual knowledge of the person who borrowed the money or the property pledged as security.

The Collection Period

A. Check calendar to see if payment arrived on time; if not, make note to follow-up within three days.
B. If follow-up indicates payment still overdue, then send out courtesy reminder that payment is due (*first notice*).
C. Continued late payments will be followed five to seven days after the first notice with another notice, indicating the date which terminated the grace period (*second notice*).
D. Follow-up calls to insure the borrower is aware the grace period has terminated. (*third notice*).
E. If the payment is 30 days past due, an inspection is generally ordered to determine if the property has been vacated or if there are other problems.
F. If the property appears not to have been vacated, a registered letter is sent from the legal department advising the borrower that his loan is in jeopardy of being foreclosed (*fourth notice*).
G. No response to the registered letter within seven days will cause the matter to be placed in the pre-foreclosure period.

The Pre-Foreclosure Period:

A. A notice is sent to the collection department to the effect that no payments on this loan will be processed without approval, since the loan has gone into default.

B. A second letter may be sent to the borrower asking for a conference to discuss the status of the loan and to see if anything can be done to avoid foreclosure (*fifth notice*).

C. The lender now prepares for the possible foreclosure:
  1. Note and mortgage are reviewed and sent to legal department.
  2. Records are examined; insurance and other matters pertaining to the maintenance of the file and the property are checked.
  3. A field report is made showing the status of the property (occupied, maintenance of property, etc.).

D. A review of the situation is made by the proper authority and a decision is reached on the basis of the alternatives given or proposed by the borrower. If none are offered or they are not plausible, then *foreclosure is filed.*

The Foreclosure Period

A. An appraisal of the property is made.

B. Accounting and collection departments prepare the status of the loan—total unpaid balance and other costs, indicating the bottom line needed by the association for their bid at auction, and the top line to cover their total cost bid by others.

C. The file and report are reviewed by the foreclosure panel and the top bid the association plans to make is decided; authorization is given to the officer or trustee of the association to make the bid as stated.

D. The sale takes place; the property is purchased either by the association or by another party who makes a higher bid.

The Post-Foreclosure Period

A. If the property were purchased by someone other than the lender, then the funds received are processed and the loan closed.

B. If the lender purchased the property, then the appropriate departments process the property and files to account for the change in ownership.

C. The property is then turned over to the proper department for marketing.

The four periods described vary from lender to lender. A foreclosure of a second or junior loan would require a slightly different procedure. If the first or superior mortgages are not joined in the foreclosure and the foreclosure was made subject to those loans, then the junior lender would make sure the superior loans were kept current during the entire process. Once the junior lender has made a successful bid on the property, he would take the necessary steps to assume the existing superior loans or give notice that he is the new owner.

It has been stated earlier that the lender will generally do all he can to prevent the property from going into foreclosure. Of course, there is a limit to how far he will or can go. Nonetheless, if the borrower has shown good intentions in the past and has not been late in making payments, the lender will go a long way to keep the loan from foreclosure.

Why Lenders Will Avoid Foreclosure If at All Possible

In almost all states, the foreclosure process is often long and burdensome. The time element is the most costly of all, since much can happen to the value of the property while the foreclosure grinds to the eventual sale or redemption of equity. At best, it is not a simple event. At worst, years can pass before the final document is filed and title is granted to the winning bidder at the foreclosure sale. Many arguments have been made for changes in the law and a speeding up of the process. Also, the law often seems to protect the less scrupulous mortgagor more than the one who attempts to do his best to pay back the monies owed.

If the property is an income producer, the mortgagor can slip behind in his payments, wait out the pre-foreclosure period, and prolong that by attempting to work out a settlement or payment plan. Then, in the end he will let the lender foreclose, knowing that without any debt service during this period of time he can milk the property until the lender can either foreclose or have a receiver or trustee appointed to operate it until the foreclosure is complete and settled.

Seasonal properties are most vulnerable to this type of "milking," and lenders are most cautious about lending in these areas when the equity is either vague or slight. Even then, the loan can be in jeopardy in a hurry since a milked hotel can drop 20% in value over the season. Good-will can be destroyed and the property itself left in disrepair. Hotels and other volatile properties that depend on limited times of operation (e.g., amusement parks and recreational facilities) will generally have mortgages that have strong default provisions. These provisions, however, do not always provide sufficient security to prevent "milking."

The speed with which the mortgagee can remove the mortgagor's control of the property will vary. In some states this removal can be accomplished in a relatively short time, while in others the time required will be longer. It may be possible for a mortgagor to claim that the mortgage interest is usurious or other aspects of the loan are onerous, and hence request the loan to be set aside. Such actions may cause the entire matter to go to court. But in the meanwhile, the mortgagor may be left in control of the property. Because the matter of foreclosure is a legal one, lawyers can often find many ways to delay the process. Lenders know this, of course, and while they may ultimately win the case, it may be only a paper victory.

It is often thought that the only type of property immune to the effect of mortgagor control is vacant land. Today, however, vacant land can become a victim of the timekeeper as well. In many communities there are movements to change zoning. Usually, zoning changes have considerable effect on the value of property. Since most zoning changes affect vacant land, they can make the land gain as well as lose value. Most rezoning provisions allow for a time period of adjustment. They usually permit an owner to file for building permits under the old zoning by a cutoff date. However, it is obvious that if the land is in the midst of a foreclosure this would not be possible. And once the foreclosure sale occurs the value of the land may be less than the amount of the mortgage.

In most office buildings and other income properties, where the gross income is gained from rents collected from tenants in the building, the mortgagee will have assignments of the leases. These assignments will permit him to step in and collect the rents in the event of a default. The owner and mortgagor may still have physical control of the building, but he no longer has control over the income from the property. The mortgagee will generally deduct from those rents the payments due and turn over the balance to the mortgagor while the foreclosure is proceeding. Keep in mind that once the mortgage has gone into default and a foreclosure has been filed, the only redemption may be for the mortgagee to pay off the entire loan and not just to bring the payments up-to-date.

OPTIONS OPEN TO THE LENDER AND THE BORROWER
IN THE EVENT OF A DEFAULT ON A MORTGAGE

1. The lender agrees to wait for the payment or payments.
2. The borrower brings the mortgage current for interest but holds up on the principal portion of the payment.
3. A partial payment of interest is made.
4. A lump sum of interest and principal is made and the mortgage is adjusted to change the overall terms to provide relief for later payments.
5. The mortgagor turns over all income, less operational expenses gained on the property, for application against the debt service.
6. The lender agrees to refinance the loan to provide needed capital to bring the project back to its feet.
7. The lender advances funds on a secondary loan to cover the debt service.
8. The mortgagor adds additional security, the loan is extended into a blanket mortgage, and additional cash is added by the lender to cover the debt service.

9. The mortgagor can give up partial ownership in favor of the lender for a reduction of the debt.

10. A portion of the property can be deeded over to the lender as a partial or full satisfaction of the debt.

11. The mortgagee allows you time to try to sell your interest in the property to someone else.

12. Seek secondary financing from another lender.

13. A deed in lieu of foreclosure (often called voluntary deed) is granted by the mortgagor to the lender and the debt is satisfied.

14. Foreclosure.

The first twelve of these options can occur alone or in combinations. The willingness of the lender or the mortgagor to enter into any of these options will depend on the nature of the property and the history of the mortgagor. If the property is not worth the mortgagor's efforts to pull it out of default or he has a history of going into default in the past, then the matter may be mute and the lender may look to only the last two options.

The deed in lieu of foreclosure is a most attractive way out for the lender in many situations. The borrower may also look to this as a way of saving face in the community or meeting his moral obligations if all else fails, especially if the impending foreclosure suit does not appear to offer the opportunity for the mortgagor to gain in overage at the sale. After all, by the time the property is about to go into foreclosure, most mortgagors have tried almost everything to sell it so the market has been tested to some degree. Of course, if the mortgagor is behind in the payments by a wide margin, the cost to bring the property current, just in past due interest alone, may make the sale preforeclosure difficult. More on this aspect later.

A deed in lieu of foreclosure is a way the mortgagor can get out from under the mess of foreclosure and allow the mortgagee to enter the property without a long battle. If the property has several mortgages, all in default, and the first mortgage holder takes the property back by deed in lieu, then that mortgagee is assuming the obligations of the junior mortgagees. In foreclosure and a forced sale, the junior mortgagees would have to either protect their interest by bidding in above the first mortgagee or hope other buyers bid in sufficiently to cover their position. Often, this will not happen. Hence, the first mortgagee must decide if the junior mortgagee will in fact protect his interest by bidding in or attempting to obtain a deed in lieu himself, thereby assuming the existing mortgage or foreclosing subject to the superior mortgage and keeping that mortgage current. Frequently, the circumstances do not favor the first mortgagee allowing the property to foreclose if he can obtain a deed in lieu, even if that means he is assuming the junior mortgages.

If the property is seasonal in nature and the season is just around the corner, the mortgagee may pay the mortgagor to sell the deed in lieu of foreclosure. The fact that the mortgagor is behind in payments and owes the mortgagee money, does not mean that the mortgagor has any equity in the property. To avoid the cost and time of foreclosure and the loss of seasonal income, the payment to the defaulting mortgagor can expedite the end result and perhaps allow him to receive some cash out of the mess.

WHAT A MORTGAGOR SHOULD DO TO HOLD OFF FORECLOSURE

When all good planning and hope fails, and the cash just isn't there for the next mortgage payment, there are several things the mortgagor can do to hold off foreclosure.

Steps To Hold Off Foreclosure

The Preventive Measures

1. Develop a good pay-back record. This means more than just paying on time. Whenever possible, get in the habit of paying early. Mortgages, credit card payments, and the like all fall into this category. If you have never borrowed large sums of money before, you have no real credit rating with the banks on your pay-back ability. One client of mine has never had to borrow money, but he has made it a practice to borrow up to $50,000 at once from one of the commercial banks in the area. He does this on his own signature and asks for the money for six months, but he pays it back in less than a month. The total cost to him is not much since he manages to get interest on the amount borrowed from another bank. He says he doubts the bank would ever turn him down now if he really needed money. I don't recommend that you follow this lead, but a loan every once in a while will establish a good credit rating if you pay the money back promptly or early.

2. Don't attempt to overextend the loan to value ratio. Remember, the best way to keep from going into default is to be able to afford the debt service in the first place. Naturally, few investors would be able to carry all or at least a major portion of the debt service, so look to a prudent demand rate and safe mix of extension and leverage. When you buy, try to take into account the possibility of a reduced income, look at the break-even point, and be ready to risk some capital.

3. Know your abilities. This means staying away from investments you know nothing about unless you are sure you can rely on your advisors and/or partners. Most bad real estate investments are really good investments, but are made by underexperienced investors. Don't look

across the fence and think the grass is greener on the other side. Those investors who are experts in their field make their jobs look easy. In fact, however, some areas of real estate are very difficult and take years of training and experience to understand and master. In Florida, as I am sure elsewhere, bars, lounges, motels, and restaurants are the big thing. Investors often feel that anyone can run a bar, lounge, and so on. Wrong!

4. Get to know the lenders you are dealing with. It is a good idea to be on speaking terms with them. Keep an account at all banks or savings and loans where you borrow. Drop in every now and then and talk to the officers about anything except foreclosure. If you are on friendly terms with them when you are making your payments, that rapport will carry over to a pre-foreclosure period if it should ever come along.

What to do when default is on the way but has not yet occurred

1. If you know you won't be able to make the next payment on time, there are two things you can do. First, if the payments are over short periods, such as monthly or quarterly, it is a good idea to call the bank or savings and loan president and let him know you have a problem. This is just to inform him that you are concerned about your inability to pay on time. Second, if the payments are over long periods, such as semi-annually or annually, you may not want to give prior notice that you may be late: Lenders who wait for long time periods between mortgage payments have a tendency to become very nervous when informed that a payment for which they have waited a whole year may not be in on time. These lenders will think the worst right away and may start planning what they will do the very moment the payment is not in.

   The rapport between the mortgagor and the mortgagee is very important. The record of past performance is likewise crucial, since a poor record will cause the lender to be most unsympathetic to tales of economic problems. Keep in mind that lenders have heard every story that exists, so keep the sob stories to a minimum, even if they are true. Remember, honesty usually works best when all else fails.

2. If you think you will be delayed in making your next payment, send the lender a letter outlining very briefly your inability to make the payment on time. If there is a good reason for the delay, state it. If not, then merely say that you will be unable to make the payment on time but that you hope to have the money before the grace period is up.

3. Review your situation and look at all the possible alternatives you may be able to use to solve your problem. The fourteen options listed

previously are open to you. Look at each one and play with the figures to see if any are plausible.

What to do when default comes and you have no real prospect of pulling out without help:

1. By now, you may have tried to sell your interest but to no avail. This is the time for you to make the decision to hold onto the property or to attempt to make a settlement with the lender which will allow you to back out. Many mortgagors hang on too long, even when the property is not worth the effort or aggravation. The time to settle on a deed in lieu will depend on the property of course, but you should make that decision early in the default rather than wait until foreclosure is already filled, since it may be too late by then. On a very large property, however, your lawyer may advise you that if you do hang on you may be able to pull the loose ends together.

2. Assuming you decide to try to keep the property, this is a good time to sit down with the lender and work out a deal which will give you time or release you from the burden of the debt service, perhaps by some alteration of the mortgage. Sitting back and ignoring the lender's letters will not help your situation at all, and could show a lack of good faith on your part. If you are willing to cooperate, this probably will work to your advantage.

3. Have a plausible program which you feel will work. You may need help in putting this program together, so seek it. If you are representing a client in such a predicament, then you will do all you personally can to find a solution and will speak to those contacts you feel can help as well.

4. If there is a valuable equity in the property, and you have a reasonable solution which will solve the problem but the lender refuses to go along, you may want to look to bankruptcy as another alternative. A Chapter 11, for example, if acceptable in your situation, would hold off foreclosure and permit a settlement of the economic problems. This possibility should be considered at any rate, at least so you will know what the option is and how it will affect you. Don't feel that bankruptcy is something you should avoid, especially if it is your only chance to protect all the creditors. Remember, if the first mortgage forecloses and the market sale does not produce an overage above it, then those creditors may be wiped out. The bankruptcy, however, may allow a partial settlement as a minimum for those creditors.

APPENDIX

USE OF THE CONSTANT TABLES SHOWN
IN THE APPENDIX

The following two constant rate tables may be used for many different shortcuts in calculating different mortgage payments, discounts and the like. Once you have understood how the Constants work, you can, with any simple hand-held calculator, ascertain a great deal of financial data by using these tables.

The first step is to understand how to read the tables. There are two such tables. Table A is to be used for the usual mortgage calculation where the mortgage is monthly. Table B is for mortgages which have but one annual payment. In each table the mortgage must be *amortizing* of Principal and Interest, rather than a mortgage which may be interest only, or have set payments of Principal each month plus interest on the balance. In the amortizing mortgage the monthly payment will be the same throughout the life of the mortgage. Yet within that payment the amount allocated to principal and the amount charged as interest will change each month. This occurs because in the early years of the mortgage the amount of interest charged against the amount owed is much greater than in the later years, as the mortgage is continually reduced. For example, if the loan was $100,000 for a 25-year period at 12%, amortized then over a total of 300 payments, the monthly payment would be $1,053.25 per month. Of this payment the amount of interest for the first payment would be $1,000 and only the balance of $53.25 would be principal. On the other hand, the very last payment would also be a total of $1,053.25 but the allocation to interest would be only $10.43, and the amount of Principal reduction to the mortgage would be $1,042.82. Sometime during this 25-year term the amount charged against interest and the allocation to Principal were equal.

In a mortgage of 25 years at 12% as indicated above, where the amount borrowed is $100,000 the loan officer of the lending institution would ascertain the monthly payment you would have to pay by using a table such as Table A. By looking under the year column (25) and moving down the page to the interest rate of 12(%), you would find the number 12.639 which would be the *constant rate* for that mortgage at the day it was to begin. The interest is 12% as shown earlier, but the charge which would reflect both interest and principal payback would be this slightly higher amount of 12.639 percent. By multiplying the gross loan outstanding by the constant rate ($100,000 × 12.639%) we would end up with an annual amount of $12,639. To get the monthly payment simply divide that amount ($12,639) by 12 to end up with $1,053.25 per month.

It is critical that you remember that these constant tables are an annual percentage figure. To get the monthly payment you would use Table A only (as Table B is for single annual payments per year). Always divide the annual payment by 12 to end up with the correct monthly payment of principal and interest.

When doing a math problem with a percentage amount, remember to move the decimal point two places to the left (the same as dividing by 100). For example, in the multiplication of $100,000 by the constant for 12% interest at 25 years you found the constant rate to be 12.639%. In the actual multiplication you would have used $100,000 times .12639 to end with $12,639.

If you have a calculator that will multiply by percentages you would not have to move the decimal over to the left. If you aren't sure about your calculator then do this following problem:

1. Make sure your calculator is cleared.
2. Multiply $100,000 by .12639
3. Check the results: It should be 12,639 (or 12,639.00). If it is, then you don't have to worry.

To check out the table, follow along with this exercise. Find the Constant Rate for a mortgage that is 30 years long at 15 percent interest, with monthly payments.

1. Look for the 30-year column in Table A.
2. Go down the page for the 15 percent interest indication.
3. Make note of the Constant Rate: 15,173

With this information you could multiply the math number of .15173 times any loan amount (for that rate and duration) and divide the annual amount by 12 to get the monthly rate. E.g. $100,000 loan, times .15173 = $15,173 divided by 12 = $1,264.42 rounded up from a slightly larger number.

Find the interest rate for a mortgage of $80,000.00 over 22 years, with 12 payments per year with a payment of $805.80 per month. In this situation you will use the table to help you establish terms on a mortgage to suit a transaction you are working on. You might have discovered that there are existing mortgages on a property you want to buy that will be fully paid off in 22 years. You want the seller to hold a mortgage for the balance of the deal for that term. He wants $80,000 to make the deal. You only can afford a monthly payment of $805.80. What's the interest rate?

FINDING THE INTEREST RATE WHEN YOU KNOW YEARS AND AMOUNT OWED

1. Arrive at the annual payment by multiplying the monthly payment by 12. ($805.80 times 12 = $9,669.60)
2. Divide the annual payment by the Loan Amount Owed That Day. ($9,669.60 divided by $80,000 = .12087) Note: It is important here that you make sure your calculator will write at least three numbers to the right of the decimal point. If you round off at 12.01 then you will not have a very accurate number to work with. Either get a new calculator or divide by a smaller number, for example 800, and omit the next step.
3. Take the number you have ended up with (Step 2) and move the decimal over two places to the right. .12087 will become 12.087.
4. Go to Table A and find the 22-year column.
5. Go down that column until you find the constant rate of 12.087% or the closest possible rate. You will notice that 12.087 percent is a constant rate for 11 percent interest.

FIND THE MORTGAGE AMOUNT WHEN YOU KNOW THE TERM OF YEARS, THE INTEREST RATE, AND THE MONTHLY PAYMENT

This is a rather common problem that comes from different circumstances. You may be working with a seller who doesn't know the amount he owes on his mortgage. He can tell you the payment (make sure it is principal and interest only and that it does not include taxes and insurance, etc.), he knows how long it has to run, and even the interest rate. For example: It has 20 years to go, the monthly payment is $805, and the interest rate is 10.5%. Okay. Are you ready for this one?

1. Get annual payment again ($805 times 12 = $9,660.00).
2. Go to the 20-year column at 10.5 percent interest and see the constant rate which would be: 11.670 percent.
3. Divide the annual payment by the constant. ($9,660.00 divided by .11670 = $82,776.35, rounded up from a slightly larger number.)

FIND THE TERM OF YEARS FOR A MORTGAGE WHEN YOU KNOW THE AMOUNT TO BE OWED, THE INTEREST RATE AND THE MONTHLY PAYMENT

When you are negotiating on a deal you may find that the flexibility of a mortgage term might bring the payment into reach. In this situation you might be fixed at having to pay off a $90,000 mortgage at 12.5 percent interest, with only $970 per month available from the current income of the property to support the added debt service. You and the seller agree to set the mortgage so that the $970 will pay out the mortgage. But what is the term?

1. Get the annual payment again ($970 times 12 = $11,640)
2. Divide the annual payment by the amount of the loan owned that day ($11,640 divided by $90,000 = .12933).
3. Move the decimal place over to the right two places (.12933 then will become 12.933).
4. Go to Table A, and look at the interest rate charged in the mortgage. (In this case 12.5 percent.) Move along the line until you find the same or closest rate to match the number you found in line 3 above. (12.933 is the rate you will try to match. However you will not find that rate exactly.) Under the 27.5-year column you will find 12.923 constant at the 12.5 interest rate, and at the 27th year 12.951 constant. The answer you need would fall between these two time periods. As a buyer you might try to settle for a 27 year payout at $970 per month, or 27.5 years at the 12.923 constant rate. As a seller you'd opt for the $970 for 27.5 years, or the 12.951 percent constant for the 27 years.

USING CONSTANTS AS A SHORT CUT TO DEALING
WITH MORTGAGES AT A DISCOUNT

When you are dealing with mortgages at a discount, you will find that almost any problem which you can think of dealing with mortgage discounts can be ascertained using the constants.

Look at this question: When I sell my property, if I take back a second mortgage that is for $50,000 payable over 10 years in equal monthly payments calculated at an amortization of principal and interest, with interest at 10%, and I want to sell the mortgage, what price will I get?

Now this is a very good question. A $50,000 second mortgage, 10 years in monthly payments at 10%. Buyers of mortgages usually want a discount to increase the yield of the mortgage for that buyer. For example if the buyer of the above-mentioned mortgage wanted a 15 percent return rather than the 10 percent rate on the mortgage, he would have to buy the mortgage at a discount price that would accurately provide that yield.

To begin with, find the constant rate for the mortgage as it now stands. To do this, look in the ten years column of Table A, and go down to the 10 percent interest rate line. You will find a constant rate of 15.858 percent. This indicates an annual payment (the total of 12 monthly payments) of $50,000 times .15858 or $7,929. This relates to a monthly payment of $660.75.

Now find the constant rate the buyer of the mortgage (at a discount) requires. The same number of years is in effect, so go to the ten-year column, and go down to the 15 percent line. The constant rate for this yield is 19.360 percent.

The relationship between these constants is as follows: If you take the constant of the existing contract rate (10% interest, and a constant of 15.858 percent) and divide that by the constant for the desired rate (15% interest desired, and a constant rate of 19.360 percent) and move the decimal two places to the right, you will end up with the percent of discount needed to discount the mortgage to permit the desired yield.

$\underline{\text{Existing constant}}$ which $\underline{15.868}$ = .8197 converted
Desired constant   is   19.360
to a percent would then be: 81.97 percent

Multiply this percent of discount by the face amount of the mortgage at the day of the discount, and you will have the amount the buyer would pay under these circumstances to obtain a yield of 15% on a mortgage that has a contract rate of only 10 percent interest

Amount of the mortgage times discount percentage = Price
        $50,000   ×   .8197   = $40,985

This same mathematical sequence can be turned around to find any part of this type of problem as long as you have sufficient data to close the circle.

For example, Charles may own a mortgage with six years to go of $35,000 payable monthly at an interest rate of 11 percent interest per annum. He might just offer it to you at a price of $25,000. Would it be a good deal? You would want to know your yield (as well as much more about the security, the mortgagor, etc.).

Here's how you find the solution to the above problem.

1. Find the constant at the contract rate in Table A. Go to the six-year column at 11 percent interest. You will find a constant rate of 22.841 percent.

2. Find the *discount percentage*. To find this, divide the *price* of the mortgage ($25,000), by the face amount owed at the day of the discount ($35,000).

$$\frac{\text{Price of Mortgage}}{\text{Amount Owed}} \text{ or } \frac{\$25,000}{\$35,000} = .7143 \text{ or } 71.43 \text{ percent.}$$

3. Now take the constant rate found in step one (22.841 percent) and divide that by the discount percent (71.43 percent)

$$\frac{\text{Existing Constant Rate}}{\text{Discount Percentage}} \text{ or } \frac{22.841}{71.43} = .3198 \text{ or } 31.98 \text{ percent.}$$

4. This new percentage (31.98 percent) is the new constant rate for the discounted mortgage. If you then look down the sixth-year column until you find a rate equal to or close to this new rate, it will correspond to the yield on that mortgage. In this case, you will find 31.958 percent under the six years column at 24.5 percent interest. In essence at $25,000 the purchase of this $35,000 mortgage would yield you over 24.5 percent interest should the mortgage go to its full term.

Mortgages rarely go the full term, however, and whenever you have purchased a mortgage at a discount, and that mortgage pays off sooner than the contracted term, a bonus will be in store.

For example: If you paid $25,000 for that mortgage which has a face value of $35,000, and you held the mortgage for one year and the mortgagor then paid the mortgage off, you would get the following:

1. One year's payments of $7,994.35.

2. At the end of the year there is still an outstanding balance on the mortgage of $30,640.26. This is found by taking the constant rate for the mortgage for the remaining term (5 years) at 11 percent interest

(26.091 percent) and dividing that into the annual total payment ($7,994.35).

$$\frac{\$7,994.35}{.26091} = \$30,640.25 \text{ is the payoff amount at the end of year 1.}$$

This little step can be most useful in other financing problems as well.

3. Add the total payments gained, and the payoff.

$$\$7,994.35 + \$30,640.25 = \$38,634.60$$

4. Subtract the amount paid to buy the mortgage: $25,000.00

Return of other than principal: $13,634.60

5. Divide by the number of years you held this mortgage.

$$\frac{\$13,634.60}{1} = \$13,634.60 \text{ (this mortgage might have been held longer)}$$

This amount is your average return of interest per year.

6. Divide the *average return* ($13,634.60) by the *price you paid* for the mortgage to get the average yield actually earned.

$$\frac{\text{Average Return}}{\text{Price You Paid}} \text{ or } \frac{\$13,634.60}{\$25,000.00} = .5454 \text{ or } 54.54 \text{ percent.}$$

This indicates that you have actually averaged a 54.54 percent yield on this mortgage. Remember, the contract rate is still only 11 percent.

By playing around with the constants in these few problems I've provided for in this section of the book, you will find many new ways to use the constant formulas to solve your specific problems.

Note 1

Calculations will result in slight error if mortgages calculated are less than annual payments. However, the error will not be sufficient to warrant that the table not be used.

Note 2

A constant annual payment percentage is that percentage which when multiplied by the loan balance will give an amount representing the annual payment of principal including interest. The table given will allow the user to take the interest rate to be paid, locate the term of years, and determine the constant annual percentage. This percentage multiplied by the principal owed will give the total annual payment which, in the case of Table A, is made up of 12 monthly installments. It is important to remember that the constant interest rate changes each year whereas the amount paid does not. This is due to the fact that the principal owed and years remaining diminish each successive year of the loan.

TABLE A.

Constant Annual Percents Expressing the Sum of 12 Equal Monthly Payments Needed to Amortize a Principal Amount for the Term of Years Shown

% INTEREST	.5	1	1.5	2	2.5	3	3.5	4
8	204.694	104.387	70.969	54.273	44.266	37.604	32.853	29.296
8.25	204.836	104.523	71.104	54.409	44.403	37.742	32.992	29.436
8.5	204.991	104.666	71.244	54.548	44.542	37.882	33.133	29.578
8.75	205.139	104.805	71.381	54.685	44.680	38.021	33.273	29.720
9	205.287	104.944	71.518	54.823	44.819	38.160	33.414	29.863
9.25	205.433	105.083	71.656	54.960	44.957	38.300	33.555	30.005
9.5	205.578	105.220	71.793	55.098	45.095	38.440	33.696	30.148
9.75	205.729	105.361	71.931	55.236	45.235	38.580	33.838	30.292
10	205.879	105.502	72.070	55.375	45.375	38.722	33.981	30.436
10.25	206.021	105.639	72.207	55.512	45.513	38.862	34.123	30.579
10.5	206.171	105.779	72.345	55.652	45.653	39.003	34.266	30.724
10.75	206.318	105.918	72.484	55.790	45.793	39.145	34.409	30.869
11	206.464	106.057	72.622	55.929	45.933	39.286	34.552	31.015
11.25	206.615	106.199	72.762	56.069	46.075	39.429	34.697	31.161
11.5	206.766	106.340	72.902	56.210	46.216	39.572	34.842	31.307
11.75	206.911	106.479	73.040	56.348	46.357	39.714	34.986	31.454
12	207.060	106.620	73.179	56.489	46.498	39.858	35.131	31.601
12.25	207.204	106.758	73.317	56.628	46.639	40.000	35.276	31.748
12.5	207.356	106.900	73.458	56.769	46.782	40.145	35.422	31.896
12.75	207.503	107.040	73.597	56.909	46.923	40.288	35.568	32.044
13	207.654	107.182	73.738	57.051	47.066	40.433	35.715	32.193
13.25	207.800	107.322	73.877	57.191	47.209	40.578	35.861	32.342
13.5	207.946	107.461	74.017	57.332	47.351	40.722	36.008	32.491
13.75	208.099	107.605	74.158	57.474	47.495	40.868	36.156	32.642
14	208.248	107.746	74.299	57.616	47.639	41.014	36.304	32.792
14.25	208.396	107.887	74.440	57.758	47.782	41.159	36.452	32.943
14.5	208.544	108.028	74.580	57.900	47.926	41.305	36.601	33.094
14.75	208.691	108.168	74.720	58.041	48.070	41.451	36.749	33.245
15	208.841	108.310	74.862	58.184	48.214	41.599	36.899	33.397
15.25	208.991	108.453	75.004	58.327	48.359	41.746	37.049	33.549
15.5	209.141	108.595	75.145	58.470	48.504	41.893	37.199	33.702
15.75	209.287	108.735	75.286	58.612	48.649	42.040	37.349	33.855
16	209.435	108.876	75.427	58.755	48.794	42.188	37.499	34.008
16.25	209.587	109.020	75.570	58.900	48.940	42.337	37.651	34.162
16.5	209.738	109.163	75.713	59.044	49.087	42.486	37.802	34.317
16.75	209.885	109.304	75.854	59.187	49.233	42.634	37.954	34.471
17	210.035	109.447	75.997	59.331	49.379	42.784	38.106	34.626
17.25	210.182	109.588	76.138	59.475	49.525	42.933	38.258	34.781
17.5	210.331	109.731	76.281	59.619	49.672	43.082	38.411	34.937
17.75	210.483	109.874	76.425	59.765	49.820	43.233	38.564	35.094
18	210.632	110.017	76.567	59.909	49.967	43.383	38.717	35.250
18.25	210.780	110.159	76.710	60.054	50.115	43.534	38.871	35.407
18.5	210.931	110.303	76.854	60.200	50.263	43.685	39.025	35.564
18.75	211.078	110.444	76.996	60.344	50.411	43.836	39.179	35.722

TABLE A (continued)

% INTEREST	YEARS							
	.5	1	1.5	2	2.5	3	3.5	4
19	211.228	110.588	77.140	60.490	50.559	43.987	39.334	35.880
19.25	211.381	110.732	77.285	60.637	50.709	44.139	39.490	36.039
19.5	211.530	110.875	77.428	60.783	50.857	44.291	39.645	36.198
19.75	211.679	111.018	77.572	60.929	51.006	44.444	39.801	36.357
20	211.827	111.161	77.716	61.075	51.155	44.596	39.957	36.516
20.25	211.976	111.304	77.860	61.221	51.305	44.749	40.113	36.676
20.5	212.129	111.450	78.005	61.369	51.456	44.903	40.270	36.837
20.75	212.279	111.594	78.150	61.516	51.606	45.057	40.428	36.998
21	212.427	111.737	78.294	61.663	51.756	45.210	40.585	37.159
21.25	212.576	111.880	78.439	61.810	51.906	45.364	40.742	37.320
21.5	212.726	112.024	78.583	61.958	52.057	45.518	40.900	37.482
21.75	212.880	112.170	78.730	62.106	52.209	45.674	41.060	37.645
22	213.029	112.314	78.875	62.254	52.360	45.829	41.218	37.807
22.25	213.180	112.459	79.021	62.403	52.512	45.984	41.377	37.971
22.5	213.328	112.602	79.166	62.550	52.663	46.140	41.537	38.134
22.75	213.478	112.747	79.311	62.699	52.815	46.295	41.697	38.298
23	213.628	112.891	79.457	62.848	52.968	46.452	41.857	38.462
23.25	213.780	113.037	79.604	62.997	53.121	46.608	42.017	38.626
23.5	213.930	113.181	79.750	63.146	53.273	46.765	42.178	38.791
23.75	214.081	113.327	79.896	63.296	53.427	46.922	42.339	38.957
24	214.230	113.471	80.042	63.445	53.580	47.079	42.501	39.122
24.25	214.381	113.617	80.189	63.595	53.733	47.237	42.663	39.288
24.5	214.534	113.763	80.337	63.746	53.888	47.395	42.825	39.455
24.75	214.685	113.908	80.484	63.896	54.042	47.554	42.987	39.622
25	214.835	114.053	80.630	64.046	54.196	47.712	43.150	39.789

TABLE A (continued)

% INTEREST	4.5	5	5.5	6	6.5	7	7.5	8
8	26.535	24.332	22.534	21.040	19.780	18.704	17.774	16.964
8.25	26.677	24.475	22.679	21.186	19.928	18.853	17.925	17.117
8.5	26.821	24.620	22.825	21.334	20.077	19.004	18.078	17.271
8.75	26.964	24.765	22.972	21.482	20.227	19.155	18.231	17.425
9	27.108	24.910	23.119	21.631	20.377	19.307	18.384	17.580
9.25	27.252	25.056	23.266	21.780	20.528	19.460	18.538	17.736
9.5	27.396	25.202	23.414	21.930	20.679	19.613	18.693	17.893
9.75	27.542	25.349	23.563	22.080	20.832	19.767	18.849	18.051
10	27.687	25.497	23.712	22.231	20.985	19.922	19.006	18.209
10.25	27.833	25.644	23.861	22.383	21.138	20.077	19.163	18.368
10.5	27.980	25.793	24.012	22.535	21.292	20.233	19.321	18.528
10.75	28.126	25.942	24.162	22.688	21.447	20.390	19.479	18.689
11	28.274	26.091	24.314	22.841	21.602	20.547	19.639	18.850
11.25	28.422	26.241	24.466	22.995	21.758	20.705	19.799	19.012
11.5	28.570	26.392	24.619	23.150	21.915	20.864	19.960	19.176
11.75	28.719	26.542	24.771	23.305	22.072	21.023	20.121	19.339
12	28.868	26.694	24.925	23.460	22.230	21.183	20.284	19.504
12.25	29.017	26.845	25.078	23.616	22.388	21.344	20.447	19.668
12.5	29.168	26.998	25.233	23.774	22.548	21.506	20.610	19.835
12.75	29.318	27.150	25.388	23.931	22.707	21.668	20.775	20.001
13	29.470	27.304	25.544	24.089	22.868	21.831	20.940	20.169
13.25	29.621	27.458	25.700	24.248	23.029	21.994	21.106	20.337
13.5	29.772	27.612	25.857	24.407	23.190	22.158	21.272	20.506
13.75	29.925	27.767	26.015	24.567	23.353	22.323	21.440	20.676
14	30.078	27.922	26.172	24.727	23.516	22.488	21.607	20.846
14.25	30.231	28.078	26.331	24.888	23.679	22.654	21.776	21.017
14.5	30.385	28.234	26.490	25.049	23.843	22.821	21.945	21.189
14.75	30.538	28.391	26.649	25.211	24.008	22.988	22.115	21.361
15	30.693	28.548	26.809	25.374	24.173	23.156	22.286	21.535
15.25	30.848	28.706	26.969	25.537	24.339	23.325	22.457	21.709
15.5	31.004	28.864	27.130	25.701	24.506	23.494	22.629	21.883
15.75	31.159	29.022	27.292	25.865	24.673	23.664	22.802	22.058
16	31.316	29.182	27.454	26.030	24.840	23.834	22.975	22.234
16.25	31.473	29.341	27.616	26.196	25.009	24.006	23.149	22.411
16.5	31.630	29.502	27.780	26.362	25.178	24.178	23.324	22.589
16.75	31.787	29.662	27.943	26.528	25.347	24.350	23.499	22.767
17	31.945	29.823	28.107	26.696	25.518	24.523	23.675	22.946
17.25	32.104	29.985	28.272	26.863	25.688	24.697	23.852	23.125
17.5	32.263	30.147	28.437	27.031	25.859	24.871	24.029	23.305
17.75	32.422	30.309	28.603	27.200	26.031	25.046	24.207	23.486
18	32.582	30.472	28.769	27.369	26.204	25.221	24.385	23.668
18.25	32.742	30.636	28.935	27.539	26.377	25.398	24.565	23.850
18.5	32.903	30.800	29.103	27.710	26.550	25.574	24.744	24.033
18.75	33.063	30.964	29.270	27.881	26.724	25.752	24.925	24.216
19	33.225	31.129	29.438	28.052	26.899	25.930	25.106	24.401
19.25	33.387	31.294	29.607	28.224	27.075	26.108	25.288	24.586
19.5	33.549	31.460	29.776	28.397	27.251	26.287	25.470	24.771
19.75	33.712	31.626	29.946	28.570	27.427	26.467	25.653	24.957
20	33.875	31.793	30.116	28.743	27.604	26.647	25.837	25.144
20.25	34.039	31.960	30.287	28.917	27.781	26.828	26.021	25.331

TABLE A (continued)

% INTEREST	YEARS							
	4.5	5	5.5	6	6.5	7	7.5	8
20.5	34.203	32.128	30.458	29.092	27.960	27.010	26.206	25.519
20.75	34.367	32.296	30.630	29.268	28.139	27.192	26.391	25.708
21	34.532	32.464	30.802	29.443	28.318	27.375	26.577	25.897
21.25	34.697	32.633	30.974	29.619	28.497	27.558	26.764	26.087
21.5	34.863	32.802	31.147	29.796	28.678	27.742	26.951	26.278
21.75	35.029	32.973	31.321	29.974	28.859	27.926	27.139	26.469
22	35.196	33.143	31.495	30.151	29.040	28.111	27.327	26.661
22.25	35.363	33.314	31.670	30.330	29.222	28.297	27.516	26.853
22.5	35.530	33.485	31.845	30.509	29.405	28.483	27.706	27.046
22.75	35.698	33.656	32.020	30.688	29.588	28.669	27.896	27.239
23	35.866	33.828	32.197	30.868	29.771	28.857	28.087	27.433
23.25	36.035	34.001	32.373	31.048	29.955	29.044	28.278	27.628
23.5	36.203	34.174	32.550	31.229	30.140	29.233	28.470	27.823
23.75	36.373	34.348	32.728	31.410	30.325	29.422	28.662	28.019
24	36.543	34.521	32.905	31.592	30.511	29.611	28.855	28.216
24.25	36.713	34.696	33.084	31.775	30.697	29.801	29.049	28.413
24.5	36.884	34.871	33.263	31.958	30.884	29.992	29.243	28.610
24.75	37.055	35.046	33.442	32.141	31.071	30.182	29.438	28.809
25	37.226	35.222	33.622	32.325	31.259	30.374	29.633	29.007

TABLE A (continued)

% INTEREST	8.5	9	9.5	10	10.5	11	11.5	12
8	16.252	15.623	15.062	14.559	14.107	13.699	13.328	12.989
8.25	16.406	15.778	15.219	14.718	14.268	13.860	13.491	13.154
8.5	16.562	15.935	15.378	14.878	14.429	14.024	13.656	13.321
8.75	16.718	16.093	15.537	15.039	14.592	14.188	13.822	13.488
9	16.875	16.252	15.697	15.201	14.756	14.353	13.988	13.657
9.25	17.033	16.411	15.858	15.364	14.920	14.519	14.156	13.826
9.5	17.191	16.571	16.020	15.528	15.085	14.686	14.325	13.997
9.75	17.351	16.733	16.183	15.693	15.252	14.855	14.495	14.168
10	17.511	16.895	16.347	15.858	15.420	15.024	14.666	14.341
10.25	17.672	17.057	16.512	16.025	15.588	15.194	14.838	14.515
10.5	17.834	17.221	16.677	16.192	15.757	15.365	15.011	14.690
10.75	17.996	17.386	16.844	16.361	15.928	15.538	15.185	14.866
11	18.160	17.551	17.011	16.530	16.099	15.711	15.360	15.043
11.25	18.324	17.717	17.180	16.700	16.271	15.885	15.537	15.221
11.5	18.489	17.885	17.349	16.872	16.444	16.060	15.714	15.400
11.75	18.655	18.052	17.519	17.044	16.618	16.236	15.892	15.580
12	18.821	18.221	17.690	17.217	16.794	16.414	16.071	15.761
12.25	18.989	18.391	17.861	17.390	16.969	16.591	16.251	15.943
12.5	19.157	18.561	18.034	17.565	17.146	16.771	16.432	16.126
12.75	19.326	18.732	18.207	17.741	17.324	16.950	16.614	16.310
13	19.496	18.904	18.382	17.917	17.503	17.131	16.797	16.496
13.25	19.666	19.077	18.557	18.095	17.682	17.313	16.981	16.682
13.5	19.837	19.251	18.733	18.273	17.863	17.496	17.166	16.869
13.75	20.010	19.425	18.910	18.452	18.044	17.680	17.352	17.057
14	20.182	19.601	19.087	18.632	18.227	17.864	17.539	17.246
14.25	20.356	19.777	19.266	18.813	18.410	18.049	17.726	17.435
14.5	20.530	19.953	19.445	18.994	18.594	18.236	17.915	17.626
14.75	20.705	20.131	19.625	19.177	18.779	18.423	18.104	17.818
15	20.881	20.309	19.806	19.360	18.964	18.611	18.295	18.011
15.25	21.058	20.488	19.987	19.544	19.151	18.800	18.486	18.204
15.5	21.235	20.668	20.170	19.729	19.338	18.990	18.678	18.399
15.75	21.413	20.849	20.353	19.915	19.526	19.180	18.871	18.594
16	21.592	21.030	20.537	20.102	19.715	19.372	19.065	18.790
16.25	21.771	21.213	20.722	20.289	19.905	19.564	19.260	18.987
16.5	21.952	21.396	20.908	20.477	20.096	19.757	19.455	19.185
16.75	22.133	21.579	21.094	20.666	20.288	19.951	19.652	19.384
17	22.314	21.764	21.281	20.856	20.480	20.146	19.849	19.583
17.25	22.496	21.949	21.469	21.046	20.673	20.342	20.047	19.783
17.5	22.679	22.134	21.657	21.237	20.867	20.538	20.245	19.985
17.75	22.863	22.321	21.847	21.430	21.061	20.735	20.445	20.187
18	23.048	22.508	22.037	21.622	21.257	20.933	20.646	20.389
18.25	23.233	22.696	22.227	21.816	21.453	21.132	20.847	20.593
18.5	23.419	22.885	22.419	22.010	21.650	21.331	21.049	20.797
18.75	23.605	23.074	22.611	22.205	21.847	21.531	21.251	21.002
19	23.792	23.264	22.804	22.401	22.046	21.732	21.455	21.208
19.25	23.980	23.455	22.998	22.597	22.245	21.934	21.659	21.415
19.5	24.169	23.647	23.192	22.794	22.445	22.137	21.864	21.622
19.75	24.358	23.839	23.387	22.992	22.645	22.340	22.070	21.831
20	24.548	24.032	23.583	23.191	22.847	22.544	22.276	22.039
20.25	24.738	24.225	23.779	23.390	23.048	22.748	22.483	22.249

TABLE A (continued)

% INTEREST	YEARS							
	8.5	9	9.5	10	10.5	11	11.5	12
20.5	24.929	24.420	23.977	23.590	23.251	22.954	22.691	22.459
20.75	25.121	24.614	24.174	23.791	23.455	23.160	22.900	22.670
21	25.314	24.810	24.373	23.992	23.659	23.366	23.109	22.882
21.25	25.507	25.006	24.572	24.194	23.863	23.573	23.319	23.094
21.5	25.700	25.203	24.772	24.396	24.069	23.781	23.529	23.307
21.75	25.895	25.400	24.972	24.600	24.275	23.990	23.740	23.521
22	26.090	25.598	25.173	24.804	24.481	24.200	23.952	23.735
22.25	26.285	25.797	25.375	25.008	24.689	24.410	24.165	23.950
22.5	26.481	25.996	25.577	25.213	24.897	24.620	24.378	24.165
22.75	26.678	26.196	25.780	25.419	25.105	24.831	24.592	24.381
23	26.876	26.397	25.984	25.626	25.315	25.043	24.806	24.598
23.25	27.074	26.598	26.188	25.833	25.524	25.256	25.021	24.815
23.5	27.272	26.800	26.393	26.041	25.735	25.469	25.237	25.033
23.75	27.471	27.002	26.598	26.249	25.946	25.683	25.453	25.252
24	27.671	27.205	26.804	26.458	26.158	25.897	25.670	25.471
24.25	27.872	27.409	27.011	26.667	26.370	26.112	25.887	25.691
24.5	28.073	27.613	27.218	26.877	26.583	26.327	26.105	25.911
24.75	28.274	27.817	27.426	27.088	26.796	26.543	26.323	26.132
25	28.476	28.023	27.634	27.299	27.010	26.760	26.542	26.353

TABLE A (continued)

% INTEREST	YEARS							
	12.5	13	13.5	14	14.5	15	15.5	16
8	12.680	12.397	12.136	11.896	11.674	11.468	11.277	11.099
8.25	12.847	12.565	12.306	12.067	11.846	11.642	11.452	11.276
8.5	13.015	12.734	12.477	12.239	12.020	11.817	11.629	11.454
8.75	13.184	12.905	12.649	12.413	12.195	11.994	11.807	11.633
9	13.354	13.076	12.822	12.587	12.371	12.171	11.986	11.814
9.25	13.525	13.249	12.996	12.763	12.549	12.350	12.167	11.996
9.5	13.697	13.423	13.172	12.940	12.727	12.531	12.349	12.180
9.75	13.870	13.598	13.348	13.119	12.908	12.712	12.532	12.365
10	14.045	13.774	13.526	13.299	13.089	12.895	12.717	12.551
10.25	14.220	13.952	13.705	13.479	13.271	13.079	12.902	12.738
10.5	14.397	14.130	13.886	13.661	13.455	13.265	13.089	12.927
10.75	14.575	14.310	14.067	13.844	13.640	13.451	13.278	13.117
11	14.754	14.490	14.249	14.029	13.826	13.639	13.467	13.308
11.25	14.934	14.672	14.433	14.214	14.013	13.828	13.658	13.500
11.5	15.115	14.855	14.618	14.401	14.202	14.018	13.850	13.694
11.75	15.297	15.039	14.804	14.588	14.391	14.210	14.043	13.889
12	15.480	15.224	14.991	14.777	14.582	14.402	14.237	14.085
12.25	15.664	15.410	15.179	14.967	14.773	14.596	14.432	14.282
12.5	15.849	15.597	15.368	15.158	14.966	14.790	14.629	14.480
12.75	16.035	15.785	15.558	15.350	15.160	14.986	14.826	14.679
13	16.223	15.975	15.749	15.543	15.355	15.183	15.025	14.880
13.25	16.411	16.165	15.941	15.737	15.551	15.381	15.225	15.081
13.5	16.600	16.356	16.134	15.932	15.748	15.580	15.425	15.284
13.75	16.790	16.548	16.329	16.129	15.946	15.780	15.627	15.488
14	16.981	16.741	16.524	16.326	16.146	15.981	15.830	15.692
14.25	17.173	16.935	16.720	16.524	16.346	16.183	16.034	15.898
14.5	17.366	17.130	16.917	16.723	16.547	16.386	16.239	16.105
14.75	17.560	17.326	17.115	16.923	16.749	16.590	16.445	16.313
15	17.755	17.523	17.314	17.124	16.952	16.795	16.652	16.521
15.25	17.950	17.721	17.514	17.327	17.156	17.001	16.860	16.731
15.5	18.147	17.920	17.715	17.530	17.361	17.208	17.069	16.941
15.75	18.344	18.120	17.917	17.733	17.567	17.416	17.278	17.153
16	18.543	18.320	18.120	17.938	17.774	17.624	17.489	17.365
16.25	18.742	18.522	18.323	18.144	17.981	17.834	17.700	17.579
16.5	18.942	18.724	18.528	18.350	18.190	18.045	17.913	17.793
16.75	19.143	18.928	18.733	18.558	18.399	18.256	18.126	18.008
17	19.345	19.132	18.939	18.766	18.610	18.468	18.340	18.224
17.25	19.548	19.336	19.146	18.975	18.821	18.681	18.555	18.440
17.5	19.751	19.542	19.354	19.185	19.033	18.895	18.770	18.658
17.75	19.956	19.749	19.563	19.396	19.245	19.110	18.987	18.876
18	20.161	19.956	19.772	19.607	19.459	19.325	19.204	19.095
18.25	20.367	20.164	19.983	19.820	19.673	19.541	19.422	19.315
18.5	20.573	20.373	20.194	20.033	19.888	19.758	19.641	19.535
18.75	20.781	20.583	20.406	20.247	20.104	19.976	19.861	19.757
19	20.989	20.793	20.618	20.461	20.321	20.195	20.081	19.979
19.25	21.198	21.004	20.831	20.677	20.538	20.414	20.302	20.201
19.5	21.408	21.216	21.046	20.893	20.756	20.634	20.524	20.425
19.75	21.618	21.429	21.260	21.110	20.975	20.854	20.746	20.649
20	21.829	21.642	21.476	21.327	21.194	21.076	20.969	20.874
20.25	22.041	21.856	21.692	21.545	21.414	21.297	21.193	21.099

TABLE A (*continued*)

% INTEREST	12.5	13	13.5	14	14.5	15	15.5	16
	Years							
20.5	22.254	22.071	21.909	21.764	21.635	21.520	21.417	21.325
20.75	22.467	22.287	22.126	21.984	21.857	21.743	21.642	21.552
21	22.681	22.503	22.345	22.204	22.079	21.967	21.868	21.779
21.25	22.895	22.719	22.563	22.425	22.302	22.192	22.094	22.007
21.5	23.111	22.937	22.783	22.646	22.525	22.417	22.321	22.235
21.75	23.327	23.155	23.003	22.869	22.749	22.643	22.548	22.464
22	23.543	23.374	23.224	23.091	22.974	22.869	22.776	22.693
22.25	23.760	23.593	23.445	23.315	23.199	23.096	23.005	22.924
22.5	23.978	23.813	23.667	23.539	23.424	23.323	23.234	23.154
22.75	24.196	24.034	23.890	23.763	23.651	23.551	23.463	23.385
23	24.415	24.255	24.113	23.988	23.878	23.780	23.693	23.617
23.25	24.635	24.476	24.337	24.214	24.105	24.009	23.924	23.849
23.5	24.855	24.699	24.561	24.440	24.333	24.239	24.155	24.081
23.75	25.076	24.922	24.786	24.667	24.561	24.469	24.387	24.314
24	25.297	25.145	25.011	24.894	24.790	24.699	24.619	24.548
24.25	25.519	25.369	25.237	25.122	25.020	24.930	24.851	24.782
24.5	25.742	25.594	25.464	25.350	25.250	25.162	25.085	25.016
24.75	25.965	25.819	25.691	25.579	25.480	25.394	25.318	25.251
25	26.188	26.044	25.918	25.808	25.711	25.626	25.552	25.486

TABLE A (continued)

% INTEREST	16.5	17	17.5	18	18.5	19	19.5	20
8	10.934	10.779	10.635	10.500	10.373	10.254	10.142	10.037
8.25	11.112	10.958	10.815	10.682	10.556	10.439	10.328	10.225
8.5	11.291	11.140	10.998	10.866	10.742	10.625	10.516	10.414
8.75	11.472	11.322	11.182	11.051	10.928	10.813	10.706	10.605
9	11.655	11.506	11.367	11.237	11.116	11.003	10.897	10.797
9.25	11.838	11.691	11.554	11.426	11.306	11.194	11.089	10.990
9.5	12.023	11.877	11.742	11.615	11.497	11.386	11.283	11.186
9.75	12.210	12.065	11.931	11.806	11.689	11.580	11.478	11.382
10	12.397	12.255	12.122	11.998	11.883	11.775	11.675	11.580
10.25	12.586	12.445	12.314	12.192	12.078	11.972	11.872	11.780
10.5	12.777	12.637	12.507	12.387	12.274	12.170	12.072	11.981
10.75	12.968	12.830	12.702	12.583	12.472	12.369	12.273	12.183
11	13.161	13.025	12.898	12.781	12.671	12.570	12.475	12.386
11.25	13.355	13.220	13.095	12.979	12.872	12.771	12.678	12.591
11.5	13.550	13.417	13.294	13.180	13.073	12.975	12.883	12.797
11.75	13.747	13.615	13.494	13.381	13.276	13.179	13.089	13.005
12	13.944	13.815	13.695	13.583	13.480	13.385	13.296	13.213
12.25	14.143	14.015	13.897	13.787	13.686	13.591	13.504	13.423
12.5	14.343	14.217	14.100	13.992	13.892	13.799	13.713	13.634
12.75	14.544	14.419	14.304	14.198	14.100	14.009	13.924	13.846
13	14.746	14.623	14.510	14.405	14.308	14.219	14.136	14.059
13.25	14.950	14.828	14.717	14.613	14.518	14.430	14.349	14.273
13.5	15.154	15.034	14.924	14.823	14.729	14.643	14.562	14.488
13.75	15.359	15.242	15.133	15.033	14.941	14.856	14.777	14.705
14	15.566	15.450	15.343	15.245	15.154	15.071	14.993	14.922
14.25	15.773	15.659	15.554	15.457	15.368	15.286	15.210	15.141
14.5	15.982	15.869	15.766	15.671	15.583	15.503	15.428	15.360
14.75	16.191	16.080	15.978	15.885	15.799	15.720	15.647	15.580
15	16.402	16.292	16.192	16.100	16.016	15.938	15.867	15.801
15.25	16.613	16.506	16.407	16.317	16.234	16.158	16.088	16.024
15.5	16.826	16.720	16.623	16.534	16.453	16.378	16.309	16.247
15.75	17.039	16.934	16.839	16.752	16.672	16.599	16.532	16.470
16	17.253	17.150	17.057	16.971	16.893	16.821	16.755	16.695
16.25	17.468	17.367	17.275	17.191	17.114	17.044	16.979	16.921
16.5	17.684	17.585	17.494	17.412	17.336	17.267	17.204	17.147
16.75	17.901	17.803	17.714	17.633	17.559	17.492	17.430	17.374
17	18.118	18.022	17.935	17.855	17.783	17.717	17.657	17.602
17.25	18.336	18.242	18.156	18.078	18.007	17.943	17.884	17.830
17.5	18.556	18.463	18.379	18.302	18.233	18.169	18.112	18.059
17.75	18.776	18.685	18.602	18.527	18.459	18.397	18.341	18.289
18	18.996	18.907	18.826	18.752	18.686	18.625	18.570	18.520
18.25	19.218	19.130	19.050	18.978	18.913	18.854	18.800	18.751
18.5	19.440	19.354	19.276	19.205	19.141	19.083	19.031	18.983
18.75	19.663	19.578	19.502	19.433	19.370	19.313	19.262	19.215
19	19.887	19.803	19.728	19.661	19.599	19.544	19.494	19.448
19.25	20.111	20.029	19.956	19.889	19.829	19.775	19.726	19.682
19.5	20.336	20.256	20.184	20.119	20.060	20.007	19.959	19.916
19.75	20.562	20.483	20.412	20.349	20.291	20.240	20.193	20.151
20	20.788	20.711	20.642	20.579	20.523	20.473	20.427	20.386
20.25	21.015	20.939	20.871	20.810	20.755	20.706	20.662	20.622

TABLE A (continued)

% INTEREST	YEARS							
	16.5	17	17.5	18	18.5	19	19.5	20
20.5	21.242	21.168	21.102	21.042	20.988	20.940	20.897	20.858
20.75	21.471	21.398	21.333	21.274	21.222	21.175	21.133	21.095
21	21.699	21.628	21.564	21.507	21.456	21.410	21.369	21.332
21.25	21.929	21.859	21.796	21.740	21.690	21.646	21.605	21.569
21.5	22.158	22.090	22.029	21.974	21.925	21.882	21.842	21.807
21.75	22.389	22.322	22.262	22.209	22.161	22.118	22.080	22.046
22	22.620	22.554	22.496	22.443	22.397	22.355	22.318	22.285
22.25	22.851	22.787	22.730	22.679	22.633	22.593	22.556	22.524
22.5	23.083	23.020	22.964	22.914	22.870	22.830	22.795	22.764
22.75	23.316	23.254	23.199	23.151	23.107	23.069	23.034	23.004
23	23.549	23.488	23.435	23.387	23.345	23.307	23.274	23.244
23.25	23.782	23.723	23.671	23.624	23.583	23.546	23.514	23.485
23.5	24.016	23.958	23.907	23.862	23.821	23.786	23.754	23.726
23.75	24.251	24.194	24.144	24.100	24.060	24.025	23.995	23.967
24	24.485	24.430	24.381	24.338	24.299	24.266	24.235	24.209
24.25	24.721	24.666	24.619	24.576	24.539	24.506	24.477	24.451
24.5	24.956	24.903	24.857	24.815	24.779	24.747	24.718	24.693
24.75	25.192	25.141	25.095	25.055	25.019	24.988	24.960	24.936
25	25.429	25.378	25.334	25.294	25.260	25.229	25.202	25.179

TABLE A (*continued*)

% INTEREST	YEARS							
	20.5	21	21.5	22	22.5	23	23.5	24
8	9.938	9.845	9.757	9.674	9.596	9.521	9.451	9.385
8.25	10.127	10.035	9.948	9.867	9.789	9.716	9.647	9.582
8.5	10.318	10.227	10.142	10.061	9.985	9.913	9.845	9.781
8.75	10.510	10.420	10.336	10.257	10.182	10.111	10.045	9.982
9	10.703	10.615	10.532	10.454	10.381	10.311	10.246	10.184
9.25	10.898	10.811	10.730	10.653	10.581	10.513	10.449	10.388
9.5	11.095	11.009	10.929	10.854	10.783	10.716	10.653	10.593
9.75	11.293	11.209	11.130	11.056	10.986	10.920	10.858	10.800
10	11.492	11.409	11.332	11.259	11.191	11.126	11.066	11.009
10.25	11.693	11.612	11.535	11.464	11.397	11.334	11.274	11.219
10.5	11.895	11.815	11.740	11.670	11.604	11.542	11.484	11.430
10.75	12.099	12.020	11.947	11.878	11.813	11.753	11.696	11.642
11	12.304	12.226	12.154	12.087	12.023	11.964	11.908	11.856
11.25	12.510	12.434	12.363	12.297	12.235	12.177	12.123	12.072
11.5	12.717	12.643	12.573	12.509	12.448	12.391	12.338	12.288
11.75	12.926	12.853	12.785	12.721	12.662	12.606	12.554	12.506
12	13.136	13.064	12.998	12.935	12.877	12.823	12.772	12.725
12.25	13.347	13.277	13.211	13.150	13.093	13.040	12.991	12.945
12.5	13.560	13.491	13.426	13.367	13.311	13.259	13.211	13.166
12.75	13.773	13.705	13.643	13.584	13.530	13.479	13.432	13.388
13	13.988	13.921	13.860	13.803	13.750	13.700	13.654	13.611
13.25	14.203	14.138	14.078	14.022	13.970	13.922	13.877	13.835
13.5	14.420	14.356	14.298	14.243	14.192	14.145	14.101	14.061
13.75	14.638	14.576	14.518	14.465	14.415	14.369	14.327	14.287
14	14.856	14.796	14.739	14.687	14.639	14.594	14.553	14.514
14.25	15.076	15.017	14.962	14.911	14.864	14.820	14.780	14.742
14.5	15.297	15.239	15.185	15.135	15.089	15.047	15.007	14.971
14.75	15.519	15.462	15.409	15.361	15.316	15.274	15.236	15.201
15	15.741	15.685	15.634	15.587	15.543	15.503	15.466	15.431
15.25	15.965	15.910	15.860	15.814	15.771	15.732	15.696	15.662
15.5	16.189	16.136	16.087	16.042	16.000	15.962	15.927	15.894
15.75	16.414	16.362	16.314	16.270	16.230	16.193	16.159	16.127
16	16.640	16.589	16.543	16.500	16.461	16.424	16.391	16.361
16.25	16.867	16.817	16.772	16.730	16.692	16.657	16.624	16.595
16.5	17.094	17.046	17.002	16.961	16.924	16.890	16.858	16.830
16.75	17.322	17.275	17.232	17.193	17.156	17.123	17.093	17.065
17	17.551	17.505	17.463	17.425	17.390	17.358	17.328	17.301
17.25	17.781	17.736	17.695	17.658	17.624	17.592	17.564	17.538
17.5	18.011	17.968	17.928	17.891	17.858	17.828	17.800	17.775
17.75	18.242	18.200	18.161	18.126	18.093	18.064	18.037	18.012
18	18.474	18.433	18.395	18.360	18.329	18.300	18.274	18.251
18.25	18.706	18.666	18.629	18.596	18.565	18.538	18.512	18.489
18.5	18.939	18.900	18.864	18.832	18.802	18.775	18.751	18.729
18.75	19.173	19.135	19.100	19.068	19.039	19.013	18.990	18.968
19	19.407	19.370	19.336	19.305	19.277	19.252	19.229	19.208
19.25	19.642	19.605	19.572	19.543	19.516	19.491	19.469	19.449
19.5	19.877	19.842	19.810	19.781	19.754	19.731	19.709	19.690
19.75	20.113	20.078	20.047	20.019	19.994	19.971	19.950	19.931
20	20.349	20.315	20.285	20.258	20.233	20.211	20.191	20.173
20.25	20.586	20.553	20.524	20.497	20.473	20.452	20.432	20.415

TABLE A (*continued*)

% INTEREST	20.5	21	21.5	22	22.5	23	23.5	24
				YEARS				
20.5	20.823	20.791	20.763	20.737	20.714	20.693	20.674	20.657
20.75	21.060	21.030	21.002	20.977	20.955	20.934	20.916	20.900
21	21.298	21.269	21.242	21.218	21.196	21.176	21.159	21.143
21.25	21.537	21.508	21.482	21.458	21.437	21.419	21.402	21.386
21.5	21.776	21.748	21.722	21.700	21.679	21.661	21.645	21.630
21.75	22.015	21.988	21.963	21.941	21.922	21.904	21.888	21.874
22	22.255	22.228	22.205	22.183	22.164	22.147	22.132	22.118
22.25	22.495	22.469	22.446	22.426	22.407	22.391	22.376	22.363
22.5	22.736	22.710	22.688	22.668	22.650	22.634	22.620	22.607
22.75	22.976	22.952	22.930	22.911	22.894	22.878	22.865	22.852
23	23.217	23.194	23.173	23.154	23.137	23.123	23.109	23.097
23.25	23.459	23.436	23.416	23.398	23.381	23.367	23.354	23.343
23.5	23.701	23.679	23.659	23.641	23.626	23.612	23.599	23.588
23.75	23.943	23.921	23.902	23.885	23.870	23.857	23.845	23.834
24	24.185	24.164	24.146	24.129	24.115	24.102	24.090	24.080
24.25	24.428	24.408	24.390	24.374	24.360	24.347	24.336	24.326
24.5	24.671	24.651	24.634	24.619	24.605	24.593	24.582	24.573
24.75	24.914	24.895	24.878	24.863	24.850	24.839	24.828	24.819
25	25.158	25.139	25.123	25.109	25.096	25.085	25.075	25.066

TABLE A (continued)

% INTEREST	YEARS							
	24.5	25	25.5	26	26.5	27	27.5	28
8	9.322	9.262	9.205	9.151	9.100	9.051	9.005	8.961
8.25	9.520	9.461	9.406	9.353	9.303	9.255	9.210	9.167
8.5	9.720	9.663	9.608	9.557	9.508	9.461	9.417	9.375
8.75	9.922	9.866	9.812	9.762	9.714	9.669	9.625	9.585
9	10.126	10.070	10.018	9.969	9.922	9.878	9.836	9.796
9.25	10.331	10.277	10.226	10.177	10.131	10.088	10.047	10.008
9.5	10.537	10.484	10.434	10.387	10.343	10.300	10.260	10.223
9.75	10.745	10.694	10.645	10.599	10.555	10.514	10.475	10.438
10	10.955	10.904	10.857	10.812	10.769	10.729	10.691	10.656
10.25	11.166	11.117	11.070	11.026	10.985	10.946	10.909	10.874
10.5	11.378	11.330	11.285	11.242	11.202	11.164	11.128	11.094
10.75	11.592	11.545	11.501	11.459	11.420	11.383	11.348	11.315
11	11.807	11.761	11.718	11.678	11.639	11.603	11.570	11.538
11.25	12.024	11.979	11.937	11.897	11.860	11.825	11.792	11.761
11.5	12.241	12.198	12.157	12.118	12.082	12.048	12.016	11.986
11.75	12.460	12.418	12.378	12.340	12.305	12.272	12.241	12.212
12	12.680	12.639	12.600	12.563	12.529	12.497	12.467	12.439
12.25	12.901	12.861	12.823	12.788	12.755	12.724	12.695	12.667
12.5	13.124	13.084	13.047	13.013	12.981	12.951	12.923	12.897
12.75	13.347	13.309	13.273	13.240	13.208	13.179	13.152	13.127
13	13.571	13.534	13.499	13.467	13.437	13.409	13.382	13.358
13.25	13.797	13.760	13.727	13.695	13.666	13.639	13.613	13.589
13.5	14.023	13.988	13.955	13.925	13.896	13.870	13.845	13.822
13.75	14.250	14.216	14.184	14.155	14.127	14.102	14.078	14.056
14	14.478	14.445	14.414	14.386	14.359	14.334	14.311	14.290
14.25	14.707	14.675	14.645	14.618	14.592	14.568	14.546	14.525
14.5	14.937	14.906	14.877	14.850	14.825	14.802	14.781	14.761
14.75	15.168	15.138	15.110	15.084	15.059	15.037	15.016	14.997
15	15.399	15.370	15.343	15.318	15.294	15.273	15.253	15.234
15.25	15.632	15.603	15.577	15.552	15.530	15.509	15.490	15.472
15.5	15.865	15.837	15.811	15.788	15.766	15.746	15.728	15.711
15.75	16.098	16.071	16.047	16.024	16.003	15.984	15.966	15.950
16	16.333	16.307	16.283	16.261	16.241	16.222	16.205	16.189
16.25	16.568	16.542	16.519	16.498	16.479	16.461	16.444	16.429
16.5	16.803	16.779	16.757	16.736	16.717	16.700	16.684	16.669
16.75	17.039	17.016	16.994	16.975	16.957	16.940	16.925	16.910
17	17.276	17.254	17.233	17.214	17.196	17.180	17.165	17.152
17.25	17.514	17.492	17.472	17.453	17.436	17.421	17.407	17.394
17.5	17.752	17.730	17.711	17.693	17.677	17.662	17.649	17.636
17.75	17.990	17.970	17.951	17.934	17.918	17.904	17.891	17.879
18	18.229	18.209	18.191	18.175	18.160	18.146	18.133	18.122
18.25	18.468	18.449	18.432	18.416	18.401	18.388	18.376	18.365
18.5	18.708	18.690	18.673	18.658	18.644	18.631	18.619	18.609
18.75	18.949	18.931	18.915	18.900	18.886	18.874	18.863	18.853
19	19.189	19.172	19.157	19.142	19.129	19.118	19.107	19.097
19.25	19.431	19.414	19.399	19.385	19.373	19.362	19.351	19.342
19.5	19.672	19.656	19.642	19.628	19.617	19.606	19.596	19.587
19.75	19.914	19.899	19.885	19.872	19.861	19.850	19.841	19.832
20	20.156	20.141	20.128	20.116	20.105	20.095	20.086	20.078
20.25	20.399	20.385	20.372	20.360	20.349	20.340	20.331	20.323

TABLE A (continued)

% INTEREST	YEARS							
	24.5	25	25.5	26	26.5	27	27.5	28
20.5	20.642	20.628	20.616	20.604	20.594	20.585	20.577	20.569
20.75	20.885	20.872	20.860	20.849	20.839	20.831	20.823	20.816
21	21.129	21.116	21.104	21.094	21.085	21.076	21.069	21.062
21.25	21.373	21.360	21.349	21.339	21.330	21.322	21.315	21.308
21.5	21.617	21.605	21.594	21.585	21.576	21.568	21.561	21.555
21.75	21.861	21.850	21.840	21.830	21.822	21.815	21.808	21.802
22	22.106	22.095	22.085	22.076	22.068	22.061	22.055	22.049
22.25	22.351	22.340	22.331	22.322	22.315	22.308	22.302	22.296
22.5	22.596	22.586	22.577	22.569	22.561	22.555	22.549	22.544
22.75	22.841	22.832	22.823	22.815	22.808	22.802	22.796	22.791
23	23.087	23.078	23.069	23.062	23.055	23.049	23.044	23.039
23.25	23.333	23.324	23.316	23.309	23.302	23.296	23.291	23.287
23.5	23.579	23.570	23.562	23.555	23.549	23.544	23.539	23.535
23.75	23.825	23.817	23.809	23.803	23.797	23.792	23.787	23.783
24	24.071	24.063	24.056	24.050	24.044	24.039	24.035	24.031
24.25	24.318	24.310	24.303	24.297	24.292	24.287	24.283	24.279
24.5	24.565	24.557	24.551	24.545	24.540	24.535	24.531	24.528
24.75	24.811	24.804	24.798	24.792	24.788	24.783	24.779	24.776
25	25.058	25.052	25.046	25.040	25.036	25.031	25.028	25.025

TABLE A (continued)

% INTEREST	YEARS							
	28.5	29	29.5	30	30.5	31	31.5	32
8	8.919	8.879	8.841	8.805	8.771	8.738	8.706	8.676
8.25	9.126	9.087	9.050	9.015	8.982	8.950	8.919	8.890
8.5	9.335	9.297	9.261	9.227	9.194	9.163	9.134	9.106
8.75	9.546	9.509	9.474	9.440	9.409	9.379	9.350	9.323
9	9.758	9.722	9.688	9.656	9.625	9.596	9.568	9.541
9.25	9.972	9.937	9.904	9.872	9.842	9.814	9.787	9.762
9.5	10.187	10.153	10.121	10.090	10.061	10.034	10.008	9.983
9.75	10.404	10.371	10.339	10.310	10.282	10.255	10.230	10.206
10	10.622	10.590	10.560	10.531	10.504	10.478	10.454	10.431
10.25	10.841	10.810	10.781	10.753	10.727	10.702	10.679	10.657
10.5	11.062	11.032	11.004	10.977	10.952	10.928	10.905	10.884
10.75	11.284	11.255	11.228	11.202	11.177	11.154	11.132	11.112
11	11.508	11.480	11.453	11.428	11.404	11.382	11.361	11.341
11.25	11.732	11.705	11.679	11.655	11.632	11.611	11.591	11.572
11.5	11.958	11.932	11.907	11.884	11.862	11.841	11.821	11.803
11.75	12.185	12.160	12.135	12.113	12.092	12.072	12.053	12.035
12	12.413	12.388	12.365	12.343	12.323	12.304	12.286	12.269
12.25	12.642	12.618	12.596	12.575	12.555	12.537	12.519	12.503
12.5	12.872	12.849	12.827	12.807	12.788	12.770	12.754	12.738
12.75	13.103	13.081	13.060	13.040	13.022	13.005	12.989	12.974
13	13.335	13.313	13.293	13.274	13.257	13.241	13.225	13.211
13.25	13.567	13.547	13.527	13.509	13.492	13.477	13.462	13.448
13.5	13.801	13.781	13.762	13.745	13.729	13.714	13.700	13.686
13.75	14.035	14.016	13.998	13.981	13.966	13.951	13.938	13.925
14	14.270	14.252	14.234	14.218	14.204	14.190	14.177	14.165
14.25	14.506	14.488	14.472	14.456	14.442	14.429	14.416	14.405
14.5	14.742	14.725	14.709	14.695	14.681	14.668	14.656	14.645
14.75	14.980	14.963	14.948	14.934	14.921	14.908	14.897	14.887
15	15.217	15.202	15.187	15.173	15.161	15.149	15.138	15.128
15.25	15.456	15.441	15.427	15.414	15.401	15.390	15.380	15.370
15.5	15.695	15.680	15.667	15.654	15.643	15.632	15.622	15.613
15.75	15.934	15.920	15.907	15.895	15.884	15.874	15.865	15.856
16	16.174	16.161	16.149	16.137	16.127	16.117	16.108	16.100
16.25	16.415	16.402	16.390	16.379	16.369	16.360	16.351	16.343
16.5	16.656	16.644	16.632	16.622	16.612	16.603	16.595	16.588
16.75	16.898	16.886	16.875	16.865	16.856	16.847	16.839	16.832
17	17.140	17.128	17.118	17.108	17.099	17.091	17.084	17.077
17.25	17.382	17.371	17.361	17.352	17.343	17.336	17.329	17.322
17.5	17.625	17.614	17.605	17.596	17.588	17.581	17.574	17.568
17.75	17.868	17.858	17.849	17.840	17.833	17.826	17.819	17.813
18	18.111	18.102	18.093	18.085	18.078	18.071	18.065	18.059
18.25	18.355	18.346	18.338	18.330	18.323	18.317	18.311	18.306
18.5	18.599	18.591	18.583	18.575	18.569	18.563	18.557	18.552
18.75	18.844	18.835	18.828	18.821	18.815	18.809	18.804	18.799
19	19.089	19.081	19.073	19.067	19.061	19.055	19.050	19.046
19.25	19.334	19.326	19.319	19.313	19.307	19.302	19.297	19.293
19.5	19.579	19.572	19.565	19.559	19.554	19.549	19.544	19.540
19.75	19.825	19.818	19.811	19.806	19.800	19.796	19.791	19.787
20	20.070	20.064	20.058	20.052	20.047	20.043	20.039	20.035
20.25	20.316	20.310	20.304	20.299	20.294	20.290	20.286	20.283

TABLE A (*continued*)

% INTEREST	28.5	29	29.5	30	30.5	31	31.5	32
20.5	20.563	20.557	20.551	20.546	20.542	20.538	20.534	20.531
20.75	20.809	20.803	20.798	20.793	20.789	20.785	20.782	20.779
21	21.056	21.050	21.045	21.041	21.037	21.033	21.030	21.027
21.25	21.303	21.297	21.293	21.288	21.284	21.281	21.278	21.275
21.5	21.550	21.545	21.540	21.536	21.532	21.529	21.526	21.524
21.75	21.797	21.792	21.788	21.784	21.780	21.777	21.774	21.772
22	22.044	22.040	22.035	22.032	22.029	22.026	22.023	22.021
22.25	22.292	22.287	22.283	22.280	22.277	22.274	22.271	22.269
22.5	22.539	22.535	22.531	22.528	22.525	22.522	22.520	22.518
22.75	22.787	22.783	22.780	22.776	22.774	22.771	22.769	22.767
23	23.035	23.031	23.028	23.025	23.022	23.020	23.018	23.016
23.25	23.283	23.279	23.276	23.273	23.271	23.268	23.266	23.265
23.5	23.531	23.528	23.525	23.522	23.519	23.517	23.515	23.514
23.75	23.779	23.776	23.773	23.770	23.768	23.766	23.764	23.763
24	24.027	24.024	24.022	24.019	24.017	24.015	24.013	24.012
24.25	24.276	24.273	24.270	24.268	24.266	24.264	24.263	24.261
24.5	24.524	24.522	24.519	24.517	24.515	24.513	24.512	24.510
24.75	24.773	24.770	24.768	24.766	24.764	24.762	24.761	24.760
25	25.022	25.019	25.017	25.015	25.013	25.012	25.010	25.009

TABLE A (continued)

% INTEREST	YEARS							
	32.5	33	33.5	34	34.5	35	35.5	36
8	8.648	8.621	8.595	8.570	8.546	8.523	8.501	8.481
8.25	8.862	8.836	8.811	8.787	8.764	8.742	8.721	8.701
8.5	9.079	9.053	9.029	9.006	8.983	8.962	8.942	8.923
8.75	9.297	9.272	9.249	9.226	9.205	9.184	9.165	9.146
9	9.516	9.492	9.470	9.448	9.428	9.408	9.389	9.372
9.25	9.737	9.714	9.692	9.672	9.652	9.633	9.615	9.598
9.5	9.960	9.938	9.917	9.896	9.877	9.859	9.842	9.826
9.75	10.184	10.162	10.142	10.123	10.104	10.087	10.071	10.055
10	10.409	10.388	10.369	10.350	10.333	10.316	10.300	10.285
10.25	10.636	10.616	10.597	10.579	10.562	10.546	10.531	10.517
10.5	10.863	10.844	10.826	10.809	10.793	10.778	10.763	10.749
10.75	11.092	11.074	11.057	11.040	11.025	11.010	10.996	10.983
11	11.322	11.305	11.288	11.272	11.258	11.243	11.230	11.218
11.25	11.554	11.537	11.521	11.506	11.491	11.478	11.465	11.453
11.5	11.786	11.769	11.754	11.740	11.726	11.713	11.701	11.690
11.75	12.019	12.003	11.989	11.975	11.962	11.950	11.938	11.927
12	12.253	12.238	12.224	12.211	12.198	12.187	12.176	12.165
12.25	12.488	12.473	12.460	12.447	12.436	12.424	12.414	12.404
12.5	12.724	12.710	12.697	12.685	12.674	12.663	12.653	12.644
12.75	12.960	12.947	12.935	12.923	12.912	12.902	12.893	12.884
13	13.197	13.185	13.173	13.162	13.152	13.142	13.133	13.125
13.25	13.435	13.424	13.412	13.402	13.392	13.383	13.374	13.366
13.5	13.674	13.663	13.652	13.642	13.633	13.624	13.616	13.608
13.75	13.914	13.903	13.892	13.883	13.874	13.866	13.858	13.851
14	14.154	14.143	14.133	14.124	14.116	14.108	14.101	14.094
14.25	14.394	14.384	14.375	14.366	14.358	14.351	14.344	14.337
14.5	14.635	14.626	14.617	14.609	14.601	14.594	14.587	14.581
14.75	14.877	14.868	14.859	14.852	14.844	14.838	14.831	14.826
15	15.119	15.110	15.102	15.095	15.088	15.082	15.076	15.070
15.25	15.362	15.353	15.346	15.339	15.332	15.326	15.321	15.315
15.5	15.605	15.597	15.590	15.583	15.577	15.571	15.566	15.561
15.75	15.848	15.841	15.834	15.827	15.822	15.816	15.811	15.807
16	16.092	16.085	16.078	16.072	16.067	16.062	16.057	16.053
16.25	16.336	16.329	16.323	16.317	16.312	16.307	16.303	16.299
16.5	16.581	16.574	16.568	16.563	16.558	16.553	16.549	16.545
16.75	16.826	16.819	16.814	16.809	16.804	16.800	16.796	16.792
17	17.071	17.065	17.060	17.055	17.050	17.046	17.043	17.039
17.25	17.316	17.311	17.306	17.301	17.297	17.293	17.290	17.286
17.5	17.562	17.557	17.552	17.548	17.544	17.540	17.537	17.534
17.75	17.808	17.803	17.799	17.795	17.791	17.787	17.784	17.781
18	18.054	18.050	18.045	18.042	18.038	18.035	18.032	18.029
18.25	18.301	18.296	18.292	18.289	18.285	18.282	18.279	18.277
18.5	18.548	18.543	18.540	18.536	18.533	18.530	18.527	18.525
18.75	18.794	18.790	18.787	18.784	18.781	18.778	18.775	18.773
19	19.042	19.038	19.034	19.031	19.028	19.026	19.024	19.021
19.25	19.289	19.285	19.282	19.279	19.277	19.274	19.272	19.270
19.5	19.536	19.533	19.530	19.527	19.525	19.522	19.520	19.518
19.75	19.784	19.781	19.778	19.775	19.773	19.771	19.769	19.767
20	20.032	20.029	20.026	20.024	20.021	20.019	20.017	20.016
20.25	20.280	20.277	20.274	20.272	20.270	20.268	20.266	20.265

TABLE A (*continued*)

% INTEREST	32.5	33	33.5	34	34.5	35	35.5	36
				YEARS				
20.5	20.528	20.525	20.523	20.520	20.518	20.517	20.515	20.514
20.75	20.776	20.773	20.771	20.769	20.767	20.765	20.764	20.763
21	21.024	21.022	21.020	21.018	21.016	21.014	21.013	21.012
21.25	21.273	21.270	21.268	21.266	21.265	21.263	21.262	21.261
21.5	21.521	21.519	21.517	21.515	21.514	21.512	21.511	21.510
21.75	21.770	21.768	21.766	21.764	21.763	21.762	21.760	21.759
22	22.018	22.017	22.015	22.013	22.012	22.011	22.010	22.009
22.25	22.267	22.265	22.264	22.262	22.261	22.260	22.259	22.258
22.5	22.516	22.514	22.513	22.511	22.510	22.509	22.508	22.507
22.75	22.765	22.763	22.762	22.761	22.760	22.759	22.758	22.757
23	23.014	23.012	23.011	23.010	23.009	23.008	23.007	23.006
23.25	23.263	23.262	23.260	23.259	23.258	23.257	23.257	23.256
23.5	23.512	23.511	23.510	23.509	23.508	23.507	23.506	23.505
23.75	23.761	23.760	23.759	23.758	23.757	23.756	23.756	23.755
24	24.011	24.009	24.008	24.007	24.007	24.006	24.005	24.005
24.25	24.260	24.259	24.258	24.257	24.256	24.255	24.255	24.254
24.5	24.509	24.508	24.507	24.506	24.506	24.505	24.504	24.504
24.75	24.759	24.758	24.757	24.756	24.755	24.755	24.754	24.754
25	25.008	25.007	25.006	25.006	25.005	25.004	25.004	25.003

TABLE A (continued)

% INTEREST	YEARS							
	36.5	37	37.5	38	38.5	39	39.5	40
8	8.461	8.442	8.424	8.406	8.390	8.374	8.358	8.344
8.25	8.682	8.664	8.646	8.629	8.613	8.598	8.584	8.570
8.5	8.905	8.887	8.870	8.854	8.839	8.824	8.810	8.797
8.75	9.129	9.112	9.096	9.081	9.066	9.052	9.039	9.026
9	9.355	9.338	9.323	9.308	9.294	9.281	9.268	9.256
9.25	9.582	9.566	9.552	9.538	9.524	9.512	9.499	9.488
9.5	9.810	9.795	9.781	9.768	9.755	9.743	9.732	9.721
9.75	10.040	10.026	10.012	10.000	9.988	9.976	9.965	9.955
10	10.271	10.258	10.245	10.233	10.221	10.210	10.200	10.190
10.25	10.503	10.490	10.478	10.466	10.455	10.445	10.435	10.426
10.5	10.736	10.724	10.712	10.701	10.691	10.681	10.672	10.663
10.75	10.971	10.959	10.948	10.937	10.927	10.918	10.909	10.901
11	11.206	11.195	11.184	11.174	11.165	11.156	11.147	11.140
11.25	11.442	11.431	11.421	11.412	11.403	11.395	11.387	11.379
11.5	11.679	11.669	11.659	11.651	11.642	11.634	11.627	11.619
11.75	11.917	11.907	11.898	11.890	11.882	11.874	11.867	11.860
12	12.156	12.146	12.138	12.130	12.122	12.115	12.108	12.102
12.25	12.395	12.386	12.378	12.370	12.363	12.357	12.350	12.344
12.5	12.635	12.627	12.619	12.612	12.605	12.599	12.593	12.587
12.75	12.876	12.868	12.861	12.854	12.847	12.841	12.836	12.830
13	13.117	13.110	13.103	13.096	13.090	13.084	13.079	13.074
13.25	13.359	13.352	13.345	13.339	13.333	13.328	13.323	13.318
13.5	13.601	13.595	13.588	13.583	13.577	13.572	13.568	13.563
13.75	13.844	13.838	13.832	13.827	13.822	13.812	13.812	13.808
14	14.088	14.082	14.076	14.071	14.066	14.062	14.058	14.054
14.25	14.331	14.326	14.321	14.316	14.311	14.307	14.303	14.299
14.5	14.576	14.570	14.565	14.561	14.557	14.553	14.549	14.546
14.75	14.820	14.815	14.811	14.806	14.802	14.799	14.795	14.792
15	15.065	15.061	15.056	15.052	15.048	15.045	15.042	15.039
15.25	15.311	15.306	15.302	15.298	15.295	15.291	15.288	15.286
15.5	15.556	15.552	15.548	15.545	15.541	15.538	15.535	15.533
15.75	15.802	15.798	15.795	15.791	15.788	15.785	15.783	15.780
16	16.049	16.045	16.041	16.038	16.035	16.033	16.030	16.028
16.25	16.295	16.292	16.288	16.285	16.283	16.280	16.278	16.276
16.5	16.542	16.538	16.535	16.533	16.530	16.530	16.526	16.524
16.75	16.789	16.786	16.783	16.780	16.778	16.776	16.773	16.772
17	17.036	17.033	17.030	17.028	17.026	17.024	17.022	17.020
17.25	17.283	17.281	17.278	17.276	17.274	17.272	17.270	17.268
17.5	17.531	17.528	17.526	17.524	17.522	17.520	17.518	17.517
17.75	17.779	17.776	17.774	17.772	17.770	17.768	17.767	17.765
18	18.027	18.024	18.022	18.020	18.019	18.017	18.016	18.014
18.25	18.275	18.272	18.270	18.269	18.267	18.266	18.264	18.263
18.5	18.523	18.521	18.519	18.517	18.516	18.514	18.513	18.512
18.75	18.771	18.769	18.768	18.766	18.765	18.763	18.762	18.761
19	19.020	19.018	19.016	19.015	19.013	19.012	19.011	19.010
19.25	19.268	19.266	19.265	19.264	19.262	19.261	19.260	19.259
19.5	19.517	19.515	19.514	19.513	19.511	19.510	19.509	19.508
19.75	19.766	19.764	19.763	19.762	19.760	19.759	19.759	19.758
20	20.014	20.013	20.012	20.011	20.010	20.009	20.008	20.007
20.25	20.263	20.262	20.261	20.260	20.259	20.258	20.257	20.257

TABLE A (*continued*)

% INTEREST	YEARS							
	36.5	37	37.5	38	38.5	39	39.5	40
20.5	20.512	20.511	20.510	20.509	20.508	20.507	20.507	20.506
20.75	20.761	20.760	20.759	20.758	20.758	20.757	20.756	20.756
21	21.011	21.009	21.009	21.008	21.007	21.006	21.006	21.005
21.25	21.260	21.259	21.258	21.257	21.256	21.256	21.255	21.255
21.5	21.509	21.508	21.507	21.507	21.506	21.505	21.505	21.504
21.75	21.758	21.757	21.757	21.756	21.755	21.755	21.754	21.754
22	22.008	22.007	22.006	22.006	22.005	22.004	22.004	22.004
22.25	22.257	22.256	22.256	22.255	22.255	22.254	22.254	22.253
22.5	22.507	22.506	22.505	22.505	22.504	22.504	22.503	22.503
22.75	22.756	22.755	22.755	22.754	22.754	22.753	22.753	22.753
23	23.006	23.005	23.004	23.004	23.004	23.003	23.003	23.003
23.25	23.255	23.255	23.254	23.254	23.253	23.253	23.253	23.252
23.5	23.505	23.504	23.504	23.503	23.503	23.503	23.502	23.502
23.75	23.754	23.754	23.753	23.753	23.753	23.752	23.752	23.752
24	24.004	24.004	24.003	24.003	24.003	24.002	24.002	24.002
24.25	24.254	24.253	24.253	24.253	24.252	24.252	24.252	24.252
24.5	24.503	24.503	24.503	24.502	24.502	24.502	24.502	24.501
24.75	24.753	24.753	24.753	24.752	24.752	24.752	24.752	24.751
25	25.003	25.003	25.002	25.002	25.002	25.002	25.001	25.001

TABLE B.

Constant Annual Percents for Loans with Annual Payments

*To be used only in the event of 1 payment
made annually or semiannually.*

% Interest	Years							
	1	1.5	2	2.5	3	3.5	4	4.5
6	106.001	71.692	54.544	44.261	37.411	32.522	28.859	26.014
6.25	106.250	71.901	54.735	44.441	37.584	32.691	29.025	26.177
6.5	106.501	72.112	54.926	44.622	37.758	32.860	29.190	26.340
6.75	106.751	72.323	55.118	44.803	37.932	33.029	29.357	26.504
7	107.001	72.533	55.309	44.983	38.105	33.198	29.523	26.669
7.25	107.251	72.744	55.501	45.164	38.280	33.368	29.690	26.834
7.5	107.500	72.954	55.693	45.345	38.454	33.538	29.857	26.999
7.75	107.751	73.166	55.885	45.526	38.629	33.709	30.024	27.164
8	108.000	73.376	56.077	45.708	38.803	33.879	30.192	27.330
8.25	108.251	73.588	56.270	45.890	38.979	34.050	30.360	27.497
8.5	108.501	73.799	56.462	46.072	39.154	34.221	30.529	27.664
8.75	108.750	74.010	56.654	46.254	39.330	34.393	30.698	27.831
9	109.001	74.221	56.847	46.436	39.506	34.565	30.867	27.998
9.25	109.250	74.432	57.040	46.618	39.682	34.737	31.036	28.166
9.5	109.501	74.644	57.233	46.801	39.858	34.909	31.206	28.334
9.75	109.750	74.855	57.426	46.984	40.035	35.082	31.377	28.503
10	110.001	75.067	57.619	47.167	40.212	35.255	31.547	28.672
10.25	110.250	75.278	57.812	47.350	40.389	35.428	31.718	28.841

TABLE B (continued)

% Interest	Years							
	5	5.5	6	6.5	7	7.5	8	8.5
6	23.740	21.882	20.336	19.031	17.914	16.947	16.104	15.361
6.25	23.901	22.043	20.496	19.190	18.073	17.107	16.263	15.521
6.5	24.064	22.204	20.657	19.351	18.233	17.267	16.424	15.682
6.75	24.226	22.366	20.818	19.511	18.394	17.428	16.585	15.843
7	24.389	22.528	20.980	19.673	18.555	17.590	16.747	16.006
7.25	24.553	22.690	21.142	19.835	18.718	17.752	16.910	16.169
7.5	24.717	22.853	21.305	19.997	18.880	17.915	17.073	16.332
7.75	24.881	23.017	21.468	20.161	19.043	18.078	17.237	16.497
8	25.046	23.181	21.632	20.324	19.207	18.243	17.401	16.662
8.25	25.211	23.346	21.796	20.489	19.372	18.408	17.567	16.828
8.5	25.377	23.511	21.961	20.654	19.537	18.573	17.733	16.995
8.75	25.543	23.676	22.126	20.819	19.703	18.739	17.900	17.163
9	25.709	23.843	22.292	20.985	19.869	18.906	18.068	17.331
9.25	25.876	24.009	22.458	21.152	20.036	19.074	18.236	17.500
9.5	26.044	24.176	22.625	21.319	20.204	19.242	18.405	17.670
9.75	26.211	24.343	22.793	21.486	20.372	19.411	18.574	17.840
10	26.380	24.511	22.961	21.655	20.541	19.580	18.744	18.012
10.25	26.548	24.680	23.129	21.823	20.710	19.750	18.915	18.183

TABLE B (*continued*)

% INTEREST	YEARS							
	9	9.5	10	10.5	11	11.5	12	12.5
6	14.702	14.115	13.587	13.111	12.679	12.287	11.928	11.599
6.25	14.863	14.275	13.748	13.273	12.842	12.450	12.092	11.763
6.5	15.024	14.437	13.911	13.436	13.006	12.614	12.257	11.929
6.75	15.186	14.600	14.074	13.600	13.170	12.780	12.423	12.096
7	15.349	14.763	14.238	13.764	13.336	12.946	12.590	12.264
7.25	15.512	14.927	14.403	13.930	13.502	13.113	12.759	12.434
7.5	15.677	15.092	14.569	14.097	13.670	13.282	12.928	12.604
7.75	15.842	15.258	14.735	14.264	13.838	13.451	13.098	12.775
8	16.008	15.425	14.903	14.433	14.008	13.621	13.270	12.948
8.25	16.175	15.593	15.071	14.602	14.178	13.793	13.442	13.121
8.5	16.342	15.761	15.241	14.773	14.349	13.965	13.615	13.296
8.75	16.511	15.930	15.411	14.944	14.522	14.139	13.790	13.471
9	16.680	16.101	15.582	15.116	14.695	14.313	13.965	13.648
9.25	16.850	16.271	15.754	15.285	14.869	14.488	14.141	13.825
9.5	17.021	16.443	15.927	15.463	15.044	14.664	14.319	14.004
9.75	17.192	16.615	16.100	15.637	15.220	14.841	14.497	14.183
10	17.364	16.789	16.275	15.813	15.396	15.019	14.676	14.364
10.25	17.537	16.963	16.450	15.989	15.574	15.198	14.857	14.545

TABLE B (*continued*)

% INTEREST	YEARS							
	13	13.5	14	14.5	15	15.5	16	16.5
6	11.296	11.017	10.759	10.519	10.296	10.089	9.895	9.714
6.25	11.462	11.183	10.926	10.687	10.465	10.259	10.066	9.886
6.5	11.628	11.351	11.094	10.856	10.635	10.430	10.238	10.059
6.75	11.796	11.519	11.264	11.027	10.807	10.602	10.411	10.233
7	11.965	11.689	11.435	11.199	10.979	10.776	10.586	10.408
7.25	12.135	11.860	11.607	11.372	11.154	10.951	10.762	10.586
7.5	12.306	12.033	11.780	11.546	11.329	11.127	10.939	10.764
7.75	12.479	12.206	11.954	11.721	11.505	11.305	11.118	10.944
8	12.652	12.380	12.130	11.898	11.683	11.483	11.298	11.125
8.25	12.827	12.556	12.306	12.076	11.862	11.663	11.479	11.307
8.5	13.002	12.733	12.484	12.255	12.042	11.845	11.661	11.491
8.75	13.179	12.911	12.663	12.435	12.223	12.027	11.845	11.675
9	13.357	13.089	12.843	12.616	12.406	12.211	12.030	11.862
9.25	13.535	13.269	13.025	12.799	12.590	12.396	12.216	12.049
9.5	13.715	13.450	13.207	12.982	12.774	12.582	12.404	12.238
9.75	13.896	13.633	13.390	13.167	12.960	12.769	12.592	12.427
10	14.078	13.816	13.575	13.353	13.147	12.958	12.782	12.618
10.25	14.261	14.000	13.760	13.539	13.336	13.147	12.972	12.810

TABLE B (*continued*)

% INTEREST	17	17.5	18	18.5	19	19.5	20	20.5
				YEARS				
6	9.545	9.385	9.236	9.095	8.962	8.837	8.718	8.607
6.25	9.717	9.559	9.410	9.270	9.138	9.014	8.896	8.785
6.5	9.891	9.733	9.585	9.446	9.316	9.192	9.076	8.966
6.75	10.066	9.910	9.763	9.625	9.495	9.372	9.257	9.148
7	10.243	10.087	9.941	9.804	9.675	9.554	9.439	9.331
7.25	10.421	10.266	10.121	9.985	9.857	9.737	9.624	9.516
7.5	10.600	10.447	10.303	10.168	10.041	9.922	9.809	9.703
7.75	10.781	10.629	10.486	10.352	10.226	10.108	9.997	9.891
8	10.963	10.812	10.670	10.537	10.413	10.296	10.185	10.081
8.25	11.146	10.996	10.856	10.724	10.601	10.485	10.375	10.273
8.5	11.331	11.182	11.043	10.913	10.790	10.675	10.567	10.465
8.75	11.517	11.370	11.231	11.102	10.981	10.867	10.760	10.660
9	11.705	11.558	11.421	11.293	11.173	11.060	10.955	10.855
9.25	11.893	11.748	11.612	11.485	11.367	11.255	11.150	11.052
9.5	12.083	11.939	11.805	11.679	11.561	11.451	11.348	11.251
9.75	12.274	12.131	11.998	11.874	11.757	11.648	11.546	11.450
10	12.466	12.325	12.193	12.070	11.955	11.847	11.746	11.651
10.25	12.660	12.520	12.389	12.267	12.153	12.047	11.947	11.854

TABLE B (*continued*)

% INTEREST	21	21.5	22	22.5	23	23.5	24	24.5
				YEARS				
6	8.500	8.400	8.305	8.214	8.128	8.046	7.968	7.894
6.25	8.680	8.580	8.486	8.396	8.311	8.230	8.153	8.079
6.5	8.861	8.763	8.669	8.580	8.496	8.416	8.340	8.267
6.75	9.044	8.947	8.854	8.766	8.683	8.604	8.528	8.457
7	9.229	9.132	9.041	8.954	8.871	8.793	8.719	8.648
7.25	9.415	9.319	9.229	9.143	9.062	8.984	8.911	8.841
7.5	9.603	9.508	9.419	9.334	9.254	9.177	9.105	9.036
7.75	9.792	9.699	9.610	9.526	9.447	9.372	9.301	9.233
8	9.983	9.891	9.803	9.721	9.642	9.568	9.498	9.431
8.25	10.176	10.084	9.998	9.916	9.839	9.766	9.697	9.631
8.5	10.370	10.279	10.194	10.113	10.037	9.965	9.897	9.832
8.75	10.565	10.476	10.391	10.312	10.237	10.166	10.099	10.035
9	10.762	10.674	10.591	10.512	10.438	10.368	10.302	10.240
9.25	10.960	10.873	10.791	10.714	10.641	10.572	10.507	10.446
9.5	11.159	11.074	10.993	10.917	10.845	10.777	10.713	10.653
9.75	11.360	11.276	11.196	11.121	11.050	10.984	10.921	10.862
10	11.562	11.479	11.401	11.327	11.257	11.192	11.130	11.072
10.25	11.766	11.684	11.606	11.534	11.465	11.401	11.340	11.283

TABLE B (*continued*)

% INTEREST	YEARS							
	25	25.5	26	26.5	27	27.5	28	28.5
6	7.823	7.755	7.690	7.629	7.570	7.513	7.459	7.408
6.25	8.009	7.943	7.879	7.818	7.760	7.704	7.651	7.600
6.5	8.198	8.132	8.069	8.010	7.952	7.898	7.845	7.795
6.75	8.389	8.324	8.262	8.203	8.147	8.093	8.041	7.992
7	8.581	8.517	8.456	8.398	8.343	8.290	8.239	8.191
7.25	8.775	8.712	8.652	8.595	8.541	8.489	8.439	8.392
7.5	8.971	8.909	8.850	8.794	8.740	8.689	8.641	8.594
7.75	9.169	9.108	9.050	8.994	8.942	8.892	8.844	8.798
8	9.368	9.308	9.251	9.196	9.145	9.096	9.049	9.004
8.25	9.569	9.510	9.454	9.400	9.350	9.301	9.256	9.212
8.5	9.771	9.713	9.658	9.606	9.556	9.509	9.464	9.421
8.75	9.975	9.918	9.864	9.813	9.764	9.718	9.674	9.632
9	10.181	10.125	10.072	10.021	9.974	9.928	9.885	9.844
9.25	10.388	10.333	10.281	10.231	10.184	10.140	10.098	10.058
9.5	10.596	10.542	10.491	10.443	10.397	10.354	10.312	10.273
9.75	10.806	10.753	10.703	10.655	10.611	10.568	10.528	10.490
10	11.017	10.965	10.916	10.870	10.826	10.784	10.745	10.708
10.25	11.229	11.178	11.130	11.085	11.042	11.002	10.963	10.927

TABLE B (*continued*)

% INTEREST	YEARS				
	29	29.5	30	35	40
6	7.358	7.310	7.265	6.897	6.646
6.25	7.552	7.505	7.460	7.101	6.857
6.5	7.747	7.702	7.658	7.306	7.069
6.75	7.945	7.900	7.857	7.514	7.284
7	8.145	8.101	8.059	7.723	7.501
7.25	8.346	8.303	8.262	7.935	7.720
7.5	8.550	8.508	8.467	8.148	7.940
7.75	8.755	8.714	8.674	8.363	8.162
8	8.962	8.921	8.883	8.580	8.386
8.25	9.170	9.131	9.093	8.799	8.611
8.5	9.381	9.342	9.305	9.019	8.838
8.75	9.592	9.555	9.519	9.241	9.066
9	9.806	9.769	9.734	9.464	9.296
9.25	10.020	9.984	9.950	9.688	9.527
9.5	10.236	10.201	10.168	9.914	9.759
9.75	10.454	10.420	10.387	10.141	9.992
10	10.673	10.640	10.608	10.369	10.226
10.25	10.893	10.860	10.830	10.598	10.461

Table C: ANNUAL SINKING FUND TABLES
WRAP-AROUND YIELD CALCULATION FOR 6-30YEARS

YEARS	6%	6¼%	6½%	6¾%	7%	7¼%	7½%	7¾%	8%	8¼%	8½%
1	1.000000	1.000000	1.000000	1.000000	1.000000	1.000000	1.000000	1.000000	1.000000	1.000000	1.000000
	.485437	.484848	.484262	.483676	.483092	.482509	.481928	.481348	.480769	.480192	.479616
	.314110	.313341	.312576	.311812	.311052	.310293	.309538	.308784	.308034	.307285	.306539
	.228591	.227745	.226903	.226064	.225228	.224396	.223568	.222742	.221921	.221103	.220288
	.177396	.176513	.175635	.174760	.173891	.173025	.172165	.171308	.170456	.169609	.168766
6	.143363	.142463	.141568	.140679	.139796	.138918	.138045	.137177	.136315	.135459	.134607
	.119135	.118230	.117331	.116439	.115553	.114674	.113800	.112933	.112072	.111218	.110369
	.101036	.100133	.099237	.098349	.097468	.096594	.095727	.094867	.094015	.093169	.092331
	.087022	.086126	.085238	.084358	.083486	.082623	.081767	.080919	.080080	.079248	.078424
	.075868	.074982	.074105	.073237	.072378	.071527	.070686	.069853	.069029	.068214	.067408
11	.066793	.065919	.065055	.064201	.063557	.062522	.061697	.060882	.060076	.059280	.058493
	.059277	.058417	.057568	.056730	.055902	.055085	.054278	.053481	.052695	.051919	.051153
	.052960	.052116	.051283	.050461	.049651	.048852	.048064	.047288	.046522	.045767	.045023
	.047585	.046757	.045940	.045137	.044345	.043565	.042797	.042041	.041297	.040564	.039842
	.042963	.042151	.041353	.040567	.039795	.039035	.038287	.037552	.036830	.036119	.035420
16	.038952	.038158	.037378	.036611	.035858	.035118	.034391	.033678	.032977	.032289	.031614
	.035445	.034668	.033906	.033159	.032425	.031706	.031000	.030308	.029629	.028964	.028312
	.032357	.031598	.030855	.030126	.029413	.028714	.028029	.027359	.026702	.026059	.025430
	.029621	.028880	.028156	.027447	.026753	.026074	.025411	.024762	.024128	.023507	.022901
	.027185	.026462	.025756	.025067	.024393	.023735	.023092	.022465	.021852	.021254	.020671
21	.025005	.024300	.023613	.022943	.022289	.021651	.021029	.020423	.019832	.019256	.018695
	.023046	.022360	.021691	.021040	.020406	.019788	.019187	.018602	.018032	.017478	.016939
	.021278	.020611	.019961	.019329	.018714	.018116	.017535	.016971	.016422	.015889	.015372
	.019679	.019029	.018398	.017784	.017189	.016611	.016050	.015506	.014978	.014466	.013970
	.018227	.017595	.016981	.016387	.015811	.015252	.014711	.014186	.013679	.013187	.012712
26	.016904	.016290	.015695	.015119	.014561	.014021	.013500	.012995	.012507	.012036	.011580
	.015697	.015100	.014523	.013965	.013426	.012905	.012402	.011917	.011448	.010996	.010560
	.014593	.014013	.013453	.012913	.012392	.011890	.011405	.010938	.010489	.010056	.009639
	.013580	.013017	.012474	.011952	.011449	.010964	.010498	.010050	.009619	.009204	.008806
	.012649	.012103	.011577	.011072	.010586	.010120	.009671	.009241	.008827	.008431	.008051

YEARS	8¾%	9%	9¼%	9½%	9¾%	10%	10¼%	10½%	10¾%	11%	11¼%
1	1.000000	1.000000	1.000000	1.000000	1.000000	1.000000	1.000000	1.000000	1.000000	1.000000	1.000000
	.479042	.478469	.477897	.477327	.476758	.476190	.475624	.475059	.474496	.473934	.473373
	.305796	.305055	.304136	.303580	.302846	.302115	.301386	.300659	.299935	.299213	.298494
	.219477	.218669	.217864	.217063	.216265	.215471	.214680	.213892	.213108	.212326	.211548
	.167927	.167092	.166262	.165436	.164615	.163797	.162984	.162175	.161371	.160570	.159774
6	.133761	.132920	.132084	.131253	.130428	.129607	.128792	.127982	.127177	.126377	.125581
	.109527	.108691	.107860	.107036	.106218	.105405	.104599	.103799	.103004	.102215	.101432
	.091499	.090674	.089857	.089046	.088241	.087444	.086653	.085869	.085092	.084321	.083557
	.077607	.076799	.075998	.075205	.074419	.073641	.072870	.072106	.071350	.070602	.079860
	.066610	.065820	.065039	.064266	.063502	.062745	.061997	.061257	.060525	.059801	.059085
11	.055715	.056947	.056187	.055437	.054696	.053963	.053240	.052525	.051819	.051121	.050432
	.050397	.049651	.048914	.048188	.047471	.046763	.046565	.045377	.044697	.044027	.043366
	.044289	.043567	.042854	.042152	.041460	.040779	.040107	.039445	.038793	.038151	.037518
	.039132	.038433	.037745	.037068	.036402	.035746	.035101	.034467	.033842	.033228	.032624
	.034734	.034059	.033396	.032744	.032103	.031474	.030855	.030248	.029651	.029065	.028490
16	.030951	.030300	.029661	.029035	.028420	.027817	.027225	.026644	.026075	.025517	.024969
	.027673	.027046	.026432	.025831	.025241	.024664	.024099	.023545	.023003	.022471	.021952
	.024815	.024212	.023623	.023046	.022482	.021930	.021391	.020863	.020347	.019843	.019350
	.022309	.021730	.021165	.020613	.020074	.019547	.019033	.018531	.018041	.017563	.017096
	.020102	.019546	.019005	.018477	.017962	.017460	.016970	.016493	.016028	.015576	.015134
21	.018149	.017617	.017098	.016594	.016102	.015624	.015159	.014707	.014266	.013838	.013421
	.016415	.015905	.015409	.014928	.014460	.014005	.013563	.013134	.012718	.012313	.011920
	.014870	.014382	.013909	.013449	.013004	.012572	.012153	.011747	.011353	.010971	.010601
	.013489	.013023	.012571	.012134	.011710	.011300	.010903	.010519	.010147	.009787	.009439
	.012251	.011806	.011376	.010959	.010557	.010168	.009792	.009429	.009079	.008740	.008413
26	.011140	.010715	.010305	.009909	.009527	.009159	.008804	.008461	.008131	.007813	.007506
	.010140	.009735	.009345	.008969	.008606	.008258	.007922	.007599	.007288	.006989	.006702
	.009238	.008852	.008481	.008124	.007781	.007451	.007134	.006830	.006538	.006257	.005988
	.008423	.008056	.007703	.007364	.007040	.006728	.006429	.006143	.005868	.005605	.005354
	.007686	.007336	.007001	.006681	.006373	.006079	.005798	.005528	.005271	.005025	.004789

Table C (cont.)

YEARS	11½%	11¾%	12%	13%	14%	15%	16%	17%	18%	19%	20%
1	1.000000	1.000000	1.000000	1.000000	1.000000	1.000000	1.000000	1.000000	1.000000	1.000000	1.000000
	.472813	.472255	.471698	.469483	.467290	.465116	.462963	.460829	.458715	.456621	.454545
	.297776	.297062	.296349	.293522	.290731	.287976	.285257	.282573	.279923	.277308	.274725
	.210774	.210003	.209234	.206194	.203205	.200265	.197375	.194533	.191738	.188991	.186289
	.158982	.158194	.157410	.154314	.151284	.148315	.145409	.142564	.139778	.137050	.134380
6	.124791	.124006	.123226	.120153	.117158	.114236	.111390	.108615	.105910	.103274	.100706
	.100655	.099884	.099118	.096111	.093192	.090360	.087613	.084947	.082362	.079855	.077424
	.082799	.082048	.081303	.078387	.075570	.072850	.070224	.067690	.065243	.062885	.060609
	.069126	.068399	.067679	.064869	.062168	.059574	.057083	.054690	.052395	.050192	.048079
	.058377	.057677	.056984	.054290	.051714	.049252	.046901	.044657	.042515	.040471	.038523
11	.049751	.049079	.048415	.045841	.043394	.041068	.038861	.036765	.034776	.032891	.031104
	.042714	.042071	.041437	.038986	.036669	.034480	.032415	.030466	.028628	.026896	.025265
	.036895	.036282	.035677	.033350	.031164	.029110	.027184	.025378	.023686	.022102	.020620
	.032030	.031446	.030871	.028668	.026609	.024688	.022898	.021230	.019678	.018235	.016893
	.027924	.027369	.026824	.024742	.022809	.021017	.019358	.017822	.016403	.015092	.013882
16	.024432	.023906	.023390	.021426	.019615	.017947	.016414	.015004	.013710	.012523	.011436
	.021443	.020944	.020457	.018608	.016915	.015366	.013952	.012662	.011485	.010414	.009440
	.018868	.018397	.017937	.016201	.014621	.013186	.011885	.010706	.009639	.008676	.007805
	.016641	.016196	.015763	.014134	.012663	.011336	.010142	.009067	.008103	.007237	.006462
	.014705	.014286	.013879	.012354	.010986	.009761	.008667	.007690	.006820	.006045	.005357
21	.013016	.012623	.012240	.010814	.009545	.008416	.007416	.006530	.005746	.005054	.004444
	.011539	.011169	.010811	.009480	.008303	.007265	.006353	.005550	.004846	.004229	.003690
	.010243	.009896	.009560	.008319	.007231	.006278	.005447	.004721	.004090	.003542	.003065
	.009103	.008778	.008463	.007308	.006303	.005429	.004673	.004019	.003454	.002967	.002548
	.008098	.007794	.007500	.006426	.005498	.004699	.004013	.003423	.002919	.002487	.002119
26	.007210	.006926	.006652	.005655	.004800	.004069	.003447	.002918	.002467	.002086	.001762
	.006425	.006159	.005904	.004979	.004193	.003526	.002963	.002487	.002087	.001750	.001467
	.005730	.005482	.005244	.004387	.003665	.003010	.002548	.002121	.001765	.001468	.001221
	.005112	.004881	.004660	.003867	.003204	.002651	.002192	.001810	.001494	.001232	.001016
	.004564	.004349	.004144	.003411	.002803	.002300	.001886	.001545	.001264	.001034	.000846

YEARS	21%	22%	23%	24%	25%	26%	27%	28%	29%	30%
1	1.000000	1.000000	1.000000	1.000000	1.000000	1.000000	1.000000	1.000000	1.000000	1.000000
	.452489	.450450	.448430	.446429	.444444	.442478	.440529	.438596	.436681	.434783
	.272175	.269658	.267173	.264718	.262295	.259902	.257539	.255206	.252902	.250627
	.183632	.181020	.178451	.175926	.173442	.170999	.168598	.166236	.163913	.161629
	.131765	.129206	.126700	.124248	.121847	.119496	.117196	.114944	.112739	.110582
6	.098203	.095764	.093389	.091074	.088819	.086623	.084484	.082400	.080371	.078394
	.075067	.072782	.070568	.068422	.066342	.064326	.062374	.060482	.058649	.056874
	.058415	.056299	.054259	.052293	.050399	.048573	.046814	.045119	.043487	.041915
	.046053	.044111	.042249	.040465	.038756	.037119	.035551	.034049	.032612	.031235
	.036665	.034895	.033208	.031602	.030073	.028616	.027231	.025912	.024657	.023463
11	.029411	.027807	.026289	.024852	.023493	.022207	.020991	.019842	.018755	.017729
	.023730	.022285	.020926	.019648	.018448	.017319	.016260	.015265	.014331	.013454
	.019234	.017939	.016728	.015598	.014544	.013559	.012641	.011785	.010987	.010244
	.015647	.014491	.013418	.012423	.011501	.010647	.009856	.009123	.008445	.007818
	.012766	.011738	.010791	.009919	.009117	.008379	.007701	.007077	.006405	.005978
16	.010441	.009530	.008697	.007936	.007241	.006606	.006027	.005499	.005017	.004577
	.008555	.007751	.007021	.006359	.005759	.005216	.004723	.004277	.003874	.003509
	.007020	.006313	.005676	.005102	.004586	.004122	.003705	.003331	.002994	.002692
	.005769	.005148	.004593	.004098	.003656	.003261	.002909	.002595	.002316	.002066
	.004745	.004202	.003720	.003294	.002916	.002581	.002285	.002023	.001792	.001587
21	.003906	.003432	.003016	.002649	.002327	.002045	.001796	.001578	.001387	.001219
	.003218	.002805	.002446	.002132	.001858	.001620	.001412	.001232	.001074	.000937
	.002652	.002294	.001984	.001716	.001485	.001284	.001111	.000961	.000832	.000720
	.002187	.001877	.001611	.001382	.001186	.001018	.000874	.000750	.000644	.000554
	.001804	.001536	.001308	.001113	.000948	.000807	.000688	.000586	.000499	.000426

Index